DEBATING DEMOCRACY

A Reader in American Politics

Third Edition

Bruce Miroff
STATE UNIVERSITY OF NEW YORK–ALBANY

Raymond Seidelman
SARAH LAWRENCE COLLEGE

Todd Swanstrom
STATE UNIVERSITY OF NEW YORK–ALBANY

Houghton Mifflin Company   Boston   New York

To our parents: Martin and Sophie Miroff, Herb and Thelma Seidelman, and Beatrice and Glenn Swanstrom

Sponsoring Editor: Melissa Mashburn
Senior Associate Editor: Fran Gay
Project Editor: Amy Johnson
Associate Production/Design Coordinator: Lisa Jelly
Senior Manufacturing Coordinator: Sally Culler
Senior Marketing Manager: Sandra McGuire

Cover Image Concept and Design: Harold Burch, Harold Burch Design, NYC

Text credits appear on p. 386

Library of Congress Catalog Card Number: 00-133822

ISBN: 0-618-05455-3

123456789-HP-04 03 02 01 00

However unwillingly a person who has a strong opinion may admit the possibility that his opinion may be false, he ought to be moved by the consideration that, however true it may be, if it is not fully, frequently, and fearlessly discussed, it will be held as a dead dogma, not as a living truth.

John Stuart Mill, *On Liberty* (1859)

CONTENTS

PREFACE

We have been very pleased by readers' and reviewers' enthusiastic reactions to the first two editions of *Debating Democracy*. They warmly endorsed our belief in the need for a reader for courses in American politics that makes democracy its unifying theme. Of course, Americans agree in the abstract about democracy, but in practice we often disagree about democracy's meaning and implications. To explore these crucial disagreements, the third edition is constructed around a series of debates about democracy in America.

Special Features of *Debating Democracy*

Debating Democracy is different from other readers in American politics. The selections in our reader are organized around a common theme. All the chapters address the meaning and improvement of American democracy. Thus, reading through the selections has a cumulative effect, helping students to think more clearly and deeply about democracy.

Our experience as teachers of introductory courses in American politics suggests that debate-type readers can leave students confused, wondering how to respond to a bewildering array of different arguments. Many students conclude that political debates are just a matter of opinion, that there is no cumulative knowledge generated by debating the issues. To prevent such confusion, we provide an Introduction, highly praised by reviewers of the first two editions, that gives students a framework for evaluating democratic debates. This framework is designed to help students develop their own political philosophies and critical abilities for analyzing political issues. In the end, we believe, engaging students in these democratic debates will help them to understand that democracy is a complex and contested idea and that although there is no One Truth, the search for democratic truths is well worth the effort.

In order to engage students in the search for democratic truths, we have included lively and clearly written selections from political leaders, journalists, and scholars. In each case we have chosen two contrasting views on a controversial topic. To help students in evaluating the selections, we introduce each debate with a short essay that places the issue in a meaningful context and alerts the reader to be on the lookout for contrasting values and hidden assumptions.

Debating Democracy seeks to generate further debate. After each set of selections we include questions that can be used by readers to analyze the issues or by teachers to spark class discussions. We end with suggested readings and web sites that students can use to pursue the topic further.

Each chapter in the book can be used as the basis for a structured in-class debate. Our own introductory lecture courses have discussion sections of ten to twenty students led by teaching assistants. The TA divides the class in two and assigns each group one side in the debate. The students are asked to meet outside of class and prepare their arguments based on the readings. A session of the discussion section is then devoted to a formal debate. We do two or three of these structured debates in the course of a semester. Students enjoy these debates and often report that this is the high point of the course for them.

Following the formal debates, each student is required to write a short paper setting out the arguments of her or his side and rebutting the arguments of the other side. We are convinced that this exercise helps students to achieve what is often an important goal in introductory American politics courses: improving writing skills. Requiring students to take a stand on a political issue and develop a coherent argument for their position in a thematic essay is an effective way, we believe, to teach writing.

Structure of *Debating Democracy*

Debating Democracy has been structured to fit with almost all introductory texts in American politics. We cover topics usually covered in an introductory text, but we have also included debates on political economy and political activism because we believe these are important subjects for an understanding of American democracy.

The editors of this book make no claim to being impartial observers of democratic debates. We support the extension of democratic decision making into broader spheres of the economy and society with greater emphasis on equality and community. Our participatory democratic inclinations are evident in our textbook, *The Democratic Debate: An Introduction to American Politics,* Second Edition (Houghton Mifflin, 1998).

Although we make no claim to impartiality, we have made every effort in the chapters that follow to select the strongest arguments on both sides of the issues. The reader can be used with any textbook in American government, no matter what the political inclinations of the professor. The reader can also stand by itself as an introduction to the critical issues facing American democracy at the beginning of the twenty-first century.

New to the Third Edition

In response to readers' and reviewers' suggestions and the changing landscape of American politics, about one-third of the selections in the third edition are new.

There are four new chapters:

Chapter 2   Democracy: Overrated or Undervalued?

Chapter 4   Culture Wars: Are We Facing a Moral Collapse?

Chapter 17   Economic Inequality: A Threat to Democracy?

Chapter 18   The United States and the Global Economy: Serving Citizens or Corporate Elites?

In addition, there are two new debates in existing chapters:

Chapter 6   Civil Liberties: Does the First Amendment Permit Religious Expression in Public Institutions?

Chapter 9   The New Media: Corporate Wasteland or Democratic Frontier?

Other new features include:

■ A new essay by Clawson, Neustadtl, and Weller, debating Bradley A. Smith on campaign finance reform (Chapter 11).

■ Additional or updated web sites for further research at the end of each chapter.

Acknowledgments

We are grateful to all of those who helped us to carry forward our original hopes for *Debating Democracy*. At SUNY, Albany, skillful research assistance was supplied by Molly Flynn, Paul Goggi, Timothy Gordinier, Christopher Latimer, Liu Runyu, Jordan Wishy, and Christopher Witko. At Sarah Lawrence, Amanda Slagle and Claire Landiss made helpful suggestions and conducted editorial work on the manuscript. The folks at Houghton Mifflin— especially Fran Gay, Melissa Mashburn, and Jean Woy—brought just the right blend of professional expertise and good cheer to the project.

The outside reviewers selected by Houghton Mifflin, whose names are listed in the following paragraphs, were of more than usual help. Their incisive suggestions led us to change some selections, add new subjects, and improve our pedagogical framework.

Six scholars provided helpful criticisms of the draft manuscript for the first edition: John L. Anderson, University of Nebraska at Kearney; Edmond Costantini, University of California at Davis; William R. Lund, University of

Idaho; David J. Olson, University of Washington; Marvin L. Overby, University of Mississippi; and Gregory G. Rocha, University of Texas at El Paso.

The following individuals gave us valuable feedback in response to the first edition and in preparation for the second: Stephen Baker, Jacksonville University; Jennifer Disney, John Jay College of Criminal Justice; Thomas Hensley, Kent State University; William J. Hughes, Southern Oregon University; Fredrick Paul Lee, Winona State University; Suzanne Marilley, Capital University; Noelle Norton, University of San Diego; Larry Schwab, John Carroll University; Dennis Shea, State University of New York College at Oneonta; Kevin Smith, University of Nebraska, Lincoln; and Kenneth F. Warren, St. Louis University.

And we are grateful to the following reviewers of the second edition, who gave us valuable suggestions for this revision: Stephen C. Baker, Jacksonville University; Dana K. Glencross, Oklahoma City Community College; Paula L. O'Loughlin, University of Minnesota at Morris; Kevin Smith, University of Nebraska at Lincoln; Linda O. Valenty, San Jose State University; and Stephen Wiener, University of California at Santa Barbara.

Finally, we continue to depend on the love, the support, and especially the patience of our families: Melinda, Nick, and Anna; Fay, Eva, and Rosa; Katie, Jessica, Madeleine, and Eleanore.

B. M.

R. S.

T. S.

How to Read
This Book

One of the more revealing exchanges in the recent race for president occurred on *Meet the Press,* a well-known Sunday morning political talk show. This particular program featured a debate between Vice President Al Gore and his challenger for the Democratic nomination, former U.S. Senator Bill Bradley. During a discussion of unregulated campaign contributions (called "soft money"), Gore made a surprising proposal: that both candidates agree to eliminate all television and radio commercials and instead debate twice a week until the nomination was decided.[1]

Bradley reacted to Gore's offer with disdain, calling it a "ridiculous proposal." "The point is," Bradley explained, "a political campaign is not just a performance for people which is what this is, but it is rather, a dialogue . . . with people, Al."

Gore persisted: "We could call it the 'Meet the Press' agreement," Gore said. "We could have two debates every single week and get rid of the television and radio commercials. I'm willing to do it right now, if you're willing to shake on it." Sitting just inches away from Bradley, Gore held out his hand.

"Al, that's good. I like that hand," said Bradley, spurning Gore's outstretched hand and then dismissing Gore's offer as "nothing but a ploy."

"Debates aren't ploys," Gore said.

"No," Bradley replied, "to come out here and shake my hand, that's nothing but a ploy."

Whether Gore's proposal was a cynical ploy or a sincere offer, the exchange tells us much about the limits of democratic debates in the midst of a political campaign. Ironically, Bradley tried to base his run for the presidency on being a new type of candidate—an antipolitician politician, someone who would stick to the issues, articulate his vision of where the country should go, and never "go negative." A centerpiece of his run for president was campaign finance reform designed to reduce the role of big money in elections.

At the same time that he campaigned against the role of money in elections, however, Bradley knew that he needed all the money he could get his hands on to have a chance of winning. The reason is simple: Bradley's name recognition was far behind Vice President Gore's and the only way to make up for that was to spend lots of money on ads. Gore knew that Bradley depended on ads and therefore could never agree to give them up. Gore's outstretched hand, however, would provide an irresistible photo opportunity, with the message that Bradley said he wanted to reform the campaign finance system, but when offered an opportunity to do just that by Gore, he refused. Gore's ploy put Bradley on the defensive.

Gore hardly came off as the pure reformer, however. His criticism of ads became itself a kind of ad focused on image more than substance. Voters are cynical about politicians, and therefore Gore was vulnerable to Bradley's charge that his offer was insincere, representing "nothing but a ploy" to manipulate symbols instead of talking about substance.

As democratic debates, presidential debates leave much to be desired. The candidates treat them as opportunities to project a presidential image instead of explaining their political philosophies and policy positions. The candidates and their handlers devote endless amounts of time and money to finding out what the voters want to hear. Drilled on what to say, instead of debating each other, the candidates often speak past each other in order to stay "on message." The media cover the debates like sporting contests, focusing not on substance but on who won or lost the image contest. Following each debate, the "spin meisters" rush out to convince the media that their candidate won.

The debates that we have gathered together in this book are far different from what we are used to in political debates. In the real world no debate is perfectly free and fair, if only because one side has more resources to make itself heard. Nevertheless, we can approximate conditions of a free and fair debate, as we have attempted to do in the pages that follow. We present arguments by authors who are experts on the issues. They concentrate on the issue at hand, not on their image. Each gets equal time. For the most part, they avoid begging (avoiding) the question, mudslinging, or manipulating stereotypes. The contest is decided not by who has the most money or who projects the best image but by who has the best arguments using logical reasoning and facts.

Political debates are not just methods for acquiring information in elections; they are the heart of a democratic system. In a true democracy, debates do not just concern who will be elected to office every few years; they address the issues of everyday life, and they occur every day, extending from television studios to dinner tables, from shop floors to classrooms. Even though political debates can become heated because they involve our most deeply held beliefs, democracies do not deny anyone the right to disagree. In a democracy we recognize that no one has a monopoly on the truth. Debates are not tangential to democracy; they are central to its meaning. "Agreeing to disagree" is the essence of democracy.

Debate as the Lifeblood of Democracy

Debate as dialogue, not demagoguery, is the lifeblood of democracy. Democracy is the one form of government that requires leaders to give reasons for their decisions and defend them in public. Some theorists argue that free and fair deliberation, or debate, is not only a good method for arriving at democratic decisions but is the essence of democracy itself.[2]

Debate is crucial to a democracy not just because it leads to better decisions but because it helps to create better citizens. Democratic debate requires that we be open-minded, that we listen to both sides. This process of listening attentively to different sides and examining their assumptions helps us to clarify and critically examine our own political values. As the nineteenth-century British political philosopher John Stuart Mill wrote:

> So essential is this discipline [attending equally and impartially to both sides] to a real understanding of moral and human subjects that, if opponents of all-important truths do not exist, it is indispensable to imagine them and supply them with the strongest arguments which the most skillful devil's advocate can conjure up.[3]

According to Mill, if we are not challenged in our beliefs, they become dead dogmas instead of living truths. (Consider what happened to communist ideologies in Eastern Europe, where they were never tested in public debate.) Once we have honed our skills analyzing political debates, we are less vulnerable to being manipulated by demagogues. By hearing the rhetoric and manipulation in others' speech, we are better able to purge it from our own.[4] Instead of basing our beliefs on unconscious prejudices or ethnocentric values, our political beliefs become consciously and freely chosen.

In order for a debate to be truly democratic it must be free and fair. In a free and fair debate the only power that is exerted is the power of reason. We are moved to adopt a position not by force but by the persuasiveness of the argument. In a democratic debate proponents argue for their positions not by appealing to this or that private interest but by appealing to the public interest, the values and aspirations we share as a democratic people. Democracy is not simply a process for adding up individual preferences that citizens bring with them to the issues to see which side wins. In a democratic debate people are required to frame their arguments in terms of the public interest.[5] And as citizens deliberate about the public interest through debates, they are changed.[6]

In this book we have gathered two contrasting arguments on each of the most pressing issues facing democracy in the United States. The reader's task is to compare the two positions and decide which argument is most persuasive. After reading the selections, readers may feel frustrated seeing that opponents can adopt diametrically opposed stands on the same issue depending on their point of view. It may seem as if political positions on the issues are simply based on your values, as if political judgments are simply a matter of opinion. Being able to understand divergent viewpoints other than our own, however, is the beginning of political toleration and insight. There is no One Truth on political issues that can be handed to you on a platter by experts. On the other hand, making public choices is *not* simply a matter of opinion. There are fundamental political values that Americans subscribe to and that we struggle to achieve in our political decisions. Political stands are not just a matter of opinion, because some decisions will promote the democratic public interest better than others.

The purpose of this introduction is to give you, the reader, tools for evaluating democratic debates. The agreements and disagreements in American politics are not random; they exhibit patterns, and understanding these patterns can help orient you in the debates. In the pages that follow we draw a preliminary map of the territory of democratic debates in the United States to guide readers in negotiating this difficult terrain. Your goal should not be just to take a stand on this or that issue but to clarify your own values and chart your own path in pursuit of the public interest of American democracy.

Democratic Debates: Conflict Within Consensus

In order for a true debate to occur, there has to be both conflict and consensus. If there were no consensus, or agreement on basic values or standards of evaluation, the debaters would talk past each other, like two people speaking foreign tongues. Without some common standard of evaluation, there is no way to settle the debate. On the other hand, if there were no fundamental disagreements, the debate would be trivial and boring. Factual disagreements are not enough. Consider a debate between two political scientists about this question: How many people voted in the last election? The debate might be informative, but few people would care about the outcome because it does not engage deeply held values or beliefs. Factual disputes are important, but they rarely decide important political debates. Democratic debates are interesting and important when they engage us in struggles over the meaning and application of our basic values.

Judging a political debate is tricky. Political reasoning is different from economic reasoning or individual rational decision making. Political debates are rarely settled by toting up the costs and benefits of alternative courses of action and choosing the one that maximizes benefits over costs. It is not that costs and benefits do not matter; rather, what we see as benefits or costs depends on how we frame the issue. In political debates each side tries to get the audience to see the issue its way, to frame the issue in language that reinforces its position. On the issue of abortion, for example, is your position best described as pro-choice or pro-life? Should programs to help minorities be characterized as affirmative action or reverse discrimination? Clearly, the terms we use to describe a political position make a difference. Each term casts light on the issue in a different way, highlighting different values that are at stake in the controversy. The terms used to describe the abortion issue, for example, emphasize either the right of the unborn fetus or the right of the woman to control her body.

As the above examples illustrate, in political debates the outcome frequently hinges on the standard of evaluation itself, on what values and principles will be applied to the decision at hand. In political debates the issue is always what is good for the community as a whole, the public interest, not just some segment of the community. The selections that follow are all examples of debates over the meaning of the public interest in American democracy. In the United States, political debates, with the notable exception of slavery, have been characterized by consensus on basic democratic principles *combined with* conflicts over how best to realize those principles in practice.

As conflicts within a consensus, democratic debates in this country go back to its founding and the original debate over the U.S. Constitution more than two hundred years ago. Americans worship the Constitution as an almost divinely inspired document that embodies the highest ideals of democracy. Yet throughout history Americans have disagreed vehemently on what the Constitution means. This is not surprising. The Constitution was born as much in conflict and compromise as in consensus. In the words of former Supreme Court Justice William J. Brennan, Jr., the framers "hid their differences in cloaks of generality."[7] The general language of the Constitution left many conflicts over specifics to later generations. The Constitution, for example, gave the federal government the power to provide for the "general welfare," but we have been debating ever since what this should include. Thus the Constitution is both a source of consensus, by embodying our ideals, and a source of conflict, by failing to specify exactly how those ideals should be applied in practice.[8]

Three Sources of Conflict

Behind the words of the Constitution lie three ideals that supposedly animate our system of government: *democracy, freedom,* and *equality.* Americans agree that we should have a government of, by, and for the people (as President Lincoln so eloquently put it), a government that treats everybody equally, and a government that achieves the maximum level of freedom consistent with an ordered society. These ideals seem simple, but they are not. While Americans are united in their aspirations, they are divided in their visions of how to achieve those aspirations.[9] Democracy, freedom, and equality are what political theorists call "essentially contested concepts."[10]

I. Democracy

Democracy comes from the Greek words *demos,* meaning "the people," and *kratein,* meaning "to rule." Hence, democracy means, simply, "rule by the people." Americans agree that democracy is the best form of government. They disagree, however, on what this means.

Elite (Limited) Democracy   For some, democracy is basically a method for making decisions. According to this minimalist definition of democracy, a decision is democratic if it is made according to the criterion of majority rule. Of course, there are other requirements of democratic decision making, such as open nominations for office and free speech, but once the basic conditions have been met, the resulting decision is by definition democratic.

Following this limited definition, the most important characteristic of a democracy is free and fair elections for choosing government officials. Democracy basically means the ability of citizens to choose their leaders.[11] Elites compete for the votes to win office, but once in office they have substantial autonomy to rule as they see fit. According to this view, ultimate power rests in the hands of the people at election time, but between elections they cede decision-making authority to elites who have the expertise and experience to make the right decisions in a technologically complex and dangerous world. We call this school of democracy *elite democracy.*[12]

Elite democrats favor a minimal definition of democracy not because it is ideal but because it is the only type of democracy that is achievable in large modern nation-states. Thus, as you will see in the selection by Richard Neustadt on the presidency in Chapter 14, elite democrats are more comfortable with a powerful president who can energize the system. In response, Bruce Miroff, representing the popular democratic side, argues that the presidency has deeply rooted elitist tendencies, driven by many factors, including the need to maintain the confidence of business elites and amass huge campaign war chests.

Popular (Expansive) Democracy   Opponents of elite democrats adopt a more demanding definition of democracy. They argue that you cannot call a decision democratic just because it came out of a democratic process. Democratic decisions must also respect certain values such as tolerance, a respect for individual freedom, and the attainment of a basic level of social and economic equality. If the majority rules in such a way as to violate people's rights or the policies result in tremendous inequalities of wealth, the system cannot be called democratic. For this group, democracy means more than a political system with free and fair elections; it means an economy and society that reflect a democratic desire for equality and respect for differences.

For adherents of an expansive definition of democracy, democracy means more than going to the polls every few years; it means citizens participating in the institutions of society, including corporations, unions, and neighborhood associations. In Chapter 5, Samuel Bowles and Michael Edwards represent this position, calling for expanding democratic decision making into the economy. Countering the view of elite democrats that people are not interested in or capable of governing effectively, those who advocate a more participatory system argue that in an atmosphere of toleration, respect, and rough equality, citizens are capable of governing themselves fairly and effectively. We call those who advocate a more participatory conception of democracy *popular democrats*.[13]

II. Freedom

Most of us have a basic intuitive idea of freedom: to be free means being able to do what we want, without someone telling us what to do. Any time we are forced to do something against our will by somebody else, our freedom is reduced. Freedom seems like an exceedingly simple idea. Once again, however, we find that there is plenty of room for disagreement.

Negative (Freedom From)   The central issue for freedom is deciding where to draw the line between the power of the group and the freedom of the individual. In other words, how far should government power extend, for any time the government imposes a tax or passes a law it limits someone's freedom. In a justly famous essay, *On Liberty,* the English political theorist John Stuart Mill argues that the only justification for government power over individuals is self-protection: "[T]he only purpose for which power can be rightfully exercised over any member of a civilized community, against his will, is to prevent harm to others."[14] In other words, your freedom to swing your arm ends where my nose begins.

Under Mill's view the purpose of government is to maximize individual freedom. Freedom is understood negatively, as freedom from external constraints. Since government actions always reduce individual freedom, their only justification is to counter other restrictions on our freedom, as when the government passes laws against robbery or assault. Clearly, this view places severe limits on what democracies can legitimately do, even under the principle of majority rule. If the majority passes laws that restrict someone's freedom, without being justified by the principle of self-protection, then it is no longer a true democracy because it is violating a basic democratic value.

Positive (Freedom To)   In contrast to the negative conception of freedom—freedom *from*—there is an equally compelling positive definition of freedom—freedom *to*.[15] The positive conception of freedom recognizes that in order to have freedom, to exercise meaningful choice, we need to possess certain resources and to have certain capacities. Education, for example, increases our freedom because it increases our ability to imagine alternatives and find solutions to problems. Freedom, therefore, is not simply the absence of external coercion but freedom to get an education, travel to foreign countries, or receive expert medical care.

A positive conception of freedom justifies an expanded role for government and for citizens acting together in other ways. When government taxes us, it reduces negative freedom, but when it uses the money to build a highway or a public library, it gives us a greater positive freedom to do things we previously were unable to do. Under the positive conception of freedom, the scope of freedom is increased when the capacity of individuals to act is enhanced by government action, whether that be protecting the right of workers to join a union (giving workers the ability to bargain over wages and working conditions) or requiring buildings to be handicapped accessible (thus giving the handicapped access to places they were previously excluded from).[16]

Whether one subscribes to a positive or a negative conception of freedom will make a big difference in one's political philosophy. The negative conception of freedom is conducive to limited government and highlights the more acquisitive and competitive side of human nature. Under this view, the expansion of power in one part of society necessarily leads to a reduction of freedom in some other part of society. The selection by Milton Friedman on political economy in Chapter 5 is based on a negative conception of freedom. Friedman warns that too much government leads to coercion and a reduction in individual freedom, which is maximized by free competition in the marketplace. The positive conception of freedom emphasizes the more cooperative side of human beings. According to the positive conception of freedom, government as a form of social cooperation can actually expand the realm of freedom by bringing more and more matters of social importance under human control.

III. Equality

Like democracy and freedom, equality seems like an exceedingly simple idea. Equality marches forward under banners that read "Treat everybody equally" or "Treat like cases alike." These are not working definitions, however, but political rhetoric that hides serious ambiguities in the concept of equality. In truth, how we apply the idea of equality depends on how we envision it in a broader context.

Process Orientation   For some people, equality is basically generated by a fair process. So long as the competition is fair—everybody has an equal opportunity to succeed—then the results are fair, even if the resulting distribution is highly unequal. Inequalities that reflect differences among people in intelligence, talent, ambition, or strength are said to be legitimate. On the other hand, inequalities that result from biases in the rules of the competition are unjustified and should be eliminated.

The process orientation toward equality is best reflected in free market theory. According to market theory, the distribution of income and wealth is fair if it is the result of a process of voluntary contracting among responsible adults. As long as the requirements for a free market are met (perfect competition, free flow of information, no coercion or manipulation, and so on), no one exerts power over the market and market outcomes are just and fair. Market theorists, like Milton Friedman, stress equal opportunity, not equal results. The role of government, in this view, is to serve as a neutral umpire, enforcing the rules and treating everyone alike.[17]

Results Orientation   Opponents argue that if the government treats everybody equally the results will still be highly unequal, because people start the race from very different positions. Some have a head start in the race, while others enter with serious handicaps. To ignore these differences is to perpetuate inequalities. Treating unequals equally is, in effect, unequal. The French writer Anatole France discussed what he called "the majestic egalitarianism of the law, which forbids rich and poor alike to sleep under bridges, to beg in the streets, and to steal bread."[18] Even though the law formally treats everyone alike, it is clear that only certain people will suffer the consequences.

Those who take a results orientation toward equality don't deny the importance of equal opportunity but argue that equal opportunity means the ability of everyone to participate equally in the decisions that affect their lives. They charge that their opponents elevate the individual over the community and privileged elites over ordinary citizens, as if the wagon train could only make it to the promised land if some of the weak and frail were left behind alongside the trail. Those who support a results orientation argue that it is possible for everyone to make it together.

Those who support a results orientation do not believe in a strict leveling of society but argue that certain resources are necessary for people to participate fully in society and realize their potential. In other words, government cannot just stand aside and watch people compete; it must establish the conditions for community and equal participation. At a minimum, many would argue, adequate nutrition, good education, safety, and decent health care are necessary for a fulfilling life.

American Ideologies: Patterns in Political Stands

With two contrasting positions on each of the three issues discussed above— democracy, equality, and freedom—there are eight possible combinations of issue positions. Stands on the three issues are not random, however; they correlate in ways that generate distinct patterns that are characteristic of American political ideologies.

One of the clearest ideological distinctions in American politics is between those who favor markets and those who favor government. As Charles Lindblom has noted: "Aside from the difference between despotic and libertarian governments, the greatest distinction between one government and another is in the degree to which market replaces government or government replaces market."[19] A central issue in American politics is where to draw the line between the public and private sectors. If you believe that the market is basically free and fair, then you will support only a limited role for government. Generally, those who favor the market subscribe to a negative conception of freedom and a process orientation toward equality. This position corresponds to what we call *free market conservatism.* On the other hand, if you believe that markets are penetrated by relations of power and are prone to discrimination, then you will support an expanded role for political participation and democratic government. Those who advocate an increased role for government generally subscribe to a positive conception of freedom and favor a results orientation toward equality. These views correspond to what is commonly called *liberalism.*

Usually, we think of social conservatives as adhering to a more elite view of democracy and social liberals as being more inclined toward popular democracy. In the 1960s, for example, *left-wing populists* supported maximum feasible participation by poor people to solve poverty and advocated democratic control of corporations. In recent years, however, because they support a large role for the federal government in Washington, D.C., liberals have been accused by conservatives of being, in effect, elitist. A *right-wing populist* movement has arisen that combines popular democratic appeals with a negative conception of individual freedom and a process approach to equality, opposing the redistribution of wealth through government. To add to the complexity, however, right-wing populists do not always favor limiting the role of government. The *religious right* generally wants the government to interfere less in the economy but more in society—exerting more democratic control over moral issues, such as abortion and pornography.

Although there are these distinct patterns in American politics on the issues of democracy, freedom, and equality, they are not fixed in stone. It is possible to mix and match different positions in putting together your own political philosophy. In developing your own political philosophy you will need to address a fundamental question: what are human beings capable of; that is, what is your conception of human nature?

Human Nature: The Big Debate

Throughout history political philosophers have debated different conceptions of human nature. Human nature is the clay out of which all political systems must be constructed. The nature of this clay, its elasticity or hardness, its ability to assume different shapes and hold them, largely determines what we can and cannot do in politics. Since the original debate over the U.S. Constitution, Americans have disagreed about human nature and therefore about politics.

The Private View   Many argue that Americans are quintessentially individualistic, well suited to the marketplace and private pursuits but not well suited to democratic citizenship. The framers of the Constitution, the

Federalists, argued that the common people were self-interested and passionate creatures who should not be entrusted with all of the reins of government. Thus, as you will see in Chapter 1, James Madison argues in "Federalist No. 10" that the greatest danger in a democracy is tyranny of the majority, especially taking away the property of wealthy elites by the majority of common people. Madison recommended various checks on majority rule that would guarantee the rights of minorities and give elites substantial autonomy to rule in the public interest.

This view of human nature is reflected in contemporary debates. In the United States the debate shifts from human nature to the nature of Americans as a people and whether we are different from other people. According to the theory of exceptionalism, Americans are more individualistic and self-interested than other people.[20] As a nation of immigrants, we fled feudal systems and traditional cultures in search of greater freedom and assimilated into an American value system that stressed upward mobility through individual effort. The pursuit of fortune in the marketplace is the special genius of Americans. Whether this is good or bad depends on your view of markets and governments.

The Social View   During the debate over the Constitution in the 1780s, a group of dissenters, the Anti-federalists, argued that the Constitution placed too many limits on citizen participation. (We have included a selection by the Anti-federalist Brutus in Chapter 1.) The Anti-federalists argued that the common people could overcome or check their selfish inclinations through democratic participation and education in civic virtue. As much power as possible, therefore, should be placed in the hands of the people at the grassroots level. The main threat to democracy, Anti-federalists believed, came not from the masses of common people but from power-hungry elites. The best way to protect against elite tyranny was to have the people participate directly in deciding important issues. The Anti-federalists founded the tradition of popular (expansive) democracy that is still alive in the United States.

Even today, when Americans seem caught up in acquisitive pursuits and politics seems so mean-spirited, some observers argue that there are important sources of social commitment in American culture. An influential book by Robert Bellah and colleagues, *Habits of the Heart,* argues that Americans are attached to powerful civic traditions that pull us out of our individualistic orientations. These civic traditions are rooted in religion and republicanism, both of which emphasize commitments to public service. Americans exhibit lively commitments to grassroots participation and public service. In Chapter 12, one selection argues that young people have withdrawn from political involvements in response to the failures of government over the past generation. The other selection disagrees, arguing that the voluntary commitments of young people are a valuable contribution to civil society.

Conclusion: A Guide to Critical Thinking

Everyone has a political philosophy. Whether we recognize it or not, we bring certain assumptions about democracy, freedom, equality, and human nature to political debates. The goal is not to give up these assumptions but to convert them from unconscious prejudices into carefully chosen elements of a political philosophy. A good way to develop a thoughtful political philosophy is to analyze political debates like those included here. Clever debaters, for example, will appear as if they are supporting equality in general, but in order to make their argument work, they must adopt one conception of equality over another. Readers must get behind the rhetoric and evaluate these assumptions, as well as the logic and evidence of the argument itself.

As a guide to critical thinking we suggest that readers keep in mind five questions and evaluate the evidence that supports their answers. (Some questions may not apply to some selections.)

1. What is the author's concept of democracy, elite (limited) or popular (expansive)?
2. What is the author's concept of freedom, negative (freedom from) or positive (freedom to)?
3. What is the author's concept of equality—process or results?
4. How would you classify each author's ideology?
5. What concept of human nature, individualist or social, lies behind the author's argument?

In conclusion, it often may seem as if Americans disagree so much (Republicans versus Democrats, conservatives versus liberals, populists versus elitists) that our society will fly apart in conflict. But there is one thing that finally does unite us: the belief that open and public debate is the best, in fact the only, democratic way to settle our differences.

NOTES

1. Richard L. Berke, "No Television or Radio Advertising? No way, Bradley says," *New York Times,* December 20, 1999.

2. See Jon Elster, ed., *Deliberative Democracy* (New York: Cambridge University Press, 1998). The German political theorist Jürgen Habermas has spent many years developing a theory of the ideal speech situation as the foundation of democracy. See especially his *The Theory of Communicative Action,* 2 vols. (Boston: Beacon Press, 1984–1987).

3. John Stuart Mill, *On Liberty,* ed. and with an introduction by Currin V. Shields (Indianapolis, Ind.: Bobbs-Merrill, 1956), p. 46.

4. See Stephen L. Esquith, *Intimacy and Spectacle: Liberal Theory as Political Education* (Ithaca, N.Y.: Cornell University Press, 1994).

5. Amy Gutmann and Dennis Thompson call this the principle of reciprocity—that in a democratic debate citizens appeal to reasons that can be mutually acceptable to

other citizens. See *Democracy and Disagreement* (Cambridge, Mass.: Harvard University Press, 1996).

6. Cohen, "Deliberation and Democratic Legitimacy," *The Good Polity: Normative Analysis of the State,* (Oxford: Basil Blackwell, 1989), p. 29.

7. Justice William J. Brennan, Jr., "Federal Judges Properly and Inevitably Make Law Through 'Loose' Constitutional Construction," in *Debating American Government,* ed. Peter Woll (2d ed.; Glenview, Ill.: Scott, Foresman, 1988), p. 338.

8. It is neither possible nor desirable for a constitution to specify every application. If it did, it would be a rigid constitution that would be incapable of adapting to new conditions.

9. The following discussion of the sources of democratic disagreements in the United States draws heavily on Deborah A. Stone, *Political Paradox: The Art of Political Decision Making* (New York: Norton, 1997), and Frances Moore Lappé, *Rediscovering America's Values* (New York: Ballantine Books, 1989).

10. For an insightful discussion of essentially contested concepts, see William E. Connolly, *The Terms of Political Discourse* (2d ed.; Princeton, N.J.: Princeton University Press, 1983).

11. For the most famous definition of democracy along these lines, see Joseph A. Schumpeter, *Capitalism, Socialism, and Democracy* (3d ed.; New York: Harper, 1950), p. 269.

12. For elaboration on the concepts of elite and popular democracy, see Bruce Miroff, Raymond Seidelman, and Todd Swanstrom, *The Democratic Debate: An Introduction to American Politics* (2d ed.; Boston: Houghton Mifflin, 1998).

13. Robert A. Dahl is the most influential contemporary political scientist who has written on the ideas of elite and popular democracy. Dahl began his career by defending a version of elite democratic theory in *A Preface to Democratic Theory* (Chicago: University of Chicago Press, 1956) and *Who Governs? Democracy and Power in an American City* (New Haven, Conn.: Yale University Press, 1961). In later works, Dahl shifted dramatically to a more popular democratic position. See *A Preface to Economic Democracy* (Berkeley: University of California Press, 1985) and *Democracy and Its Critics* (New Haven, Conn.: Yale University Press, 1989).

14. Mill, *On Liberty*, p. 13.

15. The classic statement on positive and negative freedom is Isaiah Berlin's "Two Concepts of Liberty," in *Four Essays on Liberty* (New York: Oxford University Press, 1969), pp. 118–172.

16. For an eloquent defense of a positive conception of freedom, see President Franklin D. Roosevelt's speech to Congress on "An Economic Bill of Rights," in *Documents of American History,* ed. Henry Steele Commager (New York: Appleton-Century-Crofts, 1963), Vol. 2, pp. 483–485.

17. One of the best statements of a process orientation toward equality is Robert Nozick, *Anarchy, State and Utopia* (New York: Basic Books, 1974).

18. *The Oxford Dictionary of Quotations* (3d ed.; Oxford, Eng.: Oxford University Press, 1979), p. 217.

19. Charles Lindblom, *Politics and Markets: The World's Political-Economic Systems* (New York: Basic Books, 1977), p. ix.

20. For an influential statement on American exceptionalism, see Louis Hartz, *The Liberal Tradition in American Thought* (New York: Harcourt, Brace, 1955).

1

The Founding: Debating the Constitution

Although Americans relish political controversy in the present, we project onto the distant past of our nation's origins a more dignified political consensus. The founders of our republic—Washington, Adams, Jefferson, Hamilton, Madison—are cast in stone monuments and treated as political saints. Their ideas are invoked as hallowed truths that should inspire us. Seldom are these ideas treated as arguments that we should ponder and debate.

In fact, consensus was not the hallmark of the era in which the American republic was founded. Passionate political controversies raged during the American Revolution and its aftermath. These controversies ranged over the most basic issues of political life. The most profound was the debate over the ratification of the Constitution. The supporters of the Constitution, known as Federalists, and its opponents, known as Anti-federalists, disagreed over what kind of a republic Americans should have. Although their debate took place over two hundred years ago, it still illuminates the core dilemmas of our democratic society.

The readings that follow highlight some of the fundamental issues debated by Federalists and Anti-federalists. They pit the greatest thinker among the Federalists, James Madison, against a New York Anti-federalist who used the pseudonym of Brutus in an argument over the appropriate scale of democratic political life. (Scholars are not absolutely certain who Brutus was; the most likely candidate is Robert Yates, a New York judge. The pseudonym, by recalling the Roman republican who killed the tyrant Julius Caesar, evokes the threat allegedly posed by the Constitution to republican liberty.)

In his classic essay, "Federalist No. 10," Madison favors the large, national republic established by the Constitution over small republics (state governments). In small republics, Madison warns, selfish factions can attain majority status and will use their power over the government to oppress minorities (such as the wealthy or those who hold unorthodox religious beliefs). Small republics thus allow the worst qualities in human nature to prevail: they allow irrational passion to overwhelm reasoned deliberation and injustice to supplant the public good.

The large republic created by the new Constitution, Madison prophesies, will be more rational and more just. Elected in large districts, representatives will likely be the most-distinguished and patriotic citizens, and they will "refine and enlarge the public views" by filtering out the most selfish and shortsighted popular impulses. There will also be a greater diversity of factions in the large republic, making it unlikely that a majority can come together except on the basis of the common good. In Madison's essay, the chief threat to republican liberty comes, ironically, from the people themselves. His solution is to create a large republic in which the people will be divided into so many different interest groups that they can do little harm, while a small number of decision makers at the top take care of their common needs.

Brutus's essay (the first in a series that he wrote) takes issue with Madison on every count. He predicts that the large republic established by the Constitution will be run by aristocratic rulers who will eagerly expand their powers and oppress the common people. The greater distance from voters that Madison thinks will promote deliberation and public spirit in representatives will instead, Brutus argues, foster corruption and self-seeking in them. The diversity of the large republic is also, for Brutus, an unwelcome development since it will increase selfish factionalism, conflict, and stalemate.

Whereas Madison sees small republics as scenes of turbulence and misery, Brutus portrays them in a favorable light. In the smaller political scale of a state, the people will share common economic and social characteristics. Electoral districts will be smaller, so voters will personally know and trust their representatives and these representatives in turn will mirror their constituents' values and sentiments. Rather than breeding tyrannical majorities, small republics, as Brutus depicts them, educate law-abiding and virtuous citizens. In sum, Brutus rests his political hopes on the mass of ordinary people in the small republic, whose political impulses Madison fears, while directing his criticisms against a national elite, to whom Madison looks for wise political rule.

Anti-federalist fears that the Constitution would create an oppressive government, fatal to republican liberty, strike us today as grossly exaggerated. Yet in at least one respect these fears were fortunate—they helped produce the Bill of Rights. Initially, Federalists such as Madison and his collaborator on *The Federalist Papers,* Alexander Hamilton, claimed that a national Bill of Rights was both unnecessary and undesirable. By establishing a national government that possessed only enumerated, limited powers, they insisted, the Constitution had not granted any authority to invade the liberties and rights of the people; but if a list of particular rights was nonetheless appended to the Constitution, it might imply that the government *could* invade rights that had not been listed. These arguments were brushed aside by the Anti-federalists, who continued to argue that without specific guarantees the liberties for which Americans had fought in the Revolution might be usurped by a government of their own creation. To conciliate the Anti-federalists and win greater public support for the new Constitution, Madison dropped his objections and took the lead in pushing for the Bill of Rights in the first Congress.

Although Federalists and Anti-federalists could ultimately find common ground in a Bill of Rights, the philosophical and political differences between them remained profound. Their disagreements began the American debate between elite democracy and popular democracy. Nowhere is this more evident than in the contrast between Madison's reliance on a deliberative elite and Brutus's regard for the capacities of ordinary citizens. But it can also be seen in the difference between Madison's belief that liberty will inevitably produce inequality of property and Brutus's belief that in a small republic large-scale inequalities can be avoided.

The Federalists and Anti-federalists debated basic questions about democracy, and their disagreements still echo in our politics today. Thinking about the issues in their debate can help to clarify your own perspective toward democracy in the United States. Do you believe, with Madison, that it is only at the national level that selfish majorities can be blocked and government policies can be framed by deliberative and public-spirited representatives? Do you believe, with Brutus, that we should prefer state and local governments in order to promote greater civic participation and to enhance the trust between representatives and their constituents? Even more fundamentally, do you agree with Madison that ordinary citizens are too uninformed and self-seeking to be trusted with great political influence and that decisions are best left to elected representatives who can "refine and enlarge" what the people think? Or do you agree with Brutus that elites pose the greater danger to democracy and that democracy only flourishes when conditions are established that encourage ordinary citizens to involve themselves in the search for the public good?

Federalist No. 10

JAMES MADISON

Among the numerous advantages promised by a well-constructed Union, none deserves to be more accurately developed than its tendency to break and control the violence of faction.[1] The friend of popular governments never finds himself so much alarmed for their character and fate as when he contemplates their propensity to this dangerous vice. He will not fail, therefore, to set a due value on any plan which, without violating the principles to which he is attached, provides a proper cure for it. The instability, injustice, and confusion introduced into the public councils have, in truth, been the mortal diseases under which popular governments have everywhere perished, as they continue to be the favorite and fruitful topics from which the adversaries to liberty derive their most specious declamations. The valuable improvements made by the American constitutions on the popular models, both ancient and modern, cannot certainly be too much admired; but it would be an unwarrantable partiality to contend that they have as effectually obviated the danger on this side, as was wished and expected. Complaints are everywhere heard from our most considerate and virtuous citizens, equally the friends of public and private faith and of public and personal liberty, that our governments are too unstable, that the public good is disregarded in the conflicts of rival parties, and that measures are too often decided, not according to the rules of justice and the rights of the minor party, but by the superior force of an interested and overbearing majority. However anxiously we may wish that these complaints had no foundation, the evidence of known facts will not permit us to deny that they are in some degree true. It will be found, indeed, on a candid review of our situation, that some of the distresses under which we labor have been erroneously charged on the operation of our governments; but it will be found, at the same time, that other causes will not alone account for many of our heaviest misfortunes; and, particularly, for that prevailing and increasing distrust of public engagements and alarm for private rights which are echoed from one end of the continent to the other. These must be chiefly, if not wholly, effects of the unsteadiness and injustice with which a factious spirit has tainted our public administration.

---

1. In modern terms, both interest groups and political parties are examples of Madison's factions. Note that by the definition Madison offers later, no faction can legitimately claim to represent the public interest.

By a faction I understand a number of citizens, whether amounting to a majority or minority of the whole, who are united and actuated by some common impulse of passion, or of interest, adverse to the rights of other citizens, or to the permanent and aggregate interests of the community.

There are two methods of curing the mischiefs of faction: the one, by removing its causes; the other, by controlling its effects.

There are again two methods of removing the causes of faction: the one, by destroying the liberty which is essential to its existence; the other, by giving to every citizen the same opinions, the same passions, and the same interests.

It could never be more truly said than of the first remedy that it was worse than the disease. Liberty is to faction what air is to fire, an aliment without which it instantly expires. But it could not be a less folly to abolish liberty, which is essential to political life, because it nourishes faction than it would be to wish the annihilation of air, which is essential to animal life, because it imparts to fire its destructive agency.

The second expedient is as impracticable as the first would be unwise. As long as the reason of man continues fallible, and he is at liberty to exercise it, different opinions will be formed. As long as the connection subsists between his reason and his self-love, his opinions and his passions will have a reciprocal influence on each other; and the former will be objects to which the latter will attach themselves. The diversity in the faculties of men, from which the rights of property originate, is not less an insuperable obstacle to a uniformity of interests. The protection of these faculties is the first object of government. From the protection of different and unequal faculties of acquiring property, the possession of different degrees and kinds of property immediately results; and from the influence of these on the sentiments and views of the respective proprietors ensues a division of the society into different interests and parties.

The latent causes of faction are thus sown in the nature of man; and we see them everywhere brought into different degrees of activity, according to the different circumstances of civil society. A zeal for different opinions concerning religion, concerning government, and many other points, as well of speculation as of practice; an attachment to different leaders ambitiously contending for pre-eminence and power; or to persons of other descriptions whose fortunes have been interesting to the human passions, have, in turn, divided mankind into parties, inflamed them with mutual animosity, and rendered them much more disposed to vex and oppress each other than to co-operate for their common good. So strong is this propensity of mankind to fall into mutual animosities that where no substantial occasion presents itself the most frivolous and fanciful distinctions have been sufficient to kindle their unfriendly passions and excite their most violent conflicts. But the most common and durable source of factions has been the various and unequal distribution of property. Those who hold and those who are without property have ever formed distinct interests in society. Those who are creditors, and those who are debtors, fall under a like discrimination. A landed interest, a manufacturing interest, a mercantile interest, a moneyed interest, with many lesser interests, grow up of necessity in civilized nations, and divide them into different classes, actuated by different sentiments and views. The regulation of these various and interfering interests forms the principal task of modern legislation and involves the spirit of party and faction in the necessary and ordinary operations of government.

No man is allowed to be a judge in his own cause, because his interest would certainly bias his judgment, and, not improbably, corrupt his integrity. With equal, nay with greater reason, a body of men are unfit to be both judges and parties at the same time; yet what are many of the most important acts of legislation but so many judicial determinations, not indeed concerning the rights of single persons, but concerning the rights of large bodies of citizens? And what are the different classes of legislators but advocates and parties to the causes which they determine? Is a law proposed concerning private debts? It is a question to which the creditors are parties on one side and the debtors on the other. Justice ought to hold the balance between them. Yet the parties are, and must be, themselves the judges; and the most numerous party, or in other words, the most powerful faction must be expected to prevail. Shall domestic manufacturers be encouraged, and in what degree, by restrictions on foreign manufacturers? are questions which would be differently decided by the landed and the manufacturing classes, and probably by neither with a sole regard to justice and the public good. The apportionment of taxes on the various descriptions of property is an act which seems to require the most exact impartiality; yet there is, perhaps, no legislative act in which greater opportunity and temptation are given to a predominant party to trample on the rules of justice. Every shilling with which they overburden the inferior number is a shilling saved to their own pockets.

It is in vain to say that enlightened statesmen will be able to adjust these clashing interests and render them all subservient to the public good. Enlightened statesmen will not always be at the helm. Nor, in many cases, can such an adjustment be made at all without taking into view indirect and remote considerations, which will rarely prevail over the immediate interest which one party may find in disregarding the rights of another or the good of the whole.

The inference to which we are brought is that the *causes* of faction cannot be removed and that relief is only to be sought in the means of controlling its *effects*.

If a faction consists of less than a majority, relief is supplied by the republican principle, which enables the majority to defeat its sinister views by regular vote. It may clog the administration, it may convulse the society; but it will be unable to execute and mask its violence under the forms of the Constitution. When a majority is included in a faction, the form of popular government, on the other hand, enables it to sacrifice to its ruling passion or interest both the public good and the rights of other citizens. To secure the public good and private rights against the danger of such a faction, and at the same time to preserve the spirit and the form of popular government, is then the great object to which our inquiries are directed. Let me add that it is the great desideratum by which alone this form of government can be rescued from the opprobrium under which it has so long labored and be recommended to the esteem and adoption of mankind.

By what means is this object attainable? Evidently by one of two only. Either the existence of the same passion or interest in a majority at the same time must be prevented, or the majority, having such coexistent passion of interest, must be rendered, by their number and local situation, unable to concert and carry into effect schemes of oppression. If the impulse and the opportunity be suffered to coincide, we well know that neither moral nor religious motives can be relied on as an adequate control. They are not found to be such on the injustice and violence of individuals, and lose their efficacy in proportion to the number combined together, that is, in proportion as their efficacy becomes needful.

From this view of the subject it may be concluded that a pure democracy, by which I mean a society consisting of a small number of citizens, who assemble and administer the government in person, can admit of no cure for the mischiefs of faction. A common passion or interest will, in almost every case, be felt by a majority of the whole; a communication and concert results from the form of government itself; and there is nothing to check the inducements to sacrifice the weaker party or an obnoxious individual. Hence it is that such democracies have ever been spectacles of turbulence and contention; have ever been found incompatible with personal security or the rights of property; and have in general been as short in their lives as they have been violent in their deaths. Theoretic politicians, who have patronized this species of government, have erroneously supposed that by reducing mankind to a perfect equality in their political rights, they would at the same time be perfectly equalized and assimilated in their possessions, their opinions, and their passions.

A republic, by which I mean a government in which the scheme of representation takes place, opens a different prospect and promises the cure for which we are seeking. Let us examine the points in which it varies from pure democracy, and we shall comprehend both the nature of the cure and the efficacy which it must derive from the Union.

The two great points of difference between a democracy and a republic are: first, the delegation of the government, in the latter, to a small number of citizens elected by the rest; secondly, the greater number of citizens and greater sphere of country over which the latter may be extended.

The effect of the first difference is, on the one hand, to refine and enlarge the public views by passing them through the medium of a chosen body of citizens, whose wisdom may best discern the true interest of their country and whose patriotism and love of justice will be least likely to sacrifice it to temporary or partial considerations. Under such a regulation it may well happen that the public voice, pronounced by the representatives

of the people, will be more consonant to the public good than if pronounced by the people themselves, convened for the purpose. On the other
hand, the effect may be inverted. Men of factious tempers, of local prejudices, or of sinister designs, may, by intrigue, by corruption, or by other
means, first obtain the suffrages, and then betray the interests of the people. The question resulting is, whether small or extensive republics are most
favorable to the election of proper guardians of the public weal; and it is
clearly decided in favor of the latter by two obvious considerations.

In the first place it is to be remarked that however small the republic
may be the representatives must be raised to a certain number in order to
guard against the cabals of a few; and that however large it may be they
must be limited to a certain number in order to guard against the confusion
of a multitude. Hence, the number of representatives in the two cases not
being in proportion to that of the constituents, and being proportionally
greatest in the small republic, it follows that if the proportion of fit characters be not less in the large than in the small republic, the former will present a greater option, and consequently a greater probability of a fit choice.

In the next place, as each representative will be chosen by a greater
number of citizens in the large than in the small republic, it will be more
difficult for unworthy candidates to practise with success the vicious arts by
which elections are too often carried; and the suffrages of the people being
more free, will be more likely to center on men who possess the most attractive merit and the most diffusive and established characters.

It must be confessed that in this, as in most other cases, there is a mean,
on both sides of which inconveniencies will be found to lie. By enlarging
too much the number of electors, you render the representative too little
acquainted with all their local circumstances and lesser interests; as by reducing it too much, you render him unduly attached to these, and too little
fit to comprehend and pursue great and national objects. The federal Constitution forms a happy combination in this respect; the great and aggregate
interests being referred to the national, the local and particular to the State
legislatures.

The other point of difference is the greater number of citizens and extent of territory which may be brought within the compass of republican
than of democratic government; and it is this circumstance principally
which renders factious combinations less to be dreaded in the former than
in the latter. The smaller the society, the fewer probably will be the distinct
parties and interests composing it; the fewer the distinct parties and interests, the more frequently will a majority be found of the same party; and
the smaller the number of individuals composing a majority, and the
smaller the compass within which they are placed, the more easily will they
concert and execute their plans of oppression. Extend the sphere and you
take in a greater variety of parties and interests; you make it less probable
that a majority of the whole will have a common motive to invade the
rights of other citizens; or if such a common motive exists, it will be more
difficult for all who feel it to discover their own strength and to act in

unison with each other. Besides other impediments, it may be remarked that, where there is a consciousness of unjust or dishonorable purposes, communication is always checked by distrust in proportion to the number whose concurrence is necessary.

Hence, it clearly appears that the same advantage which a republic has over a democracy in controlling the effects of faction is enjoyed by a large over a small republic—is enjoyed by the Union over the States composing it. Does this advantage consist in the substitution of representatives whose enlightened views and virtuous sentiments render them superior to local prejudices and to schemes of injustice? It will not be denied that the representation of the Union will be most likely to possess these requisite endowments. Does it consist in the greater security afforded by a greater variety of parties, against the event of any one party being able to outnumber and oppress the rest? In an equal degree does the increased variety of parties comprised within the Union increase this security. Does it, in fine, consist in the greater obstacles opposed to the concert and accomplishment of the secret wishes of an unjust and interested majority? Here again the extent of the Union gives it the most palpable advantage.

The influence of factious leaders may kindle a flame within their particular States but will be unable to spread a general conflagration through the other States. A religious sect may degenerate into a political faction in a part of the Confederacy; but the variety of sects dispersed over the entire face of it must secure the national councils against any danger from that source. A rage for paper money, for an abolition of debts, for an equal division of property, or for any other improper or wicked project, will be less apt to pervade the whole body of the Union than a particular member of it, in the same proportion as such a malady is more likely to taint a particular county or district than an entire State.[2]

In the extent and proper structure of the Union, therefore, we behold a republican remedy for the diseases most incident to republican government. And according to the degree of pleasure and pride we feel in being republicans ought to be our zeal in cherishing the spirit and supporting the character of federalists.   PUBLIUS

---

2. The examples of factional objectives (for example, paper money's benefiting debtors at the expense of creditors) that Madison cites are drawn from the economic conflicts that pervaded the states in the 1780s. The movement for a new national Constitution aimed to put an end to the possibility that radical factional goals might be achieved in the states.

Anti-federalist Paper
18 October 1787

BRUTUS

To the Citizens of the State of New-York.

Perhaps this country never saw so critical a period in their political concerns. We have felt the feebleness of the ties by which these United-States are held together, and the want of sufficient energy in our present confederation, to manage, in some instances, our general concerns. Various expedients have been proposed to remedy these evils, but none have succeeded. At length a Convention of the states has been assembled, they have formed a constitution which will now, probably, be submitted to the people to ratify or reject, who are the fountain of all power, to whom alone it of right belongs to make or unmake constitutions, or forms of government, at their pleasure. The most important question that was ever proposed to your decision, or to the decision of any people under heaven, is before you, and you are to decide upon it by men of your own election, chosen specially for this purpose. If the constitution, offered to your acceptance, be a wise one, calculated to preserve the invaluable blessings of liberty, to secure the inestimable rights of mankind, and promote human happiness, then, if you accept it, you will lay a lasting foundation of happiness for millions yet unborn; generations to come will rise up and call you blessed. . . . But if, on the other hand, this form of government contains principles that will lead to the subversion of liberty—if it tends to establish a despotism, or, what is worse, a tyrannic aristocracy; then, if you adopt it, this only remaining asylum for liberty will be shut up, and posterity will execrate your memory. . . .

With these few introductory remarks, I shall proceed to a consideration of this constitution:

The first question that presents itself on the subject is, whether a confederated government be the best for the United States or not. Or in other words, whether the thirteen United States should be reduced to one great republic, governed by one legislature, and under the direction of one executive and judicial; or whether they should continue thirteen confederated republics, under the direction and control of a supreme federal head for certain defined national purposes only?

This enquiry is important, because, although the government reported by the convention does not go to a perfect and entire consolidation,[1] yet it

---

1. The Anti-federalists charged that the proposed Constitution aimed not at federalism (a division of powers between the national government and the state governments) but at consolidation (the centralization of all powers in the national government).

approaches so near to it, that it must, if executed, certainly and infallibly terminate in it.

This government is to possess absolute and uncontrolable power, legislative, executive and judicial, with respect to every object to which it extends, for by the last clause of section 8th, article 1st, it is declared "that the Congress shall have power to make all laws which shall be necessary and proper for carrying into execution the foregoing powers, and all other powers vested by this constitution, in the government of the United States; or in any department or office thereof." And by the 6th article, it is declared "that this constitution, and the laws of the United States, which shall be made in pursuance thereof, and the treaties made, or which shall be made, under the authority of the United States, shall be the supreme law of the land; and the judges in every state shall be bound thereby, any thing in the constitution, or law of any state to the contrary notwithstanding." It appears from these articles that there is no need of any intervention of the state governments, between the Congress and the people, to execute any one power vested in the general government, and that the constitution and laws of every state are nullified and declared void, so far as they are or shall be inconsistent with this constitution, or the laws made in pursuance of it, or with treaties made under the authority of the United States.—The government then, so far as it extends, is a complete one, and not a confederation. It is as much one complete government as that of New-York or Massachusetts, has as absolute and perfect powers to make and execute all laws, to appoint officers, institute courts, declare offences, and annex penalties, with respect to every object to which it extends, as any other in the world. So far therefore as its powers reach, all ideas of confederation are given up and lost. It is true this government is limited to certain objects, or to speak more properly, some small degree of power is still left to the states, but a little attention to the powers vested in the general government, will convince every candid man, that if it is capable of being executed, all that is reserved for the individual states must very soon be annihilated, except so far as they are barely necessary to the organization of the general government. The powers of the general legislature extend to every case that is of the least importance—there is nothing valuable to human nature, nothing dear to freemen, but what is within its power. It has authority to make laws which will affect the lives, the liberty, and property of every man in the United States; nor can the constitution or laws of any state, in any way prevent or impede the full and complete execution of every power given. The legislative power is competent to lay taxes, duties, imposts, and excises—there is no limitation to this power, unless it be said that the clause which directs the use to which those taxes, and duties shall be applied, may be said to be a limitation: but this is no restriction of the power at all, for by this clause they are to be applied to pay the debts and provide for the common defence and general welfare of the United States; but the legislature have authority to contract debts at their discretion; they are the sole judges of what is necessary to provide for the common defence, and they only are to determine what is for the general welfare; this power therefore is neither more nor less, than a power to lay and collect taxes, imposts, and excises, at their pleasure; not only [is] the power to lay taxes unlimited, as to the amount they may require, but it is perfect and absolute to raise them in any mode they please. No state legislature, or any power in the state governments, have any more to do in carrying this into effect, than the authority of one state has to do with that of another. In the business therefore of laying and collecting taxes, the idea of confederation is totally lost, and that of one entire republic is embraced. . . .

Let us now proceed to enquire, as I at first proposed, whether it be best the thirteen United States should be reduced to one great republic, or not? It is here taken for granted, that all agree in this, that whatever government we adopt, it ought to be a free one; that it should be so framed as to secure the liberty of the citizens of America, and such an one as to admit of a full, fair, and equal representation of the people. The question then will be, whether a government thus constituted, and founded on such principles, is practicable, and can be exercised over the whole United States, reduced into one state?

If respect is to be paid to the opinion of the greatest and wisest men who have ever thought or wrote on the science of government, we shall be constrained to conclude, that a free republic cannot succeed over a country of such immense extent, containing such a number of inhabitants, and these encreasing in such rapid progression as that of the whole United States. Among the many illustrious authorities which might be produced to this point, I shall content myself with quoting only two. The one is the baron de Montesquieu, spirit of laws, chap. xvi. vol. I [book VIII],[2] "It is natural to a republic to have only a small territory, otherwise it cannot long subsist. In a large republic there are men of large fortunes, and consequently of less moderation; there are trusts too great to be placed in any single subject; he has interest of his own; he soon begins to think that he may be happy, great and glorious, by oppressing his fellow citizens; and that he may raise himself to grandeur on the ruins of his country. In a large republic, the public good is sacrificed to a thousand views; it is subordinate to exceptions, and depends on accidents. In a small one, the interest of the public is easier perceived, better understood, and more within the reach of every citizen; abuses are of less extent, and of course are less protected." Of the same opinion is the marquis Beccaria.[3]

History furnishes no example of a free republic, any thing like the extent of the United States. The Grecian republics were of small extent; so also was that of the Romans. Both of these, it is true, in process of time, extended their conquests over large territories of country; and the con-

2. Baron Charles de Montesquieu was an eighteenth-century French political theorist whose ideas were highly influential in the era of the American Revolution and the Constitution.
3. Cesare Beccaria was an eighteenth-century Italian legal philosopher.

sequence was, that their governments were changed from that of free governments to those of the most tyrannical that ever existed in the world.

Not only the opinion of the greatest men, and the experience of mankind, are against the idea of an extensive republic, but a variety of reasons may be drawn from the reason and nature of things, against it. In every government, the will of the sovereign is the law. In despotic governments, the supreme authority being lodged in one, his will is law, and can be as easily expressed to a large extensive territory as to a small one. In a pure democracy the people are the sovereign, and their will is declared by themselves; for this purpose they must all come together to deliberate, and decide. This kind of government cannot be exercised, therefore, over a country of any considerable extent; it must be confined to a single city, or at least limited to such bounds as that the people can conveniently assemble, be able to debate, understand the subject submitted to them, and declare their opinion concerning it.

In a free republic, although all laws are derived from the consent of the people, yet the people do not declare their consent by themselves in person, but by representatives, chosen by them, who are supposed to know the minds of their constituents, and to be possessed of integrity to declare this mind.

In every free government, the people must give their assent to the laws by which they are governed. This is the true criterion between a free government and an arbitrary one. The former are ruled by the will of the whole, expressed in any manner they may agree upon; the latter by the will of one, or a few. If the people are to give their assent to the laws, by persons chosen and appointed by them, the manner of the choice and the number chosen, must be such, as to possess, be disposed, and consequently qualified to declare the sentiments of the people; for if they do not know, or are not disposed to speak the sentiments of the people, the people do not govern, but the sovereignty is in a few. Now, in a large extended country, it is impossible to have a representation, possessing the sentiments, and of integrity, to declare the minds of the people, without having it so numerous and unwieldly, as to be subject in great measure to the inconveniency of a democratic government.

The territory of the United States is of vast extent; it now contains near three millions of souls, and is capable of containing much more than ten times that number. Is it practicable for a country, so large and so numerous as they will soon become, to elect a representation, that will speak their sentiments, without their becoming so numerous as to be incapable of transacting public business? It certainly is not.

In a republic, the manners, sentiments, and interests of the people should be similar. If this be not the case, there will be a constant clashing of opinions; and the representatives of one part will be continually striving against those of the other. This will retard the operations of government, and prevent such conclusions as will promote the public good. If we apply this remark to the condition of the United States, we shall be convinced that it forbids that we should be one government. The United States includes a variety of climates. The productions of the different parts of the union are very variant, and their interests, of consequence, diverse. Their manners and habits differ as much as their climates and productions; and their sentiments are by no means coincident. The laws and customs of the several states are, in many respects, very diverse, and in some opposite; each would be in favor of its own interests and customs, and, of consequence, a legislature, formed of representatives from the respective parts, would not only be too numerous to act with any care or decision, but would be composed of such heterogenous and discordant principles, as would constantly be contending with each other.

The laws cannot be executed in a republic, of an extent equal to that of the United States, with promptitude.

The magistrates in every government must be supported in the execution of the laws, either by an armed force, maintained at the public expence for that purpose; or by the people turning out to aid the magistrate upon his command, in case of resistance.

In despotic governments, as well as in all the monarchies of Europe, standing armies are kept up to execute the commands of the prince or the magistrate, and are employed for this purpose when occasion requires: But they have always proved the destruction of liberty, and [are] abhorrent to the spirit of a free republic. In England, where they depend upon the parliament for their annual support, they have always been complained of as oppressive and unconstitutional, and are seldom employed in executing of the laws; never except on extraordinary occasions, and then under the direction of a civil magistrate.

A free republic will never keep a standing army to execute its laws. It must depend upon the support of its citizens. But when a government is to receive its support from the aid of the citizens, it must be so constructed as to have the confidence, respect, and affection of the people. Men who, upon the call of the magistrate, offer themselves to execute the laws, are influenced to do it either by affection to the government, or from fear; where a standing army is at hand to punish offenders, every man is actuated by the latter principle, and therefore, when the magistrate calls, will obey: but, where this is not the case, the government must rest for its support upon the confidence and respect which the people have for their government and laws. The body of the people being attached, the government will always be sufficient to support and execute its laws, and to operate upon the fears of any faction which may be opposed to it, not only to prevent an opposition to the execution of the laws themselves, but also to compel the most of them to aid the magistrate; but the people will not be likely to have such confidence in their rulers, in a republic so extensive as the United States, as necessary for these purposes. The confidence which the people have in their rulers, in a free republic, arises from their knowing them, from their being responsible to them for their conduct, and from the power they have of displacing them when they misbehave: but in a republic of the extent of this continent, the people in general would be acquainted with very few of their rulers: the people at large would know little of their proceedings, and it would be extremely difficult to change them. . . . The consequence will be, they will have no confidence in their legislature, suspect them of ambitious views, be jealous of every measure they adopt, and will not support the laws they pass. Hence the government will be nerveless and inefficient, and no way will be left to render it otherwise, but by establishing an armed force to execute the laws at the point of the bayonet—a government of all others the most to be dreaded.

In a republic of such vast extent as the United-States, the legislature cannot attend to the various concerns and wants of its different parts. It cannot be sufficiently numerous to be acquainted with the local condition and wants of the different districts, and if it could, it is impossible it should have sufficient time to attend to and provide for all the variety of cases of this nature, that would be continually arising.

In so extensive a republic, the great officers of government would soon become above the control of the people, and abuse their power to the purpose of aggrandizing themselves, and oppressing them. The trust committed to the executive offices, in a country of the extent of the United-States, must be various and of magnitude. The command of all the troops and navy of the republic, the appointment of officers, the power of pardoning offences, the collecting of all the public revenues, and the power of expending them, with a number of other powers, must be lodged and exercised in every state, in the hands of a few. When these are attended with great honor and emolument, as they always will be in large states, so as greatly to interest men to pursue them, and to be proper objects for ambitious and designing men, such men will be ever restless in their pursuit after them. They will use the power, when they have acquired it, to the purposes of gratifying their own interest and ambition, and it is scarcely possible, in a very large republic, to call them to account for their misconduct, or to prevent their abuse of power.

These are some of the reasons by which it appears, that a free republic cannot long subsist over a country of the great extent of these states. If then this new constitution is calculated to consolidate the thirteen states into one, as it evidently is, it ought not to be adopted. . . .

■ DISCUSSION QUESTIONS

1. How do the Federalists and the Anti-federalists view human nature? Why does Madison think individuals are "much more disposed to vex and oppress each other than to cooperate for their common good"? Why is

Brutus more hopeful that, under the proper political circumstances, citizens will cooperate for their common good? Whose perspective on human nature do you find more persuasive?

2. How do the Federalists and the Anti-federalists view participation by ordinary citizens at the local level? Why does Madison feel that "pure democracy" leads to disaster? Why does Brutus have a more positive view of politics within local communities? Do you think a "face-to-face" politics of ordinary citizens fosters individual growth and public spirit or produces ignorant decisions and unfairness to minorities?

3. How do the Federalists and the Anti-federalists view the role of elected representatives? Why does Madison want representatives to deliberate at a distance from the demands of their constituents? Why does Brutus want representatives to be closely tied to their constituents' ideas and interests? Do you think, like Madison, that representatives should be trustees who do what they think is best for the country, or do you believe, like Brutus, that representatives should be delegates who follow the expressed wishes of their constituents?

4. In what ways is the debate between Madison and Brutus reflected in today's political debates? In what ways have the arguments changed? Do contemporary defenders of a large policy role for the federal government share Madison's fundamental assumptions? Do contemporary critics of the federal government share Brutus's fundamental assumptions?

SUGGESTED READINGS AND INTERNET RESOURCES

The best source on the debate between the Federalists and the Anti-federalists is the original texts themselves. For inexpensive editions, see Clinton Rossiter, ed., *The Federalist Papers* (New York: New American Library, 1961), and Ralph Ketcham, ed., *The Anti-Federalist Papers* (New York: New American Library, 1986). On the political ideas of the founding era, see Gordon S. Wood, *The Creation of the American Republic, 1776–1787* (New York: Norton, 1972), and Jack N. Rakove, *Original Meanings: Politics and Ideas in the Making of the Constitution* (New York: Alfred A. Knopf, 1996). In *If Men Were Angels: James Madison and the Heartless Empire of Reason* (Lawrence: University Press of Kansas, 1995), Richard K. Matthews provides a provocative interpretation of the great Federalist's political theory. The most instructive commentary on the political philosophy of the Anti-federalists is Herbert J. Storing, *What the Anti-Federalists Were For* (Chicago: University of Chicago Press, 1981).

Emory Law School
http://www.law.emory.edu/FEDERAL/

A searchable index of information on the Constitution and *The Federalist Papers;* requires a forms-capable browser.

Political Theory Web Site
http://www.esu.edu/pols/texttheory.html
This web site of political theory texts includes *The Federalist Papers,* available in numerical order or by author.

CHAPTER

Democracy: Overrated or Undervalued?

Almost everybody in America believes in democracy. When Americans are asked by interviewers about basic questions of majority rule, equality of opportunity, or individual freedom, more than 95 percent profess a belief in democratic values. As our introduction to this book suggests, however, once we probe a bit deeper into what Americans think democracy means, we find that they are not at all of one mind about how far democracy should extend into political, social, and economic life. Elite democrats believe that democracy is a valuable method for selecting those who will govern us, but they are skeptical about the political capacities and interests of ordinary citizens and want important decisions left to those with experience and expertise. Popular democrats distrust elites as potentially self-serving and believe that under the right circumstances ordinary citizens are both capable of and entitled to a significant share in deciding public matters.

The debate over democracy began at the time of the nation's founding and has continued to this day. In the previous chapter, we saw Federalists and Anti-federalists arguing about whether the American experiment in self-government should rest on elite democracy or popular democracy. To James Madison, only a national republic manned by a deliberative elite, who could filter out the irrational passions of the public, could sustain the American experiment. In the eyes of Brutus, this national republic would breed an oppressive aristocracy, who would crush popular democracy, which must be rooted in law-abiding and virtuous citizens and flourish at the local and state levels.

Although the Federalists prevailed in the original American debate over democracy, securing the ratification of the Constitution, nineteenth-century America looked more like the Anti-federalists' (and Thomas Jefferson's) vision of democracy than the Federalists'. For most of the century, political and economic life was small-scale and decentralized, with the federal government in Washington, D.C., exercising only limited powers. Nineteenth-century America witnessed the establishment of the most democratic society the world had contained since the Golden Era of democracy in ancient Athens. Levels of political involvement and rates of voting among ordinary citizens were remarkably high—much higher, in fact, than they would be a century later. To be sure, this was a white man's democracy; Native Americans, African Americans, and women paid a high price for white men's freedoms, and the latter two groups had to launch long and painful struggles for democratic inclusion that would not achieve much success until the twentieth century.

The transformation of the United States between the Civil War and World War I from a largely agrarian and decentralized society into an urbanized and industrialized nation called into question the popular democratic assumptions held by the heirs of the Anti-federalists and Jefferson. Could ordinary citizens obtain, understand, and act on the increasingly complex information that characterized modern American society? America's premier journalist, Walter Lippmann, argued in the 1920s that ordinary citizens viewed the world through stereotypes, simplistic pictures that distorted reality, and that effective government for the industrial age required a greater emphasis on trained, dispassionate experts. Agreeing with Lippmann that the American public had been eclipsed by forces that seemed beyond its control, America's premier philosopher, John Dewey, warned of the elitist tendencies of Lippmann's experts. Dewey sought to revive popular democracy in "face-to-face" communities where ordinary citizens, informed by the latest findings of social science, would participate in public affairs.

In the 1950s (like the 1920s, a decade of apparent public apathy), Lippmann's argument received reinforcement from the empirical surveys conducted by political scientists. Most Americans, these surveys suggested, were not very interested in political life, did not know much about public affairs, and did not participate at very high levels in politics. Prevailing American conceptions about democracy would have to be modified, many political scientists now argued, to reflect what Robert Dahl called "citizenship without politics." But a minority of political scientists began in the 1960s to object, on both theoretical and empirical grounds, to this redefinition of democracy, claiming that the new perspective was less democratic realism than it was democratic elitism. These critics found support among the emerging political movements that would mark the 1960s as a decade of popular democratic upsurge. Students for a Democratic Society (SDS), the most important organization of the '60s New Left, gave the period its political watchword: *participatory democracy*.

Our selections in this chapter, excerpted from books published in 1999, are two of the latest versions of America's enduring debate over democracy. John Mueller attacks what he considers to be the romantic and unrealistic conception of democracy put forward by popular democrats. All that is required for democracy, Mueller contends, is a political system that eschews violence and that allows citizens to criticize, pressure, and remove those in power. Democracy, he suggests, will always consist of a messy, unequal conflict for advantage among special interests. What it will never achieve, he argues, are the misty ideals of popular democrats: political equality, participation, and an enlightened citizenry. Holding democracy to these standards only fosters cynicism. Mueller's analysis updates the classic elite democratic perspective of Madison, Lippmann, and Dahl.

Paul Rogat Loeb represents the popular democratic perspective of the Anti-federalists, Jefferson, Dewey, and SDS. He ascribes the widespread cynicism about politics in the 1990s not to the romantic ideals of popular democrats but to the skeptical views of public involvement broadcast by the dominant forces in American society. "We've all but forgotten," he writes, "that public participation is the very soul of democratic citizenship, and how much it can enrich our lives." In our selection, Loeb tells the story of Pete Knutson (one of many stories in his book), a commercial fisherman who organized his fellow fishermen, environmentalists, and Native Americans to defeat an initiative by large industries that would have destroyed salmon spawning grounds. Loeb argues that active citizenship is required both to fulfill our responsibility to take care of the common good and to grow as individuals in psychological and spiritual depth.

Evaluating the debate between Mueller and Loeb should help to clarify your own conception of democracy. Do you believe, with Mueller, that Americans have many more interesting things to do than spend their time on political pursuits? Or do you believe, with Loeb, that political involvement is necessary for a sense of freedom and personal dignity? Do you believe, with Mueller, that self-interest and inequality will always characterize democracy and that attempts to reduce their influence through political and economic reforms will inevitably fail? Or do you believe, with Loeb, that politics can also reflect our more social impulses and can redress political and economic injustices? Above all, do you agree with Mueller that acceptance of elite democracy is the only realistic perspective, or do you agree with Loeb that the abandonment of popular democracy is a surrender to cynicism?

Democracy's Romantic Myths

JOHN MUELLER

There is a famous Norman Rockwell painting that purports to portray democracy in action. It depicts a New England town meeting in which a workingman has risen in a contentious situation to present his point of view. His rustic commonsense, it appears, has cut through the indecisiveness and bickering to provide a consensual solution to the problem at hand, and the others in the picture are looking up at him admiringly.

As it happens, that misty-eyed, idealized snapshot has almost nothing to do with democracy in actual practice. Democracy is not a process in which one shining idea conquers all as erstwhile contenders fall into blissful consensus. Rather, it is an extremely disorderly muddle in which clashing ideas and interests (all of them "special") do unkempt and unequal, if peaceful, battle and in which ideas are often reduced to slogans, data to distorted fragments, evidence to gestures, and arguments to poses. Speculation is rampant, caricature is routine, and posturing is de rigueur. If one idea wins out, it is likely to be severely compromised in the process, and no one goes away entirely reconciled or happy. And there is rarely a sense of completion or finality or permanence: in a democracy, as Tod Lindberg points out, "the fat lady never sings." It's a mess, and the only saving grace is that other methods for reaching decisions are even worse.

. . . I develop an approach to democracy that contrasts substantially with the romantic Rockwell ideal. It stresses petition and lobbying—the chaotic and distinctly nonconsensual combat of "special interests"—as the dominant and central characteristic of democracy and it suggests that while elections are useful and often valuable in a democracy, they may not be absolutely necessary. I also argue that democracy in practice is not about equality, but rather about the freedom to become politically unequal, and that it functions not so much by rule by the majority as by minority rule with majority acquiescence. . . .

. . . I also contrast democracy with other governmental forms. Although the advantage is only comparative, democracy seems to do better at generating effective governments, choosing leaders, addressing minority concerns, creating a livable society, and functioning effectively with real, flawed human beings. . . .

In defining democracy, it is particularly important, I think, to separate the essential institution itself from the operating devices that are commonly associated with it—mechanisms like written constitutions, the separation of powers or "checks and balances" (including an independent judiciary), and even elections. Any definition of democracy is inadequate, I think, if it can logically be taken to suggest that Britain (which has neither a written constitution nor separation of powers) is not a democracy or that Switzerland did not become one until 1971 (when women were finally given the vote). . . .

In my view, democracy is characterized by government that is necessarily and routinely responsive—although this responsiveness is not always even, fair, or equal. It comes into effect when the people effectively agree not to use violence to replace the leadership, and the leadership effectively leaves them free to criticize, to pressure, to organize, and to try to dislodge it by any other means. This approach can be used to set up a sort of sliding scale of governmental forms. An *authoritarian* government may effectively and sometimes intentionally allow a degree of opposition—a limited amount of press disagreement, for example, or the freedom to complain privately, something sometimes known as the freedom of conversation. But it will not tolerate organized attempts to replace it, even if they are peaceful. A *totalitarian* government does not allow even those limited freedoms. On the other end of the scale is *anarchy:* a condition which holds when a government "allows" the use of violence to try to overthrow it—presumably mainly out of weakness or ineffectiveness.

Authoritarian and even totalitarian governments can sometimes be responsive as well, of course. But their responsiveness depends on the will and the mindset of the leadership. By contrast, democracy is *routinely, necessarily* responsive: because people are free to develop and use peaceful methods to criticize, pressure, and replace the leadership, the leaders must pay attention to their critics and petitioners.

It seems to me that the formal and informal institutional mechanisms variously applied in democracies to facilitate this core consideration are secondary—though this does not mean that all institutions are equally fair or efficient. One can embellish this central democratic relationship with concerns about ethos, way of life, social culture, shared goals, economic correlates, common purposes, customs, preferred policy outcomes, norms, patriotism, shared traditions, and the like. These issues are interesting, but . . . they don't seem to be essential or necessary to the functioning of democracy. . . .

Apathy

. . . One of the great, neglected aspects of free speech is the freedom not to listen. As Hubert Humphrey reportedly put it, "The right to be heard doesn't automatically include the right to be taken seriously."[1] It is no easy task to

---

1. Hubert Humphrey was a Democratic senator from Minnesota and served as vice president under President Lyndon B. Johnson.

persuade free people to agree with one's point of view, but as any experienced demagogue is likely to point out with some exasperation, what is most difficult of all is to get them to pay attention at all. People, particularly those in a free, open society, are regularly barraged by shysters and schemers, by people with new angles and neglected remedies, with purveyors of panaceas and palliatives. Very few are successful—and even those who do succeed, including Adolf Hitler, owe their success as much to luck as to skill.

. . . Apathy helps importantly with the problem that is usually called the tyranny of the majority. It is not difficult to find a place where the majority harbors a considerable hatred for a minority—indeed, it may be difficult to find one where this is not the case. Polls in the United States regularly have found plenty of people who would cheerfully restrict not only the undeserving rich, but also homosexuals, atheists, accused Communists, Nazi paraders, flag burners, and people who like to shout unpleasant words and perpetrate unconventional messages. But it is not easy to get this majority to do anything about it—after all, that would require a certain amount of work.

Because of apathy, therefore, people, sometimes despite their political predispositions, are effectively tolerant. For democracies the danger is not so much that agile demagogues will play on hatreds and weaknesses to fabricate a vindictive mob-like tyranny of the majority: the perversions of the French Revolution have proved unusual. More to be feared, it seems, is the tyranny of a few who obtain bland acquiescence from the uninterested, and essentially unaffected, many. . . .

The Quest for Political Equality

. . . The notion that all men are created equal suggests that people are *born* equal—that is, that none should necessarily be denied political opportunity merely because of their hereditary entrance into the wrong social or economic class or because they do not adhere to the visions or dictates of a particular ideological group. The notion does not, however, suggest that people must necessarily be equal in their impact on the political system, but this damaging extrapolation is often made by reformers, at least as a goal to be quested after.

An extensive study on the issue of equality by a team of political scientists finds, none too surprisingly, that people in a real democracy like the United States differ in the degree to which they affect the political system. Political effectiveness, the study concludes, depends on three varying factors: resources, especially time, money, and skills; psychological engagement with politics; and "access to networks through which individuals can be recruited to political life." The variance of effectiveness, the authors then conclude, poses a "threat to the democratic principle of equal protection of interests." Another analyst, reviewing their findings, makes a similar observation: "liberal democracies fail to live up to the norm of equal responsiveness to the interests of each citizen."

But instead of seeking to reform the system or the people who make it up, we may want instead to abandon, or at least substantially to modify, the principle and the norm. They clearly express a romantic perspective about democracy, a perspective which has now been fully and repeatedly disconfirmed in practice. Democracies are responsive and attentive to the interests of the citizenry—at least when compared to other forms of government—but they are nowhere near equally responsive to the interests of each citizen.

Related is the perennial clamor against "special interests." As the futile struggle for campaign finance reform in the United States suggests, people who want or need to influence public policy are very likely to find ways to do so no matter how clever the laws that seek to restrict them. As Gil Troy observes, "for all the pious hopes, the goal of the Watergate-era reforms—to remove the influence of money from presidential elections—was, in hard and inescapable fact, ridiculous." (He also notes that the entire cost of the 1996 election campaigns was about 25 percent of what Procter & Gamble routinely spends every year to market its products.) A rare voice of realism amid all the sanctimonious, politically correct bluster from politicians about campaign finance reform in the United States in the 1990s was that of Senator Robert Bennett of Utah: "rich people will always have influence in politics, and the solution is not to create barriers that cause the rich people to spend even more money to hire lawyers and consultants to find ways around the law to get the same results."

In the end, "special interests" can be effectively reined in only by abandoning democracy itself, because their activities are absolutely vital to the form. Indeed, it is quite incredible that two prominent Washington reporters merely deem it "simplistic" to argue that "people with common interests should not attempt to sway government policy." In a democracy the free, competitive play of "special interests" is fundamental. To reform this out of existence would be uncomprehending and profoundly antidemocratic.

Most of the agitation against political inequality is focused on the special privileges business is presumed to enjoy. For example, concern is voiced that the attention of public officials can be differently arrested: "a phone call from the CEO of a major employer in the district may carry considerably more weight than one from an unknown constituent." It is possible, of course, that the unweighty and unknown constituent has just come up with a plan which will achieve permanent worldwide bliss in the course of the next six months, but, since there are only twenty-four hours in a day, public officials (like the rest of us) are forced to ration their time, and they are probably correct to assume, as a first approximation at least, that the concerns of a major employer are likely to be of wider relevance to more people than are those of the hapless lone constituent.

But if the CEO's access advantage to a time-pressured politician is somehow reprehensible and must be reformed, what about other inequalities—that is, why focus only on economic ones? A telephone call from a big-time political columnist like David Broder of the *Washington Post* is likely to get the politician's attention even faster than that of the CEO. Should the influential David Broder hold off on his next column until the rest of us deserving unknowns have had a chance to put in our two cents in the same forum? Inequalities like these are simply and unavoidably endemic to the whole political system as, indeed, they are to life itself. It may be possible to reduce this inequality, but it is difficult to imagine a reform that could possibly raise the political impact of the average factory worker—or even of the average business executive—remotely to equal that enjoyed by Broder. . . .

The Quest for Participation

Democratic theorists, idealists, and image-makers maintain that "democratic states require . . . participation in order to flourish," or that "a politically active citizenry is a requisite of any theory of democracy," or that "democracy was built on the principle that political participation was not only the privilege of every man, but a necessity in ensuring the efficiency and prosperity of the democratic system," or that "high levels of electoral participation are essential for guaranteeing that government represents the public as a whole," or that "to make a democracy that works, we need citizens who are engaged."

But we now have over two hundred years of experience with living, breathing, messy democracy, and truly significant participation has almost never been achieved anywhere. Since democracy exists, *it simply can't be true* that wide participation is a notable requirement, requisite, guarantee, need, or necessity for it to prosper or work. Routinely, huge numbers of citizens even—in fact, especially—in "mature" democracies simply decline to participate, and the trend in participation seems to be, if anything, mostly downward. In the United States, nearly half of those eligible fail to vote even in high-visibility elections and only a few percent ever actively participate in politics. The final winner of a recent election for the mayor of Rochester, N.Y., received only about 6 percent of the vote of the total electorate. (However, he is a very popular choice: if everybody had voted, he would almost certainly have achieved the same victory.) Switzerland is Europe's oldest democracy, and it also boasts the continent's lowest voter turnout.

Statistics like these frequently inspire a great deal of concern—after all, it is argued, "political participation" is one of the "basic democratic ideals." But it may be more useful to reshape democratic theories and ideals to take notice of the elemental fact that democracy works even though it often fails to inspire very much in the way of participation from its citizenry.

And it might also be asked, why, exactly, is it so important for citizens to participate? Most analyses suggest that nonvoters do not differ all that much from voters in their policy concerns, though there are some (controversial) suggestions that leftist parties might do a bit better in some countries if everyone were forced to vote. However, once in office, responsible leftist and rightist parties both face the same constraining conditions and, despite their ideologies and campaign promises, often do not differ all that much from each other in their policies—frequently to the disillusionment and disgust of their supporters who may come to feel they have been conned.

Some hold voting to be important because "of the problem of legitimacy." The idea is that "as fewer and fewer citizens participate in elections, the extent to which government truly rests on the consent of the governed may be called into question"; moreover the "quality of the link between elites and citizens" will erode. Actually, such callings into question seem to happen mostly when a candidate, like Bill Clinton in 1992, gets less than half of the recorded *vote*—and these are principally inspired by partisan maneuvering by the losers to undercut any claim that the winner has a mandate. And in local elections, the often exceedingly low turnout and participation levels rarely even cause much notice: I have yet to hear anyone suggest that the mayor of Rochester is illegitimate or "unlinked" because hardly anybody managed to make it to the polls when he was elected.

Moreover, it really seems to strain credulity to suggest that "if people feel distant from the electoral process, they can take no pride in the successes of the government." *No* pride? It seems that even nonvoters celebrated victory in the Gulf War. Or that nonvoters "avoid responsibility for the problems facing the nation." But nonvoters seem to have no more difficulty than voters in routinely (and sometimes even correctly) blaming the politicians for whatever is wrong. And it is simply too glib to conclude that "if you don't vote, you don't count." If that were true, women would never have gotten the vote, slavery would still exist, and there would never have been prison reform or legislation aiding the homeless.

There are also claims that low turnout levels "contribute to the problem of an unrepresentative policy agenda." But it is difficult to understand what this could possibly mean—or, better, what a "representative policy agenda" would look like. Agendas are set by people actively trying to pursue their interests; they are not out there somewhere in the miasma waiting for us objectively to snap them up. As Steven Rosenstone and John Mark Hansen argue, "political participation is the product of strategic interactions of citizens and leaders." People "participate when politicians, political parties, interest groups, and activists persuade them to get involved." Thus, there will not be an "ideal" or even "normal" degree of participation. Rather, participation will increase when "salient issues reach the public agenda . . . when governments approach crucial decisions . . . when competitive election campaigns stimulate, when social movements inspire."

Hundreds of years of experience, then, suggest that the pursuit of participation for the sake of participation is rather quixotic. Instead, applying a philosophical observation attributed to impresario Sol Hurok, perhaps we should accept the fact that "if people don't want to come, nothing will stop them." Moreover, discontent and cynicism about the system itself (and consequently perhaps nonvoting) are increased when alarmists passionately lament that many people, as they have throughout democratic eternity, freely decide to pursue interests they find more pressing than politics, or manage to come up with more interesting things to do on election day than to go through the often inconsequential ritual of voting. (Sometimes, actually, nonvoters, by the very act of not voting, may be indicating their concerns and preferences more eloquently than those who actually do vote.)

The Quest for an Enlightened Citizenry

"If a nation expects to be ignorant and free," Thomas Jefferson once said, "it expects what never was and never will be." Pretty much ever since those memorable words were issued, the United States has managed to be both, and with considerable alacrity.

Fortunately for America, eternal vigilance has not proven to be the price of democracy—it can come quite a bit cheaper. In ideal democracies, James Bryce once suggested, "the average citizen will give close and constant attention to public affairs, recognizing that this is his interest as well as his duty"—but not in real ones.[2] And Horace Mann's ringing prediction that "with universal suffrage, there must be universal elevation of character, intellectual and moral, or there will be universal mismanagement and calamity" has proven untrue.[3]

Nonetheless, democratic idealists continue to insist that "democracies require responsibility." Or they contend that democracy "relies on informed popular judgment and political vigilance." Or they persist in defining democracy "as a political system in which people actively attend to what is significant." One would think it would be obvious by now that democracy works despite the fact that it often fails to inspire or require very much in the way of responsibility and knowledge from its citizenry. Democracy does feed on the bandying about of information, but that is going to happen pretty much automatically when people are free to ferret it out and to exchange it. Democracy clearly does not require that people generally be well informed, responsible, or actively attentive.

Recent surveys find that around half the American people haven't the foggiest idea which party controls the Senate or what the first ten amendments of the Constitution are called or what the Fifth Amendment does or who their congressional representative or senators are. Moreover, this lack of knowledge has generally increased (particularly when education is controlled for) since the 1940s. A month after the Republican victory in the 1994 election that propelled the vocal and energetic Newt Gingrich into the speakership of the House of Representatives and into the media stratosphere, a national poll found that 50 percent hadn't heard enough about

---

2. James Bryce was a British writer who published a classic study, *The American Commonwealth,* in the late nineteenth century.
3. Horace Mann was a nineteenth-century educational reformer.

Gingrich even to have an opinion about him. Four months later, after endless publicly over Gingrich's varying fortunes and after *Time* magazine had designated him its "Man of the Year," that number had not changed (so much for the power of the press). In a poll conducted two years later, half were still unable to indicate who the speaker was. Meanwhile, less than 20 percent guessed correctly that over the preceding twenty years air pollution and the number of the elderly living in poverty had declined, and most people were of the wildly distorted impression that foreign aid comprised a larger share of the federal budget than Medicare.

One recent analysis observes that "for the last 200 years the United States has survived as a stable democracy, despite continued evidence of an uninformed public." It also notes that "in theory, a democracy requires knowledgeable citizens." Although it then labels the contradictory condition "the paradox of modern democracy," it seems, rather, that it is the theory that should be called into question, not the reality.

Moreover, it may not be entirely clear why one should expect people to spend a lot of time worrying about politics when democratic capitalism not only leaves them free to choose other ways to get their kicks, but in its seemingly infinite quest for variety is constantly developing seductive distractions. Democratic theorists and idealists may be intensely interested in government and its processes, but it verges on the arrogant, even the self-righteous, to suggest that other people are somehow inadequate or derelict unless they share the same curious passion. Many studies have determined that it is the politically interested who are the most politically active. It is also doubtless true that those most interested in unidentified flying objects are the ones most likely to join UFO clubs. UFO enthusiasts, however, get no special credit by political theorists for servicing their particular obsession, while politics junkies are lauded because they seem to be fulfilling a higher, theory-sanctified function.

In the end, the insistence that terrible things will happen unless the citizenry becomes addicted to C-SPAN can inspire cynicism about the process when it is observed that the Beverly Hillbillies (or whatever) enjoy vastly higher ratings.

The Active Citizen

PAUL ROGAT LOEB

n the personal realm, most Americans are thoughtful, caring, generous. We try to do our best by family and friends. At times we'll even stop to help another driver stranded with a roadside breakdown, or give some spare change to a stranger. But increasingly, a wall now separates each of us from the world outside, and from others who've likewise taken refuge in their own private sanctuaries. We've all but forgotten that public participation is the very soul of democratic citizenship, and how much it can enrich our lives.

However, the reason for our wholesale retreat from social involvement is not, I believe, that most of us feel all is well with the world. I live in Seattle, a city with a seemingly unstoppable economy. Yet every time I go downtown I see men and women with signs saying "I'll work for food," or "Homeless vet. Please help." Their suffering diminishes me as a human being. I also travel extensively, doing research and giving lectures throughout the country. Except in the wealthiest of enclaves, people everywhere say, "Things are hard here." America's economic boom has passed many of us by. We struggle to live on meager paychecks. We worry about layoffs, random violence, the rising cost of health care, and the miseducation of our kids. Too stretched to save, uncertain about Social Security, many of us wonder just how we'll survive when we get old. We feel overwhelmed, we say, and helpless to change things.

Even those of us who are economically comfortable seem stressed. We spend hours commuting on crowded freeways, and hours more at jobs whose demands never end. We complain that we don't have enough time left for families and friends. We worry about the kind of world we'll pass on to our grandchildren. Then we also shrug and say there's nothing we can do.

To be sure, the issues we now face are complex—perhaps more so than in the past. How can we comprehend the moral implications of a world in which Nike pays Michael Jordan more to appear in its ads than it pays all the workers at its Indonesian shoe factories combined? Today the five hundred richest people on the planet control more wealth than the bottom three billion, half of the human population. Is it possible even to grasp the process that led to this most extraordinary imbalance? More important, how do we even begin to redress it?

Yet what leaves too many of us sitting on the sidelines is not only a lack of understanding of the complexities of our world. It's not only an absence of readily apparent ways to begin or resume public involvement. Certainly we need to decide for ourselves whether particular causes are wise or foolish—be they the politics of campaign finance reform, attempts to address the growing gap between rich and poor, or efforts to safeguard water, air, and wilderness. We need to identify and connect with worthy groups that take on these issues, whether locally or globally. But first we need to believe that our individual involvement is worthwhile, that what we might do in the public sphere will not be in vain.

This means we face a challenge that is as much psychological as political. As the Ethiopian proverb says, "He who conceals his disease cannot be cured." We need to understand our cultural diseases of callousness, shortsightedness, and denial, and learn what it will take to heal our society and heal our souls. How did so many of us become convinced that we can do nothing to affect our common future? And how have some other Americans managed to remove the cataracts from their vision and work powerfully for change?

When we do take a stand, we grow psychologically and spiritually. Pete Knutson is one of my oldest friends. During his twenty-five years as a commercial fisherman in Washington and Alaska, he's been forced, time and again, to respond to the steady degradation of salmon spawning grounds. "You'd have a hard time spawning, too, if you had a bulldozer in your bedroom," he says, explaining the destruction of once-rich salmon habitat by commercial development and timber industry clear-cutting. Pete could have simply accepted this degradation as fate, focusing on getting a maximum share of the dwindling fish populations. Instead, he's gradually built an alliance between Washington State fishermen, environmentalists, and Native American tribes, persuading them to work collectively to demand that the habitat be preserved and restored.

The cooperation Pete created didn't come easy: Washington's fishermen were historically individualistic and politically mistrustful, more inclined, in Pete's judgment, "to grumble or blame the Indians than to act." Now, with their new allies, they began to push for cleaner spawning streams, preservation of the Endangered Species Act, and an increased flow of water over major regional dams to help boost salmon runs. But large industrial interests, such as the aluminum companies, feared that these measures would raise their electricity costs or restrict their opportunities for development. So a few years ago they bankrolled a statewide initiative to regulate fishing nets in a way that would eliminate small family fishing operations.

"I think we may be toast," said Pete, when Initiative 640 first surfaced. In an Orwellian twist, its backers even presented the initiative as environmentally friendly, to mislead casual voters. It was called "Save Our Sealife," although fishermen soon rechristened it "Save Our Smelters." At first, those opposing 640 thought they had no chance of success: They were outspent, outstaffed, outgunned. Similar initiatives had already passed in Florida, Louisiana, and Texas, backed by similar industrial interests. I remember Pete sitting in a Seattle tavern with two fisherman friends, laughing bitterly and saying, "The three of us are going to take on the aluminum companies? We're going to beat Reynolds and Kaiser?"

But they refused to give up. Instead, Pete and his coworkers systematically enlisted the region's major environmental groups to campaign against the initiative. They worked with the media to explain the larger issues at stake. And they focused public attention on the measure's powerful financial backers, and their interest in its outcome. On election night, November 1995, Initiative 640 was defeated throughout the state. White fishermen, Native American activists, and Friends of the Earth staffers threw their arms around each other in victory. "I'm really proud of you, Dad," Pete's twelve-year-old son kept repeating. Pete was stunned.

"Everyone felt it was hopeless," Pete said, looking back. "But if we were going to lose, I wanted at least to put up a good fight. And we won because of all the earlier work we'd done, year after year, to build up our environmental relationships, get some credibility, and show that we weren't just in it for ourselves."

We often think of social involvement as noble but impractical. Yet as Pete's story attests, it can serve enlightened self-interest and the interests of others simultaneously, while giving us a sense of connection and purpose nearly impossible to find in purely private life. "It takes energy to act," said Pete. "But it's more draining to bury your anger, convince yourself you're powerless, and swallow whatever's handed to you. The times I've compromised my integrity and accepted something I shouldn't, the ghosts of my choices have haunted me. When you get involved in something meaningful, you make your life count. What you do makes a difference. It blows my mind that we beat 640 starting out with just a small group of people who felt it was wrong to tell lies."

In fighting to save the environment and his economic livelihood, Pete strengthened his own soul. How the rest of us might achieve something similar is not always clear. We often don't know where to start. Most of us would like to see people treated more justly, to have the earth accorded the respect it deserves, and to feel less pressure in our lives. But we find it hard to imagine having much of a role in this process. We mistrust our own ability to make a difference. The magnitude of the issues at hand, coupled with this sense of powerlessness, has led far too many of us to conclude that social involvement isn't worth the cost.

Such resignation isn't an innate response, or the creation of some inevitable fate. Rather, it's what psychologists call learned helplessness. Society has systematically taught us to ignore the ills we see, and leave them to others to handle. Understandably, we find it unsettling even to think about crises as huge and profound in their implications as the extinction of species, depletion of the ozone layer, and destruction of the rainforests. Or the desperate poverty that blights entire neighborhoods in our nation's largest cities. We're led to believe that if we can't solve every one of these kinds of problems, we shouldn't bother to become socially active at all. We're also taught to doubt our voice—to feel we lack either the time to properly learn and articulate the issues we care about, or the standing to speak out and be heard. To get socially involved, we believe, requires almost saint-like judgment, confidence, and character—a standard we can never meet. Whatever impulses toward involvement we might have, they're dampened by a culture that demeans idealism, enshrines cynicism, and makes us feel naive for caring about our fellow human beings or the planet we inhabit. . . .

Learned Helplessness

America's prevailing culture of cynicism insists that nothing we do can matter. It teaches us not to get involved in shaping the world we'll pass on to our children. It encourages us to leave such important decisions to others—whether they be corporate and government leaders, or social activists whose lifestyles seem impossibly selfless or foreign. Sadly, and ironically, in a country born of a democratic political revolution, to be American today is to be apolitical. Civic withdrawal has become our norm. To challenge this requires courage. It also requires creating a renewed definition of ourselves as citizens—something closer to the nation of active stakeholders that leaders like Thomas Jefferson had in mind.

The importance of citizens' direct participation in a democracy was expressed thousands of years ago, by the ancient Greeks. In fact, they used the word "idiot" for people incapable of involving themselves in civic life. Now, the very word "political" has become so debased in our culture that we use it to describe either trivial office power plays or the inherently corrupt world of elected leaders. We've lost sight of its original roots in the Greek notion of the polis: the democratic sphere in which citizens, acting in concert, determine the character and direction of their society. "All persons alike," wrote Aristotle, should share "in the government to the utmost." . . .

Bowling Alone

Creating any kind of activist community is harder when the civic associations and institutions that might once have offered a foundation have themselves eroded. In a much-discussed article, "Bowling Alone," the Harvard political theorist Robert Putnam observes that during the past thirty years Americans have steadily reduced their participation not only in voting, but also in traditional forms of community involvement, such as the PTA, the League of Women Voters, unions, mainstream churches, the Boy Scouts and Campfire Girls, and service clubs like the Lions and Kiwanis. We've squandered the "social capital" that allows people to work together effectively to pursue shared objectives. As a strangely poignant example of this trend, Putnam notes that local bowling leagues have seen a 40 percent decline in membership since 1980. During the same period, however, the number of individuals who actually bowl has risen until it now exceeds the number who vote in congressional elections. These trends bode ill for American democracy, Putnam argues, because the more socially isolated our citizens become, the fewer chances they have for the kinds of civic conversations that fuel involvement in crucial public concerns.

Putnam's critics, like *Atlantic Monthly* writer Nicholas Lemann, have argued that citizens are still just as likely to get involved in community social networks, but that as America's population shifts toward the suburbs, the networks have changed form. Youth soccer leagues, in which parents participate on the weekends, are booming, he says. So are Internet discussion groups and self-help associations like Alcoholics Anonymous. Organizations from NOW and the Sierra Club to the NRA and the Christian Coalition have taken the place of the old political machines.[1]

---

1. NOW is an acronym for National Organization for Women; NRA is an acronym for the National Rifle Association.

Such examples notwithstanding, I remain convinced by Putnam's basic proposition, that civic involvement has dropped off significantly. In a follow-up article, Putnam examines a number of possible causes for the decline, including suburbanization, the increased numbers of women in the workforce, and the general demands of modern life. While most of these factors seem to play some role, they don't account for the fact that the decline cuts across cities and suburbs, the married and the single, working men, working women, and stay-at-home moms. The key change during the past fifty years, Putnam concludes, is the steadily increasing influence of television. Regardless of background or current circumstances, the more people watch TV, he finds, the less they involve themselves in civic activities of any kind, and the more mistrusting and pessimistic they become about human nature. As their sense of connectedness and common purpose erodes, they find it easy to scapegoat others, to view the world in prejudicial and unforgiving terms, and to believe that ordinary citizens can do nothing to shape the history of our time. This is all the more troubling given that extensive TV watching now begins in early childhood, taking up as much time among average kids aged nine to fourteen as all other discretionary activities combined. For many adults, TV has gradually replaced nearly every social activity outside the home.

It worries me that so many of us now sit alone for hours on end, passive spectators, paying more attention to the strangers on the screen than to the real people next door. What are the consequences for ourselves and our society? The greatest misfortune, in my view, is that by focusing so much on stories scripted by others, we forfeit the opportunity to create our own.

Fishing Together

Whatever the reasons for our declining civic involvement, we need to rebuild local communities even as we work to expand their vision. Pete Knutson took this approach in working with his fellow fishermen: First he helped create a cohesive community; then he involved its members in larger public issues. Pete, the son of a plainspoken Lutheran minister, grew up in the hardscrabble mill town of Everett, Washington. He had a Barry Goldwater poster on his wall, "because Goldwater spoke his mind."[2] At first Pete supported the Vietnam War, and even got a jingoistic letter published on the *Everett Herald*'s youth page. His views changed as friends who'd enlisted came back, feeling betrayed, and told him, "Don't believe anything the military tells you. They always lie." Before long, Pete was organizing an antiwar moratorium at his high school; then he went off to Stanford, and became the only draft-age man to testify before Congress. He even got his

---

2. Barry Goldwater, a founder of modern American conservatism, was the Republican candidate for president in 1964.

fifteen minutes of fame on the national news, after Strom Thurmond stormed out when Pete had the audacity to ask a Senate committee, "If you're so eager to fight this war, why don't you pick up an M16 and lead the first wave?"

Pete began fishing to work his way through school. Soon, fishing became a way of life, as he bought his own boat, with borrowed money, to support his wife and two young sons. Because he knew his fellow fishermen were powerless in isolation, he helped build the Puget Sound Gillnetters' Association, which enabled members to market fish jointly, lobby on laws that affected them, and gain leverage against the giant canneries. "I felt we had to trust each other," he says. "If we didn't, we had no chance." The association became a base through which fishermen gradually became conversant with large ecological issues, such as the destruction of salmon habitat, upon whose outcome their livelihoods depended.

Pete worked steadily to bridge the gap between fishermen and the generally more middle-class environmentalists. That was no easy task, given long-standing mutual mistrust fed by class divides and stereotypes. Yet a coalition did in fact emerge, and the fishermen brought a powerful blue-collar presence to issues like the Endangered Species Act and habitat protection. When President Clinton visited Seattle for a Pacific Rim trade conference, a parade of fishing boats joined with Greenpeace activists to challenge his environmental timidity. Both Pete's ethical stand and pride in craft were evoked by the bumper sticker on his truck: "Jesus Was a Gillnetter."

This hard-won and unexpected alliance proved critical when Initiative 640 threatened to shut down the gillnetters' operations by banning the nets they used. The fishermen held joint press conferences with the now-supportive environmental groups, picketed a pleasure-boat company that was a prime initial backer of the initiative, and generally refused to succumb quietly to their opponents' well-financed campaign. They survived because Pete, along with a few others, had helped change their vision from one of enlightened self-interest to a more complex and sustainable ethic, best summed up when he spoke of nurturing the salmon habitat "so my kids can fish, too, and everyone's children can inherit a healthy planet." First the fishermen learned to work together, then to reach beyond their own ranks. Building their association's internal cohesion made it easier for them to tackle difficult issues later on. . . .

The Fullness of Time

However we promote social change, we do so in time: We link past, present, and future in our attempts to create a better world. Some historical eras, however, seem more pregnant with possibility than others. . . .

The 1960s were marked by a . . . sense of urgency and creative ferment. Ordinary people worldwide challenged entrenched institutions and policies. They talked of realizing a more humane and generous future. These movements then collapsed because of powerful opposition, their participants' exhaustion, and some dangerous moments of arrogance. But for a time, people unleashed powerful dreams.

Our lives today are hardly stagnant. We have access to a world of food, music, sights, sounds, and healing traditions. We can log onto Websites from Bangkok and Reykjavik to Nairobi and Calcutta. As technology changes by leaps and bounds, it alters our lives and the earth at an almost incomprehensible pace. So does the relentless global economy. Change happens so fast we can barely keep up.

But politically, we often feel powerless, incapable of moving forward. We may have witnessed citizens fighting for democracy in the streets of Prague, Berlin, and Moscow, Tiananmen Square and Soweto, Manila, and Jakarta. But we saw them from a distance on TV. People risked their lives to have a say in their common future, but the lessons seemed remote from our world. They didn't apply to us. Not here, and certainly not now.

It's tempting to gaze back longingly toward the most dramatic periods of history, while disdaining our own era as unheroic and meaningless. "People seem so stuck these days," says Ginny Nicarthy. "But things looked pretty grim in the late 1950s too, when I first got involved. A dozen of us would picket the bomb shelters or stores that were racist in their hiring, and people would yell at us, tell us to 'Go back to Russia,' 'Go back to your kitchen, where you belong.' There were no clear reasons to believe that we could change things, but somehow we did. We leaped forward, started the ball rolling, and built enough political mass that it kept going. Maybe we need to do that again."

Seeding the ground for the next round of highly visible social progress will take work. Yet major gains for human dignity are possible, even in seemingly resistant times. Indeed, our efforts may be even more critical now than in periods when the whole world seems to be watching.

The Turnings of History

Historical contexts can change shape suddenly and dramatically. As Václav Havel wrote before the epochal Eastern European revolutions, "Hope is not prognostication."[3] Richard Flacks remembers visiting Berkeley in September 1964 and hearing members of the activist student group SDS complain that their fellow students were almost terminally apathetic, uncaring, and passive. They said that nothing they could try would work. A few weeks later, the free speech movement erupted.

We can never predict when a historical mood will suddenly shift and new hopes and possibilities emerge. But we do know that this shift won't

3. Václav Havel, a prominent playwright and a dissident during Communist rule in Czechoslovakia, is now president of the Czech Republic.

occur unless someone takes action. Recall the struggle of Susan B. Anthony. She labored her entire life for women's suffrage, then died fourteen years before it was achieved. Thirty years ago, few would have thought that the Soviet bloc would crumble, thanks in part to the persistence of individuals from Havel to Lech Walesa and Andrei Sakharov, who voiced prophetic truths despite all costs. Few would have thought that South Africa would become a democracy, with Nelson Mandela its president. Few would have imagined that women throughout the world would begin to insist on shaping their own destiny. Major victories for human dignity rarely come easily or quickly. But they do come.

"When nothing seems to help," said the early twentieth-century reformer Jacob Riis, "I go and look at a stonecutter hammering away at his rock perhaps a hundred times without as much as a crack showing in it. Yet at the hundred and first blow it will split in two, and I know it was not that blow that did it—but all that had gone before. . . ."

Faith and Hope

Even if the past holds no guarantees for the future, we can still take heart from previous examples of courage and vision. We can draw hope from those who came before us, to whom we owe so much. We can remember that history unfolds in ways we can never predict, but that again and again bring astounding transformations, often against the longest of odds. Our strength can come, as I've suggested, from a radical stubbornness, from savoring the richness of our journey, and from the victories we win and the lives that we change. We can draw on the community we build.

More than anything, activists religious and secular keep going because participation is essential to their dignity, to their very identity, to the person they see in the mirror. To stay silent, they say, would be self-betrayal, a violation of their soul. Plainly stated, it would feel cheap and tacky. "That's why we were put here on this earth," they stress again and again. "What better thing can you do with your life?" "There'll be nobody like you ever again," says veteran environmentalist David Brower. "Make the most of every molecule you've got, as long as you've got a second to go. That's your charge."

This means responding to the ills of our time with what Rabbi Abraham Heschel once called "a persistent effort to be worthy of the name human." A technical editor who chaired her local Amnesty International chapter felt demeaned just by knowing about incidents of torture. To do something about it helped her recover her spirit. "When you stand in front of the Creator," says Carol McNulty, "you want to say, 'I tried to make a difference.' It isn't going to be what kind of car I had or how big a house. I'd like to think I tried."

Being true to oneself in this fashion doesn't eradicate human destructiveness. We need to live, as Albert Camus suggests, with a "double memory—a memory of the best and the worst."[4] We can't deny the cynicism and callousness of which humans are capable. We also can't deny the courage and compassion that offer us hope. It's our choice which characteristics we'll steer our lives by. . . .

DISCUSSION QUESTIONS

1. What are the most important differences between the elite democratic perspective and the popular democratic perspective? In your view, which side has the stronger case?

2. Mueller argues that "'special interests' can be effectively reined in only by abandoning democracy itself." Do you agree?

3. Mueller believes that there is no greater intrinsic value in being a "politics junky" than in any other interest or hobby, while Loeb sees public involvement as essential for personal growth. Is there anything distinctive about political participation that makes it especially worthy of our time and commitments?

4. Are most Americans too preoccupied with their private affairs to pay much attention to public ones, or can they be taught to see critical links between their own needs and interests and the shared pursuit of public goods?

SUGGESTED READINGS AND INTERNET RESOURCES

The classic work on the meaning, practices, and dilemmas of American democracy remains Alexis de Tocqueville, *Democracy in America,* Vols. 1 and 2 (New York: Vintage Books, 1990). A provocative history of American democracy, recounting a fall from genuine self-government in the nineteenth century to bureaucracy and hierarchy in the twentieth, is Robert H. Wiebe, *Self-Rule: A Cultural History of American Democracy* (Chicago: University of Chicago Press, 1995). Perhaps the greatest work of modern political science in the elite democratic vein is Robert A. Dahl, *Who Governs? Democracy and Power in an American City* (New Haven, Conn.: Yale University Press, 1961). For a fascinating study of the 1960s experiment with participatory democracy, see James Miller, *"Democracy Is in the Streets": From Port Huron to the Siege of Chicago* (Cambridge, Mass.: Harvard University Press, 1995). A prominent attempt to develop the theory of participatory democracy is Benjamin Barber, *Strong Democracy: Participatory Politics for a New Age* (Berkeley: University of California Press, 1984).

---

4. Albert Camus was a French philosopher and novelist who won the Nobel Prize for Literature.

Center for Democracy and Citizenship
http://www.hhh.umn.edu/centers/cdc
The Center for Democracy and Citizenship, located at the University of
Minnesota's Hubert H. Humphrey Institute of Public Affairs, offers information
about various citizenship projects as well as information about the Center's own
publications; it provides links to other sites on citizenship.

Institute for the Study of Civic Values
http://www.libertynet.org/edcivic.civical.html
A non-profit organization in Philadelphia, its web site provides classic articles
and lectures on American democratic values as well as information on civic
values projects.

Electronic Policy Network
http://www.epn.org/issues/civilsociety.html
This section of the Electronic Policy Network focuses on the debate over the
place of civil society in democracy that was generated by Robert Putnam's
famous article, "Bowling Alone."

}3

The New Federalism: Does It Create Laboratories of Democracy or a Race to the Bottom?[1]

merican politics often takes a peculiar form: instead of debating *what* policy should be enacted, people argue about *where* the policy decision should be made—at the federal, state, or local level. One side will proclaim its adherence to "states' rights" or "community control," while the other side touts the need for the federal government to guarantee fairness and equal protection of the laws. Often the two sides are sincere in their defense of different levels of democracy. As you might suspect, however, the debate is not just about ideals but about who will win and who will lose. This is because where decisions are made strongly affects who wins and who loses. This peculiar quality of the "game" of politics in the United States is determined by a system we call federalism.

Federalism is a system of government that divides power between a central government and state and local governments. As a concept of government, federalism was born in compromise during the struggle over the U.S. Constitution. Some of the framers of the Constitution favored a unitary government in which all significant powers would be placed in the hands of a central government. Realizing that such a system would never be approved by the

---

1. Both phrases, "laboratories of democracy" and "race to the bottom," were coined by Louis Brandeis, U.S. Supreme Court justice from 1916 to 1939.

voters, they compromised on a system that divided power between the two levels of government. As we saw in Chapter 1, the opponents of the Constitution, the Anti-federalists, still feared that too much power had been given to the federal government at the expense of the states.

The ratification of the Constitution in 1789 did not settle the federalism issue, primarily because the language in the original Constitution is exceedingly vague. The framers were themselves divided, so they left it up to future genera- tions to settle the issue. The biggest crisis of federalism occurred over slavery. In 1861, the southern states decided they had the right to secede from the United States if they did not agree with the policies of the federal government. The issue was settled in a bloody civil war: states do *not* have the right to secede unilaterally from the union; they have to work out their differences within the federal system.

Until Franklin Roosevelt's New Deal of the 1930s, the federal government was remarkably uninvolved in a wide range of domestic policy functions that we now take for granted. The halting response of states and localities to the Great Depression changed all that. Roosevelt swiftly moved the federal government into a whole range of functions, like social security, welfare, and regulating the economy, that had previously been considered off limits. For the most part, however, Washington did not take over these functions but instead funded new programs with grants that were administered by state and local governments under varied federal rules. In the 1960s, under President Lyndon Johnson's leadership, the system of intergovernmental grants expanded tremendously.

Richard Nixon's election in 1968 began a period of reaction against the expanded powers of the federal government that has continued to this day. For the most part, Nixon did not try to roll back the functions of the federal government but instead deregulated the federal grant system and gave more power over grants to states and localities. The election of Ronald Reagan inaugu- rated a more radical phase of the new federalism in which efforts were made to return to the system that existed before the New Deal when the federal gov- ernment left many domestic policy functions to the states. Although confidence in all levels of government has fallen since the 1960s, the drop in confidence has been most severe for the federal government. A 1995 CBS/*New York Times* poll found that 48 percent of the respondents felt that the federal government had "too much power," whereas only 6 percent felt that the states had too much.

The 1994 Republican takeover of Congress accelerated the trend toward devolution of federal powers to the states. In 1996, Congress passed, and Presi- dent Clinton signed, the Personal Responsibility and Work Opportunity Act, which converted welfare from a federal entitlement for individuals to a block grant to states, leaving them significant freedom to set their own eligibility criteria and conditions for aid. The Supreme Court is also moving in the direction of restricting federal power. In 1995, the Court ruled for the first time in sixty years that Congress had exceeded its authority under the Interstate Commerce Clause of the Constitution and declared the federal Gun-Free School Zone Act of 1990 unconstitutional (*U.S. v. Lopez*, 115 S. Ct. 1624). In a series of cases decided in 1999, the Supreme Court made it more difficult to enforce uniform national policies in areas like the environment and health by barring certain kinds of lawsuits against states. Those who favor devolution, however, have not completely carried the day. President Clinton pushed modest but popular expansions of federal responsibility in such areas as day care and education and appointed justices more supportive of federal power.

In their essay, "Beyond the Beltway," William Eggers and John O'Leary identify themselves with a "devolution revolution" sweeping the country at the grassroots. They stress that the purpose of devolution is not just to make the existing government programs work more efficiently but to raise the question of whether certain functions should be the responsibility of government at all. Such decisions, they maintain, are better left with those governments that are closest to the grassroots, where citizens can see immediately the costs as well as the benefits of government programs. In the book from which this essay is excerpted, Eggers and O'Leary argue that the expansion of the federal government has stifled initiative by local governments and voluntary organizations. Shrink the federal government, they say, and grassroots organizations will flourish, becoming "laboratories of democracy." In place of a "one-size-fits-all" approach of the federal government, local organizations can fine tune their policies to suit local conditions. Moreover, argue Eggers and O'Leary in a section not reprinted here, the expanded powers of the federal government violate the U.S. Constitution, which in the Tenth Amendment reserves all powers not specifically given to the federal government "to the States respectively, or to the people."

John Donahue, the author of "The Devil in Devolution," argues that the words of the Constitution are much more ambiguous about the division of power between the federal government and the states than Eggers and O'Leary admit. Moreover, Donahue argues, it is up to each generation to adapt the federal system to the imperatives of the time. Donahue is critical of the recent trend toward devolution. Whereas Eggers and O'Leary base their argument primarily on what we call in the Introduction negative freedom—getting the government out of individual's lives—Donahue stresses positive freedom, or the idea that acting together we can accomplish things we cannot accomplish separately. Donahue argues that when each state acts separately those things that we all share, what he calls the "commons," can be damaged. For example, states may pursue economic development knowing that much of the pollution produced by it will drift across its borders to other states. Donahue admits that federal bureaucracy may be wasteful, but he says the gains from decentralization have been greatly exaggerated. Moreover, the "courtship of capital" by individual states results in greater inequality. Instead of devolution resulting in "laboratories of democracy," Donahue suggests, the more likely result will be a "race to the bottom."

The contemporary debate on federalism reverberates with the same issues and arguments that have been made since the country's founding. It is unlikely that this debate will ever be completely settled. It seems as though each generation is doomed to decide anew the proper balance between

Washington, D.C., and the states and localities. Even though there is no one neat answer, this does not mean there is not a better answer for our time. It is up to the reader to decide which position will best serve the core values of American democracy.

An intriguing aspect of this debate is that both sides argue that their position is reinforced by modern technology. The reader will have to sort this out. Do you think that new technologies make it easier for decision making to be decentralized, or do they increase the interdependencies in society, thus requiring more central coordination? Note that in the debate the two sides stress different values. Eggers and O'Leary emphasize individual freedom and local democracy whereas Donahue puts more stress on national values and equality. In this debate are we forced to choose among competing values, or is there some way to slip between the horns of the dilemmas of devolution and serve all values?

Beyond the Beltway

WILLIAM D. EGGERS
AND JOHN O'LEARY

Our swollen federal government is in large measure incompatible with the demands of a modern society. In today's Information Age, there is little rationale for the federal government to control as much as it does. Large, centralized bureaucracies—whether that be IBM headquarters, the Kremlin, or Washington, D.C.—aren't well suited to an age of rapid technological change. In business, companies are decentralizing, empowering workers, and establishing autonomous business units. (It's not just trendy, it's an economic necessity.) In politics, economic reality is relegating central planning to the dustbin of history.

Washington, D.C., is becoming increasingly irrelevant. Explain authors Alvin and Heidi Toffler:

> It is not possible for a society to de-massify economic activity, communications and many other crucial processes without also, sooner or later, being compelled to decentralize government decision-making as well. There is no possibility of restoring sense, order, and management 'efficiency' to many governments without a substantial devolution of central power.

In today's rapidly changing world, the performance of the federal government looks worse and worse. There is a reason for this. As technology advances, decentralized decision making becomes more efficient in more and more cases. The problems of centralized decision making are inherent to *any* central authority, whether corporate or governmental, and are based on the relationship between knowledge, decision-making power, and technology.

As technology advances, productivity increasingly depends on knowledge. And, as communications technology advances, *general* knowledge—the kind that can be written down—becomes widely accessible. But *specific* knowledge—the kind that requires firsthand experience and that is difficult to communicate—is as difficult to obtain today as it has ever been. Other things being equal, *specific* knowledge—the kind that is dispersed throughout society—is growing in importance relative to *general* knowledge. Thus, as technology advances, it makes less and less sense to bottle up decision-making authority in a distant, centralized bureaucracy. Dictating the "one best way" from Washington, whether in education, welfare, or crime fighting, makes less and less sense. In particular cases, there may be a compelling reason for maintaining centralized control, such as the need for a coordinated national defense. But as a general principle, for efficiency's sake we should be increasingly devolving power *away* from centralized bureaucracies.

More than simply efficiency is at stake, however. We need to return to our roots as a self-governing people. Democracy is not a spectator sport. In a healthy democracy, citizens are actively involved in their own governance—and not simply on election day. Americans need to reconnect with the political process. Numerous functions now handled (and mishandled) by the federal government should be transferred back to the states and, wherever possible, to communities and individuals. Radical devolution brings government closer to home.

The Revolt Against Washington

In 1992, a highly respected economist wrote, "The federal government should eliminate most of its programs in education, housing, highways, social services, economic development, and job training."

These radical sentiments come from Alice Rivlin, then a Brookings Institution scholar and currently President Clinton's director of the Office of Management and Budget. Writing as an independent scholar, Rivlin called for a massive, radical devolution of federal programs to states.

Devolution is not a partisan issue. It is a recognition that centralized control and centralized decision making carries unacceptably high costs, both in terms of efficiency and democratic accountability. It is not a question of Democratic dictates from Washington versus Republican dictates. Following the election of 1994, Republican governors seem ready to oppose federal usurpation even when orchestrated by their fellow party members. "My priority is for Texans to be running Texas," says Texas Governor George W. Bush "We're pretty good at what we do in Texas, and we like to be left alone by the federal government as much as possible." It's time to end the unequal partnership and the whole idea of one-size-fits-all national prescriptions. The American people have said it's time to move power *and responsibility* out of Washington—for good.

Devolution would restore clearer lines of responsibility between state and federal tasks. By bringing government closer to home, citizens could once again understand what each level of government does and hold the appropriate officials accountable at election time. Radical devolution will make much of what goes on inside the Beltway redundant or unnecessary. "You have to get rid of a lot of those vested interests in Washington," says Mayor [Stephen] Goldsmith [of Indianapolis]. "There are tens of thousands of people there whose only job in life is to control what I do."

The Department of Education, for example, spends about $15 billion a year on 150 different elementary and secondary programs. Since the department was created in 1979, Washington has become fond of imposing top-down solutions on local schools. Ohio Governor George Voinovich says his state's school superintendents spend nearly half their time filling out federal forms to get money that makes up only 5 to 6 percent of their school budgets.

. . . Joann Wysocki, [a] first-grade teacher from the Los Angeles Unified School District, . . . told us that the federal government was providing money for school days lost due to the 1994 earthquake. The rules required a special form, so every teacher had to copy *by hand* the attendance register. Photocopies were not acceptable. That's the rule. Wysocki doesn't like to jump through hoops for money from Washington, "That 'federal money' is our money to begin with, on the local level," she says. "Please don't insult anyone's intelligence saying anything else. The money comes back to us with strings attached. Why should the money go in the first place? Let it stay!"

Former Education Secretary William J. Bennett concurs: "We really do not need a Department of Education. We were educating our kids better before we had a Department of Education. Why do we have to pass the dollars from the states and locales to Washington and back out again?"

Sending housing, welfare, and social service programs to the states, as Rivlin proposes, would mean that Health and Human Services (HHS) and the Department of Housing and Urban Development (HUD) can also be dramatically downsized or eliminated. Even [former] Housing Secretary Henry Cisneros has admitted that much of what HUD does is expendable. "Many aspects of this department are simply indefensible," said Cisneros. "Change is necessary."

As for the Environmental Protection Agency (EPA), state environmental agencies are better positioned to know the problems of their states. "We don't need an EPA in Washington, D.C.," says [Arizona] Governor [Fife] Symington. "We have a Department of Environmental Quality in Arizona that is better at dealing with environmental problems in our state. You don't need an EPA in Washington with a command-and-control structure dictating environmental policies to the states." Though we believe the EPA's powers should be greatly curtailed, we're not as radical as Governor

Symington in this regard. There are certain cross-border pollution issues that may require some form of federal involvement.

No More Federal Santa Claus

For radical devolution to become a reality will require a fundamental change in mind-set not only in Washington, but also among state and local politicians. Since the beginning of the Great Society, state and local officials have come to see the federal government as a kind of Santa Claus, doling out money for all sorts of programs. Many mayors and governors became professional beggars at the Capitol's steps. Programs that would never be funded with local tax dollars become "vital" so long as they are paid for with "federal" dollars.

Even more than states, big cities turned to Washington for help. Today, most cities are addicted to federal funds. Local politicians fear the loss of federal funds, but where do they imagine this money comes from in the first place? France, perhaps? Jersey City Mayor Bret Schundler, one of the few big-city mayors to oppose the crime bill, did so because he recognized that all "federal money" comes from people living in one of the 50 states to begin with. Says Shundler:

> Clinton wants to shift the burden of policing to the federal gov-
> ernment and increase taxes. After he takes his big cut, he'll give us a
> portion of the money back for local policing. What a bonehead idea.
> The solution is not to shift taxes and make us pay more. The solution is
> reducing the cost of local policing.

Washington doesn't add any value to the tax dollars it receives and then sends back down to cities and states; in fact, the federal bureaucracy subtracts value as it takes its cut before sending money back to local governments.

Less federal money flowing out of Washington should mean less money flowing into Washington from the residents of cities and states. Keeping the money closer to home will also mean more flexibility, control, and accountability. "We understand this is going to mean less dollars from Washington," says New Jersey Governor Christine Todd Whitman, "but if you relieve us of some of the most onerous mandates, we will live with that." State and local officials need to stop judging the worth of joint federal/state programs merely in terms of whether they are funded by "federal dollars." "We as Governors need to begin to ask a new question about programs," says Utah Governor Mike Leavitt. "Instead of asking is this a funded program, we should ask, should there be a federal role?"

In the transportation arena, for example, the federal government could get out of highway and airport funding by forgoing the gasoline tax and letting states raise construction money themselves—whether through a state gasoline tax, by raising landing fees or highway tolls, or by securing private

debt. This approach would allow states to avoid a host of federal mandates—including the 55-mile-per-hour speed limit, the Davis Bacon Act,
and the minimum drinking age—that accompany acceptance of federal
highway funds.

Local Money for Local Problems

In many areas the ultimate goal of policy must be to transfer as much
power, authority, and responsibility as possible from government to individuals and local communities. Once citizens see the true cost of local programs now being financed from Washington, they may not think they're
worth the tax dollars spent on them.

Consider, for example, the uproar that ensued in Manhattan Beach,
California, (where one of us lives) after the city council voted to spend
money expanding a parking garage that residents felt would benefit only
merchants. A front-page story in *The Beach Reporter* noted that "three dozen
residents . . . bombarded the Manhattan Beach City Council on Tuesday. . . ."
Another story noted:

> [M]any residents complained that they were continually having to
> come down to City Hall to protect their interests. District 4 Council-
> member Bob Pinzler told the residents that they should continue
> voicing their opinions and concerns. "You have to keep coming down
> here to protect your interests," Pinzler said, "because the special
> interest groups are here all the time."

This is democracy at its local, messy best, with vigilant residents watching over elected officials spending their tax dollars. Chances are no one in
Manhattan Beach even knew that the federal government spent $2.5 mil-
lion of tax money to build a parking garage in Burlington, Iowa. That little
item didn't make the front page of *The Beach Reporter*, and no Manhattan
Beach residents drove the 3,000-odd miles to Washington, D.C., to testify
before a congressional committee. At the federal level, organized interests
have an enormous advantage. Former Education Secretary William Bennett
estimates that 285 education lobbying groups have offices within walking
distance of the Department of Education headquarters. The average Manhattan Beach parent doesn't have a prayer.

The parking garage story illustrates the phenomenon known as "bill av-
eraging." Imagine going out to dinner by yourself. When ordering, you'll
closely watch the cost of each menu selection because you'll be paying the
entire bill. Even if you were going out to dinner with one or two friends,
you still wouldn't spend outrageously because you'd still be footing a good
portion of the bill.

Now imagine that you are going out to dinner with 75 strangers, and
that the bill is to be divided evenly. If you are like most people, you are
going to order liberally, enjoy an extra drink, maybe even dessert and

coffee. And why not? Your order will only affect your bill a minuscule amount; besides, you can bet that everyone else will be ordering big. The only way to get your "fair share" is to order lobster and Lowenbrau.

The federal government is like going to dinner with 250 million strangers. Rather than everyone paying his own way, a complex tangle of cross-subsidies obscures everyone's actual bill.

It's time to ask for separate checks. The good folks of Burlington, Iowa, got a new parking garage because Uncle Sam took about one penny from every Manhattan Beach resident—and every other American. Because local taxpayers don't feel the bite, local officials love to spend "federal dollars." Would Altoonans have approved Altoona, Pennsylvania's multimillion dollar moving sidewalk if Altoonan taxes were going to pay for it? Unlikely. But since the folks in Burlington, Iowa, and Manhattan Beach, California, are footing the bill, the Altoonans are happy to be carried along.

The Devil in Devolution

JOHN D. DONAHUE

The shift in government's center of gravity away from Washington and toward the states—a transition propelled by both popular sentiment and budget imperatives, and blessed by leaders in both major parties—reflects an uncommon pause in an endless American argument over the balance between nation and state.

This moment of consensus in favor of letting Washington fade while the states take the lead is badly timed. The public sector's current trajectory—the devolution of welfare and other programs, legislative and judicial action circumscribing Washington's authority, and the federal government's retreat to a domestic role largely defined by writing checks to entitlement claimants, creditors, and state and local governments—would make sense if economic and cultural ties reaching across state lines were *weakening* over time. But state borders are becoming more, not less, permeable.

From a vantage point three-fifths of the way between James Madison's day and our own, Woodrow Wilson wrote that the "common interests of a nation brought together in thought and interest and action by the telegraph and the telephone, as well as by the rushing mails which every express train carries, have a scope and variety, an infinite multiplication and intricate interlacing, of which a simpler day can have had no conception." Issues in which other states' citizens have no stakes, and hence no valid claim to a voice, are becoming rarer still in an age of air freight, interlinked computers, nonstop currency trading, and site-shopping global corporations. Our current enchantment with devolution will be seen one day as oddly discordant with our era's challenges.

The concept of "the commons" can help to cast in a sharper light the perils of fragmented decision-making on issues of national consequence. In a much-noted 1968 article in *Science,* biologist Garrett Hardin invoked the parable of a herdsman pondering how many cattle to graze on the village commons. Self-interest will lead the herdsman to increase the size of his herd even if the commons is already overburdened, since he alone benefits from raising an extra animal, but shares the consequent damage to the common pasture. As each farmer follows the same logic, overgrazing wrecks the commons.

Where the nation as a whole is a commons, whether as an economic reality or as a political ideal, and states take action that ignores or narrowly exploits that fact, the frequent result is the kind of "tragedy" that Hardin's metaphor predicts: Collective value is squandered in the name of a constricted definition of gain. States win advantages that seem worthwhile only because other states bear much of the costs. America's most urgent public challenges—shoring up the economic underpinnings of an imperiled middle-class culture; developing and deploying productive workplace skills; orchestrating Americans' engagement with increasingly global capital—involve the stewardship of common interests. The fragmentation of authority makes success less likely. The phenomenon is by no means limited to contemporary economic issues, and a smattering of examples from other times and other policy agendas illustrate the theme.

Environmental Regulation

Antipollution law is perhaps the most obvious application of the "commons" metaphor to policy-making in a federal system. If a state maintains a lax regime of environmental laws it spares its own citizens, businesses, and government agencies from economic burdens. The "benefits" of environmental recklessness, in other words, are collected instate. Part of the pollution consequently dumped into the air or water, however, drifts away to do its damage elsewhere in the nation. If states held all authority over environmental rule-making, the predictable result would be feeble regulations against any kinds of pollution where in-state costs and benefits of control are seriously out of balance. Even in states whose citizens valued the environment—even if the citizens of *all* states were willing to accept substantial economic costs in the name of cleaner air and water—constituents and representatives would calculate that their sacrifice could not on its own stem the tide and reluctantly settle for weaker rules than they would otherwise prefer.

A state contemplating tough antipollution rules might calculate that its citizens will pay for environmental improvements that will be enjoyed, in part, by others. Even worse, by imposing higher costs on business than do other states, it risks repelling investment, and thus losing jobs and tax revenues to states with weak environmental laws. Congress explicitly invoked the specter of a "race for the bottom"—competitive loosening of environmental laws in order to lure business—to justify federal standards that would "preclude efforts on the part of states to compete with each other in trying to attract new plants." In a series of legislative changes starting in the early 1970s, the major choices about how aggressively to act against pollution were moved to the federal government. While aspects of enforcement remained state responsibilities—introducing another level of complications that continues to plague environmental policy—the trade-off between environmental and economic values moved much closer to a single national standard.

National regulation in a diverse economy does have a downside. States differ in their environmental problems, and in the priorities of their citizens. Requiring all states to accept the same balance between environmental and economic values imposes some real costs and generates real political friction. Yet even if the tilt toward national authority is, on balance, the correct approach to environmental regulation, there is reason to doubt we got all the details right. Moreover, logic suggests that the federal role should be stronger for forms of pollution that readily cross state borders, and weaker for pollution that stays put. But federal authority is actually weaker under the Clean Air Act and the Clean Water Act than under the "Superfund" law covering hazardous waste. Toxic-waste sites are undeniably nasty things. But most of them are situated within a single state, and stay there.

Governmental Efficiency

There is an alluring a priori case for predicting that public-sector efficiency will increase as responsibilities flow to lower levels of government. Yet this *potential* advantage largely fails to pan out; there is little evidence of a significant or systematic state efficiency edge. The states share with Washington the basic operational handicaps of the public sector.

The devolution debate, moreover, is almost wholly irrelevant to the debt service and middle-class entitlements causing most of the strain on citizens' tolerance for taxation. It is safe to assert that the ascendancy of the states will have, at best, a limited impact on the cost of American government. This is not an argument based on ideology, or economic theory, or learned predictions about comparative administrative behavior. It is a matter of arithmetic. In 1996 total public spending came to about $2.3 trillion. State and local activities, funded by state and local taxes, *already* accounted for about one-third of this total. Another one-third consisted of check-writing programs like Social Security and Medicare. National defense (12 percent of the total), interest on the national debt (10 percent), and federal grants to state and local governments (another 10 percent) accounted for most of the remaining third of the public sector. All other federal domestic undertakings, taken together, claimed between 4 and 5 percent of total government spending. Suppose every last thing the federal government does, aside from running defense and foreign affairs and writing checks (to entitlement claimants, debt holders, and state and local governments) were transferred to the states—national parks and museums, air-traffic control, the FBI, the border patrol, the Centers for Disease Control, the National Weather Service, student loans, the space program, and all the rest. Suppose, then, that the states proved able to do *everything* that the federal government used to do a full 10 percent more efficiently. The cost of government would fall by a little under one-half of one percent.

Beyond the low ceiling on cost savings—and more pertinent to the hidden issue of the *quality* of government—is the similarity between most federal agencies and most state agencies on the core characteristics of scale, complexity, and administration by legislative statute and formal rules. It is rare that economic or managerial imperatives will call for the reassignment of authority away from central government, but then stop at the states. State boundaries have been drawn by a capricious history, and only occasionally (and then by accident) does a state constitute the most logical economic unit for either making policy or delivering services. The coalition between the state-sovereignty constitutionalists and the efficient-scale decentralizers is based on a misunderstanding, and will break down as soon as it begins to succeed.

More promising strategies for improving the efficiency with which public purposes are pursued usually involve going *beyond* devolution to the states. The array of options includes privatization, to enlist private-sector efficiency advantages in the service of public goals; vouchers, to assign purchasing power while letting individuals choose how to deploy it; and the empowerment (through authority and resources) of levels of government smaller than the state, including cities, towns, and school districts. None of these strategies is without its risks and limits, but together they form a far richer menu of reform possibilities than the simple switch from federal to state bureaucracy.

Devolution is often, though misleadingly, cast as a way station toward such fundamental reforms. Its popularity among those convinced of American government's shortcomings, and committed to repairing them, diverts reformist energy that could be put to better use. State governments are only slightly, if any, less bureaucratic than Washington, and no less jealous of power or resistant to change. Power dislodged from federal bureaus is likely to stick at the state level instead of diffusing further. The characteristic pattern of American intergovernmental relations is rivalry between state and local officials, and Washington more often acts as local government's shield against state hegemony than as the common oppressor of cities and states. The ascendancy of the states is thus unlikely either to liberate local governments or to unleash fundamental reform in how government operates.

Rising Inequality

It is by no means certain that America will prove able to reverse growing economic inequality and the erosion of the middle class, no matter how we structure our politics. Devolution, however, will worsen the odds. Shared prosperity, amid the maelstrom of economic change tearing away at the industrial underpinnings of middle-class culture, is an artifact of policy. Policies to shore up the middle class include work-based antipoverty efforts that become both more important and more expensive as unskilled jobs evaporate; relentless investments in education and job training; measures to strengthen employees' leverage in the workplace; and a more progressive tilt in the overall burden of taxation. The individual states—each scrambling to lure mobile capital, fearful of losing businesses and well-off residents to lower-tax rivals, anxious to minimize their burden of needy citizens—will find such policies nearly impossible to sustain. As Washington sheds responsibilities and interstate rivalry intensifies, only a small-government agenda becomes realistic. But even for principled small-government conservatives, devolution is likely to prove less satisfying than many expect. Since it has been justified in terms of improving, not shrinking, government, the ascendancy of the states represents no conclusion to the debate over the public sector's proper size and scope.

Like the run-up in federal debt in the 1980s and early 1990s, devolution short-circuits (rather than settles) deliberation over government's purpose by making activism impossible—for a time. America's federal system is sufficiently resilient that unless citizens are convinced of small government's merits, the tilt toward the states that suppress public-sector ambition will eventually be reversed, though only after an unpredictable price has been paid. The conservative intellectual Herbert Storing has argued that a strategy of crippling the activist impulse through devolution, instead of discrediting it through reasoned appeal, was "not only contrary to the best conservative tradition but also hopelessly unrealistic." By attempting to enthrone the states as the sole locus of legitimate government, conservatives muffle their own voices in the conversation over the country's future.

By the standards of those who credit any diagnosis of what ails America *other than* "big government," shifting authority to competing states is likely to solve minor problems while causing, or perpetuating, far graver ills. As states gain a greater share of governmental duties but prove reluctant or unable to tax mobile firms or well-off individuals, the burden of funding the public sector will tilt even more heavily toward middle-class taxpayers. Their resentment of government can be expected to intensify. Efforts to use state laws or regulations to strengthen employees' leverage in the workplace will often be rendered unworkable by interstate competition for business. America's largest source of fiscal imbalance—the unsustainability of middle-class entitlement programs as the baby boom generation ages—will be untouched by devolution, feeding cynicism about the imperviousness to solution of America's public problems. And the fragmentation of taxing and spending authority puts in peril the education and training agenda that defines our single most promising tactic for shoring up the middle class.

The global marketplace both gives new fuel to America's culture of opportunity *and* allows the range of economic conditions experienced within this erstwhile middle-class country to reflect, with less and less filtering, the whole planet's disparate array of fates. A middle-class national economy, within a world of economic extremes, is a precious but unnatural thing. The policies that sustain shared prosperity will be difficult, perhaps impossible, to pursue if America's center of gravity in economic policy-making continues its precipitous shift toward the separate states. Federal officials, as a class, are certainly no wiser, more farsighted, or defter at implementation than their state counterparts. But our country as a whole remains much less subject to the flight of wealth and the influx of need than are its constituent states. Policies to shrink the underclass and solidify the middle class are thus far more sustainable at the federal level.

Fixing the federal government is an intimidating proposition in the late 1990s. The trajectory of fiscal and political trends suggests that devolution will remain the focus of politicians' promises and citizens' hopes for some time to come. But the inherent limits of a fragmented approach to national adaptation will eventually inspire America to reappraise the ascendancy of the states. Not too far into the new century we will again collect the resolve to confront together our common fate. And we will once more take up, in the two-century tradition of Americans before us, the echoing challenge of George Washington's 1796 farewell address: "Is there a doubt whether a common government can embrace so large a sphere? Let experience solve it."

DISCUSSION QUESTIONS

1. Think of a policy issue that you are interested in. Which level of government do you think is the most appropriate one to make decisions on this issue? Why?

2. Which level of government do you think is the most democratic—federal, state, or local? Can privileged elites more easily dominate at the local level or at the national level?

3. Many people argue that justice should be the same no matter where you live and therefore the federal government should establish minimal standards of justice on certain issues. Do you agree or disagree? Do you think the federal government should guarantee every American medical care or a minimum income?

4. One of the problems with decentralizing decision making is that some local governments have much larger tax resources than others. Many inner cities, for example, are very poor. How would Eggers and O'Leary respond to this problem? What can be done about it?

5. Do you think that marriage law (divorce, child custody, and so on) should be decided by the federal government or the states? What about educational policy? Should the federal government establish national standards in education?

SUGGESTED READINGS AND INTERNET RESOURCES

In *New Federalism: Intergovernmental Reform from Nixon to Reagan* (Washington, D.C.: Brookings Institution, 1988), Timothy Conlan argues that Nixon and Reagan actually had very different approaches to federalism. Jeffrey M. Berry, Kent E. Portney, and Ken Thomson in *The Rebirth of American Democracy* (Washington, D.C.: Brookings Institution, 1993) present evidence that decentralizing power all the way to neighborhood governments makes sense. Grant McConnell, on the other hand, in *Private Power and American Democracy* (New York: Vintage Books, 1966) argues that decentralization of power leads to tyranny by elites. Probably the best book on the possibilities and limits of state economic development efforts is Paul Brace, *State Government and Economic Performance* (Baltimore: Johns Hopkins University Press, 1993). For an interesting change of pace, read Ernest Callenbach's *Ecotopia* (New York: Bantam Books, 1975), an entertaining novel about environmentalists who take over part of the Northwest and secede from the United States.

James Madison Institute
http://jamesmadison.org/
The James Madison Institute is a public policy research organization dedicated to promoting economic freedom, limited government, federalism, the rule of law, and individual liberty coupled with individual responsibility. Includes a list of current books and policy studies.

Center for the Study of Federalism
http://www.temple.edu/federalism/
The web site of a research and educational institute dedicated to the scholarly study of federal principles, institutions, and processes. The Center seeks to increase and disseminate knowledge about federal systems around the world. The site includes links to publications, including abstracts of articles in their journal, *Publius*.

National Council of State Governments
http://www.csg.org/
The web site of the National Council of State Governments with information on state governments and state-level public policies.

U.S. Federalism Site
http://w3.satelink.net/~kala/fed/
In addition to descriptions of the issues and overviews of major contemporary debates, the U.S. Federalism Site links to essential documents, key legal decisions, and sites where debates are currently underway as part of the unfolding debate on federalism.

Culture Wars:
Are We Facing
a Moral Collapse?

resident Clinton's impeachment trial served as a kind of lightning rod for
the cultural tensions that divided Americans at the turn of the century.
Few Americans condoned Clinton's behavior (having sex with an intern,
Monica Lewinsky, and covering over that fact in public statements). Most
Americans (polls show about two-thirds), however, were not outraged
enough to remove the president from office. Many felt that Clintons' private
behavior should be judged separately from his public acts in office. On the
other hand, about one-third of the American people were so deeply offended
by Clinton's behavior that they wanted him removed from office. Some felt
that Clinton lied, and regardless of what he lied about, this justified removing
him from office.

But the drive to remove Clinton from office was also motivated by disgust
at Clinton's sexual infidelities and personal moral failings. For many, Clinton
represented a moral threat to the country, and, for that reason, he needed to
be removed. The cultural and moral outrage behind impeachment became
clear as the case progressed. William Bennett, a top official in the Reagan and
Bush administrations, published *The Death of Outrage* in which he chastised the
American people for not more vigorously supporting Clinton's removal from office, citing this as evidence of continuing moral decline. In his summation to
the Senate, Henry Hyde, who led the prosecution, said: "I wonder if after this
culture war is over . . . an America will survive that's worth fighting to defend."

Far from signaling a lull in the culture wars, however, Clinton's acquittal seems only to have heated them up.

Americans are contradictory on the issue of morality and politics. On the one hand, we are known for being highly individualistic and believing that government should stay out of people's private affairs. "Live and let live" is an American motto. On the other hand, Americans are one of the most religious people in the world and feel strongly about protecting the moral basis of society. For this reason, U.S. politics is periodically shaken by moral crusades— the antislavery abolitionist movement, the nativist reaction against immigrants, and the prohibition movement to ban alcohol.

Most observers trace the current culture wars to the social and political upheavals of the 1960s. At that time, one social group after another asserted its rights through political protest, winning public recognition and support for its goals. The civil rights movement began in the 1950s but reached its apex, under the skilled leadership of Martin Luther King Jr., in the mid-1960s. African Americans, along with other minorities, won recognition and favorable policies, like school desegregation and affirmative action. A huge mass movement arose in opposition to the Vietnam War, splitting the country on issues of U.S. nationalism and the proper role of the military. Learning from the civil rights movement, women organized to demand their rights and won new laws protecting them from discrimination on the job and giving them more equal access to professional schools and college sports, among other things. They gay rights movement brought a group that had previously been pretty much invisible out into the public arena to demand equal treatment.

A reaction against the social movements of the 1960s set in almost immediately. Richard Nixon won the presidency twice by representing the forgotten Americans, the "Silent Majority"—traditional, hardworking, middle Americans who felt they were being pushed aside by assertive new social movements. Many men, traditional women, and whites felt that the United States no longer belonged to them and that various minorities, representing questionable moral values, were using government for their advantage. The Republican Party appealed successfully to whites who resented affirmative action and women who objected to government support for day care in place of stay-at-home moms. White southerners, who previously had voted heavily Democratic, shifted dramatically to the Republicans, at least in part because of their distaste for the cultural politics of groups affiliated with the Democratic Party.

One of the most-heated battles in the culture wars has been over government funding of the arts. The National Endowment for the arts (NEA), founded in 1965 by President Lyndon Johnson, came under attack in the late 1980s when it was revealed that it had indirectly funded art that was morally offensive. The most sensational exhibit contained a crucifix submerged in a jar of the artist's urine, entitled *Piss Christ*. An effort to defund NEA was immediately launched, and it has continued to attack government funding of the arts ever since. Opponents countered by saying that attacks on the NEA focused on a few sensational cases, misrepresenting the work of the group. The attack on the NEA, they argued, is nothing but government censorship. For its part, the NEA has striven to avoid funding controversial artists ever since but is still threatened with defunding by Congress.

The culture wars also extended to the universities. In 1988, Allan Bloom wrote a best-seller, *The Closing of the American Mind,* in which he argued that the spread of moral relativism by professors was undermining the nation's moral fabric and contributing to a precipitous decline of academic standards on college campuses. A debate soon erupted over whether college curriculums should focus on the great books of Western civilization or whether they should follow multiculturalism, exposing students to the best of other cultural and religious traditions. In 1990–91, the term *politically correct* began to be used by opponents of the multiculturalists, who maintained that, like the Stalinists of old who originated the term, tenured professors and radical students were imposing an oppressive liberal orthodoxy on college campuses. People were afraid to defend traditional values, they maintained. Opponents responded that this was a gross exaggeration; radicals had not taken over the universities which were, in fact, still dominated by conservative corporate values.

Probably the most explosive battles of the culture wars concern family rela-tions and sex. With greater affluence, the spread of birth control, and women entering the workforce in droves, it is clear that gender relations are going to change anyway. Many women no longer need to stay in unsatisfactory or abusive marriages, because they can support themselves in the job market. The issue, however, is whether the sexual revolution of the 1960s undermined tradi-tional morality about sex and marriage. One place where the issue comes to a head is over sex education in schools. Should teenagers be taught about the consequences of sex and given access to birth control, or should the message be abstinence until marriage?

In the contemporary period the one issue that crystallizes the culture wars more than any other is abortion. The 1973 Supreme Court decision in *Roe* v. *Wade* gave women a constitutional right to abortion. The abortion issue shows how divisive the culture wars can be and how immune they are to compromise. For those who believe that human life starts at conception, abortion is murder. Thus, they call their movement "right to life." For those who believe that this question should be decided by the individual woman in consultation with her doctor, bans on abortion take away a woman's "right to choose"—using government to impose the moral beliefs of one group of people on another group. In the 2000 presidential primaries, many Republican candidates made abortion the central issue of their campaign and accused George W. Bush of not being committed enough to banning abortions. On the Democratic side, Bill Bradley accused Al Gore of being soft on abortion rights. Abortion will undoubtedly have a polarizing effect on the 2000 general election.

Is there anything that unites all these disparate issues in the culture wars? James Davison Hunter, whose 1991 book, *Culture Wars,* popularized the term *culture war,* argues that there is. At the heart of the contemporary culture war, he says, are two belief systems: one he calls *orthodoxy,* the other *progressivism.* Adherents to orthodoxy believe in an external, transcendent authority, such as the Bible, that settles issues of right and wrong. Progressives, on the other hand, believe that moral ideals must be updated to contemporary life using reason and experience. If Hunter is correct, it is clear why it is so difficult to negotiate a peace in the culture wars: each side appeals to different authorities. When people believe wholeheartedly in the moral rightness of their cause, it is difficult, if not impossible, for the normal democratic processes of negotiation and bargaining to settle the issue.

Gertrude Himmelfarb, a professor emeritus at the City University of New York, argues in a selection from her 1999 book, *One Nation, Two Cultures,* that the United States went through a genuine cultural revolution beginning in the 1960s. Cultural elites, abetted by the mass media, trashed the traditional values of marriage, family, work, and religion. Himmelfarb documents the negative effects that she says were caused by the cultural revolution: rising rates of crime, divorce, out-of-wedlock births, drug addiction, welfare dependency, and abortion. Moral laxity is especially devastating for the poor, argues Himmelfarb. Wealthy elites can survive years of moral looseness and depravity, but the poor, who have nothing to fall back on when they lose their moral compass, are quickly ruined. Even though we are split into two diametrically opposed cultures, Himmelfarb maintains, we are still one nation, with a common set of political commitments. If we hearken back to the republican virtues that animated the country at its founding, there is hope that the culture wars can find a political solution.

James Morone, a professor of political science at Brown University, disagrees strongly with Himmelfarb that the culture wars are either necessary or healthy for American democracy. The idea that there is a moral collapse in this country as evidenced by a decline in religion or rise in divorce rates is nonsense, says Morone. The rhetoric of the moralists is designed to frighten people into supporting their right-wing agenda. Those who preach about the moral decline of the nation are splitting the country into warring factions and undermining the possibility for progressive public policies that could address our real problems. For Morone, contemporary moralists are selective in their morality, concentrating on poor people and minorities while ignoring the sins of powerful elites and corporations. The politics of virtue is an effort to scapegoat the most vulnerable people as responsible for society's problems.

As you read the selections, you may want to reflect on the distinction between elite and popular democracy in the Introduction. Both sides portray themselves as the friend of the common person, charging that the other side is elitist. Who is right? Did the social movements of the 1960s basically further the interests of common people, or were they orchestrated by liberal elites? Do contemporary conservative moral advocates help common people, or are they benefiting wealthy corporate elites?

One Nation, Two Cultures

GERTRUDE HIMMELFARB

I n *The Wealth of Nations,* Adam Smith described the "two different schemes or systems of morality" that prevail in all civilized societies.[1]

In every civilized society, in every society where the distinction of ranks has once been completely established, there have been always two different schemes or systems of morality current at the same time; of which the one may be called the strict or austere; the other the liberal, or, if you will, the loose system. The former is generally admired and revered by the common people: the latter is commonly more esteemed and adopted by what are called people of fashion.

The liberal or loose system is prone to the "vices of levity"—"luxury, wanton and even disorderly mirth, the pursuit of pleasure to some degree of intemperance, the breach of chastity, at least in one of the two sexes, etc." Among the "people of fashion," these vices are treated indulgently. The "common people," on the other hand, committed to the strict or austere system, regard such vices, for themselves at any rate, with "the utmost abhorrence and detestation," because they—or at least "the wiser and better sort" of them—know that these vices are almost always ruinous to them. Whereas the rich can sustain years of disorder and extravagance—indeed, regard the liberty to do so without incurring any censure or reproach as one of the privileges of their rank—the people know that a single week's dissipation can undo a poor workman forever. This is why, Smith explained, religious sects generally arise and flourish among the common people, for these sects preach that system of morality upon which their welfare depends. . . .

The moral divide that Adam Smith saw in his society, indeed, in "every civilized society," was a class divide; it separated the rich and the poor, the "people of fashion" and the "common people." The divide we are confronting today cuts through class lines, as it also does through religious, racial, ethnic, political, and sexual lines. . . .

---

1. Adam Smith (1723–1790) is considered the founder of free market economics.

The Rise of a Counterculture

The 1960s brought to a head the "cultural contradictions of capitalism," in Daniel Bell's memorable phrase: the contradictions inherent in an economy that requires, for its effective functioning, such moral restraints as self-discipline and deferred gratification, but at the same time stimulates a hedonism and self-indulgence impatient of all restraints. One of these "contradictions" was the manipulation and exploitation of capitalism by those who professed to despise it. . . . Many "hippies" proved to be skillful at commercializing their own talents and converting their countercultural activities into profitable enterprises. Thus, entire industries arose devoted to pseudo-folk art and attire, "head shops" specializing in drug paraphernalia and herb shops in "nature remedies," and avant-garde galleries and theaters that were patronized and often subsidized by the bourgeois capitalists who were being satirized.

In 1965, Lionel Trilling took the measure of the "adversary culture," as he called it. Propagated initially by modernist writers and artists, it had a deliberately "adversary intention," and "actually subversive intention," towards the traditional bourgeois culture. In the 1960s, however, it took a form that was quantitatively as well as qualitatively unique, for it now characterized not a small group but an entire class, a class that was most conspicuous in the universities but that spilled over into society at large—indeed, into the very middle class that was its ostensible enemy. Although it did not dominate the middle class, Trilling observed, it "detached a considerable force from the main body of the enemy and . . . captivated its allegiance."

Within only a few years of that prescient comment, Trilling's "adversary culture" developed into the "counterculture," embracing far more people than he anticipated at the time. It even surpassed the expectations of Theodore Roszak, who, in 1968, in an article "Youth and the Great Refusal" in *The Nation,* introduced and defined this new phenomenon: "The counter culture is the embryonic cultural base of New Left politics, the effort to discover new types of community, new family patterns, new sexual mores, new kinds of livelihood, new aesthetic forms, new personal identities on the far side of power politics, the bourgeois home, and the Protestant work ethic." The term gained wide circulation when the essay was reprinted two years later in Roszak's *The Making of a Counter Culture.* But even then he underestimated the appeal of the counterculture, for he confined it to "a strict minority of the young and a handful of their adult mentors"; in a few generations, he speculated, their heirs might "transform this disoriented civilization of ours into something a human being can identify as home."

In fact, the counterculture progressed far more rapidly and widely than even its most enthusiastic supporters predicted, for it proved to be nothing less than a cultural revolution. And this revolution was magnified by other concurrent ones: a racial revolution (inspired by the civil rights movement); a sexual revolution (abetted by the birth-control pill and feminism); a technological revolution (of which television was a notable by-product); a demographic revolution (producing a generation of baby-boomers and a powerful peer culture); a political revolution (precipitated by the Vietnam War); an economic revolution (ushering in the Great Society and the expansion of the welfare state); and what might be called a psychological revolution (the "culture of narcissism," as Christopher Lasch dubbed it). Each was momentous in itself and together they fed upon each other, fostering a growing disaffection with established institutions and authorities and a rejection of conventional modes of thought and behavior.

Blacks and women celebrate this period as the beginning of their liberation, their admission into a world of rights, liberties, and opportunities from which they had been so unjustly excluded. The celebration is warranted and the liberation much appreciated. But it was not long before anomalies emerged—the "cultural contradictions of liberation," one might say. Some women found that they were liberated from the home in more than one sense. The rise in the employment rate for women paralleled a rise in the divorce and single-parenthood rates. Many women, having gained entry into the workplace, lost their secure place in the marital home. And having become "gainfully employed" (as economists understand that term), they were often reduced to the condition of poverty that accompanies divorce and single-parenthood.

For blacks the situation turned out to be equally anomalous. Freed from the degrading conditions of segregation and discrimination, most blacks, including working-class blacks, came to enjoy a higher standard of living, more varied and desirable jobs, and better education and housing. But others, in this "post–civil rights era," as the black economist Glenn Loury calls it, found themselves in a "moral quandary," dependent upon a government-subsidized welfare system that provided for their basic needs but put them in the unfortunate condition of victimhood and dependency—a condition that might be rectified, Loury suggests, by utilizing those resources within their own community that promote a sense of self-confidence and "self-help."

Thus the counterculture, intended to liberate everyone from the stultifying influence of "bourgeois values," also liberated a good many people from those values—virtues, as they were once called—that had a stabilizing, socializing, and moralizing effect on society. It is no accident, as Marxists used to say, that the rapid acceleration of crime, out-of-wedlock births, and welfare dependency started at just the time that the counterculture got under way.

It is a much-debated question whether we could have enjoyed the good without the bad, the desirable effects of the cultural revolution without the undesirable. Revolutions, it is well known, develop a momentum of their own, often escalating beyond their original aims and ending up by consuming both their parents and their children. And the conjunction of revolutions, such as occurred in the 1960s, made it probable that the unintended consequences would eventually overwhelm the intended ones.

Thus the beneficial results of the civil rights movement were partially—fortunately only partially—negated by two other developments that coincided with it: the cultural revolution that denigrated precisely those virtues (work, thrift, temperance, self-discipline) that are conducive to economic improvement and social mobility; and the Great Society, which was meant to facilitate the entry of minorities into the open society of opportunity and self-fulfillment, but all too often drew them into a closed society of chronic dependency. . . .

Evidence for a Cultural Revolution

In poll after poll, even at the height of economic prosperity, a great majority of the American people (as many as two-thirds to three-quarters) identify "moral decay" or "moral decline" as one of the major problems, often *the* major problem, confronting the country.

In its most virulent form this "decay" manifests itself in the "moral statistics" (as the Victorians called them—"social pathology," we would say) of crime, violence, out-of-wedlock births, teenage pregnancy, child abuse, drug addiction, alcoholism, illiteracy, promiscuity, welfare dependency. Some of these statistics have improved in the last few years and there are hopeful signs for the future. . . .

Yet while there is much to be grateful for, there is little cause for complacency. If the *rate* of births to teenagers and unmarried women has decreased, partly because of a decline in the birthrate in general, the *ratio* of out-of-wedlock births (relative to all births) has only leveled off, and at a very high level: one-third of all children, two-thirds of black children, and three-fourths of the children of teenagers are born out-of-wedlock. (And the number of single-parent households with children continues to increase, from 24 percent in 1990 to 27 percent in 1996.) If there are fewer abortions, it is partly because of newer forms of contraception (such as Norplant and Depo Provera), but also because unmarried motherhood is more respectable. (And the rate of abortions is still higher than in any other Western country.) If older girls are less sexually active, younger ones (below the age of fifteen) are more so. (A new term, "tweens," has been coined to describe eight-to-twelve-year-olds, who behave more like teenagers than the "preadolescents" of old.)

If divorce is declining, it is partly because cohabitation is becoming more common; people living together without benefit of marriage can separate without benefit of divorce—and do so with greater facility and frequency. Cohabitation increased by 85 percent in the last decade alone, and eightfold since 1970; 40 percent of cohabiting couples separate before marriage; those who eventually marry have a 50 percent higher divorce rate than couples who did not live together before marriage; and the proportion of cohabiting mothers who eventually marry the child's father has declined by almost one-fourth in the last decade.

If drug use among adults has fallen, that among young, and increasingly younger, people has risen. (In 1990, 27 percent of high-school seniors reported using marijuana in the previous year; in 1997, 38.5 percent did. For college seniors in the same period the rate rose from 29.4 percent to 31.6 percent.) If the fear of AIDS is one of the factors responsible for the decline in the out-of-wedlock birthrate among black women, it has not affected black men, among whom AIDS is significantly, and disproportionately, increasing. (While the death rate from HIV infection for white males fell from 15 per 100,000 in 1990 to 12.5 in 1996, that for black males rose from 44.2 to 66.4.)

Even the notable decrease in crime, encouraging as it is, has some disconcerting aspects, criminologists warn us, for it reflects not only more effective policing and incarceration policies but also a decline in the number of teenagers. While the juvenile crime rate has fallen since 1993, juveniles are still responsible for a substantial portion of crime, and especially violent crime. (The FBI reports that while firearm killings by people above the age of twenty-five fell 44 percent between 1980 and 1997, such killings by eighteen- to twenty-four-year-olds rose by 20 percent.) Some criminologists fear that the expected rise in the "baby-boomerang" cohort (the offsprings of baby-boomers) might lead to another "youth crime wave" comparable to that of the early 1990s.

Moreover, the lowering or stabilization of some of the indices of social disarray does not begin to bring us back to the status quo ante, before their precipitous rise in the 1960s and '70s. One does not have to be nostalgic for a golden age that never was to appreciate the contrast between past and present. The ratio of out-of-wedlock births has increased sixfold since 1960 (even the rate of out-of-wedlock births is one-third higher than it was in 1980); the number of children living with one parent has risen from less than one-tenth to more than one-quarter; and the number of households consisting of unmarried couples with children under the age of fifteen has grown from less than 200,000 in 1960 to over 1,300,000 in 1995. It has often been observed that when Senator Daniel Patrick Moynihan wrote his percipient report on the breakdown of the black family in 1965, the black illegitimacy ratio was only slightly higher than the white ratio is today, and considerably lower than it is now for the country at large. The divorce rate is almost twice that of the 1950s, and half of the marriages today and well over half of the remarriages are expected to end in divorce. Sexual activity by teenage girls declined to 50 percent in 1995; but it had been less than 30 percent in 1970. The serious crime rate is still considerably higher than in the fifties; homicides, which have witnessed the most dramatic decline, are 50 percent higher than they were in 1950; and homicides by fourteen- to seventeen-year-olds, half of what they were in 1993, are still double what they were in 1984.

The statistics, moreover, good and bad, do not tell the whole story. The loss of parental authority, the lack of discipline in schools (to say nothing of knifings and shootings), the escalating violence and vulgarity on TV, the ready accessibility of pornography and sexual perversions on the Internet, the obscenity and sadism of videos and rap music, the binge-drinking and "hooking up" on college campuses, the "dumbing down" of education at all levels—these too are part of the social pathology of our time. And this pathology, which affects not only the "underclass" but the entire population, shows no signs of abating. "The morality of the cool," the cultural historian Roger Shattuck dubs a pervasive tendency in the culture, ranging from films that portray sadistic episodes in gory detail as if they were "cool," to the university, where sin and evil appear, in fashionable academic discourse, under the neutral or even positive guise of "transgression."

Affluence and education, we have discovered, provide no immunity from moral and cultural disorders. Indeed, it has been argued that the affluent and well-educated bear some responsibility for the condition of the underclass. This is the thesis of a powerful book by Myron Magnet analyzing the symbiotic relationship between the "Haves" and the "Have-Nots." It was the Haves, the cultural elites in the 1960s, who legitimized and glamorized the counterculture, which dislocated their own lives only temporarily but had a disastrous effect on those less fortunate than themselves. In disparaging the Puritan ethic, the counterculture undermined those virtues that might better have served the poor. The underclass is thus not only the victim of its own "culture of poverty"; it is also the victim of the upper-class culture around it. The kind of casual delinquency that a white suburban teenager can absorb with relative impunity may be literally fatal to a black inner city teenager. Or the child of an unmarried, affluent, professional woman (a "Murphy Brown") is obviously in a more privileged position than the child (more often, children) of an unmarried woman on welfare.[2]

The effects of the culture, however, are felt at all levels. It was only a matter of time before there emerged, as Charles Murray has demonstrated, a white underclass with much the same pathology as the black. And that pathology has affected the middle class as well. Some of the most affluent suburbs exhibit the same symptoms of teenage alcoholism, drug addiction, delinquency, and promiscuity, although not, obviously, to the same extent or with the same devastating results.

The Dissident Culture

The reaction [to the counterculture] expresses itself in different ways, in the religious revival most conspicuously, but also in more modest forms that feed into the dissident culture. Those who encourage tolerance for "alternative lifestyles"—and not only tolerance but full legitimacy and equality— have in mind the lifestyles favored by the counterculture. But there are

---

2. *Murphy Brown* was a popular television situation comedy in which Candace Bergen played a newscaster who had a child out of wedlock.

other alternatives, traditional lifestyles, that are asserting themselves and even beginning to be reflected in public policies.

The welfare reform act, for example, is not merely an alternative way of administering welfare; it is an attempt to promote a new (or the revival of an old) attitude toward chronic dependency. Educational innovations provide other alternatives: charter schools and the voucher system enable poor parents to do what the rich have always done—opt out of the public school system and send their children to the school of their choice. Implicit in these alternatives is the recognition that the dominant culture will not soon be changed. Welfare will continue, on the state and local if not national level; and the public school system is not likely to be significantly changed in the near future. But these alternatives are important, precisely because they have been legitimized by the state.

Other alternatives do not require the intervention of the state. They require only that the state forbear from intervening. Private schools, including religious schools, have long been available but are now far more numerous than ever and being utilized by different people for different reasons—cultural and moral as well as educational and religious. Jewish day schools, for example, are flourishing as never before; the largest number are still Orthodox, but others are being established for the first time by Conservative and Reform denominations. As many as forty new Jewish schools have been established since 1990, and ten Jewish high schools in one month alone in 1997; there are now more than 600 such schools in the country, enrolling about 200,000 students.

At the college level, it is evangelical institutions that have grown most dramatically. From 1990 to 1996, while the undergraduate enrollment in public colleges increased by only 4 percent and that in private colleges by 5 percent, the student body of evangelical colleges surged by 24 percent. These schools are distinguished as much by their moral and cultural character as by their religious studies. Some, like Indiana Wesleyan (which doubled in size during this period), hold their students to a rigid code that prohibits not only premarital sex and homosexuality but also alcohol, drugs, tobacco, and social dancing. The most highly regarded of these colleges, Calvin College in Michigan, is far more permissive, allowing alcohol (although not on campus), smoking (although not in buildings), and dancing; gay students are admitted and support services provided for them. In many cases, the academic quality of these institutions, which is generally lower than secular ones, is also improving; Calvin College now has half of its students receiving merit scholarships.

A more radical educational alternative is home schooling. In the past decade alone, the number of children taught at home has more than doubled and is growing by about 15 percent a year; that number is now between one and two million. Moreover, home schooling is no longer confined, as it once was, to religious fundamentalists. Dissatisfaction with the public schools, rather than religion, is the main reason now given by parents undertaking that arduous task. (Black professionals constitute one of the fastest-growing groups of home-schoolers.) Home school organizations provide parents with curricula and advice, and a Home School Legal Defense Association serves as a lobbying group and legal defense organization. It was once thought that home-schoolers would lack the credentials for higher education, but they now surpass students in both private and public schools in standardized tests and are being admitted to some of the most prestigious colleges. (A new two-year college is being planned for those who do not want to enter the mainstream colleges.)

Even the universities provide alternatives, places of refuge for dissidents. Like the media, the academic vanguard is constantly "pushing the envelope." The subhead of an article in the *New York Times Magazine* reads: "Porn theory and queer scholarship were last year's college news. The latest academic trend: whiteness studies." Before whiteness studies (which celebrate "white trash" and expose the inherent racism in being white), before porn studies (which are now taught at major universities, accompanied by performances by porn stars), before queer studies (which go beyond gay and lesbian studies to include bisexuality, transvestitism, and other sexual "orientations"), before cultural studies (which analyze comic books and sitcoms with all the solemnity once devoted to Shakespeare and Milton), there were all the other brave new heresies that are now well-established academic orthodoxies. Yet here too, in the midst of the pursuit of the novel and the trivial, there are oases of traditional study where professors and students understand knowledge to be something other than a "social construct" or struggle for "hegemony," and where they do not feel bound by the constraints of the race/class/gender trinity.

Conclusion

It is common these days to deplore the expression "culture war," as if the very term is uncivil and inflammatory, a slander upon a good, decent, pacific people. It should hardly need saying that the "culture war" is a "war" only metaphorically, just as the "cultural revolution" is a "revolution" only metaphorically. And metaphors, while not to be taken literally, do serve a serious purpose. There is an important sense—a metaphorical sense, to be sure—in which Americans have lived through such a revolution and are experiencing such a war. To deny either is to belie or trivialize much of the history of the past three decades. It is not surprising that the impeachment trial of President Clinton elicited, from commentator after commentator, references to the culture war, or that, in the midst of this controversy, two-thirds of the public found that "Americans are greatly divided when it comes to the most important values."

The Corrosive Politics of Virtue

JAMES A. MORONE

T he most influential men in America met in Boston. The nation, they agreed, faced a terrible moral crisis: rampant substance abuse, sex (even the old taboo against naked breasts seemed to be gone), illegitimacy. Public schools were languishing, the pursuit of profits was appalling, the explosion of lawsuits completely out of hand. Worst of all, parents were doing a terrible job of raising their kids—not enough discipline. "Most of the evils" that afflict our society, reported the conference, stem from "defects as to family government." The gathering published a famous call for moral reform in 1679.

More than 300 years later, the old jeremiad is still doing a brisk business. From every political quarter we hear the same story—moral failures vex the nation. Almost no one in public life demurs. The warnings of spiritual decline sound vaguely plausible. Besides, why oppose calls for more virtuous behavior?

This essay suggests why. The moral diagnosis is wrong and its political consequences are pernicious. The moralizing divides Americans into a righteous "us" and a malevolent "them." Once those lines are drawn, you can forget about social justice, progressive thinking, or universal programs. Instead, the overarching policy question becomes "How do we protect ourselves and our children?" Never mind health care—build more jails.

Contemporary moralizing stands in a long, unhappy American political tradition. When economic and social problems are transformed into declining moral standards, the hunt is on for immoral people who threaten the public good. There are always plenty of suspects (though the contemporary list is particularly skewed toward poor people's sins). In the tumult of their witch-hunts, Americans ignore an alternative moral tradition that aspires, with Abraham Lincoln, "to touch, . . . the better angels of our nature."

The Preachers

Today, the calls to virtue sound across the full spectrum of American culture. . . . Put aside the differences in tone, sophistication, and packaging, and what you find is a startling convergence in the message. From prestigious academics to fundamentalist preachers, the moralists offer very different audiences a consistent narrative about American politics and culture. It is a story in which good people try to cling to their morals despite an over-whelming, sneering, secular tide.

When "ordinary men and women . . . wish to make moral judgments," writes Wilson, "they must do so privately and in whispers." [Gertrude] Him-melfarb wonders "whether the million purchasers of William Bennett's *The Book of Virtues* had to overcome their initial embarrassment in order to utter that word." Once upon a time, the dirty pornographer or the embarrassed condom purchaser skulked about. But with the great revolution of Ameri-can mores, it is now those who would be good who sneak red-faced while pornography is everywhere and condoms (but not prayers!) are passed around in school. Reading across the literary spectrum, the tone moves from tart irony to raw outrage—much of it directed at the federal govern-ment for buying condoms while barring Christ from public schools. But the constant message boils down to this: Our society has abandoned the morals that once guided us.

And there will be hell to pay. The trends, writes Himmelfarb, bode "even worse for the future than for the present." Or, as Reverend LaHaye puts it in *The Battle for the Mind:* "For over seventy-five years, judges, legisla-tors, governors, mayors and presidents have introduced legislation based on [secular humanism] which is destructive of morality and family solidarity. We have arrived at the gates of Sodom and Gomorrah." Recall that God burned Sodom and Gomorrah to cinders in His wrath over the people's in-iquity (in fact, it's at Sodom where the Bible first raises the specter of brim-stone and fire).

How do we avoid that kind of fate? In *Strength For the Journey,* Jerry Falwell puts it directly: God needs us to "save the nation from inward moral decay."[1]

Still Holier Than Most

Has America really developed a secular culture that runs down morality and deprecates religion? No. The charge is popular fiction. Every available mea-sure suggests people in the United States continue to talk about God with a gusto unmatched in the Western world. G. K. Chesterton once described the United States as a nation with the soul of a church. The description re-mains apt.

According to surveys by the Gallup Organization, 95 percent of Ameri-cans profess a faith in God—a number that has scarcely budged in years. (The figure is 76 percent in Britain and 52 percent in Sweden.) Or take the common polling routine that probes for belief in the Ten Commandments. Again, no Western nation beats the United States. Getting back to sex, for example, 87 percent of Americans tell pollsters that adultery is "always

---

1. Jerry Falwell is a televangelist and leader of the Moral Majority.

wrong" compared to 48 percent in France. More than three-quarters of the population belong to a church, a steady 40 percent say they went this week, and 9 percent claim to go to church "several times a week." Only the last figure, reported by the National Opinion Research Center, has changed much in the past two decades—and it is up 30 percent.

The measures of American faith stretch on and on. More than one in four Americans owns at least five Bibles. The Family Channel is one of the top ten cable channels, the Christian Broadcast Network claims a million viewers a day. The pope sells out whenever he prays in an American stadium. So does Billy Graham. And mobs of weeping men go to Promise Keepers rallies and roar approval to variations of the following: Jesus is Number One and we are on His team and we are going to win.[2] . . .

Nobody out there is blushing when they whisper *"Virtues"* to the bookseller.

Nor is religious conviction in America anything new. So why all the breathless moralizing about secular humanism, bad behavior, and looming perdition? To understand, we have to look more directly at the social and political project that lurks beneath the crusade to make us good.

The Politics of Morality

The vice squad has constructed a simple story. Most Americans are good, but we are surrounded by rampant immorality. And that tide of misbehavior threatens America in fundamental ways. The jeremiad has three effects.

First, the moralizing reassures. Good people are not to blame for social troubles or economic tribulations. Quite the contrary, the entire message encourages and comforts moral folks (who manifest their morality by buying the books and calling the toll-free numbers in the first place). "Most of us have a moral sense," writes Wilson. The message resonates precisely because most Americans do consider themselves decent, religious, moral.

Second, the moralizing message drafts readers into a political fight. Each preacher would muster us into a somewhat different battle line in the great American culture war: crime, illegitimacy, divorce (Wilson); crime, welfare, educational discipline, affirmative action (Wattenberg); crime, welfare, teen pregnancy (*Newsweek*); Satan, moral permissiveness, abortion, drugs (Falwell).

Third, the message engages an enemy. And with this we arrive at the crux of the matter. The effect of all this sermonizing is to construct an often shadowy, immoral "other." These bad people explain why life is hard or why times are confusing or why America is not what it used to be. Some, like the fundamentalist preachers, name names with relish: homosexuals, abortionists, welfare mothers. Others try to pick more carefully. Wattenberg

---

2. Promise Keepers is an organization whose goal is to bring men back to Jesus and family values.

says the battle is about crime and welfare (which all good people agree on) and not about abortion and sexual preference (where his own friends no doubt disagree).

The political result is a great division: a virtuous us, a vicious them. "They" threaten us. "They" are ominous, cruel, and depraved. (I'm not making these words up.) In the real world of political passions, fine distinctions among the issues (like Wattenberg's) get lost in the tumult. The outcry against sin leads, willy-nilly, to the fight against sinners. What we get is the logic of the witch-hunt. The moral framing of our social troubles—good us, evil them—permits leaders (and demagogues) to cash in with whatever enemy resonates among the people (more on just who that really is in a moment). . . .

Of course, moral and religious divisions mark most societies. And Americans have long been split between what sociologist James Davison Hunter calls orthodox perspectives (there is one truth for everyone) and progressive views (truth is contingent, people have their own values). What is different about the great moments of moral conflict is their primacy. The culture war goes front and center on the political stage. Today's moralizers have successfully filled the Great Enemy Vacuum left by the end of the Cold War. The fate of the nation now seems to rest on moral uplift. Ironically, our politics get most ugly precisely when values come to matter most.

What is most startling about the contemporary moral cry is its bias. The celebration of virtue stops at the market's edge. The lamentations about lost values are directed largely at poor people. There is scarcely a word about what the privileged owe their society. This gospel runs lightly over the corporal works of mercy or all that trouble in the temple between Jesus and the money changers. Today, the apostles of virtue offer almost no sermons on loyalty toward workers, obligations toward the poor, or the greed of some corporate officials.

Where are the moralizers when Fleet Finance gets caught in "predatory lending practices" (that means lying to the customers about their interest rates)? And Fleet, New England's largest bank, managed to duck an even worse charge, "equity theft" (that's stealing from the customers). On a still grander scale, the savings-and-loan fiasco involved plenty of moral meltdown along with economic miscalculation. Yet scarcely a word from the political pulpits. The wrath is reserved for bad kids and their moms, not bankers or CEOs.[3]

Why? Partially because the values movement is about explaining popular anxiety. Criminal delinquents make an ominous, predatory other. More important, they fit neatly into a picture of American troubles that conservatives framed long ago: The lazy, self-indulgent, criminal poor are responsible for their own troubles, the growth of liberal welfare government, and the dwindling opportunities for the hard-working, moral us.

---

3. Chief Executive Officers of private corporations.

Inside this worldview, even the stingy contemporary welfare state is insupportable. Charity means tough love. The kinds of policies that meet the need run to more police, tougher sentences, chain gangs, and the return of death penalties. After all, the good of the nation is at stake.

What is lost is the image of shared fate against common troubles. Benedict Anderson writes that the very idea of a nation rests on "imagined communities"—an idea that people share a common experience, a common fate, and common values. When liberals call for universal programs, they are tapping into precisely such a political construction.

Moral politics wrecks the universalist impulse. Danger is lurking right at home, within our own communities. Programs that provide everyone with, say, health care, fund the very delinquents that threaten our peace. . . .

Bad People

It goes deeper than defeating new social programs. Moral panics erode liberalism itself. Remember, liberalism grew out of the bloody European religious wars; its early proponents hoped to get the religious fights out of politics by protecting private choices and individual rights. Liberalism, writes Steven Holmes . . . , insists that "no individual can claim to have [political] motives that are morally superior to his neighbors." Or in the inelegant patois of economics, we all maximize our own utilities.

The United States may have the most liberal political rules on the planet, but moral dangers introduce an often illiberal political style. Politics spill into the private sphere. Rights and protections fail to hold. After all, someone is acting in wrong and dangerous ways. Their misbehavior threatens good people. Moral politics would rule the group, their goals, or the way they act right out of the national community. (Yes, of course, there is another moral tradition, which we'll get to.)

The illiberal urge gets particularly intense when sins are projected onto racial or ethnic groups. The underlying political question becomes: Are those strange people going to slip their moral aberrations into our cultural mainstream? . . .

Which brings us to race. Nowhere has the tension between rights and morals been more intense. From the slaveholding start, white Americans justified racial suppression by imagining a black immorality that had to be controlled. Powerful stereotypes reasserted themselves across American history, both before and after the Civil War. The most troubling aspect of the new moralizing is the old racial imagery lurking just below the rhetorical surface. In many ways, the contemporary imagery of an immoral "other" recalls the racial constructions that swamped American liberalism with Jim Crow laws a century ago.[4]

---

4. Based on a nineteenth-century minstrel song title, *Jim Crow* refers to the systematic segregation and suppression of blacks in the South following Reconstruction after the Civil War.

Political scientists usually tell the Jim Crow story by analyzing its politics. Congress repealed the laws that implemented the Civil War amendments (1893); the Supreme Court accepted segregation (with *Plessy v. Ferguson,* 1896); the southern states held conventions that put the Jim Crow laws into place (1895–1905). What is far less often observed is how these maneuvers rested on moral stigma.

White southerners constructed an image of the former slaves as morally unprepared for freedom. The calumny included a standard roster of vices— laziness, dishonesty, thieving, political corruption. But the heart of the matter, endlessly repeated, was the supposed sexual lust of black men. In his popular history, *The Tragic Era,* Claude Bowers reported the prejudice as fact: "Rape is the foul daughter of Reconstruction." As Bowers told it, the story ended happily, virtue triumphant. When "the Klan began to ride . . . white women felt some sense of security."

The illiberal stereotype of dangerous, immoral African Americans gained wide currency—in the North as well as the South, in academic history, social science, and popular culture. All elevated the fiction of black lust (and the necessary discipline imposed by beleaguered whites through organizations like the Ku Klux Klan) into the standard historical narrative. . . .

There were, of course, voices on the other side. African Americans struggled to answer the critics in conferences, monographs, and books. They told the story of free men and women struggling to make new lives for themselves after the Civil War despite violence, poverty, and repression. W. E. B. Du Bois, for example, took on historians like Bowers directly in his extraordinary *Reconstruction,* published in 1935.[5] But as Du Bois lamented, his colleagues politely ignored his revisions. To the American majority, real African Americans were invisible, hidden by scary fables about "low standards of sexual morals." Americans set liberalism aside and constructed their apartheid.

The great twentieth-century civil rights movement should be read in the same moral context. It was more than a battle about southern institutions. It was a religiously inspired movement that drew on a very different American moral tradition and forced white Americans to revise their racial images.

Now the old stigmas are back, revived by the latest round of culture wars. They glint through contemporary stereotypes about crime, welfare, teen pregnancy, and underclass immorality. Amid a renewed crusade against vice, old racial images reintroduce a prefabricated racial "them."

American cities have always gathered young toughs of every nationality and color. Now, a growing literature runs criminals together with poor people, turns them black, and dubs them a menacing underclass—the ultimate amoral them. Incredibly, the construction stands for an entire race. In *The*

---

5. William Edward Burghardt Du Bois was a black intellectual and writer who cofounded the National Association for the Advancement of Colored People (NAACP).

End of Racism, Dinesh D'Souza blurts out what most of his colleagues have the wit to remain mum about: It is entirely rational for city dwellers to treat all black men as threatening members of an immoral and predatory underclass. For "taxidrivers, storekeepers, and women," writes D'Souza, "the prejudice is warranted. In this context, a bigot is simply a sociologist without credentials." Finally, "discrimination today is . . . based more on reality than on illusion." The formula is familiar. Construct a stereotype, project it onto an entire group, take protective action.

What we get is injustice and illiberality. Take, for example, what may be the most active battle line in the contemporary morality crusades, the war on drugs. African Americans constitute 12 percent of the population and an estimated 13 percent of American drug users. They account for 35 percent of the arrests for drug possession, 55 percent of all convictions for drug possession, and a whopping 74 percent of all prison sentences. A staggering number of young black men pass through the judicial system (read, jail) as a consequence of the drug war and its biases. The effect is to clear the city streets of young black men (and tough mandatory sentences will keep them off the streets). . . .

Of course, there is an entirely different side to the American racial story. The flourishing of black artists, writes Henry Louis Gates, Jr., "may truly be the renaissance to end all renaissance." And never mind the alleged underclass. Carol Stack's lyrical *Call to Home* portrays profoundly stable family networks stretching across generations, reaching from northern cities to southern roots. She pictures communities of sophisticated urbanites and their rural kin struggling with wisdom and patience against poverty and racism. In a book soon to be published by the Russell Sage Foundation, Kathryn Edin and Laura Lein offer a striking portrait of hard-working urban welfare recipients struggling to get by in *Making Ends Meet.* They join an already large and growing pile of books and articles that expose the bigoted racial stereotypes for what they are.

These eloquent accounts are so hard to hear because they are drowned out by the moralizer's message. As long as the American master narrative is one of declining values and a threatening amoral them, it is difficult to see real fellow citizens through the images of misbehavior and predation. It is precisely this framework that takes a relatively small program like Aid to Families with Dependent Children and blows it up into 40 million indolents lounging in a cart while the rest of us push hard to give them their ride.[6]

Moral Troubles

But don't we face an unprecedented moral crisis? No. And constructing our policy problems as moral meltdowns make them far more difficult to address.

---

6. Aid to Families with Dependent Children (AFDC) was the main federal welfare program from 1935 to 1996.

Start with violent crime. The most reliable statistics are for murder (which unlike, say, spouse abuse, is tough to hush up). Yes, the murder rate is high. In 1995 it was double the rate of 40 years earlier. Murders in New York City are up more than 500 percent since 1960. While other crimes are more difficult to track precisely, they roughly shadow the homicide rate. And according to some analysts, the rise in random violence, like drive-by shootings (instantly flashed in our faces via television), amplify popular anxiety about public order.

Yet the picture of a predatory class awash in ever more violence is misleading. The murder rate last year was precisely what it was 25 years ago—and down 10 percent from the peak in 1980. The murder rate was higher in 1933 than it is today. (And talking about social pathology, the 1933 rate included 28 lynchings.)

Instead of sermonizing and demonizing, a sensible policy would focus on both punishing criminals and addressing the causes of crime—"tough on crime, tough on the causes of crime," as British Labor leader Tony Blair puts it. Perhaps some liberals and progressives were queasy about punishment in the past. But most now recognize that crime makes life in poor neighborhoods especially difficult. That, after all, is where most of the victims live. In *Labor of Love, Labor of Sorrow*, Jacqueline Jones quotes one black woman on raising her family in Washington, D.C., during the 1920s: "I have lived here long enough to know that you can't grow a good potato out of bad ground. This sure is bad ground."

A sensible crime policy also has to address a vast array of underlying causes that run a wide policy spectrum. First, there is the sheer firepower available in America: lots of guns, faster guns, more powerful guns. Almost three million handguns were manufactured and marketed in the U.S. in 1993. Second, it is time for a sustained, national reevaluation of the war on drugs. Our public policies have succeeded in making them scarcer, more expensive, and ironically more lucrative (though wealth is an illusion for most of the young men in the drug business). Third, we face the still more difficult problem of declining demand for unskilled labor. Job growth has always been cyclical, but the postindustrial economy wipes out a major traditional track out of poverty. . . .

The features of an enlightened crime policy stretch on—better education, job training, urban infrastructure, a decent minimum wage. In the long run, these are the kinds of reforms that create a safer and more just society. But the moralizers' message—the resurrection of the dangerous, depraved, urban them—pushes these possibilities right off the policy agenda.

Well, what about sex? The preachers positively wallow in their denunciations of the pelvic sins—and here the academics gnash their teeth as loudly as the fundamentalists. The jeremiads all begin with the same premise: We are reaping the bitter harvest of the permissive 1960s culture. But the moralizers disagree on the consequences. Reading from political right to left, we get denunciation of homosexuality, abortion, promiscuity, illegitimacy, teen pregnancy, the collapse of marriage, and kids without dads.

Amid these hot-button issues, one theme gathers broad support: traditional families. Alarm is spreading about the growing number of children being raised by a single parent. The 1990 census puts the figure at 28 percent of all children and 60.6 percent of African American children, up from 21.5 percent and 51.9 percent respectively in 1980. Even sensible moderates gulp hard at those numbers. Surely, concludes the conventional wisdom, this is a genuine moral crisis. Or is it?

Today, divorce is the largest factor, accounting for 40 percent of all the single-parent households in 1990. We live in a "divorce culture," writes David Blankenhorn in his widely cited book *Fatherless America*. Marriage, according to Blankenhorn, has become "old fashioned, beleaguered, even quaint—a way of life primarily suitable for older or boring people." Somehow, we have got to seize our norms and restore the old marriage culture. But according to the 1990 census, more than 79 percent of the households include a married couple, down undramatically from 82.5 percent a decade earlier. Divorce culture? Hardly.

Yet look at the familiar political result. Once again a large, righteous, properly married audience is primed to tsk at (and regulate) the immoral minority that threatens the social order with its promiscuous behavior. Michigan Governor John Engler has gotten the policy crusade rolling with a proposed law that makes divorce more difficult. Supporters of such laws rest their case on a simple maxim: Divorce is bad for kids.

Of course, not all marriages work and not all families are good for children. The new proposals dust off the old divorce loopholes—alcohol, drugs, cheating, physical abuse, mental abuse. Count on prolonged arguments about what exactly constitutes mental cruelty these days. Defining mental abuse points to the buried question that lies at the very heart of the issue: What is a proper family? What is the social institution we are trying to revive?

Beneath the clamor for getting both parents under the same roof lies the agitated matter of how the family ought to be organized. Consider the range of strongly felt contemporary views. On the one side, conservative Christians insist that "a woman's call to be a wife and mother is the highest calling." Reverend Jerry Falwell spells out the implicit organizational chart. God intends "the husband . . . to be the decision maker. . . . Wives and children want to follow." For some conservatives, men who cook dinner or women who pursue careers are violating divinely ordained gender roles. Across the cultural spectrum, the organizing statement of the National Organization of Women offers a different perspective: "A true partnership between the sexes demands a different concept of marriage, an equitable sharing of responsibilities of home and children and economic burdens." And still further along on the American cultural spectrum, Heather has two moms.

What has happened is a lot more complex than the images of rampant promiscuity imply. Rather, we have lost our consensus about the nature of the family—or, more precisely, about the nature of the women's role. Nor is this a bad thing. The halcyon days of stable marriage featured dependent women without significant career options or the real prospect of support-ing themselves. It is far easier to bar the marriage door when one member of the couple is subordinate and dependent, without any meaningful exit option.

This does not mean giving up. By all means, let us find ways that en-courage stable marriages and strong parenting. Change the tax laws. Strengthen the support services that help parents. Mend our communities. But remember that the forces moralizing for marital commitment strongly disagree about what a good marriage is. And the golden era they recall was structured on an inequity that is, happily, fading.

Moreover, trying to lock people into marriage without addressing the root causes of marital breakup is likely to undermine the institution itself—more couples delaying marriage, declining marriage, and departing mar-riage without a formal divorce. Ironically, it is apt to push the rest of society toward the patterns that dominate the African American community: mothers who never got married in the first place.

Turning to black families switches the focus from divorce to out-of-wedlock births. Fifty-one percent of one-parent black families are headed by moms who never married. Only 21 percent are divorced, compared to 28 percent never-married and 40 percent divorced across all races. The obvious ques-tion is why? The obvious answers are wrong.

The stereotype pictures a soaring rate of children bearing children en-couraged by overly generous welfare handouts. But there is scant evidence that welfare benefits explain many sins: States with low benefits do not have appreciably lower rates of separation, divorce, or out-of-wedlock births. More important, pregnancy and birth rates among young black teenagers have actually declined. The pregnancy rates fell 13 percent for African American women between 15 and 17 years old in the two decades following 1970. Ironically, condemnation has been shrillest while teen pregnancy rates have declined.

Nor should we idealize past purity. In her Pulitzer Prize–winning *A Mid-wife's Tale,* Laurel Thatcher Ulrich computed the percentage of first births conceived out of wedlock in and around Hallowell, Maine between 1785 and 1812. The result was a myth-popping 38 percent.

Still, out-of-wedlock births are high and growing as a proportion of all births among African Americans (in part because births among married women have declined). More careful recent analyses point to a series of structural causes of the rise in out-of-wedlock births: the great migration to the urban north; the lack of "marriageable males" in the black community (according to William Julius Wilson, there are 84 black men for every 100 women in the black community, compared to 99 per 100 among whites); and the relatively greater economic power black women have in their rela-tions with black men (partially because of high unemployment among black males).

However, even sophisticated analyses often overlook the women themselves. As Adolf Reed commented in a review of William Julius Wilson's *The Truly Disadvantaged,* women in the inner city have devised a "network of organizational and institutional forms" that "create meaning and dignity in lives bitterly constrained by forces apparently beyond their control." Their marriage and childbearing choices are part of that struggle for meaning and dignity. This is not to say that these decisions are always ideal, but neither hectoring them with sermons nor using public policy to punish them is likely to create strong two-parent families.

What about the kids? Precisely the right question. How do we improve the lives of American children? The real answers involve sustained commitment to improving education, health care, housing, and child care; training and decent wages for parents; jobs and institutional infrastructure for communities. As a society, we went a long way to improving the life chances of our children's grandparents—the poverty rates among the elderly have declined dramatically in the past generation. The question is how to do the same for children. Addressing that question may go a long way to solving the dilemma of single parents.

The chances of succeeding at any of this are not improved one whit by the morality project. On the contrary, we will not mend our imaginary community nor restore a more generous, universalistic public spirit until we put aside the images of an immoral, unvirtuous them.

Alternative Gospels

Contemporary moralizing lays the burden for American troubles squarely on the shoulders of troublesome Americans. There is an alternative to this emphasis on corrupt individuals.

Throughout American history, religion has inspired reformers to fight against legal and economic injustice—to fight for individuals. Moral crusades rouse Americans to expand rights, overcome biases, attack inequity.

The paradigmatic cases are familiar: abolitionism after 1830, the women's movement in the second half of the nineteenth century, the civil rights movement of the twentieth century. Each invoked a higher morality to challenge exclusion and injustice. But perhaps this different kind of moral crusade is most clearly illustrated by a less familiar case.

At the end of the nineteenth century, the social gospel movement self-consciously emphasized the moral responsibilities of the powerful toward the poor. Those who profited from the new economic order were accountable for the burdens it placed on their workers. As Walter Rauschenbusch, the best-known author of the movement, put it: "During the great industrial crisis in the '90s, I . . . could hear virtue crackling and crumbling all around. If anyone has a sound reason for taking the competitive system by the throat in righteous wrath, it is the unmarried woman and the mother with girls." Drawing on religious imagery and language, Rauschenbusch scorched the inhumanity of "our industrial machine" for the moral pressures that it put on good men and women.

Charles Sheldon's *In His Steps,* an extraordinarily popular novel of the same period, pictured how a midwestern town (Topeka, Kansas) would change if all its leaders were guided by the simple question, "What would Jesus do?" There is plenty of silliness throughout the book. But Sheldon imagines the business leaders of the Gilded Age getting religion and running out to meet their workers—to shake their hands and listen to them with respect.

The sinking feeling one gets trekking across the tomes and the tapes of the contemporary morality project comes from the complete absence of even this (rather feeble) social vision. The poor ought to learn to give back to society—more church and less crime, more discipline and fewer delinquents. But rarely a word of how the society and its rules might be biased. Not a hint of going out and listening to the workers with respect— much less helping them struggle with the dislocations of economic transformation.

Despite the thunder, American spiritual life is not going to hell. What all that moralizing does is to organize American rhetoric against social justice, against progressive politics, against national community altogether. In an era when many poor Americans struggle extraordinarily hard, the preachers blame them for their own poverty, turn them on one another, turn Americans against themselves.

The story of moral depravity is well worn. Americans have survived their own unprecedented wickedness—many times. The moralizing routine was already old when the Synod of 1679 published its list of sins. The real threat is not moral decline. It is what Americans do to their own society in the name of arresting moral decline.

▮ DISCUSSION QUESTIONS

1. Do you think society was more moral or less moral in the 1950s than today? In discussing this question, how will you weight and compare different kinds of immoral behavior? Which is more important, marital infidelity or racial discrimination, drug use or environmental pollution?

2. Do you think President Clinton's affair with Monica Lewinsky is evidence of declining moral standards, or did past presidents engage in similar behavior?

3. What role does the media play in the culture wars? Is immoral behavior by public figures now simply more difficult to hide, or is it more common? Do the media play up the culture wars because conflict sells?

4. Is American democracy basically better off or worse off because of the rights-oriented movements of the past thirty years, such as the civil rights, feminist, gay rights, and handicapped rights movements? Specifically, are women better off or worse off because of feminism?

5. Is there any way to compromise or negotiate cultural or moral conflict issues in a democracy? Should people with different moral views move into different states or localities?

SUGGESTED READINGS AND INTERNET RESOURCES

In *Slouching Towards Gomorrah: Modern Liberalism and American Decline* (New York: HarperCollins, 1996), rejected Supreme Court nominee Robert H. Bork argues that the cause of our moral decline is modern liberalism, with its extreme emphasis on egalitarianism and individualism. In his *The Death of Outrage: Bill Clinton and the Assault on American Ideals* (New York: Simon and Schuster, 1998), William Bennett largely agrees with Bork and contends that the tolerant response of the public to Bill Clinton's affair and coverup is further evidence of our moral decline. In *One Nation After All* (New York: Penguin Books, 1998), Alan Wolfe argues that Americans are much more tolerant and united than the polarizing rhetoric of the culture wars suggests. Todd Gitlin criticizes both sides in the culture wars for splitting the nation with the "politics of identity" instead of uniting citizens to attack economic inequalities and racial antagonisms in *The Twilight of Common Dreams: Why America Is Wracked by Culture Wars* (New York: Henry Holt, 1995). Finally, for a more politically neutral analysis of the culture wars, see James Davison Hunter's *Culture Wars: The Struggle to Define America* (New York: Basic Books, 1991).

Culture Wars 101
http://sepwww.stanford.edu/sep/josman/culture/
This site examines America's political and cultural battles over abortion, homosexuality, and the separation of church and state. There is a large number of links, resources, and commentaries concerning the culture wars in the United States.

The Family Research Council
http://www.frc.org/
The Family Research Council is a nonprofit, nonpartisan, national educational organization promoting the traditional family unit and the Judeo-Christian value system upon which it is built.

People For the American Way
http://sepwww.stanford.edu/sep/josman/culture/frpfaw.html

The People For the American Way organizes and mobilizes Americans to fight for fairness, justice, civil rights, and the freedoms guaranteed by the Federal Constitution. The organization lobbies for progressive legislation and helps to build communities of activists.

Institute for First Amendment Studies
http://www.berkshire.net/~ifas/index.html
The Institute for First Amendment Studies is a nonprofit educational and research organization. The Institute is a national clearinghouse for information on theocratic movements in America, and gathers data and prepares newsletters and reports about groups and individuals who pose a threat to First Amendment freedoms.

5

Political Economy: How Democratic Is the Free Market Economy?

At first glance, democratic politics and free market economics seem to go together. The liberty to speak, to practice any religion or none at all, and to participate in politics has often come to be associated with the right to make as much money as we can, to succeed or fail according to our own merits in a free marketplace. Free enterprise seems as unintimidating as a yard sale or a bazaar, with many buyers and sellers, colorful haggling, and a variety of products from which to choose. In contrast, big, intrusive government with its taxes, police, laws, and bureaucracy appears to present the biggest threat to all these rights. The equation of democracy with free market capitalism seems, especially since the demise of communism, the best and now the only economic game in town. After all, aren't the most prosperous countries in the world also the most free? And even if there are sometimes problems, what would be an alternative to what we have?

At closer inspection, though, the marriage between democracy and contemporary capitalism continues to be a contentious one everywhere. In Singapore and China, for instance, the rise of the market economy has hardly led to political freedom. And in America, free enterprise capitalism and political democracy may exist at the same time, but their relationship is hardly cozy. Everywhere, free market capitalism seems to generate enormous wealth, but also wrenching instability. *Political economy* is the study of the relationship between the two in the very different countries around the globe. The two essays that follow ask what the roles of government, citizens, corporations, workers, and consumers actually *are* in America and also what they *should* be so as to best serve the public interest.

Perhaps the most important debate in political economy concerns the relationship between democracy, equality, and economic efficiency. Aristotle wrote that democracy couldn't tolerate extremes of wealth and poverty; large inequalities destroyed the spirit of self-sacrifice and fellowship necessary in a democracy. Politics became less the search for the common good than the single-minded pursuit of material interests by rich and poor alike. While the wealthy fell into luxury and decadence, the poor would sink into ignorance and envy.

For those who believe that economic and social equality are important for democratic politics, recent trends in our political economy are indeed ominous. Despite impressive economic growth, the U.S. economic system in 2000 features high levels of income and wealth inequality. The income and wealth gap has widened continuously at the expense of what was once a very large and politically predominant middle class. While the economy produced new jobs and vast new wealth, workers in the most rapidly expanding areas (home health aides, orderlies, restaurant workers) were paid very low wages and were largely deprived of health and pension benefits. In the late 1990s, nearly half the national income went to just 20 percent of the population. Most U.S. wage earners faced increased insecurity, as waves of corporate mergers, downsizing, outsourcing, and other "innovations" made companies leaner but also meaner. Is the free market really free? If it produces such results, can democracy survive such new extremes?

Many corporations and individuals as well as ordinary Americans defend such inequalities by pointing to the efficiency, growth, and technological innovation that they say are consequences of the free enterprise system. They argue that it is healthier to divide a very large economic pie unequally than to have no pie to divide at all; they go on to say that many of the new changes represent necessary and inevitable adjustments to the realities of the new global economy. The market, its many defenders claim, also preserves liberty by allowing each individual to compete fairly and consumers to choose between a wide range of new products. Free market economies are said to be meritocracies, rewarding the industrious with wealth and punishing the lazy with hardship. In George Gilder's words: "A successful economy depends on the proliferation of the rich, on creating a large class of risk-taking men who are willing to shun the easy channels of a comfortable life in order to create new enterprise, win huge profits, and invest them again."

The two essays that follow not only offer opposing views about the meanings of American democracy and capitalism; they differ about the meaning of freedom, individual liberty, and equality. They disagree profoundly about what role government actually does play in relationship to the U.S. market economy as well as about what role it should play.

The first essay is excerpted from *Capitalism and Freedom* by Nobel Prize winner Milton Friedman. It was originally written in 1962 and has since been reissued in many editions. Friedman describes himself as a "classic liberal" and tries to restore the original doctrine's political and moral meanings. Classic liberals like Friedman advocate maximum individual freedom in the face of government's tendency to tyrannize. The market economy, Friedman argues, "remov[es] the organization of economic activity from the control of political authority," thereby "eliminat[ing] the source of coercive power." Since liberty is synonymous with democracy, Friedman argues that government has only two legitimate roles. It must defend the national territory and act as an umpire, deciding the rules of the market "game" and interpreting them as necessary when free individuals compete with one another.

In the second essay, Samuel Bowles and Michael Edwards deny Friedman's claim that market capitalism and small government go together. They argue that "the growth of government is not something that happened in opposition to capitalism" but something that happened "because of capitalism." Bowles and Edwards go on to claim that a capitalist market economy is hardly a meritocracy; political and economic power are linked and establish biased rules. Unlike Friedman, they say that the marketplace concentrates both economic and political power. Hierarchical corporations determine the investments and life circumstances for workers and communities and severely limit the meaning and scope of democratic government and citizenship themselves. For Bowles and Edwards, growing economic inequality spells the effective denial of liberty to the many. Corporate power often buys undue political influence, whether it be through campaign contributions or corporate ownership of the mass media.

The authors of both essays base their arguments on the defense of democracy. While reading them, ask the following questions: How would Friedman have defended himself against the charge that the market economy produces corporations that exercise unchecked and undemocratic power? What would Bowles and Edwards say to Friedman's charge that government often poses a threat to individual freedom and choice and thus to democratic liberty? How do both essays deal with voters and citizens and their potential role in controlling the production and distribution of economic resources? How would our political economy change if each author had his way? How would it stay the same?

Capitalism and Freedom

MILTON FRIEDMAN

Introduction

The free man will ask neither what his country can do for him nor what he can do for his country.[1] He will ask rather "What can I and my compatriots do through government" to help us discharge our individual responsibilities, to achieve our several goals and purposes, and above all, to protect our freedom? And he will accompany this question with another: How can we keep the government we create from becoming a Frankenstein that will destroy the very freedom we establish it to protect? Freedom is a rare and delicate plant. Our minds tell us, and history confirms, that the great threat to freedom is the concentration of power. Government is necessary to preserve our freedom, it is an instrument through which we can exercise our freedom; yet by concentrating power in political hands, it is also a threat to freedom. Even though the men who wield this power initially be of good will and even though they be not corrupted by the power they exercise, the power will both attract and form men of a different stamp.

How can we benefit from the promise of government while avoiding the threat to freedom? Two broad principles embodied in our Constitution give an answer that has preserved our freedom so far, though they have been violated repeatedly in practice while proclaimed as precept.

First, the scope of government must be limited. Its major function must be to protect our freedom both from the enemies outside our gates and from our fellow-citizens: to preserve law and order, to enforce private contracts, to foster competitive markets. Beyond this major function, government may enable us at times to accomplish jointly what we would find it more difficult or expensive to accomplish severally. However, any such use of government is fraught with danger. We should not and cannot avoid using government in this way. But there should be a clear and large balance of advantages before we do. By relying primarily on voluntary co-operation and private enterprise, in both economic and other activities, we can insure that the private sector is a check on the powers of the governmental sector and an effective protection of freedom of speech, of religion, and of thought.

---

1. Friedman is referring to John F. Kennedy's 1961 inaugural address.

The second broad principle is that government power must be dispersed. If government is to exercise power, better in the county than in the state, better in the state than in Washington. If I do not like what my local community does, be it in sewage disposal, or zoning, or schools, I can move to another local community, and though few may take this step, the mere possibility acts as a check. If I do not like what my state does, I can move to another. If I do not like what Washington imposes, I have few alternatives in this world of jealous nations. . . .

Government can never duplicate the variety and diversity of individual action. At any moment in time, by imposing uniform standards in housing, or nutrition, or clothing, government could undoubtedly improve the level of living of many individuals; by imposing uniform standards in schooling, road construction, or sanitation, central government could undoubtedly improve the level of performance in many local areas and perhaps even on the average of all communities. But in the process, government would replace progress by stagnation, it would substitute uniform mediocrity for the variety essential for that experimentation which can bring tomorrow's laggards above today's mean. . . .

The Relation Between Economic Freedom and Political Freedom

It is widely believed that politics and economics are separate and largely unconnected; that individual freedom is a political problem and material welfare an economic problem; and that any kind of political arrangements can be combined with any kind of economic arrangements. . . . The thesis of this chapter is . . . that there is an intimate connection between economics and politics, that only certain combinations of political and economic arrangements are possible, and that in particular, a society which is socialist cannot also be democratic, in the sense of guaranteeing individual freedom.

Economic arrangements play a dual role in the promotion of a free society. On the one hand, freedom in economic arrangements is itself a component of freedom broadly understood, so economic freedom is an end in itself. In the second place, economic freedom is also an indispensable means toward the achievement of political freedom.

The first of these roles of economic freedom needs special emphasis because intellectuals in particular have a strong bias against regarding this aspect of freedom as important. They tend to express contempt for what they regard as material aspects of life, and to regard their own pursuit of allegedly higher values as on a different plane of significance and as deserving of special attention. For most citizens of the country, however, if not for the intellectual, the direct importance of economic freedom is at least comparable in significance to the indirect importance of economic freedom as a means to political freedom. . . .

Viewed as a means to the end of political freedom, economic arrangements are important because of their effect on the concentration or dispersion of power. The kind of economic organization that provides economic freedom directly, namely, competitive capitalism, also promotes political freedom because it separates economic power from political power and in this way enables the one to offset the other.

Historical evidence speaks with a single voice on the relation between political freedom and a free market. I know of no example in time or place of a society that has been marked by a large measure of political freedom, and that has not also used something comparable to a free market to organize the bulk of economic activity.

Because we live in a largely free society, we tend to forget how limited is the span of time and the part of the globe for which there has ever been anything like political freedom: the typical state of mankind is tyranny, servitude, and misery. The nineteenth century and early twentieth century in the Western world stand out as striking exceptions to the general trend of historical development. Political freedom in this instance clearly came along with the free market and the development of capitalist institutions. So also did political freedom in the golden age of Greece and in the early days of the Roman era.

History suggests only that capitalism is a necessary condition for political freedom. Clearly it is not a sufficient condition. Fascist Italy and Fascist Spain, Germany at various times in the last seventy years, Japan before World Wars I and II, tzarist Russia in the decades before World War I— are all societies that cannot conceivably be described as politically free. Yet, in each, private enterprise was the dominant form of economic organization. It is therefore clearly possible to have economic arrangements that are fundamentally capitalist and political arrangements that are not free.

Even in those societies, the citizenry had a good deal more freedom than citizens of a modern totalitarian state.[2] . . . Even in Russia under the Tzars, it was possible for some citizens, under some circumstances, to change their jobs without getting permission from political authority because capitalism and the existence of private property provided some check to the centralized power of the state. . . .

Historical evidence by itself can never be convincing. Perhaps it was sheer coincidence that the expansion of freedom occurred at the same time as the development of capitalist and market institutions. Why should there be a connection? What are the logical links between economic and political freedom? In discussing these questions we shall consider first the market as a direct component of freedom, and then the indirect relation between market arrangements and political freedom. A by-product will be an outline of the ideal economic arrangements for a free society.

---

2. A political order in which state power is held by a single political party, with no political rights accorded to individuals. Friedman here is referring to the former Soviet Union and to other Communist countries.

As liberals, we take freedom of the individual, or perhaps the family, as our ultimate goal in judging social arrangements. Freedom as a value in this sense has to do with the interrelations among people; it has no meaning whatsoever to a Robinson Crusoe on an isolated island. . . . Robinson Crusoe on his island is subject to "constraint," he has limited "power," and he has only a limited number of alternatives, but there is no problem of freedom in the sense that is relevant to our discussion. Similarly, in a society freedom has nothing to say about what an individual does with his freedom; it is not an all-embracing ethic. Indeed, a major aim of the liberal is to leave the ethical problem for the individual to wrestle with. The "really" important ethical problems are those that face an individual in a free society—what he should do with his freedom. There are thus two sets of values that a liberal will emphasize—the values that are relevant to relations among people, which is the context in which he assigns first priority to freedom; and the values that are relevant to the individual in the exercise of his freedom, which is the realm of individual ethics and philosophy.

The liberal conceives of men as imperfect beings. He regards the problem of social organization to be as much a negative problem of preventing "bad" people from doing harm as of enabling "good" people to do good; and, of course, "bad" and "good" people may be the same people, depending on who is judging them.

The basic problem of social organization is how to co-ordinate the economic activities of large numbers of people. Even in relatively backward societies, extensive division of labor and specialization of function is required to make effective use of available resources. In advanced societies, the scale on which co-ordination is needed, to take full advantage of the opportunities offered by modern science and technology, is enormously greater. Literally millions of people are involved in providing one another with their daily bread, let alone with their yearly automobiles. The challenge to the believer in liberty is to reconcile this widespread interdependence with individual freedom.

Fundamentally, there are only two ways of co-ordinating the economic activities of millions. One is central direction involving the use of coercion—the technique of the army and of the modern totalitarian state. The other is voluntary co-operation of individuals—the technique of the market place.

The possibility of co-ordination through voluntary co-operation rests on the elementary—yet frequently denied—proposition that both parties to an economic transaction benefit from it, *provided the transaction is bilaterally voluntary and informed.*

Exchange can therefore bring about co-ordination without coercion. A working model of a society organized through voluntary exchange is a *free private enterprise exchange economy*—what we have been calling competitive capitalism.

In its simplest form, such a society consists of a number of independent households—a collection of Robinson Crusoes, as it were. Each household uses the resources it controls to produce goods and services that it exchanges for goods and services produced by other households, on terms mutually acceptable to the two parties to the bargain. It is thereby enabled to satisfy its wants indirectly by producing goods and services for others, rather than directly by producing goods for its own immediate use. The incentive for adopting this indirect route is, of course, the increased product made possible by division of labor and specialization of function. Since the household always has the alternative of producing directly for itself, it need not enter into any exchange unless it benefits from it. Hence, no exchange will take place unless both parties do benefit from it. Co-operation is thereby achieved without coercion.

Specialization of function and division of labor would not go far if the ultimate productive unit were the household. In a modern society, we have gone much further. We have introduced enterprises which are intermediaries between individuals in their capacities as suppliers of service and as purchasers of goods. And similarly, specialization of function and division of labor could not go very far if we had to continue to rely on the barter of product for product. In consequence, money has been introduced as a means of facilitating exchange, and of enabling the acts of purchase and of sale to be separated into two parts.

Despite the important role of enterprises and of money in our actual economy, and despite the numerous and complex problems they raise, the central characteristic of the market technique of achieving co-ordination is fully displayed in the simple exchange economy that contains neither enterprises nor money. As in that simple model, so in the complex enterprise and money-exchange economy, co-operation is strictly individual and voluntary *provided:* (*a*) that enterprises are private, so that the ultimate contracting parties are individuals and (*b*)·that individuals are effectively free to enter or not to enter into any particular exchange, so that every transaction is strictly voluntary. . . .

So long as effective freedom of exchange is maintained, the central feature of the market organization of economic activity is that it prevents one person from interfering with another in respect of most of his activities. The consumer is protected from coercion by the seller because of the presence of other sellers with whom he can deal. The seller is protected from coercion by the consumer because of other consumers to whom he can sell. The employee is protected from coercion by the employer because of other employers for whom he can work, and so on. And the market does this impersonally and without centralized authority.

Indeed, a major source of objection to a free economy is precisely that it does this task so well. It gives people what they want instead of what a particular group thinks they ought to want. Underlying most arguments against the free market is a lack of belief in freedom itself.

The existence of a free market does not of course eliminate the need for government. On the contrary, government is essential both as a forum for determining the "rules of the game" and as an umpire to interpret and enforce the rules decided on. What the market does is to reduce greatly the range of issues that must be decided through political means, and thereby to minimize the extent to which government need participate directly in the game. The characteristic feature of action through political channels is that it tends to require or enforce substantial conformity. The great advantage of the market, on the other hand, is that it permits wide diversity. It is, in political terms, a system of proportional representation. Each man can vote, as it were, for the color of tie he wants and get it; he does not have to see what color the majority wants and then, if he is in the minority, submit.

It is this feature of the market that we refer to when we say that the market provides economic freedom. But this characteristic also has implications that go far beyond the narrowly economic. Political freedom means the absence of coercion of a man by his fellow men. The fundamental threat to freedom is power to coerce, be it in the hands of a monarch, a dictator, an oligarchy, or a momentary majority. The preservation of freedom requires the elimination of such concentration of power to the fullest possible extent and the dispersal and distribution of whatever power cannot be eliminated—a system of checks and balances. By removing the organization of economic activity from the control of political authority, the market eliminates this source of coercive power. It enables economic strength to be a check to political power rather than a reinforcement.

Economic power can be widely dispersed. There is no law of conservation which forces the growth of new centers of economic strength to be at the expense of existing centers. Political power, on the other hand, is more difficult to decentralize. There can be numerous small independent governments. But it is far more difficult to maintain numerous equipotent small centers of political power in a single large government than it is to have numerous centers of economic strength in a single large economy. There can be many millionaires in one large economy. But can there be more than one really outstanding leader, one person on whom the energies and enthusiasms of his countrymen are centered? If the central government gains power, it is likely to be at the expense of local governments. There seems to be something like a fixed total of political power to be distributed. Consequently, if economic power is joined to political power, concentration seems almost inevitable. On the other hand, if economic power is kept in separate hands from political power, it can serve as a check and a counter to political power. . . .

In a capitalist society, it is only necessary to convince a few wealthy people to get funds to launch any idea, however strange, and there are many such persons, many independent foci of support. And, indeed, it is not even necessary to persuade people or financial institutions with available funds of the soundness of the ideas to be propagated. It is only necessary to persuade them that the propagation can be financially successful; that the newspaper or magazine or book or other venture will be profitable. The competitive publisher, for example, cannot afford to publish only writing with which he personally agrees; his touchstone must be the likelihood that the market will be large enough to yield a satisfactory return on his investment. . . .

The Role of Government in a Free Society

. . . From this standpoint, the role of the market is that it permits unanimity without conformity. . . . On the other hand, the characteristic feature of action through explicitly political channels is that it tends to require or to enforce substantial conformity. . . . The typical issue must be decided "yes" or "no"; at most, provision can be made for a fairly limited number of alternatives. . . .

The use of political channels, while inevitable, tends to strain the social cohesion essential for a stable society. The strain is least if agreement for joint action need be reached only on a limited range of issues on which people in any event have common views. Every extension of the range of issues for which explicit agreement is sought strains further the delicate threads that hold society together. If it goes so far as to touch an issue on which men feel deeply yet differently, it may well disrupt the society. Fundamental differences in basic values can seldom if ever be resolved at the ballot box; ultimately they can only be decided, though not resolved, by conflict. The religious and civil wars of history are a bloody testament to this judgment.

The widespread use of the market reduces the strain on the social fabric by rendering conformity unnecessary with respect to any activities it encompasses. The wider the range of activities covered by the market, the fewer are the issues on which explicitly political decisions are required and hence on which it is necessary to achieve agreement. In turn, the fewer the issues on which agreement is necessary, the greater is the likelihood of getting agreement while maintaining a free society. . . .

Government as Rule-maker and Umpire

. . . Just as a good game requires acceptance by the players both of the rules and of the umpire to interpret and enforce them, so a good society requires that its members agree on the general conditions that will govern relations among them, on some means of arbitrating different interpretations of these conditions, and on some device for enforcing compliance with the generally accepted rules. . . . In both games and society also, no set of rules can prevail unless most participants most of the time conform to them without external sanctions; unless that is, there is a broad underlying social consensus. But we cannot rely on custom or on this consensus alone to interpret and to enforce the rules; we need an umpire. These then are the basic roles of government in a free society: to provide a means whereby we can modify the rules, to mediate differences among us on the meaning of the rules, and to enforce compliance with the rules on the part of those few who would otherwise not play the game.

The need for government in these respects arises because absolute freedom is impossible. However attractive anarchy may be as a philosophy, it is not feasible in a world of imperfect men. Men's freedoms can conflict, and when they do, one man's freedom must be limited to preserve another's—as a Supreme Court Justice once put it, "My freedom to move my fist must be limited by the proximity of your chin.". . .

Action Through Government on Grounds of Technical Monopoly and Neighborhood Effects

The role of government . . . is to do something that the market cannot do for itself, namely, to determine, arbitrate, and enforce the rules of the game. We may also want to do through government some things that might conceivably be done through the market but that technical or similar conditions render it difficult to do in that way. These all reduce to cases in which strictly voluntary exchange is either exceedingly costly or practically impossible. There are two general classes of such cases: monopoly and similar market imperfections, and neighborhood effects.

Exchange is truly voluntary only when nearly equivalent alternatives exist. Monopoly implies the absence of alternatives and thereby inhibits effective freedom of exchange. In practice, monopoly frequently, if not generally, arises from government support or from collusive agreements among individuals. With respect to these, the problem is either to avoid governmental fostering of monopoly or to stimulate the effective enforcement of rules such as those embodied in our anti-trust laws. However, monopoly may also arise because it is technically efficient to have a single producer or enterprise. I venture to suggest that such cases are more limited than is supposed but they unquestionably do arise. . . .

A second general class of cases in which strictly voluntary exchange is impossible arises when actions of individuals have effects on other individuals for which it is not feasible to charge or recompense them. This is the problem of "neighborhood effects." An obvious example is the pollution of a stream. The man who pollutes a stream is in effect forcing others to exchange good water for bad. These others might be willing to make the exchange at a price. But it is not feasible for them, acting individually, to avoid the exchange or to enforce appropriate compensation. . . .

Parks are an interesting example because they illustrate the difference between cases that can and cases that cannot be justified by neighborhood effects, and because almost everyone at first sight regards the conduct of National Parks as obviously a valid function of government. In fact, however, neighborhood effects may justify a city park; they do not justify a national park, like Yellowstone National Park or the Grand Canyon. What is the fundamental difference between the two? For the city park, it is extremely difficult to identify the people who benefit from it and to charge them for the benefits which they receive. If there is a park in the middle of the city, the houses on all sides get the benefit of the open space, and people who walk through it or by it also benefit. To maintain toll collectors at the gates or to impose annual charges per window overlooking the park would be very expensive and difficult. The entrances to a national park like Yellowstone, on the other hand, are few; most of the people who come stay for a considerable period of time and it is perfectly feasible to set up toll gates and collect admission charges. This is indeed now done, though the charges do not cover the whole costs. If the public wants this kind of an activity enough to pay for it, private enterprises will have every incentive to provide such parks. And, of course, there are many private enterprises of this nature now in existence. I cannot myself conjure up any neighborhood effects or important monopoly effects that would justify governmental activity in this area.

Considerations like those I have treated under the heading of neighborhood effects have been used to rationalize almost every conceivable intervention. In many instances, however, this rationalization is special pleading rather than a legitimate application of the concept of neighborhood effects. Neighborhood effects cut both ways. They can be a reason for limiting the activities of government as well as for expanding them. . . .

Action Through Government on Paternalistic Grounds

Freedom is a tenable objective only for responsible individuals. We do not believe in freedom for madmen or children. The necessity of drawing a line between responsible individuals and others is inescapable, yet it means that there is an essential ambiguity in our ultimate objective of freedom. Paternalism is inescapable for those whom we designate as not responsible.

The clearest case, perhaps, is that of madmen. We are willing neither to permit them freedom nor to shoot them. It would be nice if we could rely on voluntary activities of individuals to house and care for the madmen. But I think we cannot rule out the possibility that such charitable activities will be inadequate, if only because of the neighborhood effect involved in the fact that I benefit if another man contributes to the care of the insane. For this reason, we may be willing to arrange for their care through government.

Children offer a more difficult case. The ultimate operative unit in our society is the family, not the individual. Yet the acceptance of the family as the unit rests in considerable part on expediency rather than principle. We believe that parents are generally best able to protect their children and to provide for their development into responsible individuals for whom freedom is appropriate. But we do not believe in the freedom of parents to do what they will with other people. The children are responsible individuals in embryo, and a believer in freedom believes in protecting their ultimate rights.

To put this in a different and what may seem a more callous way, children are at one and the same time consumer goods and potentially responsible members of society. The freedom of individuals to use their economic resources as they want includes the freedom to use them to have children—to buy, as it were, the services of children as a particular form of consumption. But once this choice is exercised, the children have a value in and of themselves and have a freedom of their own that is not simply an extension of the freedom of the parents.

The paternalistic ground for governmental activity is in many ways the most troublesome to a liberal; for it involves the acceptance of a principle—that some shall decide for others—which he finds objectionable in most applications and which he rightly regards as a hallmark of his chief intellectual opponents, the proponents of collectivism in one or another of its guises, whether it be communism, socialism, or a welfare state. Yet there is no use pretending that problems are simpler than in fact they are. There is no avoiding the need for some measure of paternalism. . . .

Conclusion

A government which maintained law and order, defined property rights, served as a means whereby we could modify property rights and other rules of the economic game, adjudicated disputes about the interpretation of the rules, enforced contracts, promoted competition, provided a monetary framework, engaged in activities to counter technical monopolies and to overcome neighborhood effects widely regarded as sufficiently important to justify government intervention, and which supplemented private charity and the private family in protecting the irresponsible, whether madman or child—such a government would clearly have important functions to perform. The consistent liberal is not an anarchist. . . .

Is it an accident that so many of the governmental reforms of recent decades have gone awry, that the bright hopes have turned to ashes? Is it simply because the programs are faulty in detail?

I believe the answer is clearly in the negative. The central defect of these measures is that they seek through government to force people to act against their own immediate interests in order to promote a supposedly general interest. They seek to resolve what is supposedly a conflict of interest, or a difference in view about interests, not by establishing a framework that will eliminate the conflict, or by persuading people to have different interests, but by forcing people to act against their own interest. They substitute the values of outsiders for the values of participants; either some telling others what is good for them, or the government taking from some to benefit others. These measures are therefore countered by one of the strongest and most creative forces known to man—the attempt by millions of individuals to promote their own interests, to live their lives by their own values. This is the major reason why the measures have so often had the opposite of the effects intended. It is also one of the major strengths of a free society and explains why governmental regulation does not strangle it.

The Market Erodes Democratic Government

SAMUEL BOWLES AND
RICHARD EDWARDS

Government and the Economy

The Expansion of Government Economic Activity

Over the past half-century, the economic importance of the government has grown. There is no single adequate measure by which its growth could be gauged, in part because not all government activities are equally important from an economic standpoint. For this reason, measures of the size of the government—its total expenditures, total employment, or other measures—can capture only roughly the economic impact of the government. But there is little doubt that the growth has been substantial. Though the economic importance of the government has grown in the United States, it is still considerably less than in most other advanced capitalist economies. . . .

The reasons for this growth in the economic importance of the government are much debated. Some see it as a triumph by the ordinary citizen over the self-serving interests of business. Others see it as a carefully orchestrated strategy of business to provide itself with ever-greater opportunities for profit. Still others see it as a triumph of the bureaucratic mentality, which thinks that if there is a problem, there must be or should be some government office to deal with it.

But there is a more persuasive explanation. The survival and workability of capitalism as a system required the government to grow. The ceaseless search for extra profits and the ensuing social, technical, and other changes . . . created conditions that provoked demands for a more economically involved government. These demands, as we will see, have come as often from businesspeople as from workers, as often from the Chamber of Commerce as from the AFL-CIO, as often from Republicans as from Democrats.[1] The growth of government is not something that happened in *opposition* to capitalism, but rather something that happened in very large measure *because* of capitalism. . . .

---

1. The AFL-CIO is the American Federation of Labor–Congress of Industrial Organizations, the United States's largest confederation of labor unions.

Economic Concentration   Much of the growth of governmental eco-nomic activity can be explained by the growth of large corporations and the decline of small competitive producers. The enormous power of modern corporations has allowed its owners to engage more effectively in lobbying and in the formation of public opinion. Partly for this reason, big business has become more confident that it can put the government to work to raise its profits. The government involvement in the nuclear power industry and in the production of military goods are good examples of this. Corporate leaders have also supported the expansion of government regulation in those many cases in which they wanted protection from competitive pres-sures that might lower profits. Examples include regulation of the quality of meat and other food, and milk price supports. Consumers and workers have also supported an expansion of the economic activities of the government, in part to protect themselves from the power of giant corporations. . . .

International Expansion   The increasing international involvement of the large corporations and of the U.S. economy generally contributed to the development of a worldwide conception of "U.S. interests." As corporations expanded from national to international businesses, they changed from wanting the government to impose tariffs to keep out goods made abroad to insisting that the government protect "American" (their) investments around the world. They promoted an increasingly expensive military sys-tem to defend these interests. The preparation for war and the payment for past wars have accounted for much of the economic expansion of the government. Capitalism did not invent war, but the degree of international economic interdependence and rivalry produced by the expansion of capi-talism did make *world* wars more likely. After World War II, high levels of military expenditure became a permanent feature of the U.S. economy. . . .

Economic Instability   The increasing instability of the economy, marked by periods of severe unemployment and dramatized by the Great Depres-sion of the 1930s, has provided another impetus for the growing economic importance of the government. The stabilization of the economy was a major objective of the businessmen who promoted the formation of the Federal Reserve System in 1913 and the Securities and Exchange Commis-sion in 1935.[2] Much more important was the inability of the economy to revive from the Great Depression without the stimulus of massive World War II military expenditures. During the depressed 1930s, political in-stability and radical political movements spread as people came face-to-face with the failure of the capitalist system to provide for even a minimal livelihood. . . .

---

2. The Federal Reserve System (the Fed) is composed of twelve Federal Reserve Banks. It facili-tates exchanges of cash, checks, and credit; it regulates member banks and controls the nation's money supply and interest rates through the Federal Reserve Board.

   The Securities and Exchange Commission is the federal agency empowered to regulate stock markets.

Income Support During the Great Depression, large majorities of Americans became convinced that those unable to make a living should be supported, at least at some minimal level, by the government. Government programs to support poor people replaced informal support systems and private charity, both because people who fell on hard times could no longer count on their families or neighbors to tide them over and because private charity (church and private philanthropy) did not have the funds necessary to do the job. When most Americans were self-employed and families and neighborhoods formed tight communities, the families and communities provided much of the support for the handicapped, the elderly, and others unable to work or unable to find work. But as families and communities became less tightly woven, this system of support began to leave increasing numbers of people with little place to turn for help during hard times.

More recently, unemployment has inflicted a form of economic hardship for which even hard work is no remedy, and it has greatly increased the need for income supports. During the Great Depression, for instance, sources of private charity were simply overrun with people needing help. Only the government could provide income support on the scale needed.

Ironically, workers' constant moving around in search of work played a major part in undermining the ability (or perhaps the inclination) of families and neighborhoods to take care of those who did not find paying work. Equally important was that the capitalist accumulation process spelled the doom of the family farm and the small family business. For earlier generations, going home to the family farm or business had been a way of making it through a period of unemployment, but now there was no family farm or business to go home to. . . .

Public Safety Many groups have demanded that government regulate the conflict between profitability and public safety. While competition pushed firms to develop technology in the most profitable directions, advances in these developments have not always benefited society. The pharmaceutical industry dramatizes the danger of leaving economic decision making solely up to the profitability criterion—drugs dangerous to people's health may be very profitable. For example, drugs that earn big profits for drug companies may have effects that are complicated, long delayed, and potentially lethal for individual consumers. The chemical industry illustrates another conflict between profits and public safety. Some production processes, developed because they are highly profitable, may ultimately inflict brain damage, sterility, and cancer on workers; their effects often become known only after many years of exposure. . . .

Environmental Protection Many people pressed government to protect the natural environment from capitalist development. Our natural surroundings—our land, fresh water, air, and oceans—were not only being used, they were being used up. Part of the reason was that no one was charged a price for using most of these things. In many cases, the most profitable way of disposing of wastes—even very hazardous ones—was simply to throw them away, using our natural environment as a free dumping ground. . . .

Discrimination   Over the last three decades people have come to realize that the unrestricted exercise of rights in private property and in capital goods often results in racial and sexual discrimination against both customers and workers. The lunch counter sit-ins that began the civil rights movement of the 1960s posed the issue sharply—the right of owners of the restaurants and lunch counters to do what they pleased with their property, including the exclusion of black customers, versus the rights of black people to be treated equally in public places. Since 1964 the U.S. Civil Rights Commission has brought suits against companies, unions, and, other institutions, seeking to force them to eliminate discriminatory practices.

Many of these seven sources of expanded government economic activity may be understood as responses to particular aspects of the accumulation process of the capitalist economy. The growth of the government is as much a part of the capitalist economic growth process as is the growth of investment or the growth of technology.

But if government has had to grow to repair the problems and hardships caused by capitalist development, it does not follow that this has been an adequate response. It is quite debatable whether people are today more secure economically than they were a hundred years ago, or less susceptible to environmental or natural disaster, or less likely to encounter health hazards in their workplace or in their food, or better protected from the unaccountable power of the giant corporations. It seems highly unlikely, in fact, that bigger government programs have managed to keep pace with the escalating challenges posed by the pattern of capitalist economic growth. . . .

The Limits of Democratic Control of the Capitalist Economy

[Yet] can the government really control the economy? . . . Can the citizens of a democratic government control the economy? . . . The ability of the voters—even large majorities of them—to alter the course of economic events in our economy is quite limited as long as the economy remains capitalist . . . .

Our economy may be considered to be like a game in which there are two different sets of rules. One set of rules—the rules of the capitalist economy—confers power and privilege on those who own the capital . . . used in production, particularly on the owners and managers of the largest corporations. The other set of rules—the rules of the democratic government—confers substantial power on the electorate, that is, on the great majority of adult citizens. Thus our social system gives rise to two types of power: the *power of capital* and the *power of citizenry*.[3] . . . The basic idea of democratic

---

3. The power of capital is the ability of corporations in a capitalist system to influence public policies or otherwise to create conditions favorable to the interests of investors.

The power of citizenry is the ability of citizens to influence governmental policy or otherwise to create conditions favorable to their interests in a democracy.

government—that government leaders will be selected by the principle of voting, with each person having one vote, after an open competition among competing candidates and ideas—is very different from the rules that govern the capitalist economy.

The heads of a corporation—the management—are not elected by the people who work there, nor by the community in which the firm is located. In fact, they are not elected at all in the sense that we usually use the word *election*, for they are selected by those who own the corporation, with each owner having as many votes as the number of shares of stock he or she owns. Similarly, freedom of speech and other civil liberties are very limited in the workplace. The majority of businesses place restrictions on workers' freedom to post information concerning unions, for example. . . .

Those powers are often at loggerheads, as when the citizens want to restrict the power of capital to sell dangerous or environmentally destructive products. In most of these conflicts, capitalists have immense and often overwhelming advantages, despite the fact that the owners of businesses (and particularly large businesses) are greatly outnumbered. There are three sources of their power—one obvious, the others not so obvious.

One reason capitalists have great political power is that economic resources can often be translated directly into political power. This happens when businesses or wealthy individuals contribute to political campaigns; advertise to alter public opinion; hire lawyers, expert witnesses and others to influence the detailed drafting and implementation of legislation; and otherwise apply their economic resources to the political system. Corporate control of economic resources implies substantial corporate political influence over government officials.[4]

There is a second, more indirect reason for the disproportionate political power of business leaders. It is that mass communications are run by businesses: capitalists in this industry own the TV stations, newspapers, publishing houses, and other capital goods used in production. Even "public" radio and TV depend heavily on corporate contributions. Freedom of speech and of the press (which includes TV and radio) guarantees that people can say, and journalists can write, whatever they please. On the other hand, the private ownership of . . . the TV industry, for example, guarantees that what is broadcast is in the end controlled by capitalists either by the owners of the station or by owners of the major corporations that buy the advertising for the programs. These are people who understandably have little interest in seeing the idea of citizen power applied in ways that limit the freedom or profits of those who own the capital goods used in production, whether in the TV industry or elsewhere.[5]

There is a third way in which money brings power—capitalists control investment, and so they determine the fate of the economy. . . . If profits are low, businesspeople will complain of a bad *investment climate*. They will

4. See Chapter 11 of this volume.
5. See Chapter 9 of this volume.

not invest, or they will choose to invest in some other country. The result will be unemployment, economic stagnation, and perhaps a decline in living standards of the majority of the people, who will lose no time expressing their disappointment on election day.

Since capitalists control investment and hence hold one of the keys to a healthy economy, political leaders often must do what capitalists want, in order to create the right investment climate. They know that in the end it is capitalists who make the decisions on whether to invest and where to invest. Business thus holds a kind of blackmail over democratically elected political leaders.

This form of blackmail is called a *capital strike,* because it involves capital going on strike.[6] When workers strike they refuse to do their part in the economy—they do not work. When capitalists strike they also refuse to do their part—they do not invest. But here the similarity ends. When workers strike they must organize themselves so that they all strike together. A single worker cannot go on strike (that is called quitting). By contrast, when capital goes on strike, no coordination is needed. . . . Each corporation routinely studies the economic and other conditions relevant to its decision to invest. If they do not like what they see, they will simply not invest or will invest elsewhere. *Nobody* organizes a capital strike. It happens through the independent decisions of corporate leaders. If things look bad to a large number of corporations, the effect of their combined withholding of investment will be large enough to alter the course of the economy.

Capital strike severely limits what citizen power can accomplish when citizen power conflicts with the power of capital. An example may make this clear. Unemployed workers may get unemployment insurance checks for 26 weeks. Let us imagine that the voters of a particular state—we will call it Wisconsin—decide they want to provide more generous unemployment benefits, so the checks will keep coming in as long as the worker is unemployed. These payments are to be financed by a heavy tax on the profits of firms that pollute the environment on the "polluter pays principle." . . . Because a majority of the citizens support the idea, the government of the state of Wisconsin enacts the needed taxes and other programs and enforces them. So far, so good.

Now imagine that you are the chief executive officer of General Motors, or of General Electric, or of any other corporation that employs large numbers of workers in Wisconsin. Assume you are considering investing in Wisconsin (say, opening a new plant). Not only will you worry about the taxes, you will wonder how much power you will have over your employees and how hard they will work if they know they have permanent unemployment insurance, should you fire them.

---

6. In particular it involves decisions by capitalists to reduce or end their investments as the result of a "negative" business climate.

You may ask yourself what the citizenry will vote for next. You obviously will think twice before investing in Wisconsin, not necessarily because you do not like the new laws personally, but because your profit rate, both before and after taxes, will most likely be lower in Wisconsin as a result of the new laws. And if your profit rate is lower, your company's stocks will sell for less on the stock market, leading the stockholders to complain, or even to look for a new chief executive officer. You will probably put your new plant someplace else, perhaps in a state that actively advertises its favorable investment climate.

Quite independently, other businesspeople will, no doubt, come to the same conclusion. Some may even close plants or offices in Wisconsin and move elsewhere. The result will be increasing unemployment and lower incomes for the people of Wisconsin.

The hard times may bring on a state financial crisis. As unemployment increases, state expenditures on unemployment insurance will rise, as will other costs of maintaining minimum living standards. As income falls, the state's tax revenues will decline. Rising costs and falling revenues create a soaring deficit in the state budget.

But the problems have just begun. In order to spend more money than the taxes are currently bringing in, the state government will be forced to raise taxes again or to borrow more from the banks and from others with money to lend. Because of the declining state of the Wisconsin economy the banks will be unsure that their loans will be paid back promptly or even at all. If they agree to lend the money, they will do so only at high interest rates. If the loans are granted, the problem will be put off, but it will return with greater intensity when the high interest charges must be paid, in addition to the other demands on state revenues. The resulting vicious cycle is called a *state fiscal crisis*.

There are two likely outcomes. First, with repayment increasingly uncertain, the banks may refuse further loans until the state government changes its policy. If the state government is on the verge of bankruptcy—which means breaking contracts with state employees and not paying wages or bills—the banks' advice may be quite persuasive. Second, the sovereign citizens of Wisconsin may decide to elect a new government, in order to revoke the laws.[7] In either case the new laws will be repealed.

Our example was for a single state. But what is true for one state is true for all states, and more important, it is also true for the nation as a whole. . . . General Motors and General Electric do not have to locate in the United States at all.

Let's go back over our Wisconsin example. Were the citizens' voting rights or civil liberties violated? No. Did capitalists collude and deliberately undermine citizen power? No, they acted independently and in competition

---

7. Sovereignty is the ability and right to make a decision; democratic government confers it on citizens.

with each other. Did they use lobbyists to influence the government officials or campaign contributions to influence elections? Maybe they did, but they did not need to.

Did the citizens exercise control over the economy? That is a much harder question. The capitalist economy certainly imposed limits on what they could do. The citizens could vote for any policy they wanted, but they could not force businesses to invest in Wisconsin, and that severely limited what citizens could get.

Henry Ford, who was famous for his cheap, single-design, no-frills Model T, once said, "You can have any color car you want as long as it's black." In many respects, the voters of our hypothetical state of Wisconsin had a similar choice.

Where did they go wrong? The example could have turned out very differently.

One course the citizens of Wisconsin could have followed would have been to limit their expectations; they could have instructed their government to concentrate only on those programs that would benefit citizens, but would at the same time *increase* the profit rate in the state, or at least not lower it. In other words, they might have accepted from the outset that they were not "sovereign" in economic matters, and made the best of a less-than-ideal situation.

Thus, for example, they might have concentrated on eliminating those forms of pollution that reduce profits in the recreation business and lower property values. They might have designed programs to give economic security to the elderly, but not to current workers. They might have tried to increase equality of opportunity by giving all children more business-oriented schooling. And they might have voted to finance these programs by taxes that did not fall on profits. If they had done this, many Wisconsin citizens would have benefited, and the losers might not have been in position to disrupt the program. Specifically, capitalists might have looked favorably, or at worst indifferently, on these events and might not have brought about the economic decline of the state by leaving.

Again, this is just a hypothetical example, but it is similar to what actually happened in Wisconsin. Wisconsin was a leader early in this century in trying out programs to make the most of citizen power while operating within the confines of the capitalist economy. The federal government and other state and local governments now engage in many beneficial economic activities that also fit this description. Making the best of the limits of the capitalist economy is most fully developed in some European nations such as Sweden and Austria, where social democratic governments have been in power over much of the post–World War II period. However beneficial, these programs are severely limited, since many of the ways to improve living standards and the quality of life sooner or later also threaten the rate of profit or the idea of profits.

There is a second course that Wisconsin citizens could have followed which, if not likely, is at least conceivable. When General Motors and General Electric decided to close their operations in Wisconsin, the plants could have been bought by the communities in which they are located, by those who work in them, or by the state government. When a business leaves a community, what it takes, usually, is its money. Most of the plant, the machines, and the workers stay. There is no reason the workers could not continue working at their old jobs if they could find a way to purchase the firm. They could do this as part of a community-owned enterprise, a worker-owned firm, or some other organization.

What can we conclude from this example? That citizen power is severely limited in its ability to alter fundamental economic events, unless citizens are willing to change the rules that govern the workings of the capitalist economy. Thus a democratic *government* is not the same thing as a democratic *society*, for in a democratic *society* decision making in the economy, as well as in the government, would be accountable to the majority.

DISCUSSION QUESTIONS

1. In recent years, most Americans seem to have turned against "big government," yet huge majorities support Social Security and increased spending on education and environmental and consumer regulation. How would the authors of each essay deal with this apparent contradiction?

2. Friedman stresses the point that the market economy is made up of *voluntary exchanges*. No one is forced to buy a particular product or work for a particular company. What would Bowles and Edwards say about Friedman's argument?

3. There is a substantial amount of income inequality in the United States. As long as all citizens still maintain equal political rights, is such inequality necessarily harmful to democracy? How much inequality is a threat to democratic society and why? How much inequality is justified?

4. Friedman argues that the free market promotes individual liberty. Yet many citizens in democratic countries use their liberty to support government programs that limit and regulate the scope and power of the marketplace. How might Friedman have responded to this reality?

SUGGESTED READINGS AND INTERNET RESOURCES

How democratic is the U.S. capitalist system? What is and what should be the function of government and democratic citizens in creating and distributing economic resources? How efficient and how equal is our political economy, and how is each term defined? A good introduction to these questions is Frances Moore Lappé's *Rediscovering America's Values* (New York: Ballantine Books, 1989). James Galbraith's *Created Unequal: The Crisis in American Pay* (New York: Twentieth Century Fund, 1999) and Martin Marger's *Social Inequality* (Mountain View, Calif.: Mayfield, 1999) both made compelling cases against growing inequalities. For an alternative vision of a new, high-tech economy in which work is rewarded justly, see Thomas Friedman *The Lexus and the Olive Tree* (New York: Farrar, Straus, and Giroux, 1999). A brilliant treatment of how wealth inequality translates into political inequality is William Domhoff, *Who Rules America? Power and Politics in the Year 2000* (Mountain View, Calif.: Mayfield, 1999).

The Economic Policy Institute
www.epi.org
The best site for extensive data and analyses of current economic policy issues and for studies of income and wealth trends. The EPI is nonpartisan but is funded in part by labor unions.

The Heritage Foundation
www.heritage.org
Economic news and policy analyses from the premiere ultraright think tank. Good links to other conservative foundations and public policy lobbies.

Center for Budget and Policy Priorities
www.cbpp.org
Reports on policy issues from a liberal think tank that concentrates on low- and middle-income citizens.

The Cato Institute
www.cato.org
Speeches, research, and opinion from the leading libertarian think tank in the United States. Provides economic data and opinion supportive of privatization of now public functions, from environmental protection to schools.

Civil Liberties: Does the First Amendment Permit Religious Expression in Public Institutions?

The opening words of the First Amendment to the United States Constitution read: "Congress shall make no law respecting an establishment of religion, or prohibiting the free exercise thereof. . . . " These words establish a constitutional guarantee of freedom of religion in the United States; they protect religion from government interference and government from religious domination. But like many of the phrases in the Constitution, the language quoted is hardly free of ambiguity. If government and religion are to be kept separate, how strict should the separation be? Is there no place for religious expression in America's public institutions?

One common way to debate these questions is to focus on the intentions of the men who drafted and ratified the First Amendment. Those who champion a strict separation of religion and government tend to emphasize the views of James Madison, the principal drafter of the Bill of Rights, and his close friend Thomas Jefferson, whose famous words interpreted the First Amendment as "building a wall of separation between Church and State." Aiming to safeguard religious minorities from an intolerant majority and to protect religious conscience itself from the coercive powers of the state, Madison and Jefferson believed, according to Isaac Kramnick and R. Laurence Moore, in a "Godless Constitution." Opponents of this view deny that the founding generation meant to keep religious expression out of public life. The First Amendment, they argue, was designed to block Congress from establishing an official *national* religion or telling individuals which religious doctrine they must accept. But the states were still free to favor particular churches, as many of them continued to do, and the federal government was still allowed to sponsor nondenominational expressions of religious devotion, such as national days of prayer or the provision of chaplains for the armed forces.

In the last half-century the Supreme Court has generally sided with the champions of strict separation. Although a narrow 5 to 4 majority ruled in the landmark *Everson* case (1947) that a subsidy paid by the state of New Jersey for the bus fares of children attending parochial schools was constitutional, the Court allowed this practice only because it did not breach Jefferson's "wall of separation." Following the same doctrine of strict separation, a larger majority ruled in *Engel* v. *Vitale* (1962) that a brief nondenominational prayer recommended by the Board of Regents for students in New York's public schools ("Almighty god, we acknowledge our dependence upon Thee, and we beg Thy blessings upon us, our parents, our teachers, and our country") was unconstitutional. Only in recent years, with the formation of a new Court majority appointed by Republican presidents, has the Court become somewhat more favorable to religious expressions in public institutions. For example, in *Lynch* v. *Donnelly* (1984) the Court approved of a nativity scene (crèche) erected by the city of Pawtucket, Rhode Island, during the Christmas season, but only because it was accompanied by a Christmas tree, Santa's house, colored lights, and other symbols that reflected the city's secular purpose (attracting shoppers to downtown stores).

The Court's insistence on a wall of separation between church and state, particularly its ban on prayer in the schools, has evoked dismay and anger from many Americans. Americans are a more religious people than are the citizens of any other modern democratic nation. Surveys repeatedly show that about 90 percent of the population describe themselves as religious; about 80 percent of Americans believe that God still works miracles and that they will be called before Him on Judgment Day. Citing the religious faith of the majority, supporters of various constitutional amendments have proposed language that would repudiate the Court's decisions and allow prayer in the schools and other forms of religious expression in public institutions. None of these amendments have been successful so far.

Controversy over the place of religion in public life has continued to mushroom in the last few decades. The most outspoken proponents for breaking down the strict separation between religion and politics have been the leaders of the religious right. Conservative Christian organizations, such as the Reverend Jerry Falwell's Moral Majority and the Reverend Pat Robertson's Christian Coalition, have been an important force in the political successes of the Republican Party in the 1980s and 1990s. But it is a mistake to equate support for religious expression in politics exclusively with conservatives. There are numerous writers and political activists who agree with the Supreme Court on such matters as school prayer yet believe that treating religion as purely private denies the positive role it can play in political life. Some political moderates, such as Yale law professor Stephen Carter, complain that "in our sensible zeal to keep religion from dominating our politics, we have created a political and legal culture that presses the religiously faithful to be other than themselves, to act publicly, and sometimes privately as well, as though their faith does not matter to them." Overshadowed by the religious right have been the many faith-based groups that participate in causes usually identified with the political left: unionization, antipoverty programs, environmentalism, opposition to the use of American armed force abroad.

A strong sign that support for religious expression in public life is growing is the frequency of statements of faith by candidates for the presidency. In 1976, it was regarded as somewhat unusual when Democratic candidate Jimmy Carter discussed his convictions as a "born-again" Christian. In 2000, the nominees of both parties, Vice President Al Gore and Texas Governor George W. Bush, assumed that few would object and many would applaud when they highlighted the centrality of their religious beliefs to their political philosophies.

Stephen V. Monsma, author of our first selection, argues that the strict separation between church and state currently enforced by the Supreme Court has actually created a bias against religious expression in our public life. He advocates a new perspective on the relationship between church and state that he calls "positive neutrality": government must be neutral in the sense that it does not favor any particular religion or even religion over nonreligion, but it should be positive in recognizing and providing a place in public institutions for the diverse (and healthy) expressions of Americans' religious values. Applying this doctrine to the controversial issues of church-state relations considered by the Supreme Court, Monsma suggests that the Court should permit silent prayer in the schools and allow teachers to consider religion as well as secular philosophies.

Marvin Frankel, author of our second selection, defends strict separation between church and state and agrees with the thrust of Supreme Court decisions on this subject. He believes that the religious expressions prohibited by the Court, such as prayers in schools, are irrelevant to the health and functioning of religion in the United States. It is opportunistic politicians and representatives of intolerance, he charges, who have fanned the flames of controversy over the Court's decisions for their own purposes. The anecdotes that Frankel relates suggest that religious expression in public institutions will coerce those whose beliefs differ from the majority—precisely what the First Amendment was designed to preclude.

Monsma's perspective suggests that we consider religious expression as a form of positive freedom, with government playing a supportive but neutral role. Frankel insists that both individual conscience and organized religion should be viewed in light of negative freedom, with government taking a hands-off approach. How strict do you think the separation of church and state should be? Is the "wall of separation" image a proper constitutional guide, or does it create a bias against religion in public life and public institutions? Should religion be allowed to mix with politics so long as no particular religions are favored and nonbelievers are protected? Or will the mixture inevitably advantage the dominant religious groups and ostracize those holding unconventional faiths or viewpoints? Would allowing silent prayers in the schools reenforce the religious and moral values of children, or are such vehicles of religious expression better left to the home and the place of worship?

Positive Neutrality: Letting Religious Freedom Ring

STEPHEN V. MONSMA

I t was a cloudy January day when I visited the U.S. military cemetery near Florence, Italy, and walked among the row upon row of stone monuments marking the graves of over 4,000 U.S. citizens who were killed in World War II. It was an impressive, moving experience, but as I walked among the graves and reflected on the sacrifice that many had made, it also struck me that the military had handled a sensitive church-state issue more appropriately than is often done. If ever one's religious faith comes to the fore, it is in the presence of the ultimate fact of death. Thus, cemeteries are typically filled with religious symbolism. However, this was a government cemetery I was visiting: built and, even today, maintained by U.S. tax dollars. Is it appropriate—is it a constitutionally permitted breach in the wall of separation between church and state—for the government to purchase, erect, and maintain overtly religious symbols? (Remember the Christmas displays that have failed or barely managed to pass constitutional muster.) In addition, most of the men and women killed were Christians (defining "Christian" very broadly), but some, of course, were Jews. If religious symbolism is to be permitted, should it be distinctively Christian?

One solution to this situation—and one on which the Supreme Court and U.S. society have insisted in some parallel settings—would have been to ban all religious symbols and to develop a stone monument for the graves that is purely secular. A supposed neutrality among all religions and between religion and nonreligion would have been maintained. Another solution, one some have favored in parallel settings, would have been to provide Christian crosses for all, and if a family objected, its loved one would be buried off to the side and the family could purchase a marker of its choosing. Happily, the military has chosen another course of action. Thus, the cemetery is filled with the most common, powerful symbol of Christianity: the cross, which symbolizes the sacrificial death of Jesus Christ.

However, scattered throughout the cemetery, one also sees powerful symbols of the ancient Jewish faith—Stars of David—marking the graves of Jewish Americans who had made the ultimate sacrifice. In following this practice, the military, no doubt unwittingly, has moved in the direction of adopting a solution to this church-state issue that is in keeping with structural pluralism, an approach that I have termed *positive neutrality*.[1]

Under positive neutrality, government is *neutral* in that it does not recognize or favor any one religion or religious group over any other, nor does it favor or recognize religious groups or religion as a whole over secular groups or secular philosophies and mind-sets as a whole. It is evenhanded. Government takes a position of *positive* neutrality by recognizing that in practice, neutrality is often not achieved by government simply failing to do something. Positive neutrality insists that genuine religious freedom is not a negative freedom: it does not spontaneously spring into being in the absence of governmental regulations or programs. Sometimes government will have to take certain positive steps if it is to be truly neutral in the sense of assuring equal freedoms and equal opportunities for all religious persons and groups and for religious and irreligious persons and groups alike.

Thus, in the example of the military cemetery, government is neutral in that neither Christian nor Jewish religious symbols are uniformly placed onto the graves of all those who were killed in action. It is following positive neutrality in that neutrality is not gained by stripping the governmentally owned and operated cemetery of all religious symbols, but by the active, positive use of religious symbols corresponding to the religious faiths of the fallen men and women. Religion is recognized and given its due. If positive neutrality were to be more fully followed in this example, the military ought—especially in today's United States—to develop appropriate Islamic and secular symbols so that the graves of those of the Muslim faith or of no religious faith could also have their graves appropriately marked. Such an approach would break up the uniformity of rows and columns of crosses interspersed with a few Stars of David, but structural pluralism accepts and even celebrates pluralism over uniformity and diversity over conformity, even when things appear a bit messy as a result. . . .

Pluralism and a New Mind-Set

The current mind-set dominant within the Supreme Court and among the leaders of popular U.S. culture tends to see religion—at least in its particularistic manifestations, as distinct from religion-in-general—as having only a private, personal relevance and lacking a real social or political impact. In fact, it views religion, when wedded to issues of social and political import, as a divisive, intolerant, and dangerous force.

---

1. Structural pluralism is Monsma's term for the positive contributions that diverse associations—especially religious ones—make to the functioning of a democratic society.

Pluralism, in contrast, leads to a quite different perspective with which to approach church-state issues. This mind-set colors everything else, and thus is crucial in setting the context from which the more specific, concrete standard of positive neutrality emerges. Two features of this mind-set are especially important: a positive outlook on the contributions of religion in U.S. society and an unwavering commitment to full freedom of religion.

The first feature of pluralism's mind-set regarding religion and society is its perception that it is natural, healthy, and proper for the people of the United States to adhere to a great variety of faith communities and to join a wide range of churches and other religious associations, and for some to adhere to no religious faith at all. This is seen as an appropriate consequence of a free society. Structural pluralism welcomes religion in its various manifestations and in its various activities as a legitimate, contributing, integral part of U.S. society, including its political aspects. Not merely religion-in-general but also particularistic religion, whose adherents take it as an authoritative force in their lives, is respected and accepted as a part of the life of the U.S. polity. Moreover, it is not merely the individual in his or her religious dimension that pluralism accepts and honors; it is the religious structures of society—faith communities and religious associations—that are accepted and honored *as religious structures*. Catholic parochial schools, inner-city church-sponsored homeless shelters, Jewish senior citizen centers, evangelical Protestant colleges, Mormon nursing homes, Nation of Islam mosques, and those who identify with and have a close attachment to New Age thinking: all these and more are accepted and respected—including their politically relevant aspects. In dealing with them, the pluralist creatively seeks to develop political processes and public policies that will not merely tolerate faith communities and associations and their individual members, but will integrate them fully—as religious structures and persons—into the life of the body politic.

This is an enormously important shift from the mind-set that is prevalent today. . . . That mind-set sees religion largely in individual, not structural, terms, and sees particularistic religion as a force that is largely irrelevant to the realm of politics and public policies and thus with little to contribute. Religious individuals should, of course, be tolerated, and their freedom of religion should not be denied, but their religious beliefs are seen as essentially private beliefs, relevant to individuals' personal lives but irrelevant to the affairs of state. Even worse, religious diversity is seen as socially divisive, and thus a danger when allowed into the political realm. Thus, erecting a wall of separation between religion and the state does no harm to religion and benefits the body politic. Religious structures—as religious structures—must be kept out of the political realm, or, at the most, allowed in in a carefully circumscribed, limited manner. This is held to be especially true of particularistic religious groups such as conservative Protestantism, Roman Catholicism, and Mormonism. Religious structures and individuals with potentially important religiously motivated political goals and insights are thereby finessed and squeezed onto the sidelines.

Structural pluralism objects to this, seeing it as a form of religious intolerance and discrimination.

A second basic feature marking the mind-set fostered by pluralism is a commitment to full religious freedom for all faith communities and religious associations—and for persons and structures of no faith as well. Its goal is simple: full, complete freedom of religion. Pluralism has an expansive view of this freedom. It extends to believers in all religious traditions; the wide diversity of Christian religious associations and communities should have full religious freedom, but so also should native American religions, Islam, New Age beliefs, Hinduism, and more. Similarly, persons of no religious faith should have their freedom respected and guaranteed as fully as do persons of deeply held faith. In addition, religious freedom should extend not only to the development and practice of a religious structure's core religious beliefs, but also to the development and practice of the other three roles of religious associations and communities . . . : molding their members' behavior and attitudes, providing an array of services, and influencing the policy-making process. These roles define the appropriate sphere of religion, and pluralism says that if religious associations and faith communities are to be truly, fully free, their freedom of action in their sphere must be assured. Also, religious freedom should extend to the religious beliefs and practices of churches, synagogues, and other such religious associations, but should also include the beliefs and activities of religiously based agencies such as schools, child-care centers, and other service or advocacy associations. A Jewish counseling center should have as full protection for its freedom to act on the basis of its distinctive Jewish character and beliefs as a synagogue. Pluralism insists that the tent of religious freedom be broad enough to encompass all these forms. Otherwise, the freedom of religious structures and their members will be thwarted.

It is important to note that pluralism also recognizes that religious associations and faith communities have certain obligations to other religious associations and faith communities, to the state, and to the rest of society. Full religious freedom does not mean that religious structures can do whatever they want, wherever and whenever they want to. . . .

Current U.S. thinking does not hesitate to proclaim and protect full religious freedom as long as it is kept on the level of private, individual belief. Thus, a privatized religion is granted full religious freedom, but when religion moves from individual to corporate manifestations, from religion-in-general to particularistic religion, from beliefs to practice, or from a private, personal faith to one with social and political dimensions, trouble often arises. For example, the U.S. public and the U.S. legal system are fully comfortable with individual native Americans following their traditional religion in the quiet of their communities, but when that religion begins to move from individual observances to a tribal or area-wide movement, from beliefs to practices such as the use of peyote, and from private beliefs to social implications (such as questioning white society's continued use of traditionally sacred lands), doubts, fears, and challenges quickly surface.

Structural pluralism has a broader, more inclusive, more expansive view of freedom of religion.

Conventional U.S. thinking on church and state tends to see pluralism's twin goals of full religious freedom and full involvement of a wide variety of religious structures in the polity as posing an unresolvable dilemma. To the conventional mind-set, religious freedom implies governmental neutrality toward religion and neutrality implies church-state separation. After all, if government accedes to one religion's demands for certain public policies, financially supports one religious group's drug rehabilitation center, or places the symbol of one religious group in front of city hall at the time of its major religious holiday, is not the state favoring and supporting that religion, thereby compromising the religious freedom of all other religious groups and of nonbelievers? On the other hand, structural pluralism argues that by discouraging religiously based groups from influencing public policy debates, by refusing assistance to religiously based social service agencies when it is being given to all others, and by ignoring the civic contributions of religious but not secular groups, freedom of religion is also being violated. In either case, it appears impossible to have full religious freedom. Either religious freedom is violated by denying religion equal access to or equal recognition in the public realm, or it is violated by favoring one religion over another or religion over secularism.

Structural, normative pluralism and the principle of positive neutrality, which it spawns, show this dilemma to be apparent, not real. There is another way that avoids being impaled on either horn of the dilemma and does not follow an unprincipled, messy middle ground. Religious structures can be given their full due, without favoring one religion over another or religion over secularism. However, to find this new way, old categories and assumptions must be laid aside and replaced by fresh ones. . . .

Religion in the Public Schools

Some of the Supreme Court's most difficult decisions have dealt with the question of whether and in what form religion may be brought into the public schools. This issue has been extremely controversial, and Supreme Court decisions ruling against certain religious exercises in the public schools have aroused intense opposition from large segments of the public. Congressional majorities and Presidents Ronald Reagan and George Bush have paid at least lip service to proposals that organized prayer—contrary to what the Supreme Court has ruled—should be allowed in the public schools.

Intense feelings over Supreme Court decisions regarding religion in the public schools have probably been aroused, first, by the central role of the public schools in the lives of students and their families. With compulsory attendance laws, a majority of the prime daytime hours of children's lives from age five to sixteen are under the control of the public school. There certainly is time for the family and for churches and other religious associations to have a crucial influence on the lives of children, but many feel that they are in a competitive disadvantage with the schools, with their monopolization of children's daytime hours; elaborate instructional materials; professional, highly trained personnel; and high status. The degree of controversy in this area is also increased by the fact that well into the twentieth century, elements of the informal, de facto nineteenth-century Protestant establishment of religion remained in the public schools. Until after World War II, Bible reading, prayers, Christmas and Easter celebrations, and other Christian religious exercises were commonplace in many public schools. A series of Supreme Court decisions have had the effect of rooting out long-established practices. It is not surprising that opposition and controversy have accompanied these efforts.

In dealing with cases in this area, the Supreme Court has generally taken a strong position against allowing religious observations and exercises into the public schools. . . . Offering state-composed, nonsectarian prayers, Bible reading, reading of the Lord's Prayer, posting the Ten Commandments in classrooms, a minute of silence for meditation and prayer, teaching scientific evidences in support of creation along with those for evolution, and praying at graduation ceremonies are all in violation of the establishment provision of the First Amendment. On the other hand, it has ruled that released-time programs for religious instruction held off school property, objective teaching about religion, a minute of silence for meditation, and the official recognition of voluntary, student-initiated, and student-led religious clubs are all permissible under the First Amendment. As these listings reveal, what the Court has disallowed is greater than what it has allowed. The basis for these decisions has generally been the Court's insistence that the state may not engage in or support any activity that could reasonably be interpreted as advancing or endorsing religion over nonreligion. . . .

Positive neutrality begins what it considers a much more theoretically sound approach to religion in the public schools with a basic point: the inaccuracy of the underlying assumption that a true neutrality between religion and secularism is gained by the removal from the public schools of all practices or references that are favorable to specific religions or to religion generally. The absence of religion in the life of the school in any sort of a favorable context—even one as minor as a moment of silence designated for prayer or meditation—is to send the implicit message that religion as a living, controlling force is unnecessary and irrelevant to most of life. Alone among the opinions of Supreme Court justices to raise this issue in clear terms is the dissent of Justice Potter Stewart in *Abington School District v. Schempp.* . . .

> If religious exercises are held to be an impermissible activity in schools, religion is placed at an artificial and state-created disadvantage. Viewed in this light, permission of such exercises for those who want them is necessary if the schools are truly to be neutral in the matter of religion.

And a refusal to permit religious exercises thus is seen, not as the realization of state neutrality, but rather as the establishment of a religion of secularism. . . .

The response that positive neutrality makes to most church-state issues—guided by the concepts of pluralism, which inform it—is to allow the full and free play of all religious groups and of both religion and secularism. Thus, positive neutrality's approach to the posting of the Ten Commandments in the public schools would be to allow their posting, as long as comparable, key writings of other religious or secular traditions represented in the classroom and community are also periodically displayed. The basic principle is not to try to achieve a neutrality by driving all religion out of the classroom—which results in a false neutrality that, in fact, favors a secular cultural ethos, but by welcoming and recognizing all religions and secular philosophies and mind-sets alike. . . .

. . . I would suggest three additional approaches in keeping with positive neutrality that would help to assure greater pluralism in the public schools than is now the case. All three are aimed at developing appropriate means to recognize and accommodate a diversity of religious beliefs to which students and their families hold, while also recognizing and accommodating the beliefs of those of no religious faith. One approach consists of moments of meditation and prayer at the beginning of the school day, and perhaps at lunch time and the end of the day as well. Here, school children are totally free to speak (or not to speak) to the Deity in any way they please as long as they are not disruptive of others' prayer or meditation. Those who are nonreligious can meditate or reflect on the upcoming day, or, for that matter, plan their after-school television viewing.

The Supreme Court's rejection of such an option in *Wallace v. Jaffree* (1985) went squarely against the religious neutrality that the Court itself has often professed. It did so on the basis that the Alabama law implicitly (and perhaps explicitly) endorsed religion by specifically mentioning prayer along with meditation as a purpose of the minute of silence. In one sense, the Court was right. Of course, the Alabama statute endorsed prayer, but that is beside the point. . . . The norm of neutrality is not violated as long as all religions, as well as religion and secular points of view, are equally endorsed or supported. Under positive neutrality, the relevant question is whether the statute favored any one form of prayer and whether it favored prayer over nonprayer. Neutrality means evenhandedness among religions and between religion and nonreligion. By mandating a one-minute period of silence "for meditation or voluntary prayer," Alabama law was neutral. The religious individuals could pray in whatever form they wished; the irreligious could meditate on anything to which their beliefs or values would lead. Religion and secularism were equally endorsed, yet to single out the endorsement of religion—or, more specifically, religious traditions that accept the possibility and need for human communication with the Deity—as unconstitutional, and not to hold the endorsement of meditation unconstitutional, is to favor secularism and religions not believing in prayer over religions believing in prayer. In contrast, structural pluralism and positive neutrality hold that one appropriate—that is, neutral—way in which to introduce religion into the public schools is to allow times of silence for personal, individual, voluntary prayer; otherwise, due deference to the religious traditions represented in the classroom is bound to be lost. . . .

A second way in which religion can be accommodated within the existing public schools is through the equal access approach approved by the Supreme Court in *Westside Community Schools v. Mergens* (1990) and released-time programs such as the one that was rejected in *McCollum v. Board of Education* (1948). Positive neutrality says that students surely should be free to meet for religious purposes if they meet voluntarily during noninstructional times, as long as all religious traditions and similar or parallel secularly based student groups are equally free to organize and meet. They should be free to meet on school property, to invite outside speakers in, and to advertise their meetings—just as all other student groups are free to do. The key here is a neutrality or evenhandedness by the school officials. Positive neutrality says that both the majority and the dissenting justices were wrong when they decided the *Mergens* case on whether in their judgment religion was being endorsed by the school. Endorsement or nonendorsement of religion is not the issue; equal treatment of all religious points of view and religion and nonreligion is.

Similarly, a plurality of religious points of view can be recognized and given their due without any one being favored or coerced by way of released-time programs. Here, various religious groups are invited to come into the public schools and teach the students who are adherents of their faith each week during an hour or so that has been set aside for such purposes. All religious faiths are invited to teach students of their faiths. Adherents of ethical or value-oriented associations that are not technically religious organizations could also have their representatives come in to teach their students, while those of no faith would have an extra study period.

The Supreme Court, from the point of view of structural pluralism, got it wrong back in 1948 when it judged a released-time program in Champaign, Illinois, on the basis of whether religion was being helped. Of course religion was being helped, but no more so than secularism, and no one religion any more than any other religion. It was religiously neutral. However, the Court simply asserted that the "wall between Church and State . . . must be kept high and impregnable" and then went on to note that the state's tax-supported public school buildings [were being] used for the dissemination of religious doctrines." As far as the Court was concerned, that sealed the fate of Champaign's released-time program. The support or endorsement of religion was enough to find the practice unconstitutional. The question that pluralism considers to be the key one—namely, whether all religions, as well as secular perspectives, were being treated equally—was never brought up. . . .

A third and final way in which positive neutrality suggests dealing with the issue of religion in the public schools is to make certain that religion is given its full due in an objective sense and that secular philosophies and points of view are also given their due, but no more than their proper due. Public schools today often do not even give religion the recognition and consideration it can be given without running afoul of the Supreme Court's church-state doctrines. This fact came out in a 1987 District Court case in the United States District for the Southern District of Alabama (*Smith v. Board of School Commissioners of Mobile County*, No. 82-0544-BH, 1987). Although the District Court's decision—which found that certain public school textbooks used in the Alabama schools promoted the religion of secular humanism in violation of the establishment clause of the First Amendment—was attacked by many commentators and was overturned by the Federal Court of Appeals, yet it brought to light some startling facts. For example, it noted the findings of Timothy Smith of Johns Hopkins University's History Department, which documented a systematic tendency to slight the role that religion has played in U.S. history:

> The pattern in these books is the omission of religious aspects to significant American events. The religious significance of much of the history of the Puritans is ignored. The Great Awakenings are generally not mentioned. Colonial missionaries are either not mentioned or represented as oppressors of native Americans. The religious influence on the abolitionist, women's suffrage, temperance, modern civil rights and peace movements is ignored or diminished to insignificance. The role of religion in the lives of immigrants and minorities, especially southern blacks, is rarely mentioned. After the Civil War, religion is given almost no play.

Positive neutrality—with its emphasis on genuine governmental neutrality among religions and between religion and secular perspectives—says that to drive the role religion has played in U.S. and world history out of textbooks and public school classrooms and to fail to acknowledge what various religious traditions have said in regard to issues such as sexual ethics, personal values, and economic relationships is to do violence to neutrality. The goal should be the fair, unbiased, equal representation of religion's views and perspectives—as fair, unbiased, and equal as those given views and perspectives of secular origin. Positions and evidence on various sides of controversial issues should be presented honestly and accurately.

When Louisiana enacted legislation requiring that so-called creation science be taught along with evolutionary explanations of human origins, it was acting within the spirit of this third approach. Whether this particular Louisiana law was the proper way in which to go about assuring that religion and secularism were treated evenhandedly is not the crucial issue (I personally have serious doubts); however, the underlying goal of "equal time" is. Assuring that a variety of religious and secular points of view are aired and treated fairly and respectfully is a key way in which to assure that the public schools practice a genuine neutrality toward religion and do not end up supporting a secular cultural ethos due to religion being left out of the curriculum.

Piety Versus "Secular Humanism": A Phony War

MARVIN E. FRANKEL

T he decision of the Supreme Court in 1962 outlawing the bland triviality composed as a prayer by the New York Board of Regents, and then the succeeding year's ruling against Bible reading in the public schools, led to a thunder of opposition that keeps rolling and resounding over the years. There was outrage that God had been "expelled" from the public schools. A senator declared that the Supreme Court had "made God unconstitutional." Proposed constitutional amendments to overturn those decisions became staple contributions to the congressional hopper. A measure supporting public-school prayers became a central plank of the Republican platform, endorsed by President Reagan with the kind of folksy passion that lifted his high popularity ratings. While that position has never commanded the two-thirds vote in Congress required to launch an amendment, it appears steadily to enlist a large majority in American public opinion polls. It is reflected, too, in a wide and persistent defiance of the Supreme Court's ruling as local communities, especially in the South, cheer schoolteachers for their classroom prayers, promote prayers on athletic fields, and continue to act as if officially directed sanctimony might be a path to salvation.

A strong band of pious politicians have campaigned during the last third of the twentieth century for the right of students, as it is said, to engage in voluntary, silent prayer in the public schools. A number of states in the 1980s enacted statutes to implement this goal. To avoid the constitutional rule against open and explicit group prayers in the schools, legislators combined religious zeal with legal genius. A more or less standard law simply ordered a "moment of silence" during the school day, when every student individually could think about nothing, solve mathematical puzzles, fantasize about sex, or even—perhaps—pray. In a number of instances the state law said nothing at all about prayer, providing only for the brief period of silence. These paths for God's re-entry into the public schools have for the most part run into judicial roadblocks, though the cases have not been unanimous and the struggle is not yet over.

Alabama's silent-prayer law reached, and expired in, the Supreme Court in 1985. The statute struck down in that case provided for a period of silence in the public schools "for meditation or voluntary prayer." Ishmael

Jaffree, father of two second-graders and one kindergartner, sued to have that enactment invalidated. Sustaining his position (over the dissents of Chief Justice Warren Burger and Justices Byron White and William Rehnquist), the Supreme Court found that the purpose of passing the law was, as an Alabama senator put it, "to return voluntary prayer to our public schools." That violated the state's duty of neutrality with respect to religion under the Establishment Clause.

However, two of the Justices in the majority said, and four broadly intimated, that a law merely providing for a period of silence would pass constitutional muster. And that echoed a long-running debate that remains at most only partially resolved. The idea of legislatively decreed moments of silence in the public schools has appealed to the lawmakers of more than half the states. It has led to a spate of judicial opinions one way or another and a small shelf of scholarly writing. For all the devout attention they have received, these state laws exhibit only two or three salient—and to me regrettable—characteristics.

First, they all emerge in the wake of the Supreme Court's banning of officially sponsored prayer and Bible reading in the schools. Their background leaves no question about their essential purpose, to evade or fight in the rearguard against that ban.

Second, in a number of cases the sponsors of these acts make no bones about their view that the majority has taken more than an acceptable amount of guff from minorities, and that the preponderant sentiment favoring school prayer should have its way. A New Jersey state assemblyman sponsoring one of the bills was asked in debate about its effect on atheists. The question may have wrongly implied that only atheists would oppose this sort of law. The answer in its way dismissed all sorts of opponents when the assemblyman said that "they were so few in number their views could be discounted." That position is by no means rare. In an opinion upholding the Nebraska legislature's regular payment and use of a Presbyterian minister to open its sessions with a prayer, Chief Justice Burger wrote that this was "simply a tolerable acknowledgement of beliefs widely held among the people of this country." Expressions like these, made in upholding religious exercises under government sponsorship, give less than enthusiastic support to the proposition that the Religion Clauses vouchsafe minority rights, not indulgences for the majority.

A third characteristic of the moment-of-silence laws is a common claim of their sponsors: that they are merely neutral provisions for a time of repose in the school day, when students can do as they please, even pray if the spirit moves them. This has august support, in the Supreme Court and among notable legal scholars. I'll explain below my dissent from this position.

At this point, to conclude on the state of the law as of now, I report that the majority of the lower federal courts that have considered the question have held these moment-of-silence statutes unconstitutional. They have perceived usually a more or less veiled purpose to sponsor or to promote prayer. . . .

To be sure, the decreed time of silence may be used to daydream or ogle, etc. But how did it happen that in all the decades before the school-prayer cases no powerhouse of daydreamers and oglers (who represent all of us, after all) demanded laws compelling stated periods of silence? Rhetorical questions don't need answers. As a relevant tangent, however, one recalls the long stretches of silence, in study halls and classrooms, that character-ized life in public school. There was always plenty of time to pray or ogle. No law proclaimed a specific moment of silence. No occasion arose when anybody was questioned about the failure to use the silent time for praying. The moment-of-silence laws are, in one word, charades.

Ruses of this kind remind us of the essentially sleazy uses to which politicians put their professed devotion to God. The Christians among them notably forget the lesson Christ taught about this:

> Beware of practicing your piety before men in order to be seen by them; for then you will have no reward from your Father who is in heaven.

Instead, in a kind of guerrilla war against the First Amendment, periodic bursts of public religious displays by government officials are offered up as substitutes for statesmanship. A further example or two may be enough illustration.

During the Civil War, when the fate of the nation seemed precarious, the Union cause was buttressed in 1864 by the placement of the national motto, "In God We Trust," on a two-cent piece. Blessed by the Congress, that sentiment on the money continued unquestioned until it came to be noticed by President Theodore Roosevelt. It struck him as being "close to sacrilege." He noted that this form of affirmation had tended to pro-duce jokes rather than accesses of elevated faith. In a letter to a clergyman he wrote:

> Every one must remember the innumerable cartoons and articles based on phrases like "In God we trust for the other eight cents"; "In God we trust for the short weight"; "In God we trust for the thirty-seven cents we do not pay"; and so forth, and so forth.

More repelled than amused, Roosevelt ordered that the motto be deleted from the currency.

One man's sacrilege is a lot of other people's holiness. The Congress was appalled by the President's vandalism and ordered the slogan put back onto the money. Both our metal and paper forms of legal tender have been graced ever since by the religious motto.

Do you feel better protected by those words on the money? Does it per-haps help to keep the dollar sound? Do you in fact have any awareness that the words are there? Probably the answer for most of us is that by this time it is a matter of little or no consequence. If it was thought about, however, one might hope, though possibly in vain, that more of us would be ready to join in Theodore Roosevelt's sentiments. For the genuinely devout, the vote of confidence in God, on money, of all places, might fairly seem an affront. For the nonreligious or for those, like Buddhists, among others, to whom the trust in God is an alien concept, the routine affirmation by their government might grate. It is difficult to know in the end how in a country never accused of insufficiently worshipping money anyone finds strength or solace in this practice. At least in my judgment, all of us, and the still generally shared concept of God, are diminished a little by such cheap public expressions of religiosity.

The thought was put more felicitously by a sensitive Harvard law teacher in a lovely book attending devotedly to the springs of religious sentiment as well as to the sound place of democratic government. Speaking of the easy manifestations of official spirituality, he counted these as instances of "chauvinism and religiosity" combining "to produce a triumphant vulgarity" that congratulates God for the wisdom of favoring America and Americans over lesser, less godly nations. . . .

In the same class, though perhaps more debatably, I'd put the improvement on the Pledge of Allegiance fashioned by Congress in 1954. That was a year, it will be recalled, when Senator Joseph McCarthy was still exploring how low we might be sunk in his ersatz but grimly destructive crusade against "subversives." It was also a year McCarthy's colleagues found it meet to insert the words "under God" after the reference to this "one nation" in the pledge. The House Report on the bill that became this law said that "it would serve to deny the atheistic and materialistic concepts of communism with its attendant subservience of the individual." Some very brief remarks on the floor reaffirmed that inserting the words "under God" would "strengthen the national resistance to communism." The only cerebration manifested on the subject of the bill had to do with the number and placement of commas in the revised pledge—i.e., whether it should be simply "one nation under God" or "one Nation, under God," as the legislative judgment finally determined. The short debate on this subject was suitably placid. There was no debate at all on the merits of the revision and no vote against it. Who, after all, would be caught in the open excluding God?

The uses of God as a "ceremonial and patriotic" implement go forward steadily in more obtrusive and questionable forms. The insistent demand to have crèches and menorahs in public sites continues to present tough questions. . . . The legal issues are tricky enough to promise a continued supply of test cases. To oversimplify a lot, the hardest cases—where private groups want to put their crèches or menorahs in the public park or on City Hall plaza—pit the First Amendment free-speech rights of those groups against the claim of the objectors that this placement of the symbols indicates government endorsement of the religion symbolized. Without questioning the difficulty of these cases, it is fair to conjure with the question why they keep happening. The answer lies, I think, in the very nature of hostile and competitive patriotism out of which one might wish that God could have been kept. The crèche on the public square—to "put Christ back into Christmas," as its sponsors regularly say—plants the religious flag of the angry nativists winning theirs back from the alien, infidel intruders. (Who do they think they are?) The menorah sponsors are a kindred but more pathetic story. (If the *goyim* can do it, so can we.) Both are joined together as enemies of the mutual forbearance that is at the heart of religious freedom in a pluralist society.

The gist of the demand is that the muscle of your religion be displayed in the public space. The subject, as is usual with facile shows of patriotism, is power. It is put, to be sure, as a matter of free expression by the crèche and menorah advocates, but that is largely fraud or self-delusion. There are ample private spaces in every community, amply visible, for displaying religious icons. The insistence on the *public* space, the space that belongs to all of us, is to show those others, the nonadherents. The distinction is readily, if not always malevolently, blurred. Leonid Feldman, an earnest cleric, raised as an atheist and abused as a Jew in the former Soviet Union, serves now as a conservative rabbi in Florida. He says he is now "frightened by secularism" and perplexed by those, Jews and others, who oppose the installation of menorahs. He states his case in a few moving words: "I fought the KGB for the right to light a menorah. Forgive me if I don't want to eliminate menorahs from America's lawns."[1] Moving his words may be. They also reflect, in brief compass, an entire confusion about what church-state separation means in the United States.

The fear of "secularism" is a chimera. "Secular" is what our government is supposed to be. That has nothing to do with the *imposed* religion of atheism that Rabbi Feldman suffered in the U.S.S.R. As for the right to light menorahs on "America's lawns," the rabbi should surely have realized by now that it is a right fully respected under our law (leaving aside blights like private anti-Semitism and other "antis" that continue to sully religious, racial, and ethnic relationships in our country and most others).

Whatever misunderstandings may beset a recent refugee from Soviet atheism, there is no ground for similar confusion, and probably no similar confusion, among most people who want their religious symbols standing on public property. The symbols make a statement—not of religious faith. They are not needed for that. They assert simply and starkly, as I've said, power over the nonbelievers. This was underscored for me in a fleeting moment of a case that ended 4–4 in the Supreme Court, the equal division (Justice Powell was ill and absent) resulting in a defeat for the village of Scarsdale (with me as unsuccessful counsel) when it sought to deny a place for a crèche in a public circle. In the course of that proceeding, one of the sponsors of the crèche was asked about his interest in viewing it while it stood on Scarsdale's Boniface Circle during the Christmas season. To my surprise as the questioner, it turned out that he never bothered to go look at the crèche at all, let alone to admire or draw inspiration from it. But on reflection that should not have been so surprising. The crèche was not there

---

1. KGB is an acronym for the Soviet secret police.

for him to see or appreciate for its intrinsic spiritual value in his religious universe. It was there for others, who professed other religions or none, so that the clout of his religious group should be made manifest—above all to any in the sharply divided village who would have preferred that it not be there. This is the low road followed by at least a good number of those who seek for their religion and its symbols the imprimatur of government. If it is religious at all, this stance betokens a weak and self-doubting species of faith.

Much more blatant and unsettling than the crèches and menorahs, and even the tasteless evasions of moment-of-silence laws, is the ongoing course of flat-out defiance of the Supreme Court's ban against organized prayer in the public schools. It is ironic at best that in God's name, while tracing the blessings of democracy to their religion, so many people hack at the most vital of democratic organs: the rule of law, including the acceptance of authoritative decisions by those commissioned to expound the Constitution. Ironic or not, the practice continues, at a steep price in human anguish and political subversion. One more example helps to sharpen the picture.

In 1993, the Federal Court of Appeals embracing Texas heard the case of a junior-high-school basketball coach who regularly led his girls' team in a recitation of the Lord's Prayer at the beginning and end of each practice session. At games against other schools, the members of the team were brought to the center of the court, where they got on their hands and knees while the coach stood over them, and with their heads bowed, recited the Lord's Prayer. The prayer was also said before they left school for games away from home and at critical times in games like last-second buzzer-beater shots. A twelve-year-old team member objected to the prayer. When her father spoke to the assistant superintendent of schools about her objection, that official said that "unless [the father] had grandparents buried in the Duncanville Cemetery, he had no right to tell [the assistant superintendent] how to run his schools." When Jane Doe decided not to participate in the team prayers, the coach had her stand aside at games while the others prayed. Her fellow students asked, "Aren't you a Christian?" One spectator stood up after a game and yelled, "Well, why isn't she praying? Isn't she a Christian?" Her history teacher called her "a little atheist" during one class lecture.

The court upheld an injunction forbidding this practice. No one can doubt the correctness of the decision. What causes doubt and worry is that the coach and the superintendent should have found it justifiable to require that such a lawsuit be brought. If they have done useful service at all, it is to remind us of the misery inflicted by self-righteous tyrants like these on young people and others who do not share their religious convictions (assuming in their favor that people of this sort have genuine inner "convictions" rather than merely devices for oppressing their neighbors). It is doubtful that the coach, serving as backup minister, thought this performance made his team play more effectively.

But who knows? The uses to which athletes and others put their God are multifarious and often surprising. I recall, having made a note of it, the night of October 25, 1986, when the New York Mets won the critical sixth game of the World Series on a dubious fielding effort by the Boston Red Sox first baseman. As a proper Mets fan, I stayed with the telecast to hear some post-game wisdom. Two of the star Mets players gave similar explanations for their victory. Third baseman Ray Knight explained that the Good Lord had been on their side. Catcher Gary Carter attributed the victory to the favor shown the Mets by Jesus Christ. Even a Mets fan was led to wonder how the Deity had come to nurse hostility toward the Red Sox.

Seemingly more spacious and high-minded are the clerics and philosophers who do not invoke a necessarily partisan God but argue earnestly that the secularization of government in our time leaves a moral vacuum that will be filled with false, evil, probably fascistic substitutes for true religion. A lively proponent of this position is Roman Catholic Father Richard John Neuhaus, whose famous book, *The Naked Public Square: Religion and Democracy in America,* was published in 1984, when he was a Lutheran minister. When the public square becomes naked, he taught, of religious affirmations and frankly religious morality, we lose the most basic need of a good society, some "final inhibition of evil." That inhibition, he makes clear, is found in the Christian—he sometimes says "Judeo-Christian"—tradition. He faults the Supreme Court for straying in recent years from its earlier sound perception, for it remains correct in his view to acknowledge that "this is, as the Supreme Court said in 1931, a Christian people." While the majority of the Court and most legal scholars rejoice that the Court would shun a repetition of that arrogant thought (as Justice Brennan called it), Father Neuhaus deems this a tragic retreat. This epitomizes, in my opinion, the profound error of his way.

. . . It is plain wrong to aver that the fundamental morality of our strikingly diverse people is tied to Christian, or even Judeo-Christian, doctrine or observance. Throughout American history, the great politico-moral issues that have troubled and divided us have seen the Christian and Jewish clergy about as divided as everyone else. Abortion in our time, capital punishment, equal rights for women, even capitalism versus socialism have all had religious leaders on both sides. The most tragic of our national sins, slavery, saw a similar division, with the majority of ministers siding, as is usual, with the status quo throughout the centuries before emancipation. At least one thoughtful religious scholar finds the belief in an inerrant Bible, including its literal approval of slavery, a still significant strand of fundamentalist thought in the American South. None of this is to doubt for an instant the value of spiritual leaders for their followers. It is only to stress again that this is a value that should be neither enforced nor endorsed by the state.

The notion that government must somehow be religious because most of our people are religious is a gross error. The astute observer Tocqueville concluded in the 1830s that it was precisely the separation of church and

state that led to both the peaceful careers of varying sects and the flourishing of religion in general. Times have undoubtedly changed since then, but
he found among both priests and laypeople a unanimity of opinion on this
score. That opinion was sound in Tocqueville's day. We should cherish and
preserve it.

DISCUSSION QUESTIONS

1. How should we interpret the First Amendment's words on religious
    freedom? Do we emphasize the philosophical convictions of Madison and
    Jefferson or the practices of government support for religion that prevailed
    at the time and for many years afterward?

2. Should there be a strict separation between church and state, as the
    Supreme Court has proclaimed? Or should religion occupy a greater place
    in public institutions so long as measures are taken to safeguard everyone's
    freedom of conscience, including nonbelievers?

3. Should we allow prayers in the schools and religious symbols on public
    property so long as all faiths (and nonbelievers) are allowed representation,
    or would such expressions of religion favor the faiths of the majority and
    prove coercive to the minority?

4. Should religious expression be considered a normal and usually healthy
    contributor to political life, or should it be kept a personal matter lest it
    produce divisiveness or intolerance in politics?

SUGGESTED READINGS
AND INTERNET RESOURCES

For a sympathetic and wide-ranging discussion of religion's place in American
politics, see Garry Wills, *Under God: Religion and American Politics* (New York:
Simon and Schuster, 1990). For a prominent criticism of what the author
regards as the dominant culture's antipathy to public expressions of faith, see
Stephen L. Carter, *The Culture of Disbelief: How American Law and Politics
Trivialize Religious Devotion* (New York: Basic Books, 1993). A political theorist
and a historian attack the constitutional argument presented by the Christian
right and emphasize the secular intentions of America's founders in Isaac Kramnick and R. Laurence Moore, *The Godless Constitution: The Case Against Religious
Correctness* (New York: Norton, 1996). A comprehensive treatment of religious
liberty issues is John Witte Jr., *Religion and the American Constitutional Experiment:
Essential Rights and Liberties* (Boulder, Colo: Westview Press, 1999). Historical
perspective on the struggles for civil liberties and civil rights is provided in

James MacGregor Burns and Stewart Burns, *A People's Charter: The Pursuit of Rights in America* (New York: Vintage Books, 1993).

American Civil Liberties Union
http://www.aclu.org/issues/religion/hmrf.html
The ACLU, the nation's oldest civil liberties organization, highlights recent events pertinent to First Amendment religious issues, lists resources, and provides links to other religious freedom sites.

The American Center for Law and Justice
http://www.aclj.org
A Christian legal foundation; its site on "Defending the Rights of Believers" includes a booklet on student rights in the public schools, news releases, information letters, and references to important court cases.

7

Civil Rights: How Far Have We Progressed?

A lmost half a century after the U.S. Supreme Court ruled in *Brown* v. *Board of Education of Topeka* that racial segregation was a violation of the Constitution, where do relations between the races stand? And what kind of public policies are still needed to address issues of racial inequity? Have we made considerable progress toward becoming "one nation, indivisible," as claimed by Stephan Thernstrom and Abigail Thernstrom, authors of the first selection that follows? Or do pervasive racial divisions continue to make us "a country of strangers," the title of our second selection by David Shipler? Should we abandon affirmative action programs, as the Thernstroms recommend, because they impede progress toward a "colorblind" society, or do we need them, as Shipler suggests, because African Americans continue to face handicaps and prejudices in schools and workplaces?

Few Americans today question the landmark civil rights laws and court decisions of the 1950s and 1960s, even though they were enormously controversial in their day. After hundreds of years of slavery and racial segregation, the argument of the civil rights movement that racial discrimination is incompatible with democracy has at last attained official status. But since its heroic phase ended in the 1960s, with the assassination of Martin Luther King, Jr., the civil rights struggle has become embroiled in one bitter debate after another. Leaders and groups associated with the old civil rights movement have continued to call for strong legal measures to advance racial equality, including school busing and affirmative action in education and employment. Critics of the movement, black as well as white, challenge these measures, contending that they actually obstruct racial progress by undermining black self-help and by sowing fresh resentments among whites.

The dilemmas of race continued to trouble American society through the 1990s, as dramatically evidenced in the Los Angeles riots of 1992 and the antithetical reactions of African Americans and whites to the O. J. Simpson murder trial in 1994–1995. President Clinton claimed that a top priority of his second term was a national dialogue focused on these dilemmas. But critics on the left disparaged Clinton's initiative on race as talk without action, while critics to the right saw it as merely a sounding board for bankrupt liberal nostrums such as affirmative action. Race was still an issue in the presidential primaries of 2000; Democratic candidate Bill Bradley was most vocal on the urgency of improving race relations.

President Clinton was a defender of affirmative action, responding to mounting criticisms of it with the call to "mend it, don't end it." But after he became president, affirmative action programs faced a series of legal and political setbacks. In 1995, the U.S. Supreme Court ruled in *Adarand* v. *Peña* that government programs that provide preferential treatment on the basis of race are unconstitutional unless a pattern of prior discrimination against minorities can be demonstrated. In 1996, voters in California approved Proposition 209, which forbade public agencies and schools in the state to employ racial or gender preferences. That same year, a federal appeals court decided in *Hopwood* v. *Texas* that the state university could not continue to admit minorities with lower grades and test scores in the name of promoting diversity. In 1998, voters in the state of Washington approved a measure similar to California's Proposition 209.

With affirmative action eliminated in Texas and California, minority enrollments at these states' most prestigious public universities showed an immediate, sharp drop. To restore diversity, Texas adopted a program whereby the top 10 percent of graduates from each high school were guaranteed admission to the state university; California legislators contemplated a similar (though more restrictive) plan. Although this approach serves to boost minority numbers at the undergraduate level, it provides no remedy for diminished minority admissions to graduate and professional schools.

How we view civil rights policies such as affirmative action depends in large part on how we understand and evaluate relations between the races in the United States today. Stephan and Abigail Thernstrom argue in our first selection that purveyors of racial gloom have distorted public debate, particularly by obscuring the evidence that racial attitudes in the United States have been growing more tolerant for decades. Relying heavily on public opinion surveys, the Thernstroms see whites and blacks as coming increasingly closer to one another since the days of Jim Crow segregation, even forming bonds of friendship across the boundaries of race. While not denying that African Americans suffer from higher rates of crime and poverty than whites and score lower on various educational measures, they are most impressed by the signs of

African American advancement, such as the rise of a black middle class. The Thernstroms oppose affirmative action. Although it may spring from benevolent intentions, they argue, it has had pernicious consequences and has blocked further progress toward a "colorblind society."

David Shipler studies race relations differently than the Thernstroms and reaches very different conclusions. Shipler's work is based not on public opinion surveys but on interviews and observations about race relations in schools, workplaces, and communities around the nation. He believes that race continues to draw a line between white and black Americans, with uncertainty, discomfort, and anxiety on both sides. To Shipler, talk of "colorblindness" is unrealistic: "There is scarcely a consequential interaction between a black and a white in the United States in which race is not a factor."

Like many supporters of affirmative action, Shipler expresses some ambivalence, conceding that it can play into old racial stereotypes. But to him, affirmative action is needed so long as African Americans face educational and economic handicaps and subtle prejudices that undermine genuine equality of opportunity.

Race relations in the United States have profound implications for our understandings of democracy, freedom, and equality. How do you view the current state of American race relations? Are you more persuaded by the surveys cited by the Thernstroms that we are becoming a more tolerant interracial society or by the interviews and observations presented by Shipler that racial tensions and grievances continue to prevail along an American color line? What measures should our society take to deal with remaining racial inequalities? Is affirmative action still needed? If affirmative action were abolished, would we at last create a level playing field where everyone could compete on equal terms, or would white males reassert their traditional advantages?

One Nation, Indivisible

STEPHAN THERNSTROM
AND ABIGAIL THERNSTROM

I n 1991, 13 percent of the whites in the United States said that they had generally "unfavorable" opinions about black Americans. In an ideal world, that number would be zero. But such a world is nowhere to be found. In Czechoslovakia that same year, 49 percent of Czechs had "unfavorable" attitudes toward the Hungarian ethnic minority living within the boundaries of their country. Likewise, 45 percent of West Germans disliked the Turks living in Germany; 54 percent of East Germans regarded Poles negatively; 40 percent of Hungarians frowned on the Romanians who lived among them; and 42 percent of the French disdained Arab immigrants from North Africa. In only two of the dozen European countries surveyed—Britain and Spain—was the proportion of majority group members who expressed dislike for the principal minority group less than twice as high as in the United States. . . .

Against this yardstick the racial views of white Americans look remarkably good. But are seemingly tolerant whites simply more hypocritical than Czechs or French? Perhaps they have learned to keep their animus hidden from public view. We think not. Although different ways of framing questions about racial prejudice yield slightly different answers, the bulk of the evidence squares with the 1991 survey results: when it comes to intergroup tolerance, Americans rate high by international standards. . . .

America Since Myrdal

This is a profound change. When Gunnar Myrdal first trained his microscope on the American racial scene in the closing years of the Great Depression, he was struck by the radical difference between the status of immigrants and that of African Americans.[1] The United States stood out for its success in absorbing millions of immigrants from other lands into the melting pot. Myrdal believed that American social scientists were too preoccupied with "the occasional failures of the assimilation process" and the "tension" that immigration created in the society. They lacked the perspective available to "the outside observer," to whom the "first and greatest riddle to solve" was how "the children and grandchildren of these unassimilated foreigners" so quickly became "well-adjusted Americans." Part of the answer to the puzzle, Myrdal suggested, was "the influence upon the immigrant of a great national *ethos,* in which optimism and carelessness, generosity and callousness, were so blended as to provide him with hope and endurance."

In those days, the "optimism" and "generosity" Myrdal found did not extend to the descendants of enslaved Africans, though the "callousness" certainly did. Blacks had not been coaxed or coerced into the American melting pot; they had been forcibly kept out of it. Everyone was eager to "Americanize" the immigrants, Myrdal noticed, and viewed "the preservation of their separate national attributes and group loyalties as a hazard to American institutions." The recipe for African Americans was the reverse. They were "excluded from assimilation," and advised "even by their best friends in the dominant white group" to "keep to themselves and develop a race pride of their own."

In the South, where the large majority of African Americans lived, an elaborate legal code defined their position as a separate and inferior people. Poorly educated in segregated schools, and confined to ill-paid, insecure,

---

1. Gunnar Myrdal was a Swedish social scientist who published a landmark study of U.S. race relations, *An American Dilemma: The Negro Problem and American Democracy,* in 1944.

menial jobs, they were a subordinate caste in a society dedicated to white supremacy. Moreover, in countless ways blacks were daily reminded of their status as a lesser breed; they entered only the back door of a white home, never shook hands with a white person, and grown men were habitually addressed as "boy" or simply by their first names. In the North, blacks could vote, and the color line was less rigid and lacked the force of law. But many of the semiskilled and skilled industrial positions that gave immigrants the chance to climb out of poverty were off-limits, and blacks lived for the most part in a world separate from whites. A color line in the housing market confined black families to black neighborhoods; swimming in the "white" part of a public beach was dangerous; and many restaurants would not serve black customers. As Myrdal found, nine out of ten of even the most liberal and cosmopolitan northerners whom he encountered in the 1940s blanched at the thought of interracial marriage.

None of the public opinion surveys conducted in the Depression or World War II years included a specific question about whether whites had "favorable" or "unfavorable" opinions about blacks. But there can be no doubt about the answer such an inquiry would have yielded. The polling data we reviewed . . . demonstrated that large majorities of whites held strongly racist sentiments. African Americans were a stigmatized group, assumed to be a permanent caste that would forever remain beyond the melting pot.

That world has now vanished. In the spring of 1995, in the wake of attacks on affirmative action, Georgia congressman and one-time civil rights hero John Lewis complained that he sometimes felt as if he were reliving his life. "Didn't we learn?" he asked. He felt "the need to . . . tell people we've got to do battle again." But yesterday is not today, as many do recognize—including, we suspect, Lewis himself. "We black folk should never forget that our forefathers were slaves," Florida congresswoman Carrie P. Meek said in 1994. But then she added, "though my daughter says, 'Enough, Mom, enough of this sharecropper-slave stuff.'" Meek was born in 1926, and in her own lifetime the rigidly oppressive caste system delineated in *An American Dilemma* gave way to the far more fluid social order of today.

From rigid caste system to a more fluid social order . . . we reviewed decades of amazing change.

. . . We did not neglect the bad news. In 1995 half of all the murder victims in the United States were African Americans, though they comprised just one-eighth of the population; more than half of those arrested for murder were also black. The black poverty rate that same year was still 26 percent; 62 percent of children in female-headed families were poor. Perhaps most ominously, in 1994, on average, blacks aged seventeen could read only as well as the typical white child just thirteen years old. The racial gap in levels of educational performance permanently stacks the deck against too many African American youngsters as they move on to work or further schooling.

To stress the bad news is to distort the picture, however. Equally important is the story of enormous change, of much more progress than many scholars have recognized. For instance, between 1970 and 1995 the proportion of African Americans living in suburban communities nearly doubled, and residential segregation decreased in almost all the nation's metropolitan areas with the largest black populations. One of the best kept secrets of American life today is that over 40 percent of the nation's black citizens consider themselves members of the middle class. The black male unemployment rate has gotten much press, but, in fact, of those who are in the labor force (working or looking for work), 93 percent had jobs in 1995. We have let the underclass define our notion of black America; it is a very misleading picture.[2]

Over the last half century, the positions of African Americans thus improved dramatically by just about every possible measure of social and economic achievement: years of school completed, occupational levels, median incomes, life expectancy at birth, poverty rates, and homeownership rates. Much of the change took place before the civil rights movement. And while key decisions made by political and legal authorities in this early period were undeniably important (President Truman's order abolishing segregation in the armed forces, for example, and *Brown v. Board of Education*), the impersonal economic and demographic forces that transferred so many blacks from the southern countryside to the northern city were more fundamental.

In addition, white racial attitudes were gradually liberalized. Racist beliefs that were once firmly held by highly educated and uneducated whites alike lost all claim to intellectual respectability by the 1950s, and that changed racial climate finally opened doors. For instance, the door to the Brooklyn Dodgers' locker room. Had the visionary Branch Rickey believed Dodger fans were unreconstructed racists, he would not have put Jackie Robinson on the field and risked plunging ticket sales. As it was, his feel for changing racial attitudes brought championships to Brooklyn.

Social contact between the races has also increased enormously. By 1989, five out of six black Americans could name a white person whom they considered a friend, while two out of three whites said their social circle included someone who was black. By 1994 it had become not the least bit unusual for blacks and whites to have brought someone of the other race home to dine (a third of white families and a majority of the black families had done so), and most blacks and whites said someone of the other race lived in their neighborhood. When a sample of people in the Detroit metropolitan area were asked in 1992 whether they had contact on the job with people of the other race, 83 percent of blacks and 61 percent of whites said, yes. That same year, 72 percent of blacks and 64 percent of whites reported having interracial conversations on the job "frequently" or "sometimes." Even in the most intimate of relations, there had been substantial

---

2. *Underclass* refers to residents of the nation's poorest areas.

change. By 1993, 12 percent of all marriages contracted by African Americans were to a spouse of the other race.

Two Nations: Black and White, Separate, Hostile, Unequal, Andrew Hacker called his best-selling book. Our book is in many ways an answer to Hacker. *One* nation (we argue), no longer separate, much less unequal than it once was, and by many measures, less hostile. Moreover, the serious inequality that remains is less a function of white racism than of the racial gap in levels of educational attainment, the structure of the black family, and the rise in black crime.

We quarrel with the left—its going-nowhere picture of black America and white racial attitudes. But we also quarrel with the right—its see-no-evil view. It seems extraordinarily hard for liberals to say we have come a long way; the Jim Crow South is not the South of 1997. But it seems very hard for conservatives to say, yes, there was a terrible history of racism in this country, and too much remains.

Conservatives seem to think that they concede too much if they acknowledge the ugliness of our racial history and the persistence of racism (greatly diminished but not gone)—that if they do so, they will be committed to the currently pervasive system of racial preferences and indeed to reparations. And liberals, from their different perspective, also fear concession. To admit dramatic change, they seem to believe, is to invite white indifference. As if everything blacks now have rests on the fragile foundation of white guilt . . .

The Road to Progress

Much racial progress has been made. And much has *yet* to be made. How to keep moving forward? It is a question that can be answered only by knowing the route by which African Americans have come to where they are today.

There is no mystery as to how they got from there to here, most writing on racial change in recent decades assumes. The story began with the civil rights movement, which, with a boost from *Brown v. Board of Education,* created turmoil in the nation and forced Congress and the White House to act. The civil rights and voting rights legislation of the mid-1960s destroyed Jim Crow institutions and gave equal legal status to African Americans. These colorblind measures, however, failed to remedy deeper economic and social inequalities rooted in race. Color-conscious policies that set specific numerical goals and timetables attacked the underlying problems. In fact, only the adoption of preferential policies could have created a black middle class and brought about other economic and educational gains.

From this account, a simple policy conclusion flows: preferential policies are the key to future progress. And thus Supreme Court decisions and other actions that constrain the use of racial classifications by public authorities are viewed by some as truly dangerous—a threat to black well-being comparable to the end of Reconstruction.

Such alarm ignores the historical record, we have argued, although the great strides forward have since been somewhat obscured by the gains and disappointments of subsequent years. The civil rights revolution reached a climax in a burst of legislation that destroyed the Jim Crow system, but that legislation promised more than it could quickly deliver. As Dr. King and others understood, the legal fix would not tomorrow solve the problem of economic and educational inequalities so long in the making. Blacks were understandably impatient. They had already waited much too long—almost a century since the passage of the great Reconstruction Amendments to the Constitution. It was tempting to seek shortcuts, ways of accelerating social change, and thus the demand for "freedom now" soon became a call for "equality as a fact and as a result," as Lyndon Johnson put it in 1965.

That call for equality as a "fact" and "result" was the first step down the road to racial preferences. Much celebrated in the civil rights community for the benefits they have brought, preferences are in fact difficult to assess. . . . In 1995 the historian Roger Wilkins described himself as the happy recipient of racial preferences. "I'd rather be an assistant attorney general who was a beneficiary of affirmative action than a GS 14."[3] he said. It's hard to believe Wilkins is really convinced he would have been languishing at the bottom of a bureaucratic heap had he not been rescued by preferential policies. His tale certainly does not square with the larger picture, as we understand it.

In a few respects the overall rate of black progress did accelerate after preferential policies were introduced. Rates of entry into law and medical schools are one example. But lawyers and doctors are a tiny fraction of the black middle class. And by many other measures progress slowed—and in some cases stopped altogether. One recent study found that the racial gap in median wages, labor-force participation, and joblessness was wider in 1992 than in 1967. As a consequence of the huge rise in female-headed households among African Americans, the ratio of black to white family income has fallen somewhat since the 1960s. And the poverty rate for blacks in the 1990s is about as high as it was a generation ago.

Thus, on many counts the socioeconomic gains made by African Americans in the affirmative action era have been less impressive than those that occurred before preferential policies. On the basis of that historical record, however, we cannot conclude that affirmative action did nothing significant. In the 1940s and 1950s, big strides forward were relatively easy to take—blacks were so far behind whites. Thereafter, the rate of progress naturally slowed. Moreover, preferential policies may indeed have benefited some African Americans (those with better educational credentials) without dramatically improving the position of the group as a whole.

The slower growth of the American economy since the early 1970s further complicates the task of assessment. Groups on the lower rungs of the

---

3. GS stands for General Schedule, the system that classifies federal civil servants; GS14 denotes a middle-level position in the federal bureaucracy.

socioeconomic ladder usually find it far easier to improve their position when the economy is booming, as it was to an extraordinary degree in the 1950s and 1960s. And perhaps without affirmative action, the slow economy would have been even harder on African Americans than it was. It's a what-might-have-been argument that cannot be settled. But those who assume that ending affirmative action will end black progress must reconcile the history of pre-1970s progress with their fear of a future that returns to the past.

Even assuming that affirmative action rescued Roger Wilkins and others from professional oblivion, an important question remains: have the benefits outweighed the costs? The issue was implicitly raised in a surprising 1993 letter. The mayors of Minneapolis and four other large American cities wrote to Attorney General Janet Reno, calling for an end to the collection and dissemination of any crime statistics broken down by race. "We believe," the mayors said, "that the collection and use of racial crime statistics by the federal government perpetuate racism in American society." Such data, the mayors went on, were "largely irrelevant" and conveyed the erroneous impression that race and criminality were causally linked. "Racial classifications," the letter continued, were "social constructs" and had "no independent scientific validity." An earlier letter from the Minneapolis mayor had expressed concern about the " 'we' vs. 'they' mentality" that racial classifications created.

The crime statistics had wonderfully concentrated the mayors' minds. Momentarily, at least, they recalled what liberals had always believed until the late 1960s but had chosen to forget when they were converted to affirmative action: racial classifications perpetuate racism. The mayors did not object to racial body counts on principle, as liberals once had. They were simply troubled by the publication of statistics that made African Americans look bad. Racial statistics showing that black poverty and unemployment rates were higher than those of whites, that our colleges and universities did not have "enough" African American students, and that our corporations were short on black executives: these racial classifications apparently were not mere "social constructs" with "no scientific validity." They were essential to enlightened public policy. It was only the black crime rate to which the mayors objected.

But racial data used to distribute benefits inevitably creates the we-versus-they outlook that worried them. American society has paid, it seems to us, a very high price for well-intentioned race-conscious policies. Particularly those built into our law, for the law delivers messages that ripple through both the public and private sectors. And thus unlike the mayors, we hold to Justice Harlan's belief that "our Constitution is color-blind, and neither knows nor tolerates classes among citizens."[4]

---

4. Justice John Marshall Harlan was the lone dissenter to the 1896 Supreme Court decision in *Plessy* v. *Ferguson* that legitimated the "separate-but-equal" system of racial segregation.

In 1896, Justice Harlan was under no illusion that American *society* was color-blind; his was a statement about how to read the Constitution. Nor did Thurgood Marshall in 1947 suppose the country had become oblivious to race when he argued that "classifications based on race or color have no moral or legal validity in our society."[5] We're not naïve; we don't think Americans have to think twice about the color of someone they meet. And we do know that for many whites color still carries important connotations: a young black man on an urban street in the evening appears much more menacing than one who is white. Even middle-class black neighbors may still seem less appealing than white ones to too many white families. It is, in fact, precisely the problem of ongoing racism and just plain color-consciousness that makes race-blind public policy so imperative. Policies that work to heighten the sense of racial separatism spell disaster in a nation with an ugly history of racial subordination and a continuing problem, albeit dramatically diminished, of racial intolerance.

Race-conscious policies make for more race-consciousness; they carry American society backward. We have a simple rule of thumb: that which brings the races together is good; that which divides us is bad. Of course, which policies have what effect is a matter of deep contention. To tear down affirmative action "could start a race war that would make Bosnia look like a kindergarten party," Arthur Fletcher, a former assistant secretary for employment standards, said in 1995. The . . . research we have frequently cited suggests quite a different picture: a racial divide widened by preferences. Others argue that "diversity" strategies bring whites and blacks together; it is not our view. Only those policies that recognize differences among *individuals* can create a true community.

A nation in which individuals are judged as individuals: it was the dream of the 1960s, and we still cherish it. "There *is* a proper object for all the loathing in this country," *New Republic* literary editor Leon Wieseltier has said. "That object is: race. Instead of race hatred, the hatred of race. Instead of the love of what is visible about the person, the love of what is invisible about the person." Does the Wieseltier view ask black Americans to turn their back on all things "black"—to deny all cultural differences associated with group membership? Of course not. Jews haven't; Armenians haven't; Ukrainians haven't. Many Americans arrange their private lives so as to spend much of their time with others of the same background. Purging all racial distinctions from our law and our public life would pose no threat to those who wish to live in a predominantly black neighborhood, attend an all-black church, and otherwise associate primarily or even exclusively with their fellow African Americans.

Racist Americans have long said to blacks, the single most important thing about you is that you're black. Indeed, almost the only important

---

5. Justice Thurgood Marshall was the principal lawyer in the battle by the National Association for the Advancement of Colored People (NAACP) against "separate-but-equal"; later he served on the U.S. Supreme Court.

thing about you is your color. And now, black and white Americans of seeming good will have joined together in saying, we agree. It has been—and is—exactly the wrong foundation on which to come together for a better future. "There can be no empathy and persuasion across racial lines," the economist Glenn C. Loury has said, unless we understand "that the conditions and feelings of particular human beings are universally shared. Such an understanding can be had, but only if we look past race to our common humanity." Ultimately, black social and economic progress largely depend on the sense that we are one nation—that we sink or swim together, that black poverty impoverishes us all, that black alienation eats at the nation's soul, and that black isolation simply cannot work. . . .

True Equality

"The contest between white suburban students and minority inner-city youths is inherently unfair," the chancellor of the University of California at Berkeley, Chang-Lin Tien, said in the summer of 1995. It was not a very persuasive argument for the racial double standards he was defending. If inner-city youngsters are educationally deprived, surely the real solution—indeed the only effective and just solution—has to be one that attacks the problem of K–12 education directly. But in any case, most of the beneficiaries were not the inner-city youths upon whom Tien chose to focus; 30 percent of the black students in the 1994–1995 freshmen class came from families with annual incomes over $70,000. In fact, the Berkeley admissions office, studying the question, found that preferences reserved only for students from low-income families would have reduced the black enrollment by two-thirds. Relatively privileged students—by the measure of economic well-being—had acquired privileges on the basis of the color of their skin.

Affirmative action is class-blind. Students who fall into the category of protected minority will benefit whatever the occupation and income of their parents. As the *Boston Globe* has put it, "officials at even the most selective schools recruit minority scholars with the zeal of a Big 10 football coach." The overwhelming majority of four-year institutions buy expensive lists of minority students and their scores from the Educational Testing Service. Admissions counselors and a network of thousands of alumni comb the country, visiting schools and the special preparatory programs that Phillips Academy in Andover and other private high schools run. Some universities, like Tufts, start the recruitment process in the elementary school years; others, like Boston College, have been known to bring minority students, all expenses paid, for a visit, complete with a chauffeured tour of the area. And if that student can already afford the air fare and more? That's not relevant. Until 1996, when the policy was changed, the African-American student whom the Harvard Graduate School wanted automatically qualified for a Minority Prize Fellowship—even if that student was the son or daughter of a black millionaire.

It's not a process likely to encourage its beneficiaries to work hard in high school. The message is clear: color is the equivalent of good grades. If you don't have the latter, the former will often do. When the University of California regents decided in July 1995 to abolish racial and ethnic preferences in admissions, the executive director of a YWCA college-awareness program told students that the UC vote meant that their "application would be sent in with everybody else's—people who are on college tracks and are prepared." One of the minority students at the session, Jesley Zambrano, reacted at first with anger: "The schools are mostly run by white people. If they don't help us get in, how are we going to get in?" she asked. But then she answered the question herself: "I guess I have to work harder," she said.

That was exactly the point Martin Luther King had made in a speech Shelby Steele heard as a young student in Chicago.[6] "When you are behind in a footrace," King had said, "the only way to get ahead is to run faster than the man in front of you. So when your white roommate says he's tired and goes to sleep, you stay up and burn the midnight oil." As Steele went on to say, "academic parity with all other groups should be the overriding mission of black students. . . . Blacks can only *know* they are as good as others when they are, in fact, as good. . . . Nothing under the sun will substitute for this." And nothing under the sun except hard work will bring about that parity, as King had said. Challenge the students academically rather than capitulate to their demands for dorms with an ethnic theme, Steele has urged universities. And dismantle the machinery of separation, break the link between difference and power. For as long as black students see themselves as *black* students—a group apart, defined by race—they are likely to choose power over parity.

A Country of Strangers

DAVID K. SHIPLER

A line runs through the heart of America. It divides Oak Park from Chicago's West Side along the stark frontier of Austin Boulevard, splitting the two sides of the street into two nations, separating

---

6. Shelby Steele is an African-American scholar who has been one of the most prominent critics of affirmative action.

the carefully integrated town from the black ghetto, the middle class from the poor, the swept sidewalks from the gutters glistening with broken glass, the neat boutiques and trim houses from the check-cashing joints and iron-grilled liquor stores.

The line follows stretches of the Santa Monica Freeway in Los Angeles and Rock Creek Park in Washington, D.C. It runs along the white picket fence that divides the manicured grounds from the empty field where the slaves' shacks once stood at Somerset Place plantation in North Carolina. It cuts across the high, curved dais of the Etowah County Commission in Alabama, where one black member sits with five whites. It encircles the "black tables" where African-Americans cluster together during meals at Princeton University, Lexington High School in Massachusetts, and a thousand corporate cafeterias across the country.

At eleven o'clock Sunday morning, which has been called the most segregated hour in America, the line neatly separates black churches from white churches. It intertwines itself through police departments and courtrooms and jury rooms, through textbooks and classrooms and dormitories, through ballot boxes and offices, through theaters and movie houses, through television and radio, through slang and music and humor, and even through families. The line passes gently between Tony and Gina Wyatt of Florida; he is black, she is white, and they both reach gracefully across the border. It tangles the identity of their teenage son, Justin, who looks white but feels black.

"The problem of the Twentieth Century is the problem of the color-line," W. E. B. Du Bois wrote in 1901; the prophetic words became the opening declaration of his lyrical work *The Souls of Black Folk*.[1] In the succeeding decades, that line has been blurred and bent by the demise of legal segregation and the upward movement of many blacks through the strata of American opportunity. But it remains forbidding to black people left behind in poverty and to others, more successful, who may suddenly confront what Du Bois called a "vast veil"—the curtain of rejection drawn around those whose ancestors were brought in chains from Africa. Today, when sensibilities have been tuned and blatant bigotry has grown unfashionable in most quarters, racist thoughts are given subtler expression, making the veil permeable and often difficult to discern. Sometimes its presence is perceived only as a flicker across a face, as when a white patient looks up from her hospital bed to discover that an attending physician is an African-American.

And so, as the close of the century now approaches, I offer this journey along the color line. It is a boundary that delineates not only skin color and race but also class and culture. It traces the landscape where blacks and whites find mutual encounters, and it fragments into a multitude of fissures

---

1. W. E. B. Du Bois was a leading African-American scholar and political activist whose career stretched from the 1890s to the 1960s.

that divide blacks and whites not only from each other, but also among themselves.

Americans of my generation, who were youngsters when the civil rights movement began in the 1950s, grew up on awful, indelible images. I am haunted still by the cute little white girls who twisted their faces into screams of hatred as black children were escorted into schools. I saw for the first time that the face of pristine innocence could be merely a mask.

Here was the enemy. And the solution seemed obvious: Break down the barriers and let people mingle and know one another, and the importance of race would fade in favor of individual qualities. Blacks would be judged, as Martin Luther King Jr. was preaching, not by the color of their skin but by the content of their character. The perfect righteousness of that precept summoned the conscience of America. . . .

. . . As the Jim Crow segregation laws were overturned, less tractable problems were revealed, and they frustrated King toward the end of his life as he tried to bring his campaign to cities in the North. There, villainy was less easily identified. Rooted in the prejudices, the poverty, the poor education, and the culture of hopelessness that divided blacks and whites, the racial predicament proved too deeply embedded in the society to be pried out by mere personal contact and legal equality. Perhaps it was naïve to think that all that would have to happen was for people to look into each other's eyes, to give blacks as many opportunities as whites, to open the doors. I put this to Reverend Bill Lawson, the black pastor of the Wheeler Avenue Baptist Church in Houston, who had been in the movement and had a long perspective. . . .

. . . "I think that there has been a redefinition of relationships over the last, say, forty years," he said. "There has been, on the one hand, a push toward eliminating the old segregation laws and, on the other hand, a resistance to changing community and neighborhood patterns. So there has been a tension between what we felt was right and what we felt was expedient. There has been the allowance of public contacts. Blacks can ride in the fronts of buses or eat at lunch counters. There has not been a significant change in intimate, personal attitudes. There is still some feeling that we don't want to live too close together, that we don't want to have too many close connections in places [where] we worship, or that we don't want to have too much family contact. We still have some problems with dating and marriage. So in the more public relationships, there has been at least a tolerance that says, let's each one have our own freedom. But anything that becomes more intimate or personal, we tend to have a little bit more resistance."

In Birmingham, Alabama, an old civil rights warrior, Reverend Abraham Lincoln Woods of the St. Joseph Baptist Church, saw the movement's accomplishments as more cosmetic than substantive. "Birmingham has gone through tremendous changes," he said, "and the fact that we have gone from a city where blacks were shut out of the process to having a black mayor and a predominantly black city council—we now have black policemen, in fact we have a black chief now—many things have changed of that kind. But I find that in spite of what seems to be a tolerance of the races and a working together, I find still, somewhat beneath the surface, sometimes not too deeply, those same old attitudes."

But it is behavior, not attitudes, that concerns David Swanston, a white advertising executive whose wife, Walterene, is black. He sat in his handsome town house in McLean, Virginia, one evening and took the measure of America in terms of his own interracial marriage. "It was against the law in a number of states twenty-five years ago," he observed. "It just seems to me that this world was institutionally significantly more racist, overtly racist, than today. Now, each individual black and white within the country may be about the same place they were twenty-five years ago, as regarding interracial marriages and other issues. But it seems to me that's very secondary to the fact that institutionally, we are much beyond that—and it's the institutions that hurt you, that can have the impact on your lives. And by and large, if the twenty people we see in the mall don't like it, and those twenty people wouldn't have liked it twenty-five years ago, I don't really care. The fact that our marriage is recognized by the Commonwealth of Virginia, that we're not criminals, those are the areas where it just seems to me incredible change has been made." . . .

There is scarcely a consequential interaction between a black and a white in the United States in which race is not a factor. Even as it goes unmentioned, as it normally does, race is rarely a neutral element in the equation. It may provoke aversion, fear, or just awkwardness, on the one hand, or, on the other, eager friendliness and unnatural dialogue. Even in easy contacts that are fleeting and impersonal—between a diner and a waiter, a customer and a salesperson, a passenger and a bus driver—race does not always drop to zero; it possesses weight and plays some role in the chemical reaction. "There's always something there," said a young white Princeton graduate working for the *National Journal,* a Washington magazine. "It can be mitigated or it can be worsened by a lot of other factors: social class, culture, the status hierarchy in the office." But it never quite goes away, as he realized when he observed how the mixture of race, class, and hierarchy led him to feel more comfortable with the white reporters than with the black secretaries and receptionists.

If race distorts individual relations, it also magnifies most major social and policy issues facing the American public. Poverty, crime, drugs, gangs, welfare, teenage pregnancy, chronic joblessness, homelessness, illiteracy, and the failure of inner-city public schools are usually viewed through the racial prism. They are seen as black problems or as problems created by blacks. The most popular solutions—cuts in welfare for teenage mothers and long sentences for repeat offenders—are codes for cracking down on blacks' misdeeds. Where race enters the realms of politics, health care, economic injustice, and occasionally foreign policy (as in Haiti and South Africa), the debates are charged with an additional layer of emotion. Despite the upheavals brought by the Supreme Court's 1954 ruling against segregated schools in *Brown* v. *Board of Education*, by the civil rights movement, and by the resulting 1964 Civil Rights Act and the 1965 Voting Rights Act, race is still central to the American psychological experience, as it has been for more than two hundred years.

Over their entire history on this continent, African-Americans have struggled as a people in every conceivable way, short of widespread armed insurrection, to share in the pursuit of happiness. By social reflex or by calculation, by happenstance or ideology, blacks have been servile and militant, passive and hardworking, dependent and self-sufficient. They have used the church, the mosque, the schoolhouse, the university, the military, and the corporation in an effort to advance. They have tried to go back to Africa, and they have tried to function within the political system of the United States. They have tried peaceful demonstrations and violent street riots. They have tried sweet reason and angry rhetoric, assimilation and separatism. They have appealed to the nation's conscience and to its fears. It would be wrong to say that none of this has worked: Individuals have succeeded. But neither deference nor defiance has been effective for black Americans as a whole. No degree of personal success quite erases the stigma of black skin, as many achieving blacks realize when they step outside their family, neighborhood, or professional environment into a setting where their rank and station and accomplishments are not known. "I didn't come from a deprived family," says Floyd Donald, who owns a small radio station in Gadsden, Alabama. "I grew up with books. I grew up with china. I grew up with silver. My background is impeccable, so far as my education and my parents' education and their positions in life and their abilities and so forth. So I had that advantage. However, out of my community, I was just another black. You see, it doesn't make much difference about the status that a black achieves. He is black in America."

In five years of crisscrossing the country to research this book, I was struck by the ease with which most blacks I interviewed were able to discuss race and the difficulty most whites had with the subject. . . .

. . . [B]lack Americans were enormously generous of spirit and time in reaching into their experiences to lay them out for me. Gradually, I came to understand what should have been obvious at the outset: that a black person cannot go very long without thinking about race; she has already asked herself every question that I could possibly pose.

By contrast, most whites rarely have to give race much thought. They do not begin childhood with advice from parents about how to cope with racial bias or how to discern the racial overtones in a comment or a manner. They do not have to search for themselves in history books or literature courses. In most parts of America, their color does not make them feel alone in a crowd; they are not looked to as representatives of their people. And they almost never have to wonder whether they are rejected—or accepted—because of their genuine level of ability or the color of their skin. As a result, few whites I interviewed had considered the questions I put to them. Many struggled to be introspective, but most found that I was taking them into uncharted territory, full of dangers that they quickly surrounded with layers of defensiveness. . . .

Many whites are confused over how they should be thinking about racial issues now. Some adopt an air of smooth indifference, an emotional distance. They often hesitate to say what's on their minds, lest they be accused of racism. Others work quietly, sometimes in frustration, to improve blacks' opportunities in their companies or universities or military units; indeed, I have discovered that more sincere effort goes on than ever gets reflected in press portrayals of America's racial problems. But nothing adds up to a neat sum anymore. How does a white person—even a liberal—sort out the anti-white prejudices, the black self-segregation, the manipulation of history, the endless message of white guilt, the visible achievements of prominent blacks coupled with the deepening poverty and violence of the inner cities? Across much of the spectrum of white America run common themes of distress and impatience with the subject of race, a national mood of puzzlement and annoyance. . . .

The question most often asked me by whites is whether racial matters are getting better or worse. It is an odd inquiry for people to make about their own country. I am used to being asked by Americans how things are going in Russia or in the Middle East, where I have lived and traveled and they perhaps have not.[2] But to have so little feel for the situation right at home betrays the corrosive nature of our racial legacy: how it eats away at our equilibrium, our sense of direction, our navigational skills. We simply do not know where we are, and we are not even quite sure where we have been.

What's more, there is no neat answer to the question. Sometimes I ask in return, "What is your reference point? Slavery? Jim Crow? The height of the civil rights movement? The last five years? Are we measuring economic success or personal attitudes? Are we counting black college graduates or anti-black hate crimes? And what if we decide that pockets of hopefulness are tucked into the midst of despair? Shall we feel virtuous and relax?"

If any sum can be reckoned, it is one of acute contradiction. In the 1920s, the Ku Klux Klan had about two million members; by the mid-1990s, the estimated membership was down to between 2,500 and 3,000, out of 20,000 or 25,000 altogether in various hate groups, including skinheads and militias. Furthermore, prospects have improved for blacks with high skills or advanced degrees in the sciences, business, law, medicine, and other professions as more and more white-run institutions have grown eager to find talented African-American men and women to serve diverse constituencies, improve profits, and demonstrate a commitment to "equal opportunity." But other black people, dragged down by the whirlpool of

---

2. Shipler was a foreign correspondent for the *New York Times*.

poverty and drugs, have fewer and fewer exits. The United States has more black executives and more black prison inmates than a decade ago.

The answer may be that things are getting better and worse at the same time. Racially, America is torn by the crosscurrents of progress and decay. Practically every step forward is accompanied by a subtle erosion of the ground beneath. . . .

On a late summer day in the early 1990s, the dean, who was white, rose to welcome the black and Hispanic students entering one of the country's leading law schools. They had been invited a week early for special orientation, and he had a delicate message for them. His remarks were born of anguish, for he knew something that they did not: They had been admitted with lower average scores than their white classmates had earned on the Law School Aptitude Test.

He wanted to warn them but not defeat them. He could not tell them of the disparities in test scores, because his school, like virtually all others, tried to keep such information secret. So he took an oblique approach. He himself had come from a small town, not an intellectual background, he told the new students. To overcome that deprivation, he had been forced to apply enormous effort, and so would they. "If you work extremely hard," he remembered himself saying, "you can make up for differences in past credentials."

His talk was as welcome as an earthquake. "I was deeply criticized by a number of faculty who felt I had hurt these people on their first day at the institution," he said. "I felt terrible."

The issue confronted him more directly when a group of Hispanic students approached him for reassurance. They were being tormented by white classmates who insisted that Hispanics had scored lower than whites on the LSAT and did not deserve to be there. They wanted the smear refuted. "I tried to be very candid with them," the dean recalled. It was true, he told them: Their scores had been somewhat lower, but with hard work they could erase the deficiencies of their pasts.

An awful silence descended. "I just looked into their eyes as I was talking," the dean remembered, "and I thought, 'I can't bear this; it's too painful.' Their hopes and expectations about what would be said were defeated. There was just a feeling of betrayal."

So goes the conversation about one of the most critical methods used to pry open doors long locked against Hispanics, blacks, and other minorities. The truth cannot be told on any campus without stigmatizing those being aided, without giving a weapon to conservative opponents of such efforts. This law school cannot be identified, the dean cannot be named. He cannot be quoted, except anonymously, as he reveals that if only scores and not race were taken into account, only five or six blacks would be admitted each year instead of forty or fifty. A full and honest discussion of how colleges and graduate schools increase the numbers of African-Americans in their ranks cannot be had.

But why not? How shameful can it be, after generations of imprisonment in inferior educational systems, to score lower on a standardized test? How unfair can it be, after three hundred years of white advantage, to spend thirty years redressing the imbalance? And how unwise can it be, after failing to tap the vast resources of black America, to search affirmatively past the sterile test scores into a rich human potential not easily measured? . . .

Although SAT scores are reliable predictors of freshman grades, they forecast later achievement less accurately. Harvard studied alumni in its classes of '57, '67, and '77 and found that graduates with low SAT scores and blue-collar backgrounds displayed a high rate of "success"—defined by income, community involvement, and professional satisfaction. Here is where race and socioeconomic background mix; some admissions officers believe that if affirmative action were aimed particularly at lower-class students, it would generate less opposition. But it would also yield fewer blacks, since two-thirds of eighteen-year-olds below the poverty line are white. Furthermore, giving preference to students who need financial aid would cost more in scholarships than most colleges have. Consequently, some universities seek upper-middle-class blacks, who can bring diversity and also afford the tuition. However, other elite schools, such as Dartmouth, Harvard, and the Massachusetts Institute of Technology, do give a nod to lower-class applicants. "We have particular interest in students from a modest background," said Marlyn McGrath Lewis, director of admissions for Harvard and Radcliffe. "Coupled with high achievement and a high ambition level and energy, a background that's modest can really be a help. We know that's the best investment we can make: a kid who's hungry."

The two words "affirmative action" were first put together during the inauguration of President John F. Kennedy in 1961, when Vice President Lyndon Johnson, standing in a receiving line, buttonholed a young black attorney named Hobart Taylor Jr. and asked him to help advisers Arthur Goldberg and Abe Fortas write Executive Order 10925 barring federal contractors from racial discrimination in hiring. "I was searching for something that would give a sense of positiveness to performance under that executive order, and I was torn between the words 'positive action' and the words 'affirmative action,'" Taylor recalled in an interview for the Lyndon Baines Johnson Library. "And I took 'affirmative action' because it was alliterative."

From that poetic genesis has come an array of requirements and programs that stir resentment in most of white America. An elastic concept with many definitions, affirmative action is broadly seen as unnatural and unfair, yet it has begun to work its way into the standard practices of so many universities, corporations, and government agencies that it seems sustained as much now by habit and ethic as by law. Even as the courts whittle away at affirmative action's constitutional rationales, more and more institutions are following the military's lead in justifying racial diversity as pragmatic, not merely altruistic. They strive to avoid not only legal punishment but the punishment of a marketplace that is producing fewer and fewer white males as a percentage of workers and customers. As the Pentagon realized after the draft ended in 1973, if the armed services were to compete for good people and tap the entire reservoir of potential recruits, those who were not white men would have to be convinced that unfettered opportunities existed in the ranks. Some corporations have experienced a similar epiphany of self-interest, and at many universities, an admissions officer observed, "success in minority recruitment has become a kind of coin of the realm to indicate institutional success.". . .

. . . [T]he problem created by the solution of affirmative action is this: It allows whites to imagine themselves as victims. Polls find about two-thirds of Americans believing that a white has a smaller chance of getting a job or a promotion than an equally or less qualified black does. When asked why they think this, however, only 21 percent can say that they have seen it at work, 15 percent that it has happened to a friend or relative, and just 7 percent that they have experienced it personally. "With blacks, who are such a small fraction of the population," says Barbara Bergmann, an economist at American University, "the lost opportunities to white men are really minuscule."

Furthermore, some of the personal experience is suspect. Affirmative action transports long-standing biases against blacks into the realm of reasonable discussion: It gives whites permission to affirm the stereotype of blacks as less competent by saying, or thinking, that this or that African-American was not good enough to have been admitted, hired, or promoted without a racial preference. Unscrupulous white supervisors contribute to the slander either by hiring less qualified blacks, just to get their numbers up and avoid discrimination suits, or by disingenuously telling whites, "Gee, I'd love to promote you, but I have to take a black or a woman." Affirmative action thus becomes, in the first case, an excuse for sloppy recruiting and, in the second, a handy pretext to spare a manager the discomfort of telling a white colleague why he doesn't deserve to be promoted.

These are perversions of affirmative action's purpose, and they undermine its viability. In its many forms, from intensive recruiting to hiring goals to set-aside contracts for minority-owned businesses, the effort is designed to remedy unjustified exclusion by seeking out qualified people from the excluded groups and accepting the best of them. It recognizes that passive color blindness is not enough, that people do not deal with one another purely as individuals, and that even if overt discrimination is eliminated, the handicaps of poor schooling and impoverished family life, of subtle prejudice and institutional intolerance, remain severe obstacles to advancement by African-Americans.

DISCUSSION QUESTIONS

1. What is the best way to obtain information and insight into American race relations? What are the advantages and disadvantages of using public opinion surveys to gauge race relations? What are the advantages and disadvantages of using interviews and observations to gauge race relations?

2. One point of contention between the Thernstroms and Shipler concerns inter-racial friendships. Looking at the campuses or workplaces with which you are familiar, do you think that whites and blacks have grown more comfortable with one another on a personal level or that racial separatism is growing?

3. If laws and other measures bar racial discrimination, has American society treated both races with justice? Or do further steps need to be taken to compensate for past racial injustices and to counteract subtly persisting prejudices?

4. Do affirmative action programs only encourage greater white prejudice against blacks? Or do they bring whites into contact with blacks and allow them to see real individuals rather than racial stereotypes?

5. What would American society look like today if affirmative action programs had never been instituted? What would it look like tomorrow if affirmative action programs were abolished?

SUGGESTED READINGS AND INTERNET RESOURCES

Shelby Steele's *The Content of our Character* (New York: St. Martin's Press, 1990) is a passionate call for personal responsibility and an attack on affirmative action by a black scholar. Black journalist Ellis Cose provides a sober critique of the antiaffirmative action position in *Color-Blind: Seeing Beyond Race in a Race-Obsessed World* (New York: HarperCollins, 1997). For an extensive assault on affirmative action by a former member of the Reagan administration, see Terry Eastland, *Ending Affirmative Action: The Case for Colorblind Justice* (New York: Basic Books, 1996). A detailed case for affirmative action, for women as well as racial minorities, can be found in Barbara Bergmann's *In Defense of Affirmative Action* (New York: Basic Books, 1996). As its title suggests, *Two Nations: Black and White, Separate, Hostile, Unequal* (New York: Ballantine Books, 1993), by political scientist Andrew Hacker, offers a grim account, laden with numerous statistics, of American racial divisions.

Center for Equal Opportunity
http://www.ceousa.org/
A conservative organization for the promotion of "colorblind" public policies, the Center for Equal Opportunity concentrates on the issues of racial

preferences, immigration, and multicultural education; its site provides commentary and extensive access to articles and links on these issues.

National Association for the Advancement of Colored People
http://www.naacp.org/
The nation's oldest civil rights organization's official site provides commentary on current civil rights controversies and offers research tools.

American Civil Liberties Union
http://www.aclu.org/issues/racial/hmre.html
The site of a section of the ACLU that focuses on race relations and civil rights; it provides current news and extensive research tools and links.

Public Opinion: Ignorant or Wise?

Is public opinion too weak or too powerful in the United States today? Two centuries ago, some politicians were frankly elitist in their answers to this perennial question of democracy. Alexander Hamilton called opinion "a great beast." He warned stalwart political leaders to stand up against its impulsive passions and brute ignorance. Modern politicians today would never voice such sentiments openly. From beast, public opinion has seemingly moved to revered icon.

In Hamilton's time, public opinion was most often expressed through speeches, demonstrations, marches, and pamphlets. Nowadays, all these still count. Yet in the last half-century, the development of professional public opinion surveys, focus groups, and other means of testing the public's views have become commonplace. Most surveys are quickly employed by politicians and various advocacy groups to gain advantage or to plot strategy. Public opinion, in this sense, deeply matters. President Clinton's high popularity ratings throughout his 1998–99 impeachment and trial were probably responsible for his ability to remain in office. In early 2000, George W. Bush had already amassed an incredible $70 million in his fight for the Republican nomination; much of the money came in due to the sense that public opinion, even before a formal vote, had crowned him as the most likely nominee.

For any democrat, public opinion's power should be less feared than welcomed. At least in theory, government by public opinion means that the philosophies, attitudes, and policy preferences of ordinary citizens generally rule.

Yet despite its apparent power in specific circumstances, does public opinion really shape government policies all that much? The effect of public opinion depends not just on poll numbers but also on who is active and who is not. A majority of adults don't vote; politicians and candidates are much more likely to respond to those who do participate. Among those who do vote, some have louder voices than others, due either to their access to the media or to the amount of money they contribute to candidates and parties. Nonvoting and inequality of political resources mean that some people's opinions are more important than others.

Public opinion's effects are limited by a second factor. What if opinion is created or unduly influenced by elite media corporations or government, institutions with already disproportionate powers? What if the information necessary to make judgments is systematically limited? And what if, as Hamilton feared, public opinion is constantly changing and lacks consistency and foundation? And what if on most matters, public opinion is silent, contradictory, ignorant, or all three?

Asking and answering these questions forms the contours of the democratic debate. Elite democrats begin with certain assumptions about the nature of the mass public. They argue, much like modern Hamiltonians, that public opinion is largely ignorant, because most people just don't care or know much about public affairs. Moreover, the world has become more complex: ordinary citizens can't be expected to make informed judgments on complicated matters like the shape of trade policy, the appropriate interest rate charged by the Fed, or the amount of dioxin permissible in the water supply. These questions are best left to informed experts.

There is much evidence to support the idea that ordinary citizens know very little about the details of public policies, especially foreign affairs. Most people can't name their senators, draw a blank when asked to name the Chief Justice of the United States, and point to Hungary when asked to identify Serbia on a world map. Low knowledge about facts may or may not lead to skepticism about the public's ability to judge public policies, however.

Popular democrats concede that the mass public is often ignorant and confused about the details of public policies and questions. Yet they tend to attribute this to elite institutions that either mislead the public or keep it ignorant by design or for profit.

The drawn out Vietnam War provides a classic example of how government lying and media complacency creates docile public opinion. The U.S. bombing of North Vietnam in 1964 received widespread support in public opinion polls, but it was based on what turned out to be a government lie disseminated without investigation by the U.S. media. The pretext for U.S. escalation of the war was a supposed North Vietnamese attack on a U.S. destroyer in international waters; it turns out either that this attack didn't occur at all or that, if it did, it was within Vietnam's territorial waters.

Popular democrats point out that the public gradually became quite educated about the Vietnam War, so much so that by the late 1960s and early 1970s it was prepared to dissent from official U.S. policy. The indispensible prerequisites for rational public opinion were a wide range of sources and time in which to judge.

More recently, public opinion has helped to keep public campaign finance reform on the political agenda, even though most politicians and the media either don't like to talk about it or see it as an issue that bores the public. For popular democrats, this shows that public opinion can be informed and rational, at least when it is given the tools and time to make reasoned judgments.

The two essays that follow join the democratic debate by providing strong arguments for both positions. The late Robert Nisbet, a renowned conservative essayist, makes the classic case for limiting the impact of modern public opinion. Nisbet argues that under modern and complex conditions, the public can't reason and resembles a "sandheap given quick and passing shape by whatever winds may be blowing through."

Political scientists Benjamin Page and Robert Shapiro argue for an essentially rational public. Studying public opinion as it develops over time, they find that it changes gradually, usually in reasonable response to events and to new information that becomes publicized. While the public may not know many facts about public life, it does think seriously about basic directions and philosophies in public life. When the public is misled by the media or by the government, Page and Shapiro argue that it is a reflection not of stupidity but of the elite power of the experts Nisbet tends to praise. Their essay is excerpted from the final chapter of a large study.

While reading these two essays, consider the following: Why does Nisbet distrust polls while Page and Shapiro readily use them? What are the advantages and pitfalls of using polls to discern public opinion? Are there other ways of telling what the public is thinking? How might the growing concentration of ownership in the media affect the arguments of both essayists? Do you think that there is a difference between "popular" opinion and "public" opinion, or is this a distinction without a difference?

Public Opinion Versus Popular Opinion

ROBERT NISBET

O f all the heresies afloat in modern democracy, none is greater, more steeped in intellectual confusion, and potentially more destructive of proper governmental function than that which declares the legitimacy of government to be directly proportional to its roots in public opinion—or, more accurately, in what the daily polls and surveys assure us is public opinion. It is this heresy that accounts for the constantly augmenting propaganda that issues forth from all government agencies today—the inevitable effort to shape the very opinion that is being so assiduously courted—and for the frequent craven abdication of the responsibilities of office in the face of some real or imagined expression of opinion by the electorate.

Even worse is the manifest decline in confidence in elected government in the Western democracies, at all levels, and with this decline the erosion of governmental authority in areas where it is indispensable: foreign policy, the military, fiscal stability, and the preservation of law and order. For, as a moment's thought tells us, it is impossible for any government—consisting, after all, of those supposed to lead—to command respect and allegiance very long if it degrades its representative function through incessant inquiry into, and virtual abdication before, what is solemnly declared to be "the will of the people." But what is thought or cynically announced to be the will of the people so often turns out to be no more than the opinion of special-interest advocates skilled in the techniques of contrived populism—a point I shall return to later.[1]

The important point is that from the time representative government made its historic appearance in the 18th century, its success and possibility of survival have been seen by its principal philosophers and statesmen to depend upon a sharp distinction between representative government proper and the kind of government that becomes obedient to eruptions of popular opinion, real or false. This was of course the subject of one of Edmund Burke's greatest documents, his *Letter to the Sheriffs of Bristol*, in which he declared that those who govern, once elected, are responsible

---

1. Populism is a system of democratic thought that attacks concentrations of power in elites of any kind.

only to their own judgments, not those of the electors.[2] Across the Atlantic an almost identical position was taken by the authors of *The Federalist* and by others arguing for acceptance of the Constitution.[3] . . .

That a just government should rest upon the consent of the governed assuredly is as true today as it was when the Declaration of Independence was signed. Equally true is the principle that the people, when properly consulted, remain the most trustworthy source of that underlying and continuing wisdom needed when great choices have to be made—above all, choices of those representatives capable of providing leadership in political matters. But to move from these truths to the position that is now becoming so widely accepted, that opinion—of the kind that can be instantly ascertained by any poll or survey—must somehow govern, must therefore be incessantly studied, courted, flattered, and drawn upon in lieu of the judgment which true leadership alone is qualified to make in the operating details of government—this is the great heresy, and also the "fatal malady" (as Walter Lippmann called it) of modern democracies.[4]

It is worse than heresy. It is fatuous. For always present is the assumption—nowhere propagated more assiduously than by the media which thrive on it—that there really *is* a genuine public opinion at any given moment on whatever issue may be ascendant on the national or the international scene, and that, beyond this, we know exactly how to discover this opinion. But in truth there isn't, and we don't. . . .

I do not question the fact that there is in fact public opinion and that, in the modern age at least, free, democratic government must be anchored in public opinion. There is, though, as a little reflection tells us, a substantial and crucial difference between *public* opinion, properly so called, and what, following ample precedent, I shall call *popular* opinion. The difference between the two types of opinion is directly related to the differences between the collective bodies involved. Fundamentally, this is the difference between organized community on the one hand and the mass or crowd on the other.

Communities and Transitory Majorities

A true public . . . is at bottom a community: built, like all forms of community, around certain ends held in common and also around acceptance of the means proper to achievement of these ends. Not the people in their nu-

---

2. Edmund Burke was a British parliamentarian and conservative thinker, an advocate of tradition and ordered change against the claims of democratic revolutionaries, like those in France during the time he wrote.
3. *The Federalist* contains the most articulate defenses of the U.S. Constitution, written by John Jay, James Madison, and Alexander Hamilton in 1788.
4. Walter Lippmann was a prominent U.S. intellectual of the early to mid-twentieth century. He wrote skeptically about the wisdom of public opinion in the modern communications age.

merical total, not a majority, nor any minority as such represents public opinion if the individuals involved do not form some kind of community, by virtue of possessing common ends, purposes, and rules of procedure. Public opinion is given its character by genuine consensus, by unifying tradition, and by what Edmund Burke called "constitutional spirit."

Popular opinion is by contrast shallow of root, a creature of the mere aggregate or crowd, rooted in fashion or fad and subject to caprice and whim, easily if tenuously formed around a single issue or personage, and lacking the kind of cement that time, tradition, and convention alone can provide. Popular opinion is an emanation of what is scarcely more than the crowd or mass, of a sandheap given quick and passing shape by whatever winds may be blowing through the marketplace at any given time. It would be incorrect to say that popular and public opinion are totally unconnected. What proves to be public opinion in a community is commonly generated by popular opinion, whether in majority or minority form; but it is only through a process of adaptation or assimilation—by the habits, values, conventions, and codes which form the fabric of the political community—that popular opinion ever becomes what we are entitled to call public opinion, the opinion that is in fact more than opinion, that is at bottom a very reflection of national character.

The distinction I am making may seem abstract to some, but it is a very real distinction and it has been so regarded by a long line of observers and students of government beginning in this country with the Founding Fathers, most profoundly with the authors of *The Federalist*. Few things seem to have mattered more to the architects of the American political community than that government should rest upon public opinion, upon public consent and affirmation. But in reading the key writings of that age, we are struck repeatedly by the seriousness of the thought that was given to the true nature of the public and the means proper to the eliciting from this public the will that would be most faithful to the actual character of the public, the character manifest in the people conceived as community—or rather as a community of smaller communities—rather than as mere mass or multitude brought into precarious and short-lived existence by some galvanizing issue or personality.

Hence the strong emphasis in the Constitution and in *The Federalist* upon the whole set of means whereby government, without being in any way severed from the will of the people, would respond to this will only as it had become refined through subjection to constitutional processes. Behind the pervasive emphasis in the Constitution upon principles of check and balance, division of power, and intermediate levels of government and administration ascending from local community through the states to the national government . . . lay a deep distrust of the human mind, of human nature, when it had become wrenched from the social contexts which alone can provide discipline and stability, which alone can put chains upon human appetites and make possible a liberty that does not degenerate into license.

There was, in short, no want of respect among the Founding Fathers for the wisdom of the people as the sole basis of legitimate, constitutional government. Neither, however, was there any want of recognition of the ease with which any community or society can become dissolved into, in Burke's words, "an unsocial, uncivil, unconnected chaos," with destructive passion dominant where restraint and principle ordinarily prevail. There were few if any illusions present in the minds of those responsible for the American Constitution concerning any native and incorruptible goodness of human nature or any instinctual enlightenment of the people considered abstractly. . . . From *The Federalist* through the works of such profound interpreters of the American political scene as Tocqueville, down to the writings in our own time of . . . Walter Lippmann, there is a vivid and continuing awareness of the importance of the difference I have just described: the difference between public and mere aggregate, between the people as organized by convention and tradition into a community and the people as but a multitude, and between public opinion properly termed and opinion that is at best but a reflection of transitory majorities.[5] It is this awareness, forming one of the most luminous intellectual traditions in American political thought, that I shall be concerned with in what follows. . . .

Federalist Trust and Distrust

. . . There is, I think, no better single insight into the *Federalist* view of the role of public opinion in government than that afforded by Number 49 of the papers. Here Madison addresses himself respectfully but negatively to the proposal, made by Jefferson, that "whenever any two of the three branches of government shall concur in opinion, each by the voices of two thirds of their whole number, that a convention is necessary for altering the constitution, or *correcting breaches of it,* a convention shall be called for the purpose."

Madison allows that there is great force in Jefferson's reasoning and that "a constitutional road to the decision of the people ought to be marked out and kept open, for certain great and extraordinary occasions." There are nevertheless, Madison writes, "insuperable objections" to Jefferson's proposal, and it is in the careful, restrained, but none the less powerful outlining of these that we acquire our clearest sense of the *Federalist* position concerning popular or public opinion.

In the first place, Madison writes, "every appeal to the people would carry an implication of some defect in the government" and "frequent appeals would deprive the government of that veneration which time bestows on everything, and without which perhaps the wisest and freest govern-

---

5. Alexis de Tocqueville was a French aristocrat who toured the United States in the 1830s. He wrote the now classic *Democracy in America* after his visit. This book argued that the "tyranny of the majority" was the biggest threat to liberty in a democracy.

ments would not possess the requisite stability." What follows these words is central to Madison's argument and indeed to his entire political theory:

> If it be true that all governments rest on opinion, it is no less true that the strength of opinion in each individual, and its practical influence on his conduct, depend much on the number which he supposes to have entertained the same opinion. The reason of man, like man himself, is timid and cautious when left alone, and acquires firmness and confidence in proportion to the number with which it is associated. . . . In a nation of philosophers, this consideration ought to be disregarded. A reverence for the laws would be sufficiently inculcated by the voice of an enlightened reason. But a nation of philosophers is as little to be expected as the philosophical race of kings wished for by Plato. . . .

But the greatest danger Madison foresees in any elevation of the popular will through frequent recourse to it on matters best left to the government is the unhealthy increase in legislative power, at the expense of executive and judiciary, that would inevitably follow habitual references to the people of matters of state. The legislators, Madison observes, have, by virtue of their number and their distribution in the country, as well as their "connections of blood, of friendship, and of acquaintance," a natural strength that neither the executive nor the judiciary can match. . . . But, he continues, even if on occasion this proved not to be the case—if, for example, the "executive power might be in the hands of a peculiar favorite of the people"—the upshot of any soliciting of popular opinion would undoubtedly be baneful. For, irrespective of where power might lie in the result, the matter would eventually turn upon not rational consideration but emotions and passions. "The *passions*," therefore, not the *reason*, of the public would sit in judgment." . . .

Diversity and Representative Government

. . . There are, as Madison and also Hamilton make plain, contexts in which reason and common sense will tend to come to the surface, but there are also contexts in which sheer emotions or, as Madison has it, passions dominate at the expense of rational thought. Everything possible, therefore, must be done to confine deliberations on government to the former contexts and to rely upon the vital principle of division of governmental power, of checks and balances, to maintain stability and freedom alike— hence the *Federalist* apprehensions concerning too easy, too frequent, and too regular submission of issues to the people.

It is impossible to catch the flavor of the political theory in *The Federalist*, and particularly its conception of the proper role of public opinion in government, without clearly understanding the view of human nature that was taken by Hamilton and his fellow authors. Here is no Rousseauan-romantic view of man born free and good, corrupted by institutions.[6] On the contrary, what *The Federalist* offers us is a design of government for human beings who on occasion may be good, but who on occasion may also be evil, and for whom liberation from such institutions as family, local community, church, and government could only result in anarchy that must shortly lead to complete despotism. . . . Strains will exist, are bound to exist, so long as man remains what he is, invariably a compound of the good and the bad. One would look in vain for a spirit of pessimism or misanthropy in *The Federalist*. Its authors do not hate vices; they only recognize them. Edmund Burke, in his *Reflections on the Revolution in France,* would write of the French Revolutionists: "By hating vices too much, they come to love men too little." That can scarcely be said of the authors of *The Federalist.* The aim of government, free government, is simply that of providing institutions so strong, and also in such an equilibrial relationship, that neither calculated evil nor misspent goodness flowing from human nature could easily weaken or destroy them. . . .

The Federalist recognizes the inevitability of such factions and associations, with Madison declaring that "the latent causes of faction are . . . sown into the nature of man; and we see them everywhere brought into different degrees of activity, according to the different circumstances of civil society." There is to be expected a "landed interest," a "manufacturing interest," a "moneyed interest," and the like. Creditors and debtors, with their inevitably divergent interests, will always be with us. What Madison writes is: "The regulation of these various and interfering interests forms the principal task of modern legislation, and involves the spirit of party and faction in the necessary and ordinary operations of the government."

It is this recognition of the intrinsic and ineradicable diversity of the social and economic orders, of the pluralism of society, that leads the authors of *The Federalist* to their striking emphasis on *representative* institutions.[7] Direct democracy is as foreign to the spirit of *The Federalist* as it is to the Constitution. . . .

Tocqueville and the Tyranny of the Majority

. . . There is a fundamental likeness between *The Federalist* and *Democracy in America* on the role of public opinion and on the dangers which lie in direct, popular government unmediated by the representative, deliberative bodies prescribed by the Constitution. Nearly a half-century separates the America of *The Federalist* papers from the America Tocqueville and his friend Beaumont visited in 1831. Great changes had taken place. What had been prospect for

---

6. Jean-Jacques Rousseau, a French-Swiss eighteenth-century democratic philosopher, claimed that monarchies and aristocracies violated human nature. He argued forcefully for strong, local democracies in which a "general will" could be formed.
7. Pluralism is a political theory that views democracy as characterized by the ability to disperse political power among many competing interest groups.

the Founding Fathers was by now reality, and as Tocqueville's *Notebooks* make clear, there was not the slightest doubt among the Americans he talked with that America's future was a secure one. . . . And yet, hovering over all of Tocqueville's impressions and reflections on the American scene, is his concern with, his apprehensions about, the power exerted by the majority in American society, the fetters which he thought were placed upon genuine individuality by public or majority opinion.

Nowhere, he writes, does public opinion rule as in the United States. . . .

Individuality and American Society

It is in this context that Tocqueville utters one of his most frequently quoted observations: "I know of no country in which there is so little independence of mind and real freedom of discussion as in America." So great, he thought, was the influence of the majority's opinion upon the individual mind that the number of genuinely great or creative human beings was bound to diminish in the ages ahead. The first great generation of political leaders in the United States had, after all, been a product of different, even aristocratic, contexts. Moreover, "public opinion then served, not to tyrannize over, but to direct the exertions of individuals." Very different, Tocqueville thinks, are present circumstances. "In that immense crowd which throngs the avenues to power in the United States, I found very few men who displayed that manly candor and masculine independence of opinion which frequently distinguished the Americans of former times, and which constitutes the leading feature in distinguished characters wherever they may be found."

The effect of the majority is not merely to tyrannize the individual but also to diminish him. In the presence of the majority, Tocqueville observes, the individual "is overwhelmed by the feeling of his own insignificance and impotence." From the *Notebooks* it is evident that Tocqueville was genuinely distressed by his own observations, and by what was reported to him, of instances in which individual dissent, . . . even though protected thoroughly by law, could be stifled by majority opinion. He refers to "the fury of the public" directed at a man in Baltimore who happened to oppose the War of 1812, and there is a long account of an interview with a white American (the gist of which went into a footnote in *Democracy in America*) on the failure of black freedmen in a Northern city to vote in a given election—the upshot of which, Tocqueville concludes, is that although the laws permit, majority opinion deprives. The majority thus claims the right of making the laws and of breaking them as well: "If ever the free institutions of America are destroyed, that event may be attributed to the omnipotence of the majority, which may at some future time urge the minorities to desperation and oblige them to have recourse to physical force. Anarchy will then be the result, but it will have been brought about by despotism."

Immediately after this passage comes a long, fully appreciative, and re-spectful quotation from Madison's Number 51 of *The Federalist,* in which the argument is that while it is of great importance to guard a society against the oppression of its rulers, it is equally important to "guard one part of the society against the injustice of the other part."

And yet, with all emphasis upon Tocqueville's apprehensions concern-ing individuality and freedom in American society as the result of majority opinion, we are also obliged to emphasize the sections of his work which deal with "the causes which mitigate the tyranny of the majority in the United States." He cites the absence of centralized administration, the pres-ence of the frontier which made it possible for individuals to escape the conformities pressed upon them, the still-vigorous regionalism and localism of American society, the checks which executive and judiciary exert upon the majority-dominated Congress, the ascendancy of the legal profession, the institution of trial by jury, and, in many ways most important for Tocque-ville, the unlimited freedom of association. The latter, both in its political form of party and its civil form of interest-group, can be counted upon, Tocqueville thinks, so long as the principle remains vital, to protect indi-viduals from the majority and the kind of government majorities seek to create. . . .

. . . Hamilton and Madison knew, as did Tocqueville, that language as often conceals as it communicates. Hence the untrustworthiness, or at least the precariousness, of verbalized responses to verbalized questions concern-ing matters of profoundest moral, social, and political significance. We have all been struck by the shifting character of response to persisting issues as revealed in polls. But without trying to consecrate *public* opinion, I think it is fair to say that this shifting, kaleidoscopic character is in fact one aspect of *popular* opinion, as mercurial in nature as the fashions, fads, and foibles which compose it. By the very virtue of its superficiality, its topical and *ad hoc* character, popular opinion lends itself to facile expression, in the polls as well as in drawing rooms and taverns, and hence, as is the case with all fashions, to quick and often contradictory change. Very different is public opinion: It changes, to be sure, as the history of the great moral and politi-cal issues in America and other nations makes evident. But change in public opinion tends to be slow, often agonizing, and—in the deepest realms of conviction—rare. The greatest political leaders in history have known this; hence their success in enterprises which, on the basis of soundings of merely popular opinion, might have seemed suicidal.

"Public Interest Populism"

It is the ease with which popular opinion can be confused with public opin-ion that accounts in substantial degree for not only the polls in American public life but also the great power of the media. The impact, the frequently determining influence of television commentators, newspaper editors, reporters, and columnists upon individual opinions is not to be doubted. In the scores of topics and issues dealt with by the media daily, the shaping, or at least conditioning, effect of the media is apparent, certainly so far as popular opinion is concerned. In this fact lies, however, a consequence that would not, a couple of decades ago, have been anticipated by very many makers of opinion in America: the rising disaffection with, even hatred of, the media in public quarters where, though the matter may not be given verbal articulation, it is believed that the media are flouting, not reflecting, *public* opinion. . . .

There is also what Irving Kristol has admirably described as "public interest populism," a phenomenon also, I suggest, to be accounted for in terms of popular opinion.[8] Such populism can, as we have learned, be utterly at odds with the sentiments of large majorities, and yet, through the always available channels of popular opinion—newspapers and television, preeminently—take on striking force in the shaping of public policy. . . . Given, however, the variety and ingenuity of means whereby a popular opinion can be created overnight, given credence by editorial writers, columnists, and television commentators, and acquire the position of a kind of superstructure over genuine public opinion, it has not proved very difficult for a point of view to assume a degree of political strength that scarcely would have been possible before the advent of the media in their present enormous power. . . .

It is useful to conclude this essay by reference to a work that deserved better than its fate in the hands of most of its reviewers when it was published in 1955: Lippmann's *The Public Philosophy.* . . .

"The people," Lippmann writes in words reminiscent of the apprehensions of *The Federalist,* "have acquired power which they are incapable of exercising, and the governments they elect have lost powers which they must recover if they are to govern." What, we ask, are the legitimate boundaries of the people's power? Again it could be Hamilton or Madison rather than Lippmann responding: "The answer cannot be simple. But for a rough beginning let us say that the people are able to give, and to withhold, their consent to being governed—their consent to what the government asks of them, proposes to them, and has done in the conduct of their affairs. They can elect the government. They can remove it. They can approve or disapprove of its performance. But they cannot administer the government. They cannot themselves perform."

Lippmann draws a distinction respecting the public, or people, that has been present in Western thought since the very beginning of the tradition I have been concerned with. It is the distinction between the people as mere multitude or mass, a sandheap of electoral particles, and, to use Lippmann's phrasing, "*The People* as a historic community." . . .

---

8. Irving Kristol is a contemporary conservative thinker who argues for the moral and political superiority of the capitalist system and its compatibility with democracy and liberty.

In politics as in religion and elsewhere, many a leader has at times justified arbitrary and harsh rule by recourse to something along the line of what Lippmann calls *"The People,"* the people, that is, as a historic, tradition-anchored, and "corporate" nation rather than as the whole or a majority of actual, living voters.[9] None of this is to be doubted. And yet, however difficult to phrase, however ambiguous in concrete circumstance, the distinction may be—it is, I would argue—a vital one if, on the one hand, liberty is to be made secure and, on the other hand, the just authority of government is to be made equally secure.

In truth, Lippmann's distinction is but a restatement of the core of an intellectual tradition going back at very least to Burke's famous description of political society as a contract between the dead, the living, and the unborn. That description too was capable . . . of being pilloried and mocked, of being declared a mere verbal mask for opposition to all change or a rationalization of government policy flouting the interests of the governed. And yet it is, as is Lippmann's, a valid, even vital, distinction, one that lies at the heart of a philosophy—so often termed "conservative," though it is in fact liberal—which in the 20th century, under whatever name, we have discovered to be the only real alternative to the kinds of awful power which are contained in "people's governments" or are, in our own country, hinted at in declared programs of "common cause" populism. The distinction which Burke and Lippmann make between the two conceptions of "the people" is fundamental in a line of 19th and 20th century thought. . . . Basically, it is a distinction between constituted society and the kind of aggregate that, history tells us, threatens to break through the interstices of the social bond in all times of crisis, the aggregate we call the mass or crowd, always oscillating between anarchic and military forms of despotism.

Paralleling this distinction between the two conceptions of the people is the distinction . . . between public opinion and what I have called popular opinion. The one distinction is as pertinent to present reality as the other. We live, plainly, in a kind of twilight age of government, one in which the loss of confidence in political institutions is matched by the erosion of traditional authority in kinship, locality, culture, language, school, and other elements of the social fabric. The kind of mass populism, tinctured by an incessant search for the redeeming political personage, where militarism and humanitarianism become but two faces of the same coin, and where the quest for centralized power is unremitting, is very much with us. More and more it becomes difficult to determine what is genuinely public opinion, the opinion of the people organized into a constitutional political community, and what is only popular opinion, the kind that is so easily exploited by self-appointed tribunes of the people, by populist demagogues, and by all-too-many agencies of the media. The recovery of true public opinion in our age will not be easy, but along with the recovery of social

---

9. By *corporate,* Nisbet means citizens not as separate individuals but as parts of the nation or of permanent associations like business, labor, or other groups that make up society.

and cultural authority and of the proper authority of political government in the cities and the nation, it is without question among the sovereign necessities of the rest of this century.

Public Opinion Is a Wise Judge

BENJAMIN PAGE AND
ROBERT SHAPIRO

Democracy means that the people—the public—have power. It involves a connection between the policy preferences of citizens, on the one hand, and what their governments do, on the other. . . .

Many influential critiques of the idea of majoritarian democracy . . . and many arguments for restraining or ignoring the views of the general public, are based on alleged incapacities of ordinary citizens. Some critics say that ordinary people lack political information and lack the motivation or the cognitive skills to receive and process such information. They maintain that citizens may, therefore, hold policy preferences that do not correspond to their true values or to the public good, or, indeed, that citizens may have no policy preferences at all. It follows that democracy is unattainable or undesirable.

The evidence here indicates that these critics are wrong. The public, as a collectivity, has the capacity to govern. Any major defects of American democracy are more likely to be found at the elite level.

Here, we will summarize our major findings and discuss what they imply for democratic theory, organizing the discussion around a set of nine propositions. The first four propositions concern the collective capacities of the public. The next five deal with the political information and experience that are provided (or not provided) to citizens in the United States.

The Political Capacity of the Public

1. *Americans' collective policy preferences are real, knowable, differentiated, patterned, and coherent.*[1] [Some scholars] hold that ordinary citizens' policy preferences are unreal, meaningless, or at least unknowable through survey

---

1. *Collective policy preferences* is the authors' term for public opinion taken as a whole, *not* as separate individuals. Particular individuals may not evidence the same coherence as the collective policy preferences of the public.

research. If this were so, then to seek a correspondence between government policies and citizens' preferences would be to seek a will-o'-the-wisp.
Policy cannot respond to what does not exist or cannot be known.

Milder versions of this argument hold that public opinion offers no guidance on specific policy questions, or that it is incoherent or inconsistent. If
public opinion had nothing to say about the concrete issues of the day, or if it
were incoherent or self-contradictory, it might comfortably be ignored.

We have seen, however, that these indictments of public opinion are
not well founded. Despite the evidence that most individual Americans
have only limited knowledge of politics (especially of proper names and
numbers and acronyms), and that individuals' expressions of policy preferences vary markedly and somewhat randomly from one survey to the next,
collective policy preferences have very different properties.

The data we summarize here—the result of our analysis of thousands of
questions asked in national surveys covering a period of more than fifty
years—reveal that collective responses make sense; that they draw fine distinctions among different policies; and that they form meaningful patterns
consistent with a set of underlying beliefs and values. Again and again . . .
we saw that the public makes definite distinctions among policy alternatives: which spending programs to cut and which to increase, under what
conditions to permit legal abortions, when to use U.S. military force abroad,
what civil liberties to ensure for which groups, what kinds of assistance to
provide which allies, and many others. The public's choices among policies
were generally consistent with each other and with broader values, and
were usually maintained over periods of years. . . .

2. *Collective policy preferences are generally stable; they change in understandable, predictable ways.* As we have seen, some of the reasons that the authors of *The Federalist* gave for restraining the popular will—shackling it
with a powerful, indirectly elected president, an independent Senate protected by long terms in office, an appointed judiciary, and the like—had to
do with alleged "temporary errors and delusions," or "fluctuations," or
"transient impulse(s)," or "violent passions" in opinion. . . .

After closely examining hundreds of repeated survey questions, however, we can be sure that Americans' policy preferences do not in fact
change in a capricious or whimsical . . . fashion. . . . The graphs throughout
the book show that collective public opinion about policy is generally quite
stable. It rarely fluctuates. Despite the fact that many of our graphs were
chosen to illustrate exceptionally large and important opinion trends, the
overwhelming impression even from them is one of incremental change.
What the public thinks about a given policy now is a very strong indicator
of what it will think later. . . .

When collective preferences have changed, during the last fifty years,
they have generally done so in predictable and understandable ways. . . .
There have been regular patterns of responses to social and economic
trends, events, and new information. Even abrupt changes in foreign policy
preferences nearly always represent understandable reactions to sudden

events: militant and activist responses to foreign threats, for example, and more peaceful reactions when conditions improve. Opinion does not tend to "snap back" to its earlier state. Any capriciousness of opinion that may have existed in the Founders' time is certainly not common now.

For the most part, the public reacts consistently, in similar ways to similar stimuli. Particularly impressive are the systematic time series results which show regular shifts in policy preferences responding to changes in such objective indicators as rates of unemployment, inflation, and crime.

Short-term movements in public opinion, in fact, can largely be accounted for (and predicted) [by seeing] what news, from what sources, appears in the mass media. The public's reactions are so consistent that more than half the variance in opinion changes can be accounted for in this way. . . .

3. *Citizens are not incapable of knowing their own interests or the public good.* The suggestion that ordinary citizens are simply too ignorant to know their own or their country's interests lies at the heart of many objections to majoritarian democracy. The authors of the *Federalist Papers,* for example, worried not merely that public opinion vacillated but that it erred. . . .

In more recent times, Walter Lippmann . . . issued scathing denunciations of the public's capabilities, maintaining that reality differs sharply from the "stereotypes" or "pictures" in people's heads. Joseph Schumpeter declared that individuals' opinions are not "definite" or "independent" or "rational" and that on most political matters individual volition, command of fact, and method of inference are defective. . . .

Early survey research . . . seemed to bear out these low estimates of public capacity. Surveys indicated that most Americans knew little about politics, cared little, and apparently made their voting decisions on the basis of demographic characteristics or party loyalties, which scholars (perhaps too quickly) took to indicate lack of rational deliberation. . . .

The result was a wholesale revision of democratic theory. Schumpeter's weak procedural definition of democracy, in which elite leadership competes for voters' acquiescence but does not necessarily respond to their policy preferences . . . , influenced more than a generation of scholars. . . . Most of the leaders of the political science and sociology professions rejected majoritarian democracy, embracing some form of pluralistic or "polyarchical" system in which organized interest groups play an important part and in which participation by, and responsiveness to, the general public is limited. . . .

This revisionism mistakenly blamed the citizen victims, ignoring system-level influences upon peoples' behavior (apathy about elections, for example, may result from legal restrictions, repression, or lack of attractive candidates and parties rather than from defects of the citizenry); that it abandoned a worthy normative ideal and turned democratic theory into little more than a conservative ratifier of the status quo; and that it neglected the possibility that broader participation could promote political education and human development.

In particular, we believe that the revisionists misinterpreted survey research results and gave up too quickly on the public. . . .

Our work indicates that *collective* public opinion reflects a considerably higher level of information and sophistication than is apparent at the individual level. . . . In part, it reflects the logic of "information pooling": if each individual has a reasonably good (but very imperfect) chance of judging whether a particular assertion is true—or whether a particular policy will satisfy his or her interests or the common good—then, by simple operation of the laws of probability, a majority of independently judging individuals has a much higher probability of being right. . . . And, in substantial part, collective wisdom results from collective deliberation based on a division of labor. For all these reasons, collective public opinion far outshines the opinion of the average individual. It is both an aggregation of many individual opinions and the result of a process in which many individuals interact.

The role of collective deliberation also helps explain why . . . citizens' preferences reflect not only personal and group self-interest but also concerns for the common good at a national level.

Our research has led us to a view of collective public opinion that justifies the use of terms like "reasonable," "responsible," and "rational." Without claiming that we have any unique knowledge of what people's true interests are, we are convinced by the general stability, differentiation, and coherent patterning of collective policy preferences, and by their responsiveness to new situations and new information, that characterizations of public opinion as ignorant fall very wide of the mark. We do not know who is better able to judge the public interest than the public itself. Any alternative invites minority tyranny.

4. *The public generally reacts to new situations and new information in sensible, reasonable ways.* (Note that this refers to something more than the "predictable," "understandable" responses of proposition 2.) Some critiques of democracies as "ungovernable" . . . have suggested that the public cannot keep up with the complexity of an ever-changing world. Much the same theme animated Walter Lippmann's final . . . fulmination against the public, in which he argued that the liberal democracies were paralyzed with regard to the great questions of war and peace because of the "derangement" of pressure from public opinion, which not only compulsively made mistakes and was easily deceived but was too slow to react.

Our data provide little or no evidence that the American public has failed in this fashion, during Lippmann's 1950s . . . or any other time. Collective opinion has responded rapidly and in sensible ways (given the information provided) to international events, wars, and crises as well as to more subtle gradual trends in technology, the economy, and society. When there has been less money to spend, the public has been less eager to spend, and when more, more. The *consistent* responses mentioned in connection with proposition 2 have also been *reasonable:* seeking harsher court treatment of criminals when crime is a more severe problem, wanting to try wage and price controls when inflation is rampant, favoring more spending on employment policies when unemployment is high. . . .

Taking our first four propositions together, then, we see the public—at least the twentieth-century U.S. public—as considerably more *capable* and *competent* than critics of majoritarian democracy would have us believe.[2] Most of the excuses for why public opinion can be ignored, why government ought not to respond to it, have little merit.

Whether or not the public's capacities are completely realized, however—and, therefore, whether or not majoritarian democracy fully lives up to its potential—depends in part upon the political environment in which citizens find themselves, especially upon what opportunities for political learning and what quality of political information are provided to them by what we can call the "information system."

If a society provides accurate, helpful information about public policy; if it offers moral leadership, encourages participation, and in a broad sense educates its citizenry, then there is every reason to expect that citizens will rise to the occasion and democracy will flourish. If, on the other hand, the system minimizes public participation, or obscures policy-making processes so that unpopular government actions go undetected, then democratic control will be diminished, no matter how competent the public. If politicians or others regularly deceive and mislead the public, if they manipulate citizens' policy preferences so as to betray their interests and values, democracy may be a sham. Responsiveness to manipulated preferences is nothing to celebrate. Our next set of propositions, therefore, concerns how well the information system serves the public.

The Information System and Democracy

Our findings also . . . suggest that there is more reason to worry about the quality of the information system—that is, about the institutions and structures and activities at the elite level that produce and disseminate political information—than about the capacity of ordinary citizens. That is, defects in American democracy may be more the fault of elites than the public.

5. *Collective deliberation often works well.* The *Federalist Papers* argued that the "cool and deliberate sense of the community" ought ultimately to prevail in government. We agree. Democracy is most appealing if the majority's preferences are informed through public reflection, debate, and discussion, making use of a system of research and expertise. . . .

---

2. Majoritarian democracy is a kind of democracy in which the majority rules on most, if not all, important questions. Majoritarian democracy is opposed to a kind of democracy in which minorities of various kinds and individuals are afforded special protections against government power and majority will.

Does there exist in the United States a system of deliberation sufficient to ensure that the public's policy preferences embody the "cool and deliberate sense of the community"? We think the answer, generally speaking, is "yes." Certainly an elaborate system exists by which policy-relevant research is conducted and then publicized through testimony, books, articles, and debates by experts, commentators, and political leaders. The thrust of such debates tends eventually to reach the public through the media of mass communications, especially . . . by means of editorial commentary and the reporting of experts' statements. Political conversations among ordinary citizens and their friends, family members, and coworkers further refine, interpret, and disseminate political information. . . .

The process of collective deliberation . . . takes advantage of a division of labor among experts, commentators, communicators, cue givers, and attentive citizens. It is also, for the most part, pluralistic and decentralized (though this is less true of foreign policy matters than domestic). Ordinary citizens need not master the intricacies of policy analysis but can get the general drift by knowing whom to trust for a reliable conclusion—assuming, of course, that trustworthy cue givers are available.

Thus, by the time national polls are taken, public opinion has often been "refined and enlarged" through public debate. The system of collective deliberation could certainly be improved upon, as we will argue below. But it already works well enough to produce generally well-informed collective public opinion that responds to changing realities and new information, as our survey data reveal.

6. *Political education in the United States could be improved.* A judgment concerning whether political education in the United States is adequate must depend heavily upon evidence outside our scope, and upon choice of a standard of adequacy, but undoubtedly there is much room for improvement.

A number of democratic theorists have taken education of one sort or another—if not the acquisition of large amounts of information, then at least the sharpening of cognitive skills and the ability to evaluate public debate, or the development of good moral character—as a crucial prerequisite, concomitant, and/or consequence of popular rule. . . .

Thomas Jefferson, America's quintessential democrat, put a heavy emphasis on the need for universal public schooling, which he actively promoted, and for informative political debate through free and diverse newspapers.

Perhaps the most important recent voice on this subject is that of John Dewey, whose own philosophy of formal education, advocating active experience to develop capacities for thinking and reflection, was aimed at training citizens for democracy[3] . . . Dewey saw inquiry and communica-

---

3. John Dewey was a prominent twentieth century U.S. philosopher, who believed that it would be possible to create a "Great Community" of thinking and participating citizens. He proposed many educational reforms that would nurture popular democracy.

tion as the keys to the functioning of democracy, as ways to make consequences known, and to create an "organized, articulate Public." . . . Dewey
also wrote of democracy as the "truly human way of living," saying that the
participation of all is necessary not only for the social welfare but to develop human beings as individuals. Human intelligence, together with
pooled and cooperative experience, . . . produces the knowledge and wisdom needed for collective action. . . .

Education involves learning and instruction of many sorts, having to
do with facts, causal connections and interpretations, cognitive skills, moral
reasoning; it involves many individuals and institutions—families, schools,
workplaces, associations, political leadership, the mass media, and direct
participation in politics. It would not be easy for us to evaluate the American system of political education as a whole, particularly those parts of it we
have not studied directly.

What is most apparent from our work is that education does not fail
completely; in fact, it has been quite successful, in the sense that collective
public opinion does display considerable sophistication. . . . At the same
time, however, one can imagine a much higher level of political teaching.
The schools' treatment of public policy tends to be skimpy and bland. Political figures, facing electoral incentives to be ambiguous, seldom offer serious analyses of policy; they often rely on images and so-called sound bites.
Political parties fall short of the . . . ideal . . . when they are engaged in collusive ("bipartisan") policy-making or are both financed by the same special
interests. Journalism often fails to probe beneath the surface of events and
does not cover some issues at all. On many issues, neither experts nor
would-be leaders of mass movements speak clearly to the public.

Perhaps the most conspicuous deficiency is the lack of opportunity for
political learning through direct participation. In a country where only
about half the eligible citizens vote in presidential elections, where town
meetings are rare, where most workplaces are hierarchical, and where most
citizens are not mobilized by a congenial issue-oriented party or political
group, the educational potential of participation is not fully realized. . . .

In short, we see considerable room for more and better political information, more moral leadership, and more mobilization and organization of
the public for participation.

7. *Lack of available information may permit government nonresponsiveness
to public opinion.* Research by ourselves and others indicates that governmental responsiveness to public opinion is substantial but imperfect; policy
tends to be out of harmony with what the public wants roughly one-third
of the time . . . , a significant proportion. Though evidence on the matter is
limited, there are indications that government responsiveness is weaker
when public information, and hence salience and attention, are low. . . .
The level of information, then, may be an important determinant of how
well the public can control government.

The point is not merely that the public doesn't care about some issues
or is inattentive. Rather the *availability* of key facts about certain public
policies may be low, for reasons of chance or design; the public may have

no way . . . to know what is going on—to know whether or not the government is doing what the citizenry wants, for example—and may, therefore, have no way to enforce its will and ensure responsiveness.

A number of scholars and observers have concluded that lack of available information does often give elites leeway to act in unpopular ways. . . .

We do not know exactly how often these sorts of concealment or deception occur. But there does seem to be substantial slippage in democratic responsiveness, a substantial discrepancy between what citizens want and what the government does, which may result from a dim spotlight that does not direct public attention to unpopular policies—especially when there is bipartisan collusion of the sorts we have already alluded to, and when few or no dissenting elite voices speak up. (The savings and loan debacle of the 1980s comes to mind.)

8. *Elites sometimes mislead the public or manipulate its policy preferences.* Opinion manipulation, as we have said, is a crucial matter for democratic theory. If . . . elites create or influence the very wants of the public . . . preferences are "circular," with businessmen and politicians and others strongly affecting what the public wants; and if elite influence is exerted in such a way as to lead people astray from their own true interests and values, then the most responsive political machinery in the world will not produce democratic outcomes.

To be sure, this subject is full of difficulties, and our own work on it is neither complete nor conclusive. But some of the instances and patterns examined in this book have disturbing implications. The historical record indicates that government officials often mislead and sometimes lie, particularly in foreign affairs, where government control of information is great. Opposing countries and movements are commonly portrayed as aggressive and evil (and U.S. government actions as benevolent), for example, regardless of the facts, in order to mobilize public support for official policies. This tendency is not unique to the United States; it may result from the nation-state system, which gives every country's officials both the tools and the incentives to mislead their citizenry for the sake of their own power and the projection of national influence. That is, the nation-state system enables elites to create "national interests" that may diverge from what national populations would want if fully informed.

We have suggested that the information presented to the public through the mass media has certain persistent biases, slants, or value tendencies that may distort the public's picture of the world and lead its policy preferences astray. These tendencies may result from the nation-state system and official control of information, as described above. They may also reflect such factors as the capitalist character of the economy, which ensures that many powerful voices will support capitalism and oppose communism or socialism in the United States and abroad; the weakness of the American labor movement; journalists' perennial need to rely on official sources; and the tendency for expertise and commentary to change with shifts in party control of government. Hence we find anti-Communist, pro-capitalist, minimal government, pro-incumbent, and partisan biases as well as the pervasive ethnocentric or nationalistic slant.

These informational biases can arise without any government monopoly power or any conspiracy among elites; some of them probably result from the normal operation of a competitive free enterprise system and a free press. Political information is often a public or social good. Information which is of significant but small use to many different people cannot be sold efficiently. . . . Political information of value to millions of citizens, therefore, probably tends to be underproduced, whereas large, organized political actors can find out what they need to know. A large corporation, for example, with extensive resources and a big stake in political action, has a much better chance of learning how a tax bill will affect it than do many unorganized taxpayers with small, diffuse interests that (in the aggregate) add up to a great deal.

Moreover, the producers and transmitters of political information often have corporate or other interests of their own which may influence what they put out to the public. Their financial returns are affected not only by their sales of books and airtime and the like but also by the political impact of the information they disseminate. Corporations fund foundations and think tanks that produce research studies and support the "experts" seen on TV, often, presumably . . . serving corporate purposes. The mass media are mostly owned by large corporations that are distinctly uninterested in undermining the capitalist system, upsetting their own labor relations, or stirring populist tendencies among the citizenry. . . .

The good news, in any case, is that misinformation does not always succeed in actually affecting the public's policy preferences in the intended ways. Public opinion is quite resistant to being led astray, particularly when at least a few elite voices dissent, or when policy preferences are based on personal experience, or when events are inherently easy to understand. We have given several striking examples, including the failure of barrages of publicity in the late 1970s and early 1980s to dislodge Americans from their advocacy of social welfare programs and arms control, or to persuade them to aid the Nicaraguan Contras.[4] . . .

Still, there is reason for concern that democracy in the United States may be undermined to some extent by systematic distortions in the information that is provided to the public.

9. *The "marketplace of ideas" cannot always be counted upon to reveal political truth.* It is a prime tenet of liberal faith that, if all views are permitted free expression, truth will overcome falsehood through a vigorous competition of ideas. . . . Thomas Jefferson in his first inaugural address (1801) referred to "the safety with which error of opinion may be tolerated where

---

4. The U.S.-backed rebels who were attempting to overthrow the Sandinista government in Nicaragua throughout the 1980s. Aid from the United States to the contras divided public opinion in the 1980s.

reason is left free to combat it." . . . And Supreme Court Justice Oliver Wendell Holmes put it in terms of an economic metaphor: "[T]he best test of truth is the power of the thought to get itself accepted in the competition of the market." . . .

Jefferson . . . and Holmes were . . . concerned chiefly with tolerating dissent and avoiding excessive government *restraints* on speech through licensing, censorship, punishment, or the like. Their arguments seem altogether persuasive on that point: society has little to lose from hearing the odd dissenter when he or she is wrong, and much to gain when the dissenter happens to be right. The more general point also has some force: in the long run, no doubt, even under inauspicious circumstances, the truth does tend to win out.

But does it follow that a laissez-faire market in information will provide accurate, unbiased, and accessible political information to ordinary citizens?[5] Our empirical material suggests that, in fact, it does not. There are theoretical reasons for doubt, as well, even beyond the obvious points that the long run can be very long, and that as old lies are exposed new ones can be invented.

In the first place, the logic of a competitive market does not work well in the presence of monopoly or collusion. The market fails, for example, when the government holds centralized control of national security information and uses its control to propagate untruths, or when financial interests convince both parties not to compete with each other and not to reveal uncomfortable political truths.

But the problem goes deeper than that. Even in a perfectly functioning market, production and consumption are, in a sense, dominated by the consumer power of those with the most money and other resources. Thus market forces lead available political information to reflect the needs of the wealthier individuals and organizations. Economic inequality tends to overcome political equality in the information sphere, just as unequal resources to make campaign contributions may offset equal rights to vote. Furthermore . . . markets for political information may be imperfect even absent government monopoly, because of public goods problems which advantage concentrated interests and disadvantage small, diffuse consumers of information. And information producers can reap indirect (political) gains at the expense of the citizenry. For all these reasons, ordinary citizens cannot necessarily count on the market to provide easy access to the useful and correct political information they need.

When it comes to political applications, the "marketplace of ideas" remains little more than an unexamined metaphor. The natural working of free enterprise economics may lead to patterns of misleading political information that distort citizens' policy preferences and political choices.

---

5. Refers to a mass media market in which government has little or no influence and "private," usually corporate-owned, sources of information predominate.

Traditional defenses of free speech—with their emphasis upon freedom from government restraints—tend to neglect the issue of what sorts of institutional arrangements and allocations of economic resources would be necessary for *effective* expression of varying points of view and for a balanced or unbiased political discourse. To provide incentives and opportunities for such discourse might well require active policy interventions.

Improving American Democracy

It is not unusual to hear complaints from both Left and Right that democracy does not work well in the United States. If it does not, our research suggests that the American public should not be blamed. The fault is more likely to lie with officials and elites who fail to respond to the citizenry, and with defects in the system by which the public is provided with political information.

It is simply not the case that the collective policy preferences of the U.S. public are nonexistent, unknowable, capricious, inconsistent, or ignorant. Instead, they are real, meaningful, well measured by polls, differentiated, coherent, and stable. They react understandably and predictably to events and new information. The classic justifications for ignoring public opinion do not hold up. . . .

Thus our research provides little reason for anyone to fear or oppose majoritarian democracy in the United States. There is no need to sneer at politicians who "read the Gallup polls," so long as they do so correctly. In our view, in fact, government should pay more attention to what the public wants. More democratic responsiveness, rather than less, would be all to the good, and institutional changes to that end (reducing the role of money in politics, easing voter registration, strengthening political competition, broadening electoral accountability) should be encouraged.

At the same time, we have suggested that political education—in the broad sense of providing useful political experience and information and moral guidance to the citizenry—is not what it could be; that concealment of (or failure to provide) relevant information sometimes permits government to pursue unpopular policies, outside of public view; and that the public's policy preferences may sometimes be manipulated by deceptive leaders and by flows of information subject to various biases or distortions. . . .

A chief focus for improvement, we believe, should be the political information system. The public deserves better political education, more opportunities for participation, and access to better information about public policy. Thomas Jefferson expressed the point neatly, in a famous passage from his letter of September 28, 1820, to William C. Jarvis:

> I know of no safe depository of the ultimate powers of the society but the people themselves, and if we think them not enlightened enough to exercise their control with a wholesome discretion, the remedy is not to take it from them but to inform their discretion by education.

DISCUSSION QUESTIONS

1. Both essays, but especially Page and Shapiro's, think of modern public opinion as it is expressed through polls and surveys. Yet in recent years, virtually every interest group conducts polls to support its positions, and the findings often contradict each other. Are there other ways of representing public opinion that might be more effective as a guide?

2. Page and Shapiro argue that "any major defects of American democracy are more likely to be found at the elite level." Just how do they define *elite* differently than Nisbet does? Should political leaders simply obey the verdict of public opinion? Under what circumstances should they not do so?

3. The authors of both essays agree that democratic public opinion is constructed on communities and publics rather than on strangers and masses. How does each essay define community and public? Do the authors differ in their definitions?

4. The authors of both essays seem to agree that public opinion doesn't always matter but disagree about whether it should. On which issues and questions does public opinion seem to be informed and reflective? On which less so?

5. By large majorities, Americans seem to favor a more equitable division of wealth and income. Why is it that policymakers can apparently ignore this widespread concern? How would Nisbet and Page and Shapiro account for this weak articulation of the majority view?

SUGGESTED READINGS AND INTERNET RESOURCES

Many prominent scholars paint a diverse portrait of U.S. public opinion in Carol Glynn, ed., *Public Opinion* (New York: HarperCollins, 1999). The classic elite democratic argument for public opinion's defects is Walter Lippmann, *The Phantom Public* (New York: Harcourt, 1925). A contemporary study supporting the low knowledge of most Americans about public affairs is Michael X. Delli Carpini and Scott Keeter, *What Americans Know About Politics* (New Haven, Conn.: Yale University Press, 1996). Riveting case studies of government and corporate manipulation of opinion are contained in Noam Chomsky and Edward Herman, *Manufacturing Consent* (New York: Pantheon, 1988). For provocative accounts of how elites see public opinion, see Susan Herbst, *Reading Public Opinion* (Chicago: University of Chicago Press, 1998). For a comparative perspective on citizenship, see Arthur Lupia and Matthew McCubbins, *Can Citizens Learn?* (New York: Cambridge University Press, 1998).

Public Agenda
www.publicagenda.org
An outstanding source for all kinds of polling data, along with helpful
assessments about how to read surveys and their findings critically.

Pew Research Center for the People and the Press
www.people-press.org
Independent opinion research group that conducts surveys about popular
perceptions of the media, visibility of public policy issues, and public figures.
Pew is known for its in-depth analyses of basic trends in long-term public
opinion.

Gallup Poll
www.gallup.com
The site of the oldest polling organization still going in the United States, with
up-to-date surveys on contemporary issues, both political and social.

Policy.com
www.policy.com
Perhaps the best and most comprehensive site for all political news. Click on
"polling" in the subject column for links to all major national and international
polling organizations.

CHAPTER

The New Media: Corporate Wasteland or Democratic Frontier?

In this information-rich age, the mass media play a crucial and powerful set of roles in our lives. Americans read, watch, use, and listen to the mass media more than at any time in our history. What we know about others, our politics, history, and the issues confronting the country and the world depends more than ever on how all of these matters are presented by the mass media.

The crucial role of a free press is recognized by the Bill of Rights' First Amendment. The founders hoped that the press would use its special protections to educate the public and ferret out facts, opinions, and interpretations that promoted intelligent debate. At the same time, the press is supposed to reflect and express the wide range of interests and views among the citizenry, whatever they may be. For advocates of popular democracy, the media's most important role is that of speaking "truth to power." Taken singly, any media source may be incorrect. But taken together, the media have the important role of presenting different and competing versions of political truth.

Just how well or poorly have the mass media performed these democratic tasks? While we rely on the media more than ever, criticism of television, film, newspapers, and other traditional media sources abounds. The most vocal critics lampoon the media for either liberal or conservative biases. Others accuse the media of crass commercialism and sensationalism in their relentless pursuit of profits. By highlighting dramatic episodes of crime and violence and of spectacular personal scandals, the definition of news has been trivialized.

Pushed to the sidelines are in-depth stories that deal with substantive political issues. Critics charge that the mass media subject all coverage to short-term entertainment values, even as the needs of a democratic society demand that the media express and reflect alternative visions of our present and future.

The drive for big profits, critics charge, accompanies the rise of the new corporate megagiants who control most of the nation's and the world's cable and satellite television, book publishing, films, magazines, and Internet portals. In the 1980s and 1990s, merger frenzy accompanied the growth of technological innovation. Time, Inc., first became Time Warner. It then bought CNN and Turner Broadcasting, and in 2000 merged with America Online to form the largest media company on the planet. General Electric, a major producer of nuclear power plants and military weaponry, owns NBC. Disney purchased ABC, and CBS fell to Viacom with its worldwide video, film, and cable empire. If the media marketplace was producing thousands of new stations and outlets through new communications technology, it was nonetheless a marketplace dominated by fewer and fewer sellers.

Still, the case for a wide and increasingly participatory marketplace seems to be bolstered by the growth of digital communication, and most especially the Internet and World Wide Web. On the Internet, everyone can become a source of information—at least in theory—by building a web page. On the Web and through email, information and opinions travel with the speed of light. Low start-up costs allow millions of people to interchange ideas and information, whether it be to buy or sell or to communicate about politics. Above all, the Internet does provide choice and diversity—unmediated and unfiltered by established organizations, at least if the user so desires.

The two essays excerpted here provide sharply contrasting views about the political and cultural meaning of the Internet and World Wide Web. In the first essay, political scientist Anthony Corrado summarizes the case for the Internet as a tool for increased democracy. Observing the widespread disenchantment of many citizens with politics and the established media, Corrado argues that the emergence of the World Wide Web may provide citizens with a powerful new means of accessing information and influencing politicians. He warns, though, that increased participation through cyberspace may create a "vulgar democracy in which individuals simply pursue their own interests."

Douglas Rushkoff, a New York University professor and a onetime self-proclaimed "cyber optimist," tells a far grimmer tale in his essay. The Web, he claims, has been transformed from an interactive and democratic medium into a "coercive" sales and marketing vehicle for a new generation of megacorporations. Rushkoff argues that the Web, so full of democratic potential, can be revived as a populist medium, but only if new, free, public spaces are wrested from the corporate marketers and established elites who have appropriated it.

While reading these essays, the following questions may be of interest: How would Corrado respond to Rushkoff's charge that the Web has turned "interactivity" into corporate-mediated "information"? How would Rushkoff deal with Corrado's claim that millions of citizens can interact in cyberspace?

Politics in Cyberspace

ANTHONY CORRADO

E merging technologies are revolutionizing political communication. Cable television, direct broadcast satellites, electronic mail, and the Internet are creating powerful new links between citizens and politicians, offering voters access to vast amounts of information, a diversity of perspectives, and new forums for sharing ideas. Although these technologies are still in their formative stages, they are already redefining traditional forms of political activity and transforming the character of political dialogue. Indeed, digital technology may ultimately have a greater effect on the American political system than radio and television did earlier in this century. And what we are now witnessing is only the beginning.

With the development of fiber optics and digital compression, the boundaries between traditionally separate electronic media, such as television, telephony, and computer networks, are breaking down. The result will be an interactive, multimedia environment in which average citizens will have on-demand access to video, audio, text, or data transmissions with the click of a handheld remote control or portable computer keyboard. In this environment, citizens will communicate with each other and their political leaders in ways that less than 25 years ago were considered more science fiction than science fact.

These new forms of communication suggest the prospect of a revitalized democracy in which average citizens will have a powerful voice in political affairs. . . .

While most observers agree that the digital revolution will dramatically transform American politics, there is wide disagreement about the effects of these changes. Many political experts believe that the primary effect will be to promote the development of a more democratic system of government. In this view, technology will close the gap between citizens and their government, making it easier for voters to communicate with political leaders and easier for these leaders to reflect the preferences of their constituents. Individuals will play a more meaningful role in political life, in part because they will not have to rely on predigested broadcast media or broad-based political party organizations to represent their views. Interactive media will increasingly replace more passive forms of political communication, which in turn will encourage the development of a more informed and active citizenry. Individual voters will have the capacity to identify issues of common interest and organize around them. They will be better able to hold officials accountable for their actions or to act when government fails to respond to

their needs. The result will be a political system that promotes civic participation, responds to majority concerns, and provides individuals with a
meaningful voice in the governing process.

Other practitioners are not so optimistic. While they agree that new
technologies will expand public access to information, they are concerned that this information will only benefit a relatively small portion
of the electorate. Many voters will not take advantage of the opportunities to learn more about candidates and government, and millions may
not have access due to a lack of computer literacy skills or the unavail-
ability of the necessary equipment. Instead of promoting a more informed electorate and widespread participation, these experts believe
that new technologies will primarily serve to enhance the strength of organized groups and further fragment the electorate. In addition, the immediate public feedback available to politicians will essentially constitute
daily opinion polls, which may so closely tie legislators to constituent
concerns that legislative compromise and consensus may be even more
difficult to achieve than in the highly partisan, "gridlocked" governments of recent years.

The Emergence of Campaigns in Cyberspace

Electronic and digital forms of communication are rapidly emerging as important political tools, as an increasing number of citizens are gaining access to new information technologies. Over 40 million Americans already
have access to the Internet, a worldwide computer network, through their
home, school, or business, and this number is expected to grow dramatically over the next ten years. . . .

Many of those who will not have computers in their home . . . will be
able to access information networks either from their business or in some
other way. For example, in the next five years most public school systems
should be on-line. . . . To spur this growth, the federal government has
launched an initiative to have every public school wired to the network. . . .
Many local governments and private businesses are working with federal
agencies to make this goal a reality. Public libraries and hospitals are also
expanding their efforts to make computer information technology more
readily available to the public.

The expansion of on-line services and the great potential of the Internet as a means of communicating with voters has convinced many candidates, party organizations, and political groups to experiment with this
technology. While World Wide Web sites, electronic bulletin boards, and
other forms of interactive communication were regarded as novelties in
the 1994 election cycle, they . . . gained much broader use in the 1996
campaigns. Indeed, they have reached a point where they have become a
part of the presidential campaign, as well as many federal and statewide
contests. . . .

. . . Although they will not have replaced television and radio as the major sources of voter information by that time, they will be an important source of information for a significant share of the electorate and a primary component of an increasing number of campaigns.

Candidates and political groups will continue to adopt and place greater emphasis on digital, interactive means of communication for a number of reasons. Because some candidates are already employing these methods, others are following their lead either due to fear of being placed at some strategic disadvantage or because they recognize the potential of these technologies for reaching out to select groups of voters. These incentives will be even more compelling as more voters gain access to these methods. Technological developments will spur this growth by expanding availability and increasing the ways in which voters can access interactive media, while at the same time reducing equipment costs. By 2010 gaining access to digital information may be as easy as picking up a telephone or selecting a channel on a television set.

Reviving Democratic Politics

The primary reason why interactive communications will likely come to the fore in electoral and governmental politics is that candidates and voters alike are beginning to recognize and experience their advantages over television, radio, surface mail and other current methods of political outreach. These advantages are already apparent in the limited uses now being explored, and they should increase dramatically as the technology develops.

Reconnecting the Citizenry

Opinion poll after opinion poll has demonstrated that large majorities of Americans feel alienated and distant from the political process. Gone are the days when most voters personally knew an individual seeking office or had a chance to meet a candidate face-to-face. Presidential campaigns have largely become a series of tarmac photo opportunities and 30-second television ads. Even in statewide races, few voters get a chance to ask a candidate a question or discuss a particular concern.

Emerging technologies offer a means of reestablishing the connection between voters and candidates. While not as intimate as meetings in person, they allow a type of individual contact and interaction that is not possible through current campaign communications. Voters can ask specific questions of candidates and acquire information on topics of particular interest to them. Through electronic mail and town meetings they can engage in dialogues with candidates or elected officials. Furthermore, since citizens with access to the Internet will have a capacity to share their views with, potentially, millions of other voters, they can also participate in broader public dialogues about politics and elections.

Improving Voter Information

Promoting the development of an informed electorate is one of the basic objectives of a democratic political process. But most observers argue that this goal is not being fulfilled by the current system. Voters now receive the bulk of their political information from news reports or candidate-sponsored television and radio advertising, which are widely criticized as not conducive to the creation of a more enlightened public. Instead of providing voters with detailed information on policy issues and the candidates' respective positions on major public concerns, news reports increasingly tend to reduce candidate speeches or statements to brief "sound bites," emphasize the tactical and strategic aspects of political campaigns, and devote relatively little attention to the substance of policy debates. The brief, 30-second format of most campaign ads offers even less substantive information to voters. And, according to many experts, the rise of negative advertising has further diminished the quality of political discourse in this nation, while at the same time it has increased public disaffection with politics and reduced the level of political participation.

The expansion of digital communications will dramatically change the quality of the information readily available to voters. With the rise of the Internet and continuing expansion of cable television alternatives, citizens will have access to a wide range of information from a variety of sources. In fact, the materials prepared by candidates, party organizations, and other partisan groups will be but the tip of the information iceberg in the dynamic, multimedia environment of the future. These materials will be supplemented by information prepared by a wide spectrum of political groups, citizens' associations, and news organizations. This will provide voters with greater access to contrasting views and enhance their ability to compare candidates' views on particular issues. As a result, the public will be able to achieve more well-rounded views of those seeking political office.

Examples of the type of higher quality information that will be available to voters already can be seen on the World Wide Web. Project Vote Smart, a nonprofit organization, has established a web site that offers users a wide array of factual information on federal and statewide elected officials and candidates from all fifty states. The site includes biographical backgrounds, voting records, interest group ratings, and campaign finance data, as well as links to home pages of candidates, all branches of the federal government, and state government election sites. A number of news organizations have joined forces, among them, CNN and *Time Magazine,* and the *Washington Post* and ABC News, to develop multimedia sites devoted to political coverage. . . . Over time, such sites will enable voters to gain additional information on major news stories, contrast the policy views of different candidates, compare candidates' compaign pledges to their voting records in office, and track a candidate's financial support and policy positions from election to election.

Moreover, . . . much of the information that will be distributed through the Internet or other interactive means will be "unmediated"; that is, it will not go through the editorial process that currently shapes much news reporting or be oriented towards particular views or interests. Instead, voters will be able to decide for themselves what information they consider to be most important. The advent of politics in cyberspace and digital technology will thus create a revitalized arena of free political speech that will help voters develop more informed views.

Increasing Candidate Access to the Political Process

One of the primary reasons why the information environment is likely to change in the future is the reduced cost of political communications. Unlike television and radio advertising, distributing information via the World Wide Web is relatively inexpensive. Anyone with the proper software can place a message on an electronic bulletin board or newsgroup, or send thousands of electronic mail messages without the printing and postage costs of surface mail. Individuals can also post messages on web sites that solicit visitor responses or create web sites of their own. In addition, the cost to a campaign of creating and maintaining a web site is much less than the cost of producing and airing even a single television ad, and dramatically less than the cost of even a modest television advertising campaign.

Because of their low cost, new technologies will open the electoral process to groups and candidates who have traditionally been priced out of the mass political market. . . . Digital communications could make financial resources less important in electoral politics since candidates will have access to mass audiences without having to conduct expensive advertising campaigns or spend tens of thousands of dollars on direct mail. . . . It is clearly the case that emerging technologies will benefit candidates who lack significant financial resources or broad-based public support.

The Internet is already becoming a principal means of communication for those who have traditionally been unable to generate or purchase significant media attention. Among others, the Libertarian Party and Green Party are using the Internet to spread their messages, maintain contact with members, and recruit new supporters. These parties, which traditionally have not had the resources to engage in mass public advertising, can now present their candidates and their views to an audience that could potentially reach tens of millions of voters. . . .

The potential effectiveness of this approach is suggested by the experience of United We Stand America, the citizens' group formed by Ross Perot after the 1992 election, and, more recently, the Reform Party. Although atypical of other minor parties in many regards, these organizations stand as prime examples of the type of intraparty activity that can be achieved through the World Wide Web. . . . In the future, digital communications may not just facilitate the growth of current political organizations, it could also stimulate the creation of new parties and political institutions. The most basic feature of this technology is that it will allow individuals more easily to find others who share their interests or views and communicate with them, which in turn will lead to the development of new forms of "community," new political groups, and undoubtedly, new political organizations. . . . In the future the political system may no longer be dominated by the Democratic and Republican parties. Instead, a variety of political communities and party interests could emerge, many of which would transcend geographic or political boundaries. . . .

Expanding Voter Alternatives

Because a broader range of political groups and candidates will be able to reach large audiences, voters will have more candidates to choose from when they cast their ballots. This is likely to increase electoral competition and could help restore the public's faith in the American system of government. Currently, more than a third of the electorate no longer identifies with either of the two major parties, and a majority feels that the candidates who seek major office do not represent its interests or concerns. This lack of connectedness is often cited as one of the reasons why so many Americans feel alienated from politics and choose not to participate on Election Day. By expanding the choices available to the electorate, new technologies will make it more likely that groups of voters will find candidates whom they feel are more representative of their views. Interactive communications may even encourage candidates to orient their campaigns towards the representation of particular blocs of voters or to stake out clear policy positions in hopes of building new electoral coalitions. These outcomes may very well rekindle public interest in election campaigns, and make elections more competitive, which would encourage larger numbers of citizens to turn out and vote.

Increasing Civic Participation

The digital revolution could also promote civic involvement simply by making it easier to participate. Rather than relying solely on elected officials, party organizations, or organized interest groups to represent their views, citizens can present their own views through electronic messages that will provide candidates and legislators with immediate feedback. They can also take part in electronic town halls, where they can discuss political issues with citizens and government officials from their local community, region, and state, or from throughout the nation. In addition, the technology can also be used to revitalize civic life by encouraging broad participation in a variety of political activities.

Fundraising

One form of political participation that could easily be encouraged by electronic communications is the act of making a financial contribution to a candidate or political organization. Candidates and groups could solicit hundreds of thousands of potential donors through their web sites or via electronic mail without having to incur the expense of telephone campaigns or direct mail solicitations. Such methods of solicitation would dramatically reduce the cost of campaign fundraising and enhance the possibility of financing a viable political campaign through thousands of small contributions.[1]

Emerging and Future Policy Concerns

While emerging technologies offer new hope for improving the political system, they also raise many fundamental concerns. Is a new regulatory structure needed to govern the types of political activity that are possible in cyberspace? Will the new communications revolution ensure equitable access to political information? Will it provide the quality of information needed to promote a more informed citizenry? Will it undermine an individual's sense of physical community and thereby exacerbate the sense of isolation and alienation within the electorate? . . .

Ensuring Fair and Equitable Access

As an increasing amount of political activity and communication begins to take place in cyberspace, fair and equitable access to new technologies will become an increasingly important concern. . . . We face the risk of a divided electorate, split between those who have access to technology and those who do not, or a split between those who are computer literate and those who are not. If such a division does transpire, certain segments of the electorate may be disadvantaged because they will not have ready access to the same information and will not be able to participate politically in the same way as others. Such disparities in the opportunity to participate, as well as in actual participation itself, would raise serious questions about the fairness and equity of the electoral process.

Many observers believe that any inequities in the level of voter information access currently being projected will be solved in due course by market mechanisms and the sorts of public/private initiatives that are already underway. As with first radio and then television, there will be a transitional period in which a minority of voters will enjoy significantly greater access than others. But soon the technology will become commonplace and increasingly affordable. . . .

. . . Fair and equitable access is by no means guaranteed and one of the imperatives in developing these new technologies as vehicles for political communication should be to guarantee such access. . . .

---

1. In 2000, all major candidates for president effectively raised money through their web sites; Bill Bradley raised the most.

Managing the Information Environment:
New Forms of Community

One of the major drawbacks to interactive communications is that most of the methods involve time-consuming processes that require a relatively high level of motivation on the part of the user. It takes more time and commitment on the part of the individual to participate in an on-line political conversation, search for voting record information on the Internet, or correspond with an elected official by electronic means, than it does to watch the evening news broadcast, scan the newspaper headlines, or listen to a talk radio program. Will a significant number of citizens take advantage of the new technologies and spend the time needed to become better informed voters? Will they be motivated to use the information that is available to them?

This issue is likely to become more prominent as the political uses of new technologies increase and develop. As access to information continues to expand, individuals will increasingly face the problem of information overload. Their primary concern will be how to select, authenticate, interpret, and assess the information already available on demand, rather than that of how to gain access to information on government and politics. As a result, voters will have to find ways to manage information more efficiently.

To resolve this problem, voters will seek out shortcuts for obtaining the information they consider relevant and useful. This need might eventually be met through a technical solution, the use of "intelligent agents." Intelligent agents are autonomous, customizable software programs that can gather and synthesize information for their users. They can be programmed to search for information from particular sites on specific subjects, and form a digest for the individual user that can essentially serve as a daily, multimedia "newspaper." But this technology is still in its infancy, and it is unlikely that a significant portion of the electorate will have access to it any time in the near future.

The most likely response for most users will be to rely on specific web sites or sources for their information, just as they now rely on certain evening news broadcasts or newspapers. But the sources are unlikely to be such traditional intermediaries as political parties, major network news associations, schools, or local civic organizations. Instead these links between citizens and government will be replaced by a vast array of formal and informal "neo-intermediaries," that can interact with each other freely without having to rely on traditional "gatekeepers" or institutions.

These "neo-intermediaries" will include many of the institutions that currently serve as mediators between the citizenry and elected officials or government institutions. This is evident from the activities of the last year in which many traditional press organizations have established World Wide Web sites and other interactive forms of communicating with voters. . . .

While these new information vehicles and forms of community are often cast as one of the improvements that will accompany new technologies, they raise many questions that policymakers need to consider. What sorts of information will be accessible through these sites? Will they promote exposure to different perspectives and views? To what extent will they uphold notions of collective accountability and ethical standards, especially with respect to the distribution of unverified information or the acceptance of minority views? Will there be limitations or contractual rules placed upon participants?

These issues are especially important because they strike at the heart of the question of whether the digitally interactive politics of the future will actually improve the quality of American democracy. . . . Emerging communications technologies may not lead to the broader, more informed public dialogue that many advocates envision. Instead, given so many possibilities and the prospect of information overload, most voters may continue to opt for information sources that essentially reflect their own views, and participate only in on-line forums that provide settings for meeting like-minded voters who will not criticize their thinking. If so, a major effect of interactive communications may prove to be greater fragmentation and disassociation of the electorate, rather than a more broadly informed, active public. . . .

Conclusion

For close to three decades the American political system has been characterized by increasing public disaffection and declining political participation. New technologies offer a means of reversing these trends. The interactive communication systems now being developed will provide individuals with powerful new means of accessing information and sharing their views with politicians and fellow citizens. They will offer citizens the opportunity to participate in elections and governance in meaningful ways, and could promote the type of interaction between voters and elected officials that is largely missing from modern politics. Eventually, they may lead to the creation of new forms of democratic participation that will supplement, or even replace, many of the representative structures that form the framework of our current constitutional system.

Emerging technologies thus offer the prospect of a revitalized democracy characterized by a more active and informed citizenry. But the realization of this promise will depend on whether all citizens can gain fair and equal access to the essential technologies. Another factor will be the extent to which policymakers successfully adapt current regulatory structures to accommodate new methods of communication. The most important factor, however, will be the willingness of significant numbers of citizens to take advantage of these extraordinary new tools to engage in meaningful political discourse, become better informed voters, and get more involved in civic life. If these technologies do stimulate greater public participation, then their impact may truly prove to be more revolutionary than that of radio and television. . . .

In the *Federalist Papers,* James Madison warned of the dangers to free government posed by "factions," that is, groups of citizens motivated by particular interests rather than the public interest as a whole. One of the advantages of such a large country as ours, in his view, was that it inhibited individuals with "common motives" from organizing and acting on their personal interests due to the problems created by geographical distance and limited communications. These barriers have steadily eroded throughout this century and will be all but eliminated in an electronic republic. Emerging technologies will make it easy for individuals to transcend geographical barriers and organize in cyberspace with others who share their views. This will give rise to a plethora of interest groups or citizen movements that seek to influence electoral and legislative outcomes. Thus, instead of crystallizing majority views, technological innovation may increase the division of opinion throughout the nation and make consensus more difficult to achieve. This would further complicate voter decision-making, and make it harder to achieve the level of compromise needed to build electoral and legislative coalitions.

. . . The value of democracy is to be found in the civic virtue and civic spirit that it can instill in the citizenry. In the absence of these qualities, political participation produces at best a form of "vulgar democracy" in which individuals simply pursue their own self-interests. Democratic governance then becomes an accumulation of independent efforts on the part of groups of individuals to fulfill their own interests, rather than a collective effort to achieve public goods. An effective democracy thus requires not just a need for better communication, but an increase in the amount of deliberation and debate that takes place within the citizenry. How to expand the arena of discourse and motivate citizens to capitalize on the variety of perspectives that will be available through new communications methods must therefore be a fundamental concern in the future development of technologies.

The Internet: Coercion
in Cyberspace?

DOUGLAS RUSHKOFF

We sell audience, not content.

—Jonathan Sacks, general manager of The Hub, America Online

I really believed the Internet could put an end to coercion.
This was back in 1988, when I was still getting laughed at for suggesting that someday nearly everyone would be using e-mail on a daily basis. . . .

What I knew for sure back then was that the Internet would somehow irrevocably change the way we relate to our media, and to one another. Early signs showed that the change would be immensely positive. People would finally have a medium for communicating freely with one another, instead of merely absorbing the messages of advertisers. . . .

The Internet made us more aware of the process by which news and public relations are created and disseminated. As we gained access to press releases and corporate data, we . . . witnessed firsthand how public relations experts . . . write the evening news. In the early nineties, there was a participant of an electronic bulletin board who would post the transcripts of local news shows and then compare them, word for word, with the prepared press releases of the companies or individuals concerned. The results were embarrassingly similar, with whole paragraphs lifted directly from press release to newscaster's script. . . .

. . . As a happy witness to what was taking place in our culture, I began to write books celebrating our liberation through the tools of new media. *Cyberia* applauded the scientists, hackers, and spiritualists who were determined to design a better society with these new tools. The technological revolution seemed to me a populist renaissance through which real people would wake from centuries of heartless manipulation. Hierarchy and social control soon would be things of the past as every individual came to realize his or her role in the unfolding of civilization. I saw my vision confirmed as the Internet rose in popularity, and as the once-ridiculed nerds of Silicon Valley began to engineer the communications infrastructure for the world's business community. The Internet would not fade into obscurity like CB radio. It was here to stay. Our culture was hardwiring itself together.

I became fascinated and inspired by the organic and responsive qualities of this new mediaspace. . . .

. . . Huge, well-funded, mainstream publicity campaigns were becoming obsolete. Now, anyone could launch an idea that would spread by itself if it were packaged in a new, unrecognizable form of media. Mutant media got attention because it was strange. And there's nothing the media likes more than to cover new forms of itself. The Rodney King tape proliferated as much because it demonstrated the power of a new technology—the camcorder—as for the image contained within it. One of the reasons why the O.J. Simpson story became the biggest trial in history was because it began with a mutant media event: the nationally televised spectacle of the Bronco chase, during which Los Angeles TV viewers ran outside and literally onto their own TV screens as the motorcade drove by. Similarly, the media stunts of ACT UP activists, Earth First "eco-terrorists," Greenpeace, and even unorthodox political candidates received worldwide attention simply by launching their campaigns through media viruses.

The hegemony of Hearst and Murdoch were over. We had entered an age where the only limiting factor was an idea's ability to provoke us through its novel dissemination. An idea no longer depended on the authority of its originator—it would spread and replicate if it challenged our faulty assumptions. In an almost Darwinian battle for survival, only the fittest ideas would win out. These new, mutated forms of media were promoting our cultural evolution, empowering real people, and giving a voice to those who never before had access to the global stage.

Best of all, young people were the ones leading the charge. Adults were immigrants to the new realm of interactive media, but kids raised with joysticks in their hands were natives. They spoke the language of new media and public relations better than the adults who were attempting to coerce them. What media can you use to manipulate a kid when he is already more media literate than you are? He will see through any clunky attempt to persuade him with meaningless associations and hired role models. By the time this generation came into adulthood, I believed, the age of manipulation would be over. . . . Meanwhile, young computer hackers had gotten their hands on the control panel of our electronic society. Bank records and other personal data that formerly were accessible only to credit bureaus and loan officers were now within the reach of any skilled fourteen-year-old. As a result, our privacy finally became an issue to be discussed publicly. We became aware of how information about us was being gathered, bought, and sold without our consent, and we supported activists, organizations, and candidates who promised to enact policies to prevent this invasion.

. . . As the coercive effects of mainstream media became more self-evident, media awareness led to a revival of cultural literacy. Our ability to see through the shameless greed of televangelists changed the way we related to the ritual surrounding the collection plate. Our ability to deconstruct the political process as it took place on TV gave rise to independent, homespun candidates like Ross Perot and Jerry Brown, whose campaigns promised direct access and accountability.

In the meantime, television programs like "Beavis and Butthead" and "The Simpsons" were deconstructing the rest of the mediaspace for our children. With Bart as their role model, the generation growing up in the last decade has maintained a guarded relationship to the media and marketing techniques that have fooled their parents. While his dad, Homer, was suckered by every beer promotion, Bart struggled to maintain his skateboarder's aloofness and dexterity. Through Bart, our kids learned to remain moving targets.

The Battle for Cyberspace

As the Internet grew in popularity, and more and more users discovered how absorbing and rewarding it could be, media conglomerates began to panic at the way interactive channels and constant feedback were eroding their monopoly over the media-space. By the mid-1990s, the Internet already had eaten away more than ten percent of the time its users previously spent watching television, and the damage was increasing by the month.

Like covered wagons circling in defense against the onslaught of an untamed, indigenous people, media companies banded together for protection. Viacom bought Blockbuster and Paramount [and then CBS] which in turn bought Simon and Schuster; Disney bought ABC which had already bought Capital Cities; Murdoch's News Corp. bought Fox; General Electric bought NBC; Time-Warner bought CNN [and then merged with America Online in 2000]. Once consolidated, these companies were braced for battle.[1]

The war to retake the media, signaled by the creation of these corporate behemoths, manifested itself in the trenches as a step-by-step undoing of the processes that had liberated the media in the first place. The effects of the keyboard, the joystick, and the remote control had to be reversed.

While cyber optimists like me were out proclaiming the digital renaissance, other futurists with far better business credentials were busy [remaking] it for the consumption of Wall Street. As skilled as they were at hyping interactive technology, they still had some tough questions to answer before anyone would invest in their visions. How would anybody, other than the phone companies, make a profit off people merely communicating with one another? Television had commercials, and movies had an admission price. People interacting online were not buying anything, nor were they in the captive or anxious frame of mind that would render them easy targets. They were [just] having fun with one another.

This posed a serious challenge to those who wished to make money online. They could either hope that the anticommercial ethic of the early Internet would fade as more "mainstream" audiences found their way online, or else enact a public-relations campaign designed to speed up that conver-

---

1. A similar consolidation occurred in telephone, cable, and video.

sion. The slow but steady process by which the Internet was surrendered to commercial use falls somewhere between a real conspiracy and an inevitable, natural shift. The key players . . . were merely extending the already awesome power of the market into a new arena. If market forces brought down the Soviet Union and the Berlin Wall, they could surely break through the resistance of a few Internet users.

Their first job was to gain both public acceptance and financial support for the appropriation of cyberspace. They had to convince investors that there was a way to make money on-line, while showing Netizens that business could make the Internet safer, cheaper, and more fully featured. . . .

Ironically, perhaps, it was my faith in the liberating powers of cyberspace that made me one of the last people to take such efforts seriously, and to reckon with the Internet's coercive potential. I saw the computer keyboard and mouse as our best weapons in the effort to turn around the mind-numbing impact of traditional media. Just as the remote control had deconstructed the television image and the joystick demystified it, the keyboard and mouse spawned a new generation of do-it-yourself media tacticians. That's why, even as my opinions were being sought by corporations hoping to exploit these technologies for their own ends, I was incapable of seeing where their efforts would lead us.

In the early nineties, I attended several meetings at HarperCollins . . . , in which some of the executives running the company's new multimedia division wanted to know how to leverage their vast backlist to gain a foothold on the Internet. Rupert Murdoch's News Corp., which owned HarperCollins, already had an online service called Delphi. Surely there was a way to "synergize" these two subsidiaries, they thought. The question was simply how to go about it. Like most of the New York companies looking to exploit the Internet, HarperCollins and Delphi understood that the main thing they could offer consumers was content. . . . If HarperCollins could turn the Internet into a distribution channel for its massive storehouse of text, games, and other copywritten materials, it could cash in. . . .

Although businesses had failed in their efforts to capitalize on the initial surge in Internet use, the race was on to find a way to make money online. Many different companies, working independently, arrived at a similar strategy. The first step was to reverse the do-it-yourself attitude that the computer keyboard had provoked, and restore the supremacy of commercial content over social contact. The trick would be to change the perception of the Internet as a communications medium to a broadcast medium, which meant convincing users that our interactions with one another were less important than the data we could download and the things we could purchase with our new equipment. . . . That's how [the] Information Age became the label to describe the communications breakthrough. Previously, the users themselves had been the content of the Internet. Now, it would be "information."

In 1995, Nicholas Negroponte, the founder of the corporate-sponsored Media Lab at MIT and a major investor in *Wired* magazine, drew a faulty but calculated distinction between online and real-world interaction. He said that in the physical world, we exchange atoms, but that in the online world, we exchange bits—meaning units of information. Negroponte saw us entering an information age, chiefly characterized by the fact that we now would exchange units of data rather than physical objects.

The problem with reducing online interaction to an exchange of bits, and the interactive age to an information age, is that it allows cyberspace to be quantified and, ultimately, [turned into something that could be bought and sold.] The fact is that the social and emotional substance of an online interaction cannot be described in terms of bits of information. As far as . . . these cyber theorists were concerned, a social dimension to online transmissions did not exist. The Internet was not something a person engaged with; it was a set of information that could be accessed. And anything that can be accessed can be given a price tag.

The second stage of the transformation was [making] the media, which had been demystified by the advent of interactive devices like the joystick and the remote control, [mysterious again]. [The new] *Wired* [magazine] used busy graphics and wrote in a buzzword-laden style, stoking newcomers' fears that the Internet was technically complex and conceptually daunting. Without proper instruction, users would surely get lost out there. Meanwhile, more mainstream publications like *Time* magazine, themselves threatened by competition from the many news services sprouting up online, ran frightening cover stories about "cyberporn." *The New York Times* reported that innocent people were jeopardizing their health by taking advice from online holistic practitioners, while drive-time radio fed us stories about dangerous computer viruses—items lifted directly from the press releases written by the software companies selling us protection from these evils.

Once the Internet was seen as a danger zone best traveled with the help of experts, it wasn't long before a mediating filter known as World Wide Web became the preferred navigational tool. Unlike bulletin boards or chat rooms, the Web is—for the most part—a read-only medium. It is flat and opaque. You can't see through it to the activities of others. You don't socialize with anyone when you visit a Web site; you read text and look at pictures. This is not interactivity. Like a fake decibel meter at a basketball game where the crowd is led to believe its cheers are actually moving the needle, there's nothing truly participatory about it. Although anyone can publish his ideas on his own Web site—the Web did represent a tremendous leap for self-publishing—the interface is not all that conducive to conversation. But only by compromising its communicative function could the Web's developers turn the Internet into a shopping mall. . . .

Further aiding the effort to remystify new media, designers made the programs necessary to navigate the Web more complex than earlier tools. The original Internet was built and navigated by researchers and university students using "shareware"—software that was distributed and exchanged for free. These simple programs worked on the most primitive computers, and they functioned in a transparently straightforward fashion. Their no-frills designs and freely published code helped users understand how they were put together and allowed anyone to participate in their development and offer enhancements. The original Internet was a "shareware universe," expanded and maintained chiefly by its own participants.

By 1995, Netscape [Communications] had become a for-profit company, and the "browser wars" were under way. An ethic of free-market competition replaced the era of freewheeling cooperation. As if to rewrite history, many Internet experts and journalists developed a mythology that the Internet was developed not by university researchers but by the United States military. . . . [Falsely,] the Internet would forever be associated with the Cold War arms race, and its communitarian roots could be discounted more easily. Anyone who wrote articles disagreeing with the folklore of a military-built Internet or the virtues of a competitive marketplace was quickly labeled a "leftist."

As profit-seeking software companies took over where shareware developers left off, programs became correspondingly less efficient and less accessible. The code for software was no longer routinely released to the public for us to modify or improve. Even if it had been, these new programs were much too convoluted for the average user to understand. We were once again at the mercy of the companies from whom we bought our equipment and software. . . . People who wanted to use the Web were initiated into an endless cycle of upgrades. In a campaign of planned obsolescence that made the 1970s automotive industry's schemes look like child's play, computer manufacturers and software companies conspired to force more and more purchases. Imagine if automobile companies controlled the designs not only of vehicles but of the roads. By changing the kinds of surfaces we drive on, they could force us to buy new kinds of tires, and then new kinds of cars on which those tires fit. Similarly, Microsoft can use proprietary code to develop Internet sites that require new kinds of browsers, browsers that require new kinds of operating systems, and operating systems that require enhanced hardware.

The dominance of the World Wide Web also gave traditional entertainment companies, salespeople, and advertisers an Internet they could at last understand. From now on, the Internet would be treated like the broadcast media they had already mastered. The entertainment industry began to invest heavily in online video and music services in the hope of one day being able to charge people money for receiving such goods via the Internet. Salespeople understood that Web sites gave them a way to put their entire catalogs of merchandise online, and that secure credit-card transactions would allow customers to purchase whatever they wanted without leaving their homes. Marketers were delighted by the development of a more tractable mediaspace in which to peddle their wares. They bought space on the most heavily trafficked Web sites for slick "banner" ads—colorful patches begging to be clicked on, diverting Internet users to commercial Web sites.

The third way marketers co-opted the interactive mediaspace was through the manipulation of shortening attention spans. . . . The new economists announced that we had entered an "attention economy," where the only limiting factor on the business community's ability to earn money online was the number of "eyeball-hours" they could wrest from an Internet user. New methods of attention control—from graphical interfaces to Internet portals—were researched and implemented, targeting the people who had grown used to the freedom of the mouse and remote control. Meanwhile, all this focus on attention spans and resistant youth led to a flurry of news reports about attention deficit disorder, which in turn prompted worried parents to seek medications like Ritalin for their children so that they could compete effectively in the complex and highly acceler-ated marketplace of the twenty-first century.

Democracy and the Internet

Early in the summer of 1998, I was invited to join a few other writers, on-line enthusiasts, and legal activists . . . to discuss what had happened to the Internet. It seemed to us that the promise of this interactive mediaspace was fast fading as the concerns of business outweighed those of the people who stood to benefit from its existence.

The result of this and several other such meetings was a document we published online and in *The Nation* called "Technorealism." The two-page proclamation called attention to the fact that the Internet is a public space and that the public therefore has the right to decide how it should be used—in schools, in communities, and in the commercial sector. We felt that most commentary and debate about cyberspace was being dominated by those who saw market forces as the only valid method of defining online culture, and we sought to stake out a new middle ground. We believed it was possible, even necessary, to support the mindful development of cyber-culture beyond the priorities set by business interests, which had so far seemed to wreck so many other kinds of human interaction. And we meant to do so without resorting to the fearful . . . rhetoric so often heard on the six o'clock news.

The rather moderate document we generated was met with immediate ridicule and disdain. Michael Kinsley, the former *New Republic* editor who was now in Microsoft's employ as editor of their online publishing venture, *Slate*, publicly dismissed the technorealist effort as a self-serving Gen-X whine, but also admitted freely that he had never even bothered to read it. *Wired News* and *The New York Times* interviewed pro-business stalwarts . . . for their reactions, and went on to mock the technorealists for our naïveté. Some looked for agendas beneath our words. Were we just trying to pro-mote our own writing careers through a new kind of publicity stunt? Others thought we were simply killjoys or closet Marxists.

Perhaps we had already lost the war. In spite of the fact that over a thousand people had added their electronic signatures to the online document within a week of its being posted, the overwhelming sentiment in the mainstream media was that any attempt to challenge the businesses that, they believed, had paid for the technological infrastructure was futile and misguided. Libertarians and progressives alike had come to believe that cyberspace was no place to enact public policy; it was either a place to do business or one to avoid altogether. . . .

DISCUSSION QUESTIONS

1. In early 2000, the largest media company on earth (Time Warner, Inc.) joined with the largest Internet access provider (America Online). How might each author respond to this merger? Is it a technological breakthrough, a corporate takeover, or both?

2. Corrado and Rushkoff both seem to see democratic potential in the Internet. What aspects of Corrado's views allow him to ignore growing corporate control of the Internet? Why does Rushkoff seem to ignore the thousands of small web sites that can be found through this medium?

3. In what ways is the World Wide Web just an extension of the established, traditional media of print, radio, and newspapers? In what ways is it a departure?

4. Rushkoff claims that interactivity has been replaced with one-way communication of "information." How might Corrado rebut this assertion? What do you think?

SUGGESTED READINGS AND INTERNET RESOURCES

At least in part, the debate about the Internet's democratic character is related to arguments about the nature of the traditional media. Are the media lapdogs for or watchdogs of other powerful institutions? How diverse is the traditional media? What is news, and how ought it to be defined? One book that sees an independent if problematic role for journalists is James Fallows's *Breaking the News: How the Media Undermine American Democracy* (New York: Pantheon, 1995). See also Doris Graber, *The Mass Media in American Politics* (Washington, D.C.: CQ Press, 1997). For the best critical account of the effects of corporate mergers and government policy on established news organization and citizenship, see Robert McChesney, *Rich Media, Poor Democracy* (Urbana: University of Illinois Press, 1999). For discussions of the effect of the Internet on news coverage and citizen participation, see Richard Davis, *The Web of Politics* (New York: Oxford University Press, 1999), and Gary Selnow, *Electronic Whistle-Stops: The Impact of the Internet on American Politics* (Westport, Conn.: Praeger, 1998)

Fairness and Accuracy in Reporting (FAIR)
www.fair.org
This New York City–based watchdog group reports inaccuracies and biases in mainstream news programming, with an emphasis on the undemocratic effects of corporate control.

The Media Studies Center
www.freedomforum.org
Web site of the nation's biggest think tank devoted to media issues, funded and operated by the Freedom Forum. Strong on the dissemination of new media technologies and on threats to journalistic integrity from governments.

Media Access Project
www.mediaaccess.org
Web site of the only U.S. law firm dedicated to preserving public space on the increasingly commercial airwaves. Lots of data on pending questions with the Federal Communications Commission and on lawsuits over public access and against corporate monopoly.

Project Censored
www.sonoma.edu/ProjectCensored
Web site of least-covered stories by the traditional media, with documentation about which stories are and aren't covered by the corporate media. Also good for links to alternative media sites.

America's Political Parties: Channels for Voters or Conduits for Cash?

There was a time in America when political parties were about as important to people as their hometowns, their religious beliefs, their ethnic origins, or their social and economic class. That time was not so long ago. As political science professor Xandra Kayden tells us in the following essay, saying "I am a Jewish Democrat from New York City" or "a German Republican from Wisconsin" was only recently a fairly common self-designation for many Americans. Being poor or wealthy, middle- or working-class also meant identifying with a particular political party.

What did it mean to be a strong Republican or Democrat, or even to reject both in favor of a third party like the Populists of the 1890s? Partisan identities meant having a general orientation to others, to citizenship, to history, and to government. Partisan identity matched and expressed other important experiences in people's lives, both linking and distinguishing them from neighbors and strangers. At their strongest, parties included diverse groups, aggregating them to form effective national coalitions. Parties stitched together local communities to compete in elections at the state and national levels.

Nowadays, such partisan identities sound old-fashioned if not downright bizarre. Party affiliation is less important than people's beliefs and lifestyles— many of us are more inclined to see our individuality expressed through tastes in music, movies, clothes, or food. Insofar as people are involved politically, one's party affiliation may not be all that crucial. Environmentalists, feminists, and labor union activists may generally support Democratic candidates, while business executives and Christian fundamentalists may tend to support Republicans. Yet all these people now tend to form their own groups and movements, seeking to influence political parties from the outside.

Even though many citizens still vote for the candidates of the major parties, most voters report to pollsters that they don't care much about the parties, that they have a tough time identifying parties with particular ideas, and that parties are largely irrelevant to their political beliefs. Throughout most of the nineties, voters told pollsters that the formation of some kind of third party might be a good idea. Yet a variety of third parties from the Reform Party to the Greens and Libertarians, have a tough time in the United States's winner-take-all electorate system.

Many writers have properly concluded from all this that the parties are weakening. Yet at another level, the parties are most definitely not in decline. In 1995–1996, the national parties together raised and spent $263 million, a 300 percent increase over just four years before. By 1998 and 2000, the national parties were raking in even greater amounts of cash and "soft money." In the American past, parties were primarily local and state organizations; today, parties own their own buildings in Washington, D.C., gain the support of an ever-growing list of small and large contributors, and direct formidable media and advertising machines. Like never before, both parties can and do recruit candidates to run for office. In Congress and in government generally, officeholders stay loyal to their party's legislative program and join in the partisan attacks on their adversaries.

So which is it? How can the political parties be weakening and strengthen-ing at the same time, and what does it matter for American democracy? In our country's past, elite democrats have praised strong parties, and in so doing they've defined them in a very particular way as the controllers and educators of an otherwise fickle and fragmented citizenry. For elite democrats, "strong" parties provide able leaders and disciplined organizations that act on the electorate as much as they do to represent voters. Providing coherence among factions, strong parties filter conflicts and then refine them into manageable policy debates in Washington and in state governments. Parties, from this perspective, are important as organizations that help to shape and determine responsible debate among public officeholders.

For popular democrats, strong parties are defined far differently. For them, the appropriate measure is the quantity and quality of mass participation in the parties. Strong parties are the instruments by which "organized people"—voters and all their conversations and activity—have a voice. Strong parties balance "organized money" and the powerful institutions that gain influence through economic power, lobbying, and the privileged access that comes with both. Strong parties should provide the electorate with alternative visions of the public good, so that voter choices mean something. These visions should be produced through organized and widespread grass roots activity. A party's officeholders should be the instruments of the grass roots, not the other way around.

How well or poorly do the parties today perform according to these different criteria? The two essays that follow provide very different answers to this question, even as the authors both agree that parties are very important for the operation of democracy.

In the first essay, Xandra Kayden argues that American political parties haven't so much declined as they have changed to become more effective and adapted to the modern political world. Kayden finds the parties, especially the GOP, "alive and well," vigorous and effective at reaching voters and eliciting financial contributions. She even argues that the modernized parties may have the capacity to revive public interest and involvement in politics.

Journalist and author William Greider paints a very different picture of the parties in "Rancid Populism." Greider examines and criticizes the GOP. Elsewhere, he provides a similarly critical analysis of the Democrats.

The GOP's successes, Greider says, have come at the expense of grass roots democracy because they are built on money, manipulation, and demagoguery. He argues that the Republicans may win national elections, but they do so only through their success at manufacturing and selling meaningless political symbols to a cynical and disorganized electorate.

Greider notes that both parties advertise their closeness to the people but that each is remarkable for its exploitation and manipulation of voters around an elite governing agenda. "Bringing people back into the contest" is the only way to strengthen the democratic character of either party, Greider contends.

Both these essays were written at a crucial transition point in the recent history of U.S. political parties. In the 1980s and early 1990s, both the Democrats and the Republicans literally revived themselves, not by rebuilding grass roots organizations but by finding new ways to raise money and spend it. A decade later, the parties have, if anything, become more extreme versions of the organizations Kayden and Greider describe.

While reading each essay, think about the following: Do the authors give the same reasons for the importance of political parties? How would Kayden reply to Greider's claim that the parties are money driven, hierarchical, and elitist? How would Greider respond to Kayden's claim that the parties have necessarily adjusted to contemporary political realities? What does Greider mean when he says that the GOP's populism is "rancid" or "feigned"?

Alive and Well and Living in Washington: The American Political Parties

X A N D R A K A Y D E N

The American party system has gone through a [recent] metamorphosis . . . , changing from a weak, decentralized structure to a strong centralized organization possessed of new resources in money and technology. Although there is still considerable debate about the consequences of these changes, . . . it is my view that the new system represents a dramatic change from the past and that it is a positive step in bringing the processes of politics into line with the communication and opinion formation of a modern technological society. The new system is capable of recapturing the traditional functions of political parties: control of nominations and resources, and influencing public opinion and public policy. That the rebirth has coincided with turbulent political tides and a widespread contention that the parties are dying, if not already dead, has obscured the picture of what they are and what they might portend for our future. One task . . . is to consider their meaning—assuming that the new form comes out of new needs and serves new functions. What is the role of the party: as an organization, as a vehicle for expressing and influencing opinion, and as a participant in political life?

The rebirth may not have been inevitable, although an argument could be made that if the parties did not exist, they would have to be created, for they are an inherent characteristic of the modern democratic state. The circumstances that encouraged the current rebirth were: changes in campaign finance regulation . . . and the increased complexity and cost of modern campaign technology. . . . We must also credit leadership in both parties for recognizing what had to be done and making the tough decisions to do it. Finally, the remaining causes of party change must lie in the changes in the practice of politics and government.

The New Organization: A Description

. . . Both national parties consist of three committees: the national committee (which is composed of representatives of the states and is supported by a professional staff) and the campaign committees for the House and Senate.

Until the mid-1970s the national party existed principally for the function of organizing a national nominating convention to select its candidate for the presidency, and secondarily as a clearinghouse for political appointees.

In recent times, the influence of the national party has declined in the actual selection of presidential candidates—giving cause to the cry of the demise of the party—but it has *increased* in the selection of all other candidates for party office at both the federal and state levels. All three committees in both parties raise money, recruit and support candidates, develop data and techniques to affect the outcome of elections, and participate in policy debates. The strength of the committee rests in their staffs who do the work and who, in more instances than is generally recognized, influence the selection of candidates and issues upon which they will stand. The professional organization is the core of the modern party.

The decline in the role of the [presidential nominating] convention as a decision-making body reflects the decline in influence of local party bosses, rather than a weakness in the national organization. Indeed, there is little question that local parties are in danger of disappearing in many places, leaving vestiges of their structures with few volunteers willing to devote the time and energy necessary to their sustenance. The decline of local party volunteers is due to a variety of causes. These include the loss of a major function due to nonpartisan local elections, the accompanying decline of party control of patronage that promised future rewards for volunteers, and changes in lifestyle that do not permit as much time for volunteer efforts, particularly by women. . . .

The national committees have used their increased resources to enhance their role in the selection and election of candidates and to create super campaign committees. Few candidates can afford to run for federal office today without the backing of the national party. . . . The national party [also] trains candidates, campaign managers, and fund-raisers, and provides technical assistance in just about every phase of an election, including detailed information about the opposition and the voters. It has the capacity to contact registered party members, independents, and registered Democratic voters who live in districts that voted Republican in previous elections. The finely tuned message, while not as personal as a neighbor canvassing his or her block on behalf of the party, can be made more accurate and more informative than any ever before directed to American voters.

National/State Relations

The national parties used to be financed by a tithe placed on each state party. Their activities were, not surprisingly, limited. The Federal Election Campaign Act (FECA) changed this.[1] The national parties moved from dependence on the states to reliance on direct funding from millions of small contributors and thereby changed the relationship within the party

---

1. FECA is the 1970 law and its later amendments that regulate contribution levels and require disclosure for all contributors to candidates for federal office.

organization. Today, the national party supports the state parties with funds, staff, and a multitude of other resources. The congressional campaign committees are now almost entirely responsible for supporting their respective candidates, freeing the other committees to use their resources elsewhere.

Besides helping state parties, . . . both national parties recruit candidates for office. Although many still think of our system as candidate-centered, i.e., that the candidates are self-selected and independent of the parties, the reality is that very few candidates for federal and important state offices run without expecting and receiving significant aid from the national party in the form of money, advice, research on issues and the demographics of the voting district, staff and organizational support in registration and get-out-the-vote efforts, help in soliciting political action committee (PAC) and individual support, and assistance in federal and state compliance procedures.[2] No other individual or group can contribute anything closely approximating it. In many instances, it is the party which makes the first approach. . . .

Another area of national party activity, which grows out of the new resources and professionalism, is the activism of the party in policy debates. The influence of the party varies from presenting candidates for office with issue positions . . . to lobbying Congress, and even to publishing views which differ from the official party platform adopted at the nominating convention. . . .

The Party in Washington

Debates about party influence must inevitably blur the lines of participants. On one hand, this discussion has been based on the professionalism of party staffers. On the other hand, the growth of party influence in Congress includes the increased power of House and Senate party leaders. Whether their influence is due in large measure to the increased resources they can provide for the next election, and whether they are holding a carrot or a stick, it is true that voting within Congress has become markedly more partisan. . . .

. . . Both major national parties own their headquarters in Washington. These buildings on Capitol Hill are more than symbols of the new institutional strength of the parties: they are the bases of ongoing activity by individuals who have devoted themselves to party building for several years. Most of the staff in both parties are young, well educated, and well versed in modern technology. They are partisan, but they have developed the outlook of professionals and since 1980, . . . they have maintained communication with each other. As professionals they seem, in fact, to have more in common with each other stylistically than with many of their adherents out in the field. . . .

---

2. PAC is the official FECA designation for organizations that collect and administer individual donations to be used in congressional races.

The Resources of Strong National Organizations

The sources of national party money are twofold: large donors (a traditional but less important source in recent years), and small donors whose participation is solicited through the mails. It is the direct-mail fund raising which has turned out to be the key to the new strength, and ultimately, to the nationalization of the parties.[3] The shift to direct mail began paying off for the Republicans in 1974, when the FECA went into effect. The process is well suited to the law's requirements to gather information about those who contribute to federal elections. . . .

It should be noted that direct-mail fund raising by the parties does not come as an isolated phenomenon in American political life. Issue groups and individual candidates have led the way, helped in turn by the intensity and scope of the media.[4] Television brings issues to the public mind and thereby enables activists to seek support. Although many observers have criticized the trivial nature of media communication, the fact that it focuses attention makes possible the more comprehensive mail appeal. The attention also brings about the nationalization of issues, and that process strengthens the nationalization of the parties. . . .

Direct-mail appeals tend to be negative: opposing some policy, person, or action in which the appealer is in the minority. Those who view themselves in the majority are less apt to get angry, less apt to be concerned, and less apt to feel they must do something to change things or defend the status quo. Those who give large donations usually expect to gain access and the possibility of influence in return for their gift; those who give small amounts of money cannot realistically have such expectations; hence what motivates them is the sense of moral satisfaction which comes from participating in the battle. . . .

The impact of national party direct-mail fund raising extends beyond the funds brought into party headquarters. It increases the sense of loyalty to the national party itself, extending participation in its affairs . . . to far larger numbers than ever before. . . . If everything we know about the relationship between giving money and loyalty is correct, it suggests that partisanship may be increasing in intensity among larger portions of the population.

Nationalization: The Causes

Local Decline

Local party organization—the structure we usually associate with strong parties—is now the weakest link in the system. While it has not disappeared, it has certainly changed in importance and, in many instances, in the kinds of activities it undertakes.

---

3. Direct-mail fund raising is targeted soliciting of contributions by interest groups, political parties, or other associations through the mail.
4. Issue groups are associations based on the pursuit of a single cause; they can be associated with a political party but are often independent of parties.

There are many explanations for local party decline. The most important include the following:

- The reforms of the Progressive Era, principally the growth of nonpartisan elections and civil service reform.[5] . . .

- The New Deal and the assumption of governmental responsibility for the well-being of the citizenry eliminated many services and rewards that the local party customarily offered members as incentives for belonging.

- The increased levels of education and access to employment by many in the population made the old material incentive for participation less valuable.

- The women's movement . . . encouraged the women most likely to be local volunteer activists to seek full-time employment but also affected their sense of how to spend leisure time, e.g., more on family-centered and health-related activities.

- The economy itself has forced both spouses to work in order to maintain an adequate standard of living.

- The complexity of modern campaign technology has placed greater emphasis on the centralization and professionalization of politics and less value on volunteer activity.

- The sheer complexity of the FECA and its amendments became an active discouragement to local party participation in federal elections.

Parties were required to maintain separate accounts for federal and state candidates (because many states permit corporate contributions that federal law does not), and were required to report all income and expenditures on behalf of their candidates for congressional elections. There were, and are, limits as well on how much the party can spend in presidential elections, especially during the general election, which is otherwise publicly financed.

Even though many observers blamed the decline in local party activity directly on the law, it soon became clear that while the law placed some burdens on the party, it placed greater prohibitions on others, and the cumulative effect was to enhance the role of the central (national and state) party in all campaigns. . . .

Resurgence of local parties is not likely in the immediate future. For our purposes, the question is not whether or not the local party is weak, but what caused the organizational decline and what—if anything—is likely to bring about a change. . . .

---

5. The New Progressive Era was an early-twentieth-century reform period that curtailed the power of political parties in the name of the people.

The National Impetus

Local party decline and the nationalization of issues were important dynamics in the restructuring of party organization, but perhaps the most important factors were the nature of modern campaign technology and the reform of campaign finance laws. . . . Politics [used to be a] labor-intensive operation. Campaigns needed people to stuff envelopes, knock on doors, engage in a multitude of research activities, and so on. Some of the work was essential to the campaign; some of it was "make work," designed to allow volunteers to make a contribution without letting them interrupt the development and implementation of campaign strategy. Most research activities by volunteers fell into the latter category. Nonetheless, campaign headquarters were rather free-wheeling places where individual entrepreneurship counted as much as anything, and creativity and energy were usually rewarded.

Today's campaigns are dominated by professionals. Research has become a highly focused and important part of campaign strategy. Polling data are available to test the attitudes of voters to candidates, issues, and campaign tactics. Complex computer analyses now provide tremendous amounts of information about the characteristics of the voting population and about the opponent: voting records, public utterances, backers, etc., all bear scrutiny. The computer has gone a long way toward alleviating the uncertainty so characteristic of past elections.

We may not yet have reached the stage where total manipulation of the population is possible, but we can at least measure the impact of campaign advertisements and events in 24-hour tracking polls. That level of sophistication leaves little room for volunteers who want to test their political sensibilities. It requires money, complex equipment, and persons who know how to compile and analyze the data. Much of the background information on issues, voters, and opponents requires years to amass and ongoing efforts to maintain. It is usually beyond the ability of the temporary campaign organization created by a challenger, and often beyond the ability of an incumbent. Individual campaign consulting firms are more apt to maintain the skills than the data because they cannot be sure which campaigns they will run. That leaves only the party because it is a permanent organization, and because it has the resources in money and accumulated hardware and software. . . .

Party Participation

. . . The passage of [a] federal campaign finance law was not directly intended to help the parties. Its main objective was to curb the undue influence of special interests: the eternal goal of political reform. After the first two election cycles (1976 and 1978), when it seemed that the law was hurting the parties, Congress sought to correct the perceived imbalance, again in the interests of limiting the influence of other groups. Although as a nation we have always been ambivalent about the value of the parties, most observers decried the apparent party decline and applauded legislative efforts to forestall the decline. What is interesting is how difficult it has been to reach a consensus on the consequences of the changes that have taken place in the past decade and a half. Most journalists, political scientists, and even politicians believe the strength of the parties ranges somewhere from dead to dying. A minority—generally those scholars who do research in Washington or in the states by talking to politicians and party leaders— have reached a far more optimistic assessment of party strength, but they are still divided on whether or not a strong central party is a good or an evil development. Political life is so complex and depends on so many variables that it encourages the coexistence of antithetical views. For those, like myself, who have been interviewing political activists since the early 1970s, the increases in strength of the national parties between then and now are truly startling. . . .

Nationalization: The Implications

The national parties are essentially professional organizations. They are well financed, mostly through millions of small individual contributions. The law, the technology, and the nature of national politics support the activities of the parties in candidate selection, use of resources to win elections, and, as a result of candidate dependency, using resources to influence public policy. These activities are traditional functions of a party, although for many years American political scientists have tended to emphasize only the parties' role in elections.

Underlying these activities are the coalitions that make up our politics: broad segments of the population and special interest groups. Since the 1960s the political environment has appeared fragmented: candidates were self-selected; interests were all-powerful. The development of strong national parties has brought some measure of cohesion to the scene, but the order that exists is hardly uniform.

The Party Versus Candidates: Who's Boss?

In 1976 the Republican National Committee began to intervene in primary elections in support of the candidates it had recruited for office. The behavior of the national party was a departure from the past and marked a turning point in the relationship between the parties and their candidates. Since 1980, the RNC has been prohibited by party rules from intervening unless invited in by the state party, but most national participation has been taken up by the House and Senate campaign committees for Republicans and Democrats. . . . The legitimacy and resources these committees provide in federal elections make them the single largest actor in a campaign. . . .

The Party Versus the Interests

As the late California Democrat Jesse Unruh once said, "Money is the mother's milk of politics." It can come from the candidate himself, individual supporters (now limited to $1,000 contributions per election), from the party, and from the interests. The age of candidate-centered politics coincided with the perception that the interests were king and the parties dead. . . . [Yet] the dramatic changes are to be found in the nuances of these proportions and in the evidence we can compile in interviews and observation.

The participation of interests in politics is not new. What is new is that campaign contributions are disclosed, and we can get some sense of the proportionate relationship one candidate has to some interests vis-à-vis another candidate's relationship. Some observers are appalled by the process. Others argue that the disclosure provisions of the law have simply opened our eyes to what probably went on before. The fear is that the interests are more powerful than the parties: there are more formally organized interest groups today than there used to be; they are centralized; they have more funds and greater sophistication in their use of funds; and they can act in concert. Some believe they have all but replaced the party by engaging "in broader forms of political activity, including political education, grassroots lobbying, coalition building, and electoral funding through political action committees." . . .

. . . [Yet] parties, almost by definition, seek to form majorities capable of sustaining credibility for governance. Interests rarely, if ever, represent majorities. Some may be more dominant than others, but the impetus to organize comes from fear that the majority voice will dominate. Coalitions of interests which would make a majority are difficult to mount and sustain over a period of time because of the narrowness of their goals and the changing saliency of their concern in the public mind. . . .

The main objective of a political party in our system is winning elections. Those who would place any other goal above that either tend to drop out, or to change their views, becoming more conciliatory toward others. Continual losses at the polls leave the party leadership ripe for another takeover, especially if there is a chance that another candidate might win. Parties which are so much in the minority that they do not stand a chance of winning may be able to afford the luxury of retaining their issue purity; however, both major parties have become more competitive around the nation in recent years and a contest is likely to draw them toward the middle as victory is sensed within reach. . . .

National Parties and Public Opinion

The party system described here represents a marked change from the past in terms of organizational structure. The ultimate question any student of party politics must ask, however, is "So what? Does party organization make a difference in how anyone believes or behaves?"

It used to be—in the halcyon days of the 1950s and before—that, if asked, an American would define him or herself by listing religion, ethnic background, region or state, and party identification: "I am a German Lutheran Democrat from Indiana." The response provided information about the values, political orientation, and often the class of the speaker. From it, one could predict a certain amount of behavior, barring extraordinary circumstances. Much of that predictability has declined in the past quarter century; and now, some believe, political predictability (and, by implication, political stability) extends only as far as the next election: "I am a Democrat" means the speaker will probably vote Democratic in November.

Political scientists believe that one of a party's principal functions was providing the framework for understanding political events. Party members were inclined to view the world through the prism of partisanship and believed their views corresponded with the party line. The complexity of political issues and communication being what it is, pollsters frequently discovered that the views were not as compatible as asserted, but, what is important for our purposes, is that the respondents *believed* they were.

As the decline of partisanship was measured through the 1960s and 1970s, that other American virtue—independence—asserted itself and a growing portion of the population described itself as not being bound by a party. "I vote for the man, not the party" was the common cry. Deeper analyses suggested, however, that many of those who described themselves as independents leaned toward one party or the other, and that these "leaners" tended to be as consistent in their voting behavior as party identifiers.

The parties reached their nadir in the late 1960s and early 1970s, as the proportion of independents grew. Confidence in most of our institutions declined, although party identifiers were likely to be more confident than their neighbors. The situation with regard to confidence changed in the 1980s, however, and both partisan identification and confidence increased, at least until the end of the decade when political scandals began erupting in the Reagan administration.

Although the issues of the day are a significant determinant of the confidence, political identification, and partisan strength in the electorate, it nonetheless makes sense to suggest that a strong national party that spends a good part of its resources communicating to supporters and potential supporters will have an impact on public opinion. . . . We can trace the rise and fall of organizational resources. We can measure activities and observe crises. When it comes to political opinion formation—including how and why people vote the way they do—we can only speculate. I would argue that the increased communications ability of the parties, particularly to supporters and potential supporters through the mail, telephone, media advertising, and professional staff at the national, state, and sometimes local levels, has an impact on public opinion.

The positions on issues expressed in these communications are, in fact, considerably clearer than what ordinarily came from a local party representative in the past. The messages are more direct, going from national and state party to the voter, and they are finely tuned, addressed to everything market research can tell the party about the economic and social status of the recipients. They are meant to have impact. . . .

If we cannot measure the direct correlation between party activity and opinion formation, we can borrow from the experience of fund raisers in other areas who aver that belief follows money: if you can get someone to contribute money to a cause by whatever strategy (e.g., personal appeal from a friend or community leader or at a social occasion) his or her commitment to the cause will increase after the donation. Opinion, in other words, will be formed and focused by the contribution and the attachment the donor has to the contributing act.

The one thing we know with certainty about party activity and growth in the past two decades is that the number of contributors has increased dramatically. The contributors, in turn, will increase their commitment to the party and to the issues described by the party to motivate the contribution in the first place, and each contributor is likely to have an impact on the opinions of those in his or her circle of family, friends, and associates.

There are times when some issues are more divisive than others, and although parties normally seek to assemble coalitions and represent large, uncontroversial segments of the population, if the issues are significant, in time, one or the other party (in a two-party system) will move to adopt a position. These periods of political upheaval, which we like to think are reflected in significant voter realignments, clearly have a more dramatic impact on public opinion and party identification than does the less sensational work of party loyalists. But such diverse issues are not always in evidence, nor are they necessarily clearly divided up by the parties. In their absence, the work of the parties in opinion formation is the most probable cause of growth in party identity as a first step, and opinions about political issues as a second step. . . .

My argument is only intended to be stretched far enough to make the case that party strength has increased, when measured by organizational resources and behavior, and that one consequence of the improved organizational ability is, and will continue to be, an increase in the impact of parties on public opinion.

Rancid Populism

WILLIAM GREIDER

T he contemporary Republican party seems brilliantly suited to the modern age, for it has perfected the art of maintaining political power in the midst of democratic decay. The party of Lincoln has become the party of mass marketing, applying marketing's elaborate technologies to the task of winning elections. From this, it has fashioned a most improbable marriage of power—a hegemony of monied interests based on the alienation of powerless citizens.

As men of commerce, Republicans naturally understood marketing better than Democrats, and they applied what they knew about selling products to politics with none of the awkward hesitation that inhibited old-style politicians. As a result, voters are now viewed as a passive assembly of "consumers," a mass audience of potential buyers. Research discovers through scientific sampling what it is these consumers know or think and, more important, what they feel, even when they do not know their own "feelings." A campaign strategy is then designed to connect the candidate with these consumer attitudes. Advertising images are created that will elicit positive responses and make the sale.

To understand the basic approach, one has only to watch an evening of television, not the programs but the commercials. There are wondrous things to behold on TV—cars that turn into sleek panthers and stallions, or that take off and fly like jet airplanes. Beers that magically produce jiggling young women in bikinis. Basketball shoes that allow small boys to soar like gazelles. There are patriotic soaps and talking toilets and phallic deodorants. In this dimension of reality, a presidential candidate who is actually a cowboy on horseback seems quite plausible.

The essential transaction in modern marketing is that most products are separated from their intrinsic qualities—since most brands are basically not that different—and imbued with fabulous mythical attributes that attract buyers. Consumers understand (at least most do) that cars will not fly and that underarm deodorants do not increase sexual potency. Still, the advertising's fantasies provide as good a reason as any to choose one brand over another that is just the same.

"Increasingly people buy a product not because of its benefits but because they identify, or strive to identify, with the kind of people they think use it," Karen Olshan, a senior vice-president of BBDO, explained to a business-magazine writer. Paula Drillman, executive director of strategic research at McCann Erickson, emphasized that consumer emotions are a more reliable basis for selling than the "rational beliefs" of the product itself.

"Rational benefits are vulnerable," she explained, "because with today's technology it's easy to knock off a competitor's innovation quickly or play on his marketing turf. Emotional bonds, on the other hand, are hard to break."

The same logic has now become the prevailing rule for political competition in the media age. Campaign consultants and managers describe the electoral process in the same dispassionate—and amoral—terms. Elections are for selling, not for governing and certainly not for accountability. The selling depends, not on rational debate or real differences, but on concocting emotional bonds between the candidate and the audience.

"We had only one goal in the campaign and that was to elect George Bush," Lee Atwater, Bush's 1988 campaign manager, told *The New York Times*. "Our campaign was not trying to govern the country."

"Campaigns are not for educating," GOP consultant Douglas Bailey told *The Washington Post*. "They're for linking up with the public mood."

No one gets educated in election seasons—neither voters nor candidates—because provocative new ideas may disrupt the formation of emotional ties. Discussing the actual content of governing issues simply complicates the message. "Pollsters are so good that it is possible to know at every minute what people think," Doug Bailey told a Washington seminar. "No political leader needs to guess at what the people think about any issue and, therefore, there is no need ever to go out and lead."

In this realm, Democrats have had to overcome certain cultural disadvantages. Their political experience originates, for the most part, in old-fashioned organizational settings, labor unions or protest movements or good-government causes. Republican managers came from backgrounds in public relations, advertising and corporate management, all of which are familiar with the contours of advertising messages. Democrat Mike McCurry described his party's handicap: "Our idea of politics is to go out and build coalitions among different groups and so you don't get 'Big Think.' You get 'Big Think' from the corporate culture of mass communications."

Much of what currently passes for strategic planning within the Democratic party is actually a forlorn discussion about how to emulate the Republican party's mass-marketing skills. As Democrats learn to catch up, the content and relevance of election campaigns naturally becomes even less satisfying to those expecting a serious debate about governing agendas. The conduct of contemporary electoral politics is like what would happen if an automobile company decided to fire its engineers and let the advertising guys design the new model. The car they package might sell. It just wouldn't run very well. . . .

Politicians face the same dilemma: They are spending more and more money on messages that get weaker and weaker in terms of eliciting a reliable response from voters. That is the primary reason for the proliferation of negative ads in campaigns—the need to be heard, not the declining morals of candidates. Negative attacks are more exciting and, therefore, more memorable to viewers. They deliver provocative information that is more likely to stick in the minds of the audience—the buyer-voter who is besotted each evening with glossy appeals for his loyalty. Politics is merely following the negative trend in commercial advertising, where more and more companies are sponsoring their own "attack ads" on the competing products. . . .

Exhortations to conscience from the press are not likely to reverse this trend. So long as political communication depends so singularly on expensive mass media, the competition for attention will drive the most high-minded candidates to explore the low road—because it promises a more efficient use of scarce advertising dollars. Republican campaign managers seem to understand this better than Democrats, especially during presidential campaigns.

As an organization, the Republican party shares many of the Democrats' problems: a client-based Washington establishment, a very weak party structure and the same preoccupation with political money. Republicans also lack connective tissue—people in communities who are reliably linked to the people in power. Paul Weyrich, a conservative reformer who is president of the Free Congress Research and Education Foundation, remarked: "The difficulty with the Republican party is that in large areas of the country, it doesn't exist."

But the Grand Old Party is more successful than the Democrats at raising political money and at deploying it. . . . The Republican party is less burdened than Democrats by the ethical implications of these money transactions. After all, it is the party of business enterprise. . . . It has always defended propertied wealth and corporations against the political claims of workers and others, so there is not the same tension of implicit betrayal when Republicans collect huge treasuries from business interests or wealthy individuals and institutions. Indeed, if the Republican party exists mainly to defend and enhance the monied interests, it has been a spectacularly effective political institution in recent years.

The more challenging question about the Republican party is how it manages to accomplish this—since the political results seem to pose a democratic contradiction. It wins national elections, often overwhelmingly, yet it is the party that most faithfully represents the minority, namely wealth holders. The Republican hegemony of the 1980s demonstrably benefited the few over the many—in private incomes and tax burdens, as well as in the distribution of public services. Yet its electoral success was undiminished.[1] . . .

---

1. Greider wrote this essay in 1992, before Clinton's 1992 and 1996 victories, and the GOP surge in 1994. In the 1990s, the Democrats came close to equaling the GOP in amounts spent. See Chapter 11.

Nor can the contradiction be explained as public ignorance, since the public knows that the GOP is the party of money. In a *New York Times*/CBS survey, conducted in the midst of the 1988 presidential election, 64 percent of the electorate identified the Republican party as the party of the rich. Only 20 percent said it treats all classes equally; only 9 percent described Republicans as the party of the middle class. Furthermore, most people seem to have a roughly accurate sense of what Republican economic policy accomplished during the 1980s. They at least know their own tax burden grew while corporations and the wealthy enjoyed huge tax cuts.[2]

How does the GOP overcome this handicap? The Democratic party helped substantially by retreating from its own position as the party of labor and the "little guy." When there are no dramatic differences of substance between two candidates or two parties, the impact of the fantasy qualities concocted in TV ads grows even stronger. . . .

Republicans have also succeeded through marketing themes that connect powerfully and positively with the deepest national values: patriotism; America's singular sense of itself in the world; our faith in individual work and enterprise; our abundant optimism. This success, however, still does not get at the heart of the explanation.

The party of money wins power in national elections mainly by posing as the party of the disaffected. From its polling and other research data, it concocts a rancid populism that is perfectly attuned to the age of political alienation—a message of antipower. . . .

"Simply put," [former Republican campaign manager Lee Atwater has] said, "there is constantly a war going on between the two parties for the populist vote. The populist vote is always the swing vote. It's been the swing vote in every election. The Democrats have always got to nail Republicans as the party of the fat cats, in effect, the party of the upper class and privilege. And the Democrats will maintain that they are the party of the little man, the common man. To the extent they're successful, Republicans are unsuccessful."

The term "populism," so abused in modern usage, is now applied routinely to almost any idea or slogan that might actually appeal to ordinary people. In history, the Populists of the late nineteenth century constituted a specific citizens' movement that was rich in democratic promise and far-sighted ideas. Calling themselves the People's party, the farmers of the South and Middle West revolted against both major parties and the emerging dominance of corporate capitalism. They fell short of power themselves, but their far-sighted ideas lived and many were subsequently adopted in government. By that historical standard, there is very little in the trivial sentiments of modern politics that qualifies as genuinely "populist."

---

2. Polls in the late 1990s reveal that citizens still see the GOP as the party of the rich but by lesser margins.

When the term is used now, it usually means to convey not ideas, but a political mood—resentment against established power, distrust of major institutions and a sense of powerlessness. In this period of history, it is perhaps not an accident that so many of the effective political managers are southerners. The South understands alienation better than the rest of the nation. Feelings that were once peculiar to a single section of America—the defeated region within the nation—have now taken over the national mood.

Uniting alienated voters into political coalition with the most powerful economic interests has a distinctly old-fashioned flavor of southern demagoguery, since the strategy requires the party to agitate the latent emotional resentments and turn them into marketable political traits.[3] The raw materials for this are drawn from enduring social aggravations—wounds of race, class and religion, even sex.

The other party's candidate is not simply depicted as unworthy of public office, but is connected to alien forces within the society that threaten to overwhelm decent folk—libertine sexual behavior, communists, criminals, people of color demanding more than they deserve. The Republican party, thoroughly modern itself, poses as the bulwark against unsettling modernity. . . .

[Then–Vice President] George Bush's "Willie Horton" became the topic at every dinner table in 1988, just as Atwater hoped, and was actually the most interesting event in the long, dreary presidential campaign. Is this an issue of prison furloughs for convicted murderers or is it really about black men raping white women? Two years later Senator Jesse Helms won re-election in North Carolina with a devastating commercial called "White Hands"—white hands replaced by black hands. Is this an argument about affirmative-action "quotas" or is it really about white people who resent uppity black people? No one can ever settle these arguments, any more than one can prove that the Budweiser commercials exploit adolescent sexual craving to sell beer.

These Republican messages build bridges across class lines. They give people who are not themselves well-to-do and do not share the economic interests of traditional Republicans a reason to join the party of money. The Republican party cannot win without them, as it well knows, so it must assemble a set of ideas that will attract millions of voters from the lower middle stratum of the economy—disaffected Democrats with conservative social and religious values—who are persuaded to see their old party as "them" and the GOP as "us." . . .

Race is only one of the bridges, though surely the most powerful. A generation ago, the alien force threatening American values was communism, and the GOP, led by Senator Joseph McCarthy, sought to expose the "trai-

---

3. Southern demagogues are post–Civil War southern politicians who inflamed whites' racial hatreds and class resentments to win and maintain political office.

tors" lurking within the society—mostly, it seemed, within the Democratic party.[4] In the turmoil of the 1960s, the bridge was expanded to include drugs and crime and the disturbances of cultural change. In the 1980s, all those themes endured and Democrats were portrayed, not simply as wrong-headed opponents, but as enemies of the American way of life.

"Now we have a way of dividing America," [Republican] Representative Newt Gingrich of Georgia told *The Washington Post*.[5] He was referring to the "value-laden" issues of crime, drugs, education and corruption, which he attributed to the failures of Democratic liberals. "These people are sick," he told *The Wall Street Journal*. "They are destructive of the values we believe in."

The basic problem with the Republican electoral strategy is that it does not have much to do with governing, especially at the federal level. American politics has always been rich in demagogic diversions and empty appeals to nativist emotions; both parties share that history. The modern Republican hegemony, however, is most striking in the divergence it fosters between elections and governing.

Millions of voters are persuaded to cross the bridge, but they do not get much in return on the other side. Once in power, the Republican government serves the traditional Republican economic interests. The aggravations of modernity, meanwhile, persist. The fears of crime and race and decaying moral values do not abate. They merely accumulate for exploitation in the next election. . . .

The Republican hegemony, therefore, depends upon a more subtle form of betrayal. The party's method deliberately coaxes emotional responses from people—teases their anxieties over values they hold important in their own lives—but then walks away from the anger and proceeds to govern on its real agenda, defending the upper-class interests of wealth and corporate power. Government . . . is assumed to be rational and expert; the raw emotions of people are unscientific and distrusted.

The Republican government, aside from empty gestures, has no serious interest in resolving the anger it has aroused. After all, popular anger is the political commodity that it uses, again and again. Everyone in Washington understands this, Democrats and Republicans alike, and there is a professional admiration for the way in which Republicans ignite bonfires of public passion, then coolly walk away from them, without repercussions. George Bush ran against the "Harvard-boutique liberals," then appointed Harvard people to six Cabinet-level positions, plus many other second-rung government jobs. No one really minds. Everyone knows it was just a slogan.

---

4. Joseph McCarthy was a Wisconsin Republican senator who in the early 1950s led a smear campaign against supposed Communists in government and other institutions.
5. Representative Gingrich was elected House Speaker after the 1994 congressional elections and retired in early 1999 after the GOP suffered losses in the 1998 House elections.

The reason the Republicans succeed at this may be that cynical citizens do not expect much more from politics. Certainly, most voters who took the bait do not express great surprise when a succession of Republican governments fails to deliver meaningful responses to their discontent. Voters, as savvy TV viewers, are perhaps wise enough to understand that the pictures that aroused their emotions have no real connection with governing decisions, that nothing much will actually happen in Washington to deal with their fears or anger.

Possibly, people are entertained by Republican politics in the same way they are entertained by the mythical qualities that emanate from the commercial advertising. If all politicians are alike, corrupt and unreliable, you might as well vote for the one who got the patriotic music right, the one who at least talked about *your* anger, *your* fears.

People know elections, like television commercials, are not real. All that the campaign images provide them is an imagined moment of aroused feeling—a transient emotional bond with those who will hold power, a chance to identify with certain idealized qualities, but not an opportunity to connect with real governing power. If manipulated voters do not feel cheated, it is because the Republican party gives them a chance, as the perfume commercial says, to "share the fantasy." . . .

While the social issues evoke the strongest emotions, the unnatural nature of the Republican coalition is exposed most clearly on the economic questions of government.[6] In the abstract, the social conservatives have the same ideological disposition toward unfettered business enterprise and smaller government that is espoused by orthodox Republicans. In the practical terms of their own class interests, however, these voters are often on the opposite side from the Republican orthodoxy. . . .

Notwithstanding their populist phrasemaking, most conservatives in Congress faithfully vote for the business position on these divisive issues and others. Republican politicians, for instance, talk endlessly about their devotion to protecting the family (and sometimes even describe Democrats as antifamily), but most of them voted against family rights and for corporate rights when the choice came down to that. The parental leave measure that Democrats pushed for working mothers and fathers was vetoed by Bush as an excessive intrusion on management practices; the profamily conservatives . . . limply went along with the business argument.[7]

The deeper split in Republican ranks is about money. . . . The character of Ronald Reagan—particularly his videogenic skills—was important in

---

6. By social issues, Greider means abortion, school prayer, affirmative action, the death penalty, and family values.

7. The parental leave measure was legislation requiring businesses to allow unpaid leave for employees who are new parents or who need to take care of ill relatives. Such a law was passed in 1993 after President Clinton's inauguration. Parental leave was opposed by President Bush and many congressional Republicans.

obscuring the corporate power in the GOP. "Reagan was criticial," [Paul] Weyrich said. "He did not strike social conservatives as being owned by those big business people. Reagan was 50 percent different from the old Republican party, he had elements of populism. Democrats never attacked Reagan on that. If I were them, I would have said, "This guy may have come from a small town, but remember who owns him—General Electric and all that."

Democrats, if they had the will, could still break up the Republican coalition, Weyrich believes, by defining a stark opposition to Republican economics—in particular, on the trade issue and foreign competition, the continuing loss of American jobs and spreading foreign ownership of American real estate and companies. "Democrats can sound macho if they attack on that issue because it makes them sound like nationalists, but they don't seem to have it in them," Weyrich said.

The Democrats' reluctance is not simply a matter of will, of course, but of corporate political influence. In that regard, the Democratic elites and the Republican elites look very much alike. But the Republican party elites—lawyers, lobbyists, corporate managements, fundraisers—are even closer to the multinational corporations and foreign interests than the Democrats. . . .

The Republican party is not a party of conservative ideology. It is a party of conservative clients. Wherever possible, the ideology will be invoked as justification for taking care of the clients' needs. When the two are in conflict, the conservative principles are discarded and the clients are served.

The most fundamental ideological contradiction of the [1980s] was the extraordinary explosion of federal deficits and debt during the Reagan years and continuing under [President] George Bush. Nothing else conflicts more profoundly with conservative beliefs about government, for the GOP was always the party of balanced budgets and fiscal responsibility (and indeed still limply claims the mantle). Yet, twelve years after coming to power under Reagan, the supposedly conservative government produced an annual federal deficit of $390 billion.

When all of the fanciful economic argumentation is stripped away, the enormous deficits were provoked by the regressive tax cuts for business and wealthy individuals and by the rapid buildup in defense spending. Both of these actions served important clients in the Republican hierarchy, the defense industry and the wealth holders, and served them well.

Conservative anguish about the deficits was never sufficient to produce the painful action of actually reducing them, for that would have required the Republican White House to sacrifice its own clients. A third alternative—cutting Social Security and domestic social programs—was more appealing to Republicans, but Democrats were defending those clients and, as budget director David Stockman learned to his sorrow, Republicans were never very serious about this possibility anyway. "I have a new theory," Stockman declared bitterly in 1981. "There are no real conservatives in Congress."

Conservative ideology opposes federal regulation of private enterprise, and the Reagan era advanced the cause of deregulation on many fronts— mostly by making irregular deals with specific industries that amounted to de facto decisions not to enforce the law. Nevertheless, in case after case, when industries pleaded for new federal regulation as a way of preempting meddlesome state governments, the conservative government swung around to the other side and decided in favor of federal regulation.

The true loyalties of the Republican regime were demonstrated most vividly in the continuing series of financial crises. When the small farm banks in the Midwest began to fail in greater numbers in the early 1980s, the Republican administrators articulated a laissez-faire response: Let the marketplace work its will, however painful. But when Continental Illinois, eighth-largest bank in the nation, failed in 1984, the same Republicans agreed that this bank was "too big to fail," and they came to its rescue with a multi-billion-dollar bailout. Subsequently, in case after case, the largest banks in Texas, Massachusetts, Washington, D.C., and elsewhere were saved from failure and their largest depositors were protected from loss, while smaller institutions were allowed to disappear.

When some of the largest commercial banks in the nation (fine old Republican names like Chase Manhattan and Citibank) were threatened with insolvency, George Bush's White House urged federal bank regulators to bend the rules, and its domestic agenda was preoccupied with enhancing the profitability of banks. When the big money is in trouble, the Republican party finds itself acting like a compassionate liberal.

The Republican governance, in sum, could not be described as conservative in any historical sense of the word. Taken all together, the Republican policies more nearly resembled a right-wing version of the New Deal— intervening massively on behalf of worthy clients. In practical affairs, the government functioned according to principles that were closer to the liberal government of Franklin Roosevelt than to conservative creeds espoused by Robert A. Taft or Barry Goldwater. The difference with FDR's New Deal was, of course, fundamental: The modern Republicans intervened, not on behalf of struggling labor unions or distressed sharecroppers or the destitute elderly, but in order to assist the most powerful enterprises in the economy.

To understand the Republican party (or the Democratic party, for that matter), it is most efficient to look directly at the clients—or as political scientist Thomas Ferguson would call them, "the major investors." On that level, the ideological contradictions are unimportant. Political parties do function as mediating institutions, only not for voters.

Ferguson . . . analyzes political parties by identifying the major sources of their financing—the individuals from finance and industry who naturally have the greatest stake in influencing government decisions. "The real market for political parties," Ferguson says, "is defined by major investors, who generally have good and clear reasons for investing to control the state. . . . Blocs of major investors define the core of political parties and are responsible for most of the signals the party sends to the electorate." . . .

The Reagan-Bush governance, in Ferguson's portraiture, has been a running contest between two blocs of business interests with very different objectives in government policy. The "protectionists" are centered in old industries, textiles and steel for instance, that are traditionally Republican and anxious for help in the domestic markets. The "multinationals" are manufacturers and bankers as well as exporters, high-tech firms, oil companies, defense manufacturers—all interested in an aggressive global policy.

The list alone makes it clear which group has more girth and political power, but the Republican regime attempted to serve both blocs, when there was no irreconcilable conflict between them. "In effect," Ferguson wrote, "the Reagan economic coalition always had a huge seam running down its middle . . . the 'Reagan Revolution' was a giant banner under which two columns marched in different directions."

For the Republican old guard in heavy industry, the party in power mainly provided temporary relief from long-standing aggravations—relief from imports, from organized labor, from government regulation and, of course, from federal taxes. The severe recession of the early Reagan years was devastating to manufacturing, but it also smashed labor unions and provided the opportunity for corporate restructurings, free of restraints from the workers. By 1985, the Reagan administration focused its diplomatic energies on driving down the dollar's foreign-exchange rate and, thus, launched an export boom for the domestic manufacturers—just in time for the 1988 election.

For the multinationals, from Boeing and Citibank to Exxon and General Electric, the political goals were much more substantial and even historic—maintaining America's role as manager (and occasionally enforcer) in the emerging global trading system anchored also in Japan and Germany. Dating from the New Deal era, multinational corporations and investment banks had once been aligned with the Democratic party, then the party of free trade. In Ferguson's telling, American politics got interesting in the 1970s when the multinationals shifted their allegiance to the GOP.

They have been well served by the new alliance. The U.S. buildup of armaments [in the 1980s], which they had promoted, would be a significant token of leadership resolve to the competitor nations who were also allies (as well as an abundant source of contracts for the defense companies). The multinational financial institutions, banks and brokerages, benefited enormously from the rising dollar—and even from the accumulating deficits—because both produced expanded financial activity as the bankers recycled U.S. debt to Japanese lenders. . . .

While the Republican government extended trade protection to some of the old-line industrial sectors, its main energies were devoted to the multinationals—defending and extending their prerogatives in the global trading system. The close working relationships the Reagan and Bush administrations formed with Japan and Germany were integral to this objective—their governments wanted much the same outcome. But the U.S. strategy gradually turned into dependency, as America's financial position weakened and the nation became indebted to its economic competitors.

Quite apart from the economic injury done to individual classes of citizens, Republican governing—by and for the "major investors"—has not led to the general prosperity and economic stability described in the conservative rhetoric. On the contrary, while each influential sector gets what it wants, the economy overall has sunk deeper into debt and failures, dependency and competitive disadvantage.

In other words, what [political scientist Theodore] Lowi called "interest-group liberalism" has been transformed by Republicans into what might be called "interest-group conservatism."[8] From labor law to financial regulation, conservatives use the governmental forms invented by liberal reformers to serve their own clients' interests. Liberals have difficulty coming to grips with this since the economic interventions on behalf of selected sectors or enterprises are consistent with their own governing philosophy.

The deleterious effects are visible for the nation as a whole. The short-run demands of elite interests do not add up to a workable scheme for governing the economy on behalf of the nation's long-term well-being. The powerful win their narrow victories; the country loses. So long as this system is the core of how the government decides the most important questions, ordinary citizens will find ample justification for their discontent.

Organized money versus organized people—the only way to break out of this governing system is, again, to imagine a democratic renewal that brings people back into the contest. Thomas Ferguson, though quite pessimistic about the prospects, described the outlines of the solution:

"To effectively control governments, ordinary voters require strong channels that directly facilitate mass deliberation and expression. That is, they must have available to them a resilient network of 'secondary' organizations capable of spreading costs and concentrating small contributions from several individuals to act politically, as well as an open system of formally organized political parties.

"Both the parties and the secondary organizations need to be 'independent,' i.e., themselves dominated by investor-voters (instead of, for example, donors of revokable outside funds). Entry barriers for both secondary organizations and political parties must be low, and the technology of political campaigning (e.g., cost of newspaper space, pamphlets, etc.) must be inexpensive in terms of the annual income of the average voter. Such conditions result in high information flows to the grassroots, engender lively debate and create conditions that make political deliberation and action part of everyday life."

---

8. The term *interest-group liberalism* is used to describe the often incestuous relationship between government agencies and the particular clienteles they fund, regulate, and serve; it most often refers to programs developed by Democrats in the 1960s.

Those "conditions" for effective citizen control of government are what is missing from both political parties and from American democracy. So long as citizens remain unorganized, they will be prey to clever manipulation by mass marketing. So long as people must rely on empty TV images for their connection to politics, then, as Ferguson concluded, nothing can "prevent a tiny minority of the population—major investors—from dominating the political system."

DISCUSSION QUESTIONS

1. Kayden seems to argue that U.S. political parties need to spend large sums of money because the new technology of politics is expensive. In 1996, both parties raised unprecedented amounts of cash, yet together they spent less on advertising than the potato chip industry did in the same year. How would Greider deal with the argument that the parties have to keep up with modern developments in communications?

2. Why do both authors concern themselves with the question of party decline? Can't ordinary citizens now participate just as effectively in interest groups, social movements, letter writing, or other kinds of "nonpartisan" activities?

3. Talk to your parents, grandparents or other older relatives about their impressions of the parties when they were your age. Compare notes on these interviews with others in your class. In what ways have images of the parties changed since your older relatives were young?

4. Discuss the following quote: "The problem with American political parties is not that they are too weak, but that they are too strong. Citizen democracy envisioned by the Founders is less about parties than it is about the integrity of each individual. Parties crush individual participation in the name of the group."

5. Why do the Republicans seem to have a "natural" edge over the Democrats when it comes to the new forms of national party organization? Why don't the Democrats fight back by organizing and mobilizing their "natural" constituencies among the working class and poor?

SUGGESTED READINGS AND INTERNET RESOURCES

A favorable and comprehensive account of modern U.S. political parties is provided in John Green and Daniel Shea, eds., *The State of the Parties* (3d ed.; Lanham, Md.: Rowman and Littlefield, 1999). A provocative argument urging the Democrats to recapture their lost base among low- and middle-income citizens is Stanley Greenberg and Theda Skocpol, eds., *The New Majority* (New Haven, Conn.: Yale University Press, 1999). See also Frances Fox Piven, *The Breaking of the Social Contract* (New York: New Press, 1998), for a compelling set of essays on the Democrats' drift rightward. A detailed treatment of the GOP in Washington is Linda Killian, *The Freshman* (Boulder, Colo.: Westview Press, 1998).

Project Vote Smart
www.vote-smart.org
Targeted to young voters, this site includes highly accessible information on parties and virtually all their state and federal candidates. Includes surveys of youth and their political preferences, too, and neutral analyses of speeches, position papers, and money in campaigns.

Townhall.com
www.townhall.com
National umbrella site for conservative and GOP-allied groups, foundations, think tanks, and activitists of all kinds.

Electronic Policy Network
www.epn.com
A similar site to Townhall but for liberal Democrats. This site contains more nonpartisan groups than Townhall, however.

The major political parties all maintain extensive web sites. The following is a list of their national web sites:

GOP: www.rnc.org
Democrats: www.democrats.org
Greens: www.greens.org
Libertarians: www.lb.org
New Party: www.newparty.org
Reform Party: www.reformparty.org

11

Campaigns and Elections: Organized Money Versus (Dis)Organized People?

From the nineteenth century's camp meetings and torchlight parades to today's sound bites and attack ads, political campaigns are parts of American democratic folklore. Despite their hoopla and hype, electoral campaigns are serious business. Without them, voters wouldn't have a choice, couldn't get organized, and would judge their would-be rulers in ignorance and isolation.

Today, however, a chorus of critics complains about campaigns. Campaigns often seem to be personality contests that trivialize issues rather than engage the electorate. Supercharged accusations fly between candidates, without much sense of their truth value. The media often compound the problem through sensationalized coverage. Campaign professionals and spin doctors seem to orchestrate images and manipulate voters rather than respond to their deeper aspirations. Sensing that they're being used, many citizens become cynical spectators, or withdraw from the electoral process entirely.

While there are few unqualified fans of modern campaigns, there are some defenders of the process. Most of the voters, most of the time, seem to learn something from campaigns, and when voters care enough to participate, the democratic debate seems to improve. The 1992 and 1994 electoral contests, some say, were more substantive because many voters demanded precision and substance from the candidates and the parties. Perhaps campaigns are no better or worse than the society from which they emerge.

High-tech campaigns may also be inevitable. Old-style, door-to-door campaigning just isn't possible in a country of 270 million people, whose attention is constantly distracted from politics by the burdens of work, family, and the diversions of entertainment. Politicians and parties have to rely on costly and sophisticated advertising, focus groups, and public opinion polls because it is impossible to know every voter and because of the competition for attention. In any case, perhaps campaigns are no worse than they used to be; competitive elections have always been messy affairs, and perhaps today's critics romanticize the past.

Nonetheless, there are some notable developments in modern election campaigns that deserve extended scrutiny. Successful campaigns have always had ample amounts of cash, but today the new technology of politics—polls, advertising, and image-makers—requires money in amounts that seem to utterly exclude the unconnected or the unrich. Today, political campaigns may be monopolized by interests and candidates concerned less with addressing the needs of voters than of the privileged, that slender slice of American society that contributes the cash that makes campaigns effective.

Raising money has almost always mattered in U.S. campaigns, but in the 1990s and in the 2000 election, it became a feeding frenzy. In 1998, the average Senate seat cost the winner close to $6 million; to raise these amounts, the victor would have to solicit about $2,500 for every day he or she was in office. For a winning House candidate, over $1,000 a day for over two years was the norm. And for presidential races, the already high money totals of the 1980s soared into orbit by the turn of the new millennium. By New Year's Day of 2000, more than ten months before the election, George W. Bush had already raised $67 million, almost doubling the previous record just four years before. And these amounts did not even include the most rapidly expanding sources—so-called soft money—given to the national and state political parties ($263 million in 1996, a predicted $500 million or so in 2000).

The growing cash pile has prompted moves for reform both in Congress and in some states, spurred on by Senator John McCain's 2000 presidential campaign. Public opinion surveys revealed wide support for regulation of campaign money but not for any specific proposal to do so. In some states— notably Maine, Vermont, Massachusetts, and Arizona—public financing of campaigns was passed by voters. In Congress, attempts to ban soft money contributions were proposed but were blocked by the Republican leadership in both houses. By 2000, the effect of money on campaigns was still very much a public issue, but the road to reform seemed foggy.

Is the cost of money-driven campaigns too high? Or is the right to contribute money to candidates an expression of a lively democracy? Answers to these questions provide judgment about the state of American democracy itself. For people who believe in popular democracy, today's campaigns have to be judged by how well or poorly they promote talk and participation by ordinary voters. While money, advertising, polling, and professional marketing may never disappear from contemporary campaigns, do these drown out democratic activity by volunteers and organizations that have little money to give? Popular democrats look to a historical standard by which to judge modern campaigns. Which is more important: organized money or organized people? Do modern campaigns mean that only candidates who are wealthy or backed by wealthy people can succeed? And does money undermine the egalitarian spirit of one citizen, one vote, which is supposed to be the basis of democracy itself?

For elite democrats, money's corrupting role is far from clear. Money is said to promote effective free speech, for to be heard requires resources and organization. Reformers, in their zeal to create a wall between money and politics, don't understand why generations of reformers have been ineffective; no matter what the laws intend, organized money in a free society will always find a way to be heard. The best that we can hope for in a free society is that the sources of money be made known to the electorate. Existing laws passed in the 1970s could be beefed up to further disclosure, and there are already ample laws on the books to limit the size of contributions to individual candidates. Anything more than that is said to be a violation of the democratic norm of free speech and would backfire on democracy itself.

The two essays reprinted here both articulate and expand on these arguments. Bradley A. Smith, an Ohio law professor, provides a persuasive case against further efforts to regulate campaign contributions. He finds little evidence to support the charges of people who believe that campaign donations corrupt the political process, and much evidence that limits on campaign spending would prevent full debate and discussion of contentious political issues. Sociologists Dan Clawson, Alan Neustadtl, and Mark Weller respond with a careful study of what corporate contributors expect from politicians as they hand out the cash. They argue that business campaign contributions "subvert democracy" for numerous reasons, and they propose a system of public financing of campaigns to level the playing field.

While reading these essays, you might think about the following questions: How would the "Dollars and Votes" authors respond to Smith's charge that regulating campaign money never works? How would Smith deal with the problem of the amount of time politicians must devote to fund-raising? All the authors rely on an historical standard of democracy to defend their claims. What do the authors of each essay mean by the term?

Free Speech Requires Campaign Money

BRADLEY A. SMITH

I n 1974, Congress passed amendments to the Federal Elections Campaign Act that, for the first time in our nation's history, seriously undertook to regulate political campaigns. Most states followed suit, and virtually overnight, politics became a heavily regulated industry.

Yet we now see, on videotape and in White House photos, shots of the President of the United States meeting with arms merchants and drug dealers; we learn of money being laundered through Buddhist nuns and Indonesian gardeners; we read that acquaintances of the President are fleeing the country, or threatening to assert Fifth Amendment privileges to avoid testifying before Congress. Regulation, we were told two decades ago, would free our elected officials from the clutches of money, but they now seem to devote more time than ever before to pursuing campaign cash. The 1974 reforms, we were promised, would open up political competition, yet the purely financial advantage enjoyed by incumbents in congressional races has increased almost threefold. Regulation was supposed to restore confidence in government, yet the percentage of Americans who trust their government to "do what is right most of the time" is half what it was before the 1974 act, and campaigns themselves seem nastier and less informative.

Well, say apologists for the law, if we have failed, it is only because our labors have just begun. If our goals seem further away, we must redouble our efforts. We must ban political action committees (PAC's). We must prevent "bundling," a procedure whereby a group collects contributions from its members and delivers them all at once to a candidate's election committee. We must ban large contributions to political parties ("soft money"). . . .

If existing regulation has failed so spectacularly, and existing laws are being broken seemingly at will, is more regulation the solution? Before we rush off on another round, it may be worthwhile to examine the premises on which the impulse to regulate campaign finance is based. Each of them is severely flawed.

II

The first assumption underlying proposals for campaign-finance regulation is that too much money is being spent on political campaigning. The amounts are often described in near-apocalyptic terms. Candidates, we are informed, amass "huge war chests" from "fat cats" who "pour their millions" into campaigns and "stuff the pockets" of representatives in an "orgy" of contributions. Expenditures "skyrocket," leaving legislators "awash" in "obscene" amounts of cash.

Hyperbole aside, however, the amount spent each year on all political activity in the United States, from every ballot referendum to races for every office from dog catcher to President, is less than the amount spent on potato chips. Total spending on congressional races in 1995–96 was less than what is spent annually on Barbie dolls. Total PAC contributions in federal elections in 1995–96 were just about equal to the amount needed to produce the most recent *Batman* movie.

On a per-voter basis, our expenditures are equally low: less than $2.50 per eligible voter per year, or about the cost of a single video rental, for all congressional races, including all primaries. . . .

Perhaps more relevant than any of these comparisons are the amounts spent on political campaigning versus other types of advertising. In 1996, the Home Depot corporation alone spent more on advertising than federal law allowed Bill Clinton, Bob Dole, and Ross Perot put together to spend on the general election. Although Michael Huffington was roundly criticized for "exorbitant" spending in his 1994 race for a Senate seat from California, it cost him less than what Sony International spent in the same year to promote a single compact disc by Michael Jackson. . . .

The plain truth is that it costs money to communicate, and there is no reason to expect that political communication should come free. This is the crucial insight of the Supreme Court's 1976 decision in *Buckley* v. *Valeo,* a case issuing from a challenge to the 1974 Federal Elections Campaign Act by a broad coalition of groups ranging from the ACLU to the Conservative and Libertarian parties. There the Court struck down mandatory limits on campaign spending as well as limits on what a candidate could spend from his own personal funds. The Court did not say, as its critics have alleged, that money equals speech; rather, it recognized that limits on spending can restrict speech just as surely as can a direct prohibition. Imagine, for example, if newspapers were limited to $100,000 a year for publishing costs: most would go out of business, and those that remained would become very thin indeed. . . .

Spending on political advertisements is important to educate voters, increasing their interest in elections and their knowledge of candidates and issues. Repetition plays an important part in this process: the electorate's hatred of 30-second campaign ads is surpassed only by its desire to get its political information by means of those same ads. And the ads cost money.

Although campaign-finance reformers often appeal to the public's unhappiness with negative ads, negativity has long been a feature of political campaigns, and money is not the source of it. (As long ago as 1796, the presidential candidate Thomas Jefferson was attacked as "an atheist, anarchist, demagogue, coward, mountebank, trickster, and Francomaniac." . . . In fact, if the goal is to have positive campaigns, even *more* money would be needed, for the simple reason that positive ads are less memorable than negative ones and hence need to be repeated more frequently. Besides, a limit on spending would mean that candidates would have to depend more

on the media to get their message across, and the press is often more negative in its campaign coverage than the contestants themselves.

There is, finally, no objective criterion by which to measure whether
"too much" is being spent on political campaigns. But as we have seen,
spending in this country is not high. Considering the vital importance of
an informed electorate to democratic government, it is hard to discern why
it should be lower.

The hidden premise behind the idea that too much is being spent on campaigns is that money "buys" election results—a second assumption of reformers. It is true that the candidate who spends the most money wins
most of the time. But the cause-and-effect relationship between spending
and victory is nowhere near so straightforward as this might suggest.

For one thing, the formulation neglects the desire of donors to give to
candidates likely to win. In other words, it may be the prospect of victory
that attracts money, not the other way around. . . . Or a candidate's fundraising edge may simply reflect the relative status of his popularity, later to
be confirmed or disconfirmed at the polls.

Even when the ability to raise and spend money actually succeeds in
changing the outcome of a race, it is ballots, not dollars, that ultimately decide who wins, and ballots reflect the minds of voters. All that spending can
do is attempt to change those minds. It would be a strange First Amendment that cut off protection for speech at the point where speech began to
influence people's views, and it reflects a remarkable contempt for the electorate to suggest that it is incapable of weighing the arguments being ten-
dered for its consideration.

Indeed, there is ample evidence that the electorate does so discriminate,
and that higher spending in behalf of a losing argument will not necessarily
translate into electoral triumph. In the Republican takeover of Congress in
1994, for example, the 34 victorious challengers spent, on average, just two-
thirds of the amount spent by their Democratic opponents, who also enjoyed
the inherent advantage of incumbency. By contrast, in the 1996 race for the
Republican presidential nomination, Phil Gramm, who raised the most
money, was the first to have to drop out. As Michael Malbin of the Rockefeller
Institute of Government has observed, "Having money means having the
ability to be heard; it does not mean that voters will like what they hear."

The key variable in elections is not which candidate spends the most,
but whether or not challengers are able to spend enough to overcome the
advantage of incumbency and make their names and issues known to voters. Once they reach this threshold, races are up for grabs. For example, in
the 1996 House races, 40 percent of challengers who spent over $600,000
won, as opposed to just 3 percent who spent less than $600,000. Once the
threshold was crossed, it mattered little whether or not the challenger was
outspent, or by how much. The problem, if it can be called that, is not that
some candidates "buy" elections by spending too much, but that others
spend too little to get their message to the voters.

Still another assumption of reformers is that, if we truly cared about self-government and participatory democracy, we would be better off if campaigns were funded by many small contributors rather than by fewer large ones.

In fact, the burden of financing political campaigns has *always* fallen to a small minority, both in the United States and in other democracies. Nearly eighteen million Americans now make contributions to a political party, candidate, or PAC during an election cycle. Although this figure is higher than at any other time in American history, and represents a broader base of voluntary public support than has been enjoyed by any other system of campaign funding anywhere, it still comes to less than 10 percent of the voting-age population.

Which sorts of candidates are typically able to raise large sums of money in small amounts, as the reformers prefer? In the years prior to federal funding of presidential campaigns, the two most successful in this respect were Barry Goldwater and George McGovern. The former raised $5.8 million from over 400,000 contributors in 1964, only to suffer a landslide defeat, while the latter, who raised almost $15 million from donors making average contributions of about $20, lost in an even bigger landslide eight years later. More recently, Oliver North raised approximately $20 million, almost all from small contributors, for his 1994 U.S. Senate race, outspent his rival by almost four to one, and still lost to a candidate plagued by personal scandal—primarily because the electorate, rightly or wrongly, viewed him as too "extreme."

What these examples suggest is that the ability to raise large sums in small contributions can be a sign less of broad public support, as reformers assert, than of fervent backing by an ideological minority. Other groups positioned to exert influence by this means tend to be those (like unions) in possession of an ongoing structure for mobilizing their constituents or those we usually call "special interests." It is the inchoate, grass-roots public that more often fails to make its interests known, and is therefore frequently reliant on individuals with large fortunes to finance movements that will represent it. . . .

Ironically, the banning of large contributions, which means that no single gift is likely to make much difference in a political race, gives potential donors little incentive to become involved. A radical campaign can overcome this difficulty: its supporters tend to be motivated more by ideology than by rational calculations of a candidate's chances of winning. But this just further underscores the way in which banning large contributions can help render the political system more rather than less vulnerable to forces on the fringes of the mainstream—hardly, one presumes, the result the reformers have in mind.

A corollary fallacy entertained by reformers is that the financial resources placed at a candidate's disposal should ideally reflect his level of popular support. But this is to confuse the purpose of elections with the purpose of campaigns. The former do measure popular support. The latter, however, are about something else: persuading voters, and *improving* one's level of support.

This, as we have seen, requires monetary expenditures, and it is a sign of health in a democracy when such expenditures are forthcoming. . . .

Perhaps no belief is more deeply rooted in the psyche of reformers—and of the public at large—than that the money drawn into the system through political campaigns corrupts not only the campaigns themselves but, once a candidate is elected, the entire legislative process. Many office-holders have themselves complained about the influence of money in the legislature. But political scientists and economists who have studied this matter have consistently concluded otherwise. As John Lott and Stephen Bronars, the authors of one such study, conclude: "Our tests strongly reject the notion that campaign contributions buy politicians' votes. . . . Just like voters, contributors appear able to sort [out] politicians who intrinsically value the same things that they do."

The primary factors affecting a legislator's voting record are personal ideology, party affiliation, and constituent wishes—not contributions. Does anybody really think Phil Gramm would suddenly drop his opposition to gun control if the National Rifle Association (NRA) ceased contributing to his campaigns? Of course not: the NRA supports Gramm *because* he opposes gun control, and so, almost certainly, do many if not most of his Texas constituents.

This makes perfect sense. Individuals who enter politics usually do so because they have strong views on political issues; party support is almost always more important to election than any one contribution; and, to repeat, a legislator wins with votes, not dollars. For a politician to adopt an unpopular or unwise position that will cost him voter support in exchange for a $5,000 campaign contribution—the maximum amount allowed under federal law—would be counterproductive, to say the least.

This is not to say that other factors never come into play. A legislator may be concerned about how his vote will be reported in the press, or whether an opponent can easily caricature him in a negative ad. Personal friendships may affect a voting decision, as may the advice of aides and staff, itself often influenced by ideology. Money is another such secondary factor, but it is only one, and not necessarily the political commodity of greatest value. Many of the most influential Washington lobbying groups, including the American Association of Retired Persons, the National Education Association, and the American Bar Association, do not make political contributions. The NRA does have a large PAC, but it also has nearly two million members who care intensely about its issues. Although gun-control advocates complain that the NRA outspends them, the more important fact is that it also outvotes them.

Finally, most issues find well-financed lobbies on both sides. A seemingly dull proposal to introduce a one-dollar coin, for example, may line up metal companies, vending-machine manufacturers, and coin laundries on one side, paper and ink companies on the other. Similarly with higher-profile issues like tort reform, where well-financed insurance interests take one position and equally well-financed trial lawyers the other. At least one set of these contributors, and often both, will suffer enormous *losses* in the legislative process, a fact often ignored by reformers.

When push comes to shove, even the most ardent reformers are rarely able to point to a specific instance of corruption. Ask a reformer to name which of our 535 Congressmen and Senators are acting contrary to what they believe to be the public good, or to what their constituents desire, because of campaign contributions, and the answer every time is some variation of "It's the system that's corrupt." But if we cannot name individuals corrupted by the system, on what basis are we to conclude that corruption is a problem intrinsic to the "system"?

III

When it came time to fight the American Revolution, the founders of this nation did not go to the king seeking matching funds with which to finance their revolt. Instead, in the Declaration of Independence, they pledged their fortunes as well as their lives and sacred honor.

Today, in order to cure the alleged problem of fortunes in politics, reformers offer a variety of complex schemes aimed at *preventing* private citizens from demonstrating their commitment to democratic political change. Former Senator Bill Bradley and House Minority Leader Richard Gephardt claim that we need a constitutional amendment to overturn the *Buckley* decision. In Gephardt's sweeping formulation, there is a "direct conflict" between "freedom of speech and our desire for healthy campaigns in a healthy democracy," and "you can't have both." Their proposed amendment, if enacted, would grant a greater degree of protection to commercial speech, flag burning, and Internet porn than to the discussion of political candidates and issues.

Meanwhile, "moderate" reformers continue to push the McCain-Feingold bill, lately shorn of a ban on PAC's that even its sponsors admit was "probably" unconstitutional. Even so, this bill would place vast new limits on the freedom of political discussion, ban most contributions to political parties to pay for voter registration, slate cards, rallies, and get-out-the-vote drives, and restrict speech in ways directly prohibited by standing Supreme Court decisions.[1]

If it is not the case that too much money is spent on campaigns, or that money, rather than the character of a handful of elected officials, is the source of political corruption, or that large contributors buy elections or in some way frustrate "true democracy," why should we tolerate such gross infringements of traditional First Amendment freedoms? What would be accomplished by measures like those being proposed by the reformers that

---

1. Opposition from Senate Republicans and Senate Majority Leader Trent Lott (R-Mississippi) prevented the McCain-Feingold bill from reaching the Senate floor in 1998. A bill similar to the Senate version was passed by the House of Representatives over the opposition of Republican leaders.

would not be better accomplished by minimal disclosure laws that simply require the reporting of all sources of financial support?

Of course, disclosure laws may also be broken, as they appear to have been in the 1996 campaign. Character matters, and the rule has yet to be invented that someone will not succeed in violating. But what all the reformers overlook, from the most extreme to the most moderate, is that we already have, in the First Amendment, a deeply considered response to the problems inherent in democratic elections—and one that is far superior to the supposedly enlightened system of regulation with which we are now saddled.

By assuring freedom of speech and the press, the First Amendment allows for exposure of government corruption and improper favors, whether these consist of White House meetings with drug dealers or huge tax breaks for tobacco companies. By keeping the government out of the electoral arena, it allows for robust criticism of government itself, and prevents incumbents from manipulating the election-law machinery in their own favor. It frees grass-roots activists and everyday speech alike from suffocating state regulation, thereby furthering the democratic aim of political discussion. And it allows candidates to control their own message rather than having to rely on the filters of the press or the vagaries of bureaucrats and judges called upon to decide which forms of speech are to be limited as "endorsements or attacks," and which allowed as "genuine debate."

In the vast muddle that has been made by our decades-old regulatory folly, the only real question concerns whose logic we will now follow: the logic of those who gave us our existing campaign-finance laws and who, despite a disastrous record, now want license to "reform" them still further, or the logic of the founders who gave us the First Amendment. For most Americans, I suspect, the choice would be an easy one.

Dollars and Votes

DAN CLAWSON,
ALAN NEUSTADTL, AND
MARK WELLER

Imagine the November election is just a few weeks away, and your friend Sally Robeson is seriously considering running for Congress two years from now. This year the incumbent in your district, E. Chauncey DeWitt III, will (again!) be reelected by a substantial margin, but you and Sally hate Chauncey's positions on the issues and are convinced that with the right campaign he can be beaten. Sally is capable, articulate, well informed, respected in the community, politically and socially connected, charming, good at talking to many kinds of people, and highly telegenic. She has invited you and several other politically active friends to meet with her immediately after the election to determine what she would need to do to become a viable candidate.

The meeting that takes place covers a host of topics: What are the key issues? On which of these are Sally's stands popular, and on which unpopular? What attacks, and from what quarters, will be launched against her? What individuals or groups can she count on for support? How, why, and where is the incumbent vulnerable? But lurking in the background is the question that cannot be ignored: *Can Sally (with the help of her friends and backers) raise enough money to be a contender?*

This is the *money primary, the first, and, in many instances, the most important round of the contest.* It eliminates more candidates than any other hurdle. Because it eliminates them so early and so quietly, its impact is often unobserved. To make it through, candidates don't have to come in first, but they do need to raise enough money to be credible contenders. Although having the most money is no guarantee of victory, candidates who don't do well in the money primary are no longer serious contenders. . . .

How much is needed? If Sally hopes to win, rather than just put up a good fight, she, you, and the rest of her supporters will need to raise staggering amounts. (At least they are staggering from the perspective of most Americans. . . .) In order to accumulate the *average* amount for major-party congressional candidates in the general election, you will collectively need to raise $4,800 next week. And the week after. And *every* week for the next two years.

But even that is not enough. The average amount includes many candidates who were never "serious"; that is, they didn't raise enough to have a realistic hope of winning. If you and your friends want to raise the average amount spent by a *winning* candidate for the House, you'll have to come up with $6,730 next week and every single week until the election, two years away.[1]

Well, you say, your candidate is hardly average. She is stronger, smarter, more politically appealing, and more viable than the "average" challenger. You think she can win even if she doesn't raise $6,730 a week. Let's use past experience—the results of the 1996 elections—to consider the likelihood of winning for challengers, based on how much money they raised. In 1996 more than 360 House incumbents were running for reelection; only 23 of them were beaten by their challengers. The average successful challenger spent $1,045,361—that is, he or she raised an average of over $10,000 every week for two years. What were the chances of winning without big money? Only one winning challenger spent less than $500,000, 12 spent between a half-a-million and a million dollars, and 10 spent more than a million dollars. Furthermore, 13 of the 23 winning challengers outspent the incumbent. A House challenger who can't raise at least a half-million dollars doesn't have a one percent chance of winning. . . .

In the Senate, even more money is needed. Suppose your candidate were going to run for the Senate, and started fundraising immediately after an election, giving her six years to prepare for the next election. How much

---

1. In 1996; estimates for 2000 are up 20 percent.

money would she need to raise each and every week for those *six* years? The average winning Senate candidate raised approximately $15,000 per week.

For presidential candidates, the stakes are, of course, much higher: "The prevailing view is that for a politician to be considered legitimate, he or she must collect at least $20 million by the first of January 2000." Presumably any candidate who does not do so is "illegitimate" and does not belong in the race.[2]

If you collectively decide that the candidate you plan to back will need to raise $7,000 per week (for the House; $15,000 per week for the Senate), how will you do it? Suppose you hold a $10-per-person fundraiser—a barbecue in the park on Memorial Day or Labor Day. Even if 500 people attend, the affair will gross only $5,000, and net considerably less, no matter how cheap the hot dogs and hamburgers. And that takes no account of the problems of persuading 500 people to attend—just notifying them of the event is a major undertaking—or what it would mean to hold such an event every week, not just on Labor Day. In order to get through the money primary, an alternative strategy is needed, so candidates, especially incumbents, increasingly prefer to raise money at "big ticket" events. Selling 10 tickets for a $1,000-per-person fundraiser brings in more than twice as much as the 500-person barbecue in the park.

Who is likely to cough up a thousand bucks to attend a fundraiser? . . . A disproportionate number of such contributors are corporate political action committees (PACs), executives, and lobbyists. One typical version of the $1,000-per-person fundraiser is a breakfast: The candidate and 10 to 30 PAC officers and lobbyists from a particular industry (trucking, banking, oil and gas exploration). Even with a lavish breakfast, the candidate's net take is substantial. If enough lobbyists and corporate executives can be persuaded to come, perhaps the candidate could get by on one fundraiser every couple of weeks.

Coming up with the money is a major hassle; even for incumbents, it requires constant effort. *National Journal,* probably the single most authoritative source on the Washington scene, reports that "there is widespread agreement that the congressional money chase has become an unending marathon, as wearying to participants as it is disturbing to spectators," and quoted an aide to a Democratic senator as observing, "During hearings of Senate committees, you can watch senators go to phone booths in the committee rooms to dial for dollars." . . .

Long before the 1996 election, politicians felt that they had no choice: The Senate majority leader reported that "public officials are consumed with the unending pursuit of money to run election campaigns." Senators not only leave committee hearings for the more crucial task of calling people to beg for money. They also chase all over the country, because their reelection is more dependent on meeting rich people two thousand miles from home than on meeting their own constituents. Thomas Daschle, the current Democratic leader in the Senate, reports that, in the two years prior to his election to the Senate, he "flew to California more than 20 times to

---

2. The major candidates had raised more than $30 million by 2000. George W. Bush had raised $67 million by January 2000.

meet with prospective contributors," going there almost as often as he went to the largest city in his home state of South Dakota. . . .

Not only is it necessary to raise lots of money; it is important—for both incumbents and challengers—to raise it early. Senator Rudy Boschwitz, Republican of Minnesota, was clear about this as a strategy. He spent $6 million getting reelected in 1984, and had raised $1.5 million of it by the beginning of the year, effectively discouraging the most promising Democratic challengers. After the election he wrote, and typed up himself, a secret evaluation of his campaign strategy:

> Nobody in politics (except me!) likes to raise money, so I thought the best way of discouraging the toughest opponents from running was to have a few dollars in the sock. *I believe it worked. . . . From all forms of fundraising I raised $6 million plus and got 3 or 4 (maybe even 5) stories and cartoons* that irked me," he said. "In retrospect, I'm glad I had the money. . . .

The Contributors' Perspective

Candidates need money, lots of it, if they are to have any chance of winning. The obvious next question . . . is who gives, why, and what they expect for it.

Contributions are made for many different reasons. The candidate's family and friends chip in out of loyalty and affection. Others contribute because they are asked to do so by someone who has done favors for them. People give because they agree with the candidate's stand on the issues, either on a broad ideological basis or on a specific issue. Sometimes these donations are portrayed as a form of voting—people show that they care by putting their money where their mouth is, anyone can contribute, and the money raised reflects the wishes of the people. Even for these contributions, however, if voting with dollars replaces voting at the ballot box, then the votes will be very unequally distributed: the top 1 percent of the population by wealth will have more "votes" than the bottom 90 percent of the population. In the 1996 elections, less than one-fourth of one percent of the population gave contributions of $200 or more to a federal candidate. PACs and large contributors provide most of the money, however; small contributors accounted for under one-third of candidate receipts.

It is not just that contributions come from the well-to-do. Most contributors have a direct material interest in what the government does or does not do. Their contributions, most of them made directly or indirectly by business, provide certain people a form of leverage and "access" not available to the rest of us. The chair of the political action committee at one of the twenty-five largest manufacturing companies in the United States explained to us why his corporation has a PAC:

> The PAC gives you access. It makes you a player. These congressmen, in particular, are constantly fundraising. Their elections are very expensive, and getting increasingly expensive each year. So they have an ongoing need for funds. . . .

You know, some congressman has got X number of ergs of energy and here's a person or a company who wants to come see him and give him a thousand dollars, and here's another one who wants to just stop by and say hello. And he only has time to see one. Which one? So the PAC's an attention getter.

So-called soft money, where the amount of the contribution is unlimited, might appear to be an exception: Isn't $100,000 enough to buy a guaranteed outcome? . . . It is *not,* at least not in any simple and straightforward way. PAC contributions are primarily for members of Congress; they are for comparatively small amounts, but enough to gain access to individual members of Congress. The individual member, however, has limited power. Soft money donations are best thought of as a way of gaining access to the president, top party leaders, and the executive branch. These individuals are more powerful than ordinary members of Congress, so access to them comes at a higher price. . . . It does not—and is not expected to—*guarantee* a quid pro quo. . . .

Why Business?

In business–government relations most attention becomes focused on instances of scandal. The real issue, however, is not one or another scandal or conflict of interest, but rather the *system* of business–government relations, and especially of campaign finance, that offers business so many opportunities to craft loopholes, undermine regulations, and subvert enforcement. . . .

Business and the way it uses money and power . . . subverts the democratic process. This runs counter to the conventional wisdom, which treats all campaign contributions as equally problematic. A "balanced" and "objective" approach would, we are told, condemn both business and labor; each reform that primarily restricts business should be matched by one that restricts labor. We've heard these arguments, thought them over, and rejected them. They assume that what we have now is "balance" and that all changes should reinforce the existing relations of power. We see no reason to accept that as an a priori assumption.

Why are business campaign contributions more of a problem than contributions by labor (or women, or environmentalists)? First, because business contributes far more money. According to a study by the Center for Responsive Politics, in [1996] business outspent labor by an 11 to 1 margin.[3] Most reports about campaign finance give the impression that labor contributes roughly as much as business—a distortion of the reality.

Second, . . . beyond the world of campaign finance, business has far more power than labor, women's groups, or environmentalists.

Third, business uses campaign contributions in a way few other groups do, as part of an "access" process that provides corporations a chance to shape the details of legislation, crafting loopholes that undercut the stated

3. The disparity was 12 to 1 in 1998.

purpose of the law. Other groups do this on rare occasions; business does so routinely. Businesses are far more likely than other donors to give to *both* sides in a race; nearly all the soft money donors who gave to both sides were corporations. . . .

Fourth, there is a fundamental difference between corporate and labor PAC contributions. That difference is democracy; unions have it, corporations don't. This overwhelmingly important distinction is concealed by almost all public discussion. No one talks about it, no one seems to take it seriously. There is a virtual embargo on any mention of this fact, but it merits serious consideration.

The original legislation ratifying the creation of PACs, passed in 1971 and amended in 1974 after Watergate, intended that corporations and labor unions be treated in parallel fashion. In each case, the organization was permitted a special relationship to the group that democratically controlled it—stockholders in the case of corporations, members in the case of labor unions. The organization was permitted to communicate with those individuals and their families on any issue (including political issues), to conduct registration and get-out-the-vote campaigns, and to ask those people for voluntary contributions to a political action committee.

In the 1975 SUN–PAC decision, the Federal Election Commission, for almost the only time in its existence, took a bold step. In fact, it essentially threw out a key part of the law and then rewrote it, permitting corporations to solicit PAC contributions not just from their stockholders but also from their managerial employees. This had two consequences. First, corporate PACs—but no others—are able to coerce people to contribute. Second, corporate PACs are not, even in theory, democratically controlled. Each of these consequences needs to be examined.

Neither stockholders nor union members can be coerced to contribute— the organization doesn't have power over them, they have power over the organization. Managers, however, can be coerced. As a result, virtually all corporate PAC money comes from employees rather than stockholders. If your boss comes to you and asks for a contribution, saying he or she hopes that all team players will be generous, it's not easy for you, an ambitious young manager, to say no. Some companies apparently do not pressure employees to contribute, but others do. For example, at one company we studied, the head of government relations told us that each year he and the company's lobbyist go to each work unit and hold an employee meeting: "We talk about the PAC and what it means to the company and what it means to them as individuals, and we solicit their membership; if they are members, we solicit an increase in their gift." Then the employees' boss is asked "to get up and say why they are members and why they think it's important for an employee to be a member." The upper-level manager clearly has no confidentiality, which in itself sends a key message to others. A number of coercive elements converge in this solicitation: The meeting is public, employees are to commit themselves then and there in the public meeting, the boss recommends that subordinates contribute, and an impression is probably conveyed that the boss will be evaluated on the basis of his or her employees' participation rate. . . . No one is told they will be fired for failing to contribute, but it seems probable that they will assume their boss will be disappointed and that their contribution or noncontribution will be remembered at promotion time.

The second consequence of the 1975 SUN–PAC decision is even more important. Corporate PACs are *not* democratic. Many corporations have steering committees that vote to decide to whom the PAC will contribute, but the committees are appointed, the corporate hierarchy selects individuals who are expected to take the corporate purpose as their own, and managers know that they will be evaluated on their performance on the committee. As one senior vice president explained: "Policy is made by the top of the company, and it filters down. They tell you what they want, and you do it."

The internal functioning of corporate PACs suggests how they relate to and value democracy. Most aspects of the political system are beyond the *direct* control of corporations, but they *can* determine how their PACs operate and make decisions. As a result, in all but a handful of corporate PACs democratic control is not even a theoretical possibility. . . .

The only corporation that reported having *some* contested elections agreed that, in general: "It is an elected-appointive; it's kind of a pseudo-election I guess is what it amounts to."

We might expect those ideological corporations that stress general principles of support for democracy and the "free" enterprise system to be exceptions to the undemocratic organization of corporate PACs. Not at all. At one corporation that boasted about its wholehearted support of the "free enterprise system," the chair of the PAC Committee matter-of-factly noted: "If our [company] chairman said we are going to have a certain kind of PAC, then we'd have an option of resigning or doing it the way he wanted." . . .

The nondemocratic character of corporate PACs is consistent with the principles guiding the corporation as a whole. Corporations are not run on democratic principles; employees don't vote on corporate leadership or policies. Many corporate executives are dubious about democracy in general. Leonard Silk and David Vogel attended a set of meetings organized by the Conference Board for top executives. They concluded:

> While critics of business worry about the atrophy of American democracy, the concern in the nation's boardrooms is precisely the opposite. For an executive, democracy in America is working all too well—*that is the problem.*

Campaign contributions are (part of) the solution to the "problem" of democracy. . . .

Business Is Different

Power, we would argue, is not just the ability to force someone to do something against their will; it is most effective (and least recognized) when it shapes the field of action. Moreover, business's vast resources, influence on the economy, and general legitimacy place it on a different footing from other campaign contributors. Every day a member of Congress accepts a $1,000 donation from a corporate PAC, goes to a committee hearing, proposes "minor" changes in a bill's wording, and has those changes accepted without discussion or examination. The changes "clarify" the language of the bill, legalizing higher levels of pollution for a specific pollutant, or exempting the company from some tax. The media do not report this change and no one speaks against it. On the other hand, if a PAC were formed by Drug Lords for Cocaine Legalization, no member would take their money. If a member introduced a "minor" wording change to make it easier to sell crack without bothersome police interference, the proposed change would attract massive attention, the campaign contribution would be labeled a scandal, the member's political career would be ruined, and the changed wording would not be incorporated into the bill. Drug Lords may make an extreme example, but approximately the same holds true for many groups: At present, equal rights for gays and lesbians could never be a minor and unnoticed addition to a bill with a different purpose.

Even groups with great social legitimacy encounter more opposition and controversy than business faces for proposals that are virtually without public support. One example is the contrast between the largely unopposed commitment of tens or hundreds of billions of dollars for the savings and loan bailout, compared to the sharp debate, close votes, and defeats for the rights of men and women to take *unpaid* parental leaves. The classic term for something non-controversial that everyone must support is "a motherhood issue," and while it costs little to guarantee every woman the right to an *un*paid parental leave, this measure nonetheless generated intense scrutiny and controversy—going down to defeat under President Bush, passing under President Clinton, and then again becoming a focus of attack after the 1994 Republican takeover of Congress. Few indeed are the people publicly prepared to defend pollution or tax evasion. Nonetheless, business is routinely able to win pollution exemptions and tax loopholes. . . .

Corporations are unlike other "special interest" groups not only because business has far more resources, but also because of its acceptance and legitimacy. When people feel that "the system" is screwing them, they tend to blame politicians, the government, the media—but rarely business. In terms of campaign finance, while much of the public is outraged at the way money influences elections and public policy, the issue is almost always posed in terms of politicians, what they do or don't do. This is part of a pervasive double standard that largely exempts business from criticism. We, however, believe it is vital to scrutinize business as well. . . .

. . . Corporations are so different, and so dominant, that they exercise a special kind of power, what Antonio Gramsci called hegemony. Hegemony can be regarded as the ultimate example of a field of power that structures what people and groups do. It is sometimes referred to as a worldview, a way of thinking about the world that influences every action, and makes it difficult to even consider alternatives. But in Gramsci's analysis it is much more than this, it is a culture and set of institutions that structure life patterns and coerce a particular way of life. . . .

. . . Today business has enormous power and exercises effective hegemony, even though (perhaps because) this is largely undiscussed and unrecognized. *Politically,* business power today is similar to white treatment of blacks in 1959—business may sincerely deny its power, but many of the groups it exercises power over recognize it, feel dominated, resent this, and fight the power as best they can. At least until very recently, *economically,* business power was more like gender relations in 1959: Virtually no one saw this power as problematic. The revived labor movement is beginning to change this, and there are signs that a movement is beginning to contest corporate power. Nonetheless, if the issue is brought to people's attention, many still don't see a problem: "Well, so what? how else could it be? maybe we don't like it, but that's just the way things are." . . .

Everyone is talking about campaign finance reform. But what kind of reform? The answer varies. If the problem is occasional abuses by renegade fundraisers, then the only change needed is a system of improved enforcement. . . . If the problem is that the public has (momentarily? irrationally?) lost faith in the system, and now sees democracy for sale, then the solution is to address the most visible symbol of this—soft money—and make cosmetic changes elsewhere, loudly proclaiming that this is a thorough reform. For campaign finance insiders—a tiny fraction of the population, but crucial for policy decisions—the problem is that politicians are having to work too hard to raise money. The solution is to find some way to reduce the cost of campaigns (typically, through limited free television time), while seeing to it that the margin of success continues to depend on campaign contributions from big-money donors, which is, after all, the system that put these politicians into office. Most campaign finance experts analyze the issue in ways generally similar to the political insiders. Academic "expertise," and certainly media punditry, generally depends on possessing views certified as "reasonable" by those with power—that is, by politicians, the media, business, and big-money campaign contributors. For most members of the American public—and for us—the problem is an entire system that is institutionally corrupt, that coerces politicians to put dollars over voters, that buys off democracy. The solution, therefore, must be a complete overhaul and the introduction of a fundamentally new system. . . .

Public Financing

. . . As long as our society continues to have vast inequalities of wealth, income, and power, the people with the most money will be able to find ways around restrictive rules. Virtually all current [reform] proposals are intended to limit the ways in which money can be funneled into campaigns. It is extremely difficult to impose limitations, because however many rules and barriers are erected, the ingenuity of the rich, or their hirelings, will always find ways to evade the regulations. Clinton's Deputy Chief of Staff Harold Ickes explains, "Money is like water. . . . If there is a crack, water will find it.

Same way with political money." Moreover, virtually no meaningful penalties are imposed on those caught violating the rules. As a result, the regulators are always one step behind the evaders and shysters.

The alternative approach is to cut the Gordian knot of restrictions by instituting public financing of election campaigns. In the early 1990s, such proposals seemed utopian. In 1992, we argued that Congress and the president would not institute public financing unless a popular movement put a gun to their heads. As we predicted, Washington didn't budge, but state-level referendum campaigns may do what Congress would never do. In 1996, Maine voters adopted a public financing system, and Public Campaign, a new organization dedicated to taking special interest money out of elections, is spearheading a movement around the country to bring about public campaign financing, one state at a time, if necessary. Real reform, with full public financing, is no longer a utopian dream—it's on today's political agenda. Other proposals are of course possible, but Public Campaign's model law is an excellent framework, *and* it has helped mobilize and coordinate a major grassroots campaign. Our discussion therefore focuses on this proposal.

Public Campaign, and its Clean Money Campaign Reform (CMCR), are—at least for now—bypassing Congress, which has shown an amazing ability to sidetrack and frustrate reform efforts, and focusing instead on state-by-state efforts, most notably by putting referendum questions on the ballot. By taking the issue directly to the voters in a ballot referendum, it's possible to pass a full reform proposal. The normal legislative process is highly likely to bury reform in committee and then change "just a few" details in order to make the proposal "more realistic"—that is, to be sure that special interest money continues to provide a decisive margin in most contests.

State-level campaigns necessarily mean that there will be minor variations from one place to another. And any effort to present a campaign finance proposal confronts a dilemma: Readers want enough detail to be sure the proposal is viable—that it won't encounter an insoluble contradiction—but don't want to be bogged down in minor provisions of interest only to technocrats and political junkies. In its broad outlines, Clean Money Campaign Reform limits campaign spending, prohibits special interest contributions to those candidates who participate in the system, provides public financing for participating candidates, and guarantees a level playing field. The system is completely voluntary. . . .

The arguments in favor of [public financing of campaigns] are . . . powerful. . . . Elections would be far more competitive. Although challengers would still have less name recognition than incumbents, they would have enough money to mount credible campaigns, and for the first time challengers as a group would have as much to spend as incumbents.

Special interests could no longer use campaign money to increase their access and win benefits for themselves. It is not only that a member would not be indebted for a past donation. Members would also know they would never need to depend on a future donation and could never gain a campaign advantage by soliciting or accepting such a donation. Corporations would continue to have substantial clout based on their wealth, power, and respectability, their ability to maintain a staff of lobbyists, their advocacy advertising, their networks, connections, and friendships. But *one* of their major special interest weapons would have been eliminated.

The guarantee of public funding for campaigns would give members of Congress more time to spend on legislation and on keeping in touch with constituents who are *not* campaign contributors. . . .

People sometimes argue that such reforms only make the system more stable and resistant to change. Perhaps that is true in some instances. In other instances, what Andre Gorz called a "non-reformist reform" provides immediate benefits to people *and* makes it easier to win future reforms. Did the auto safety campaign Nader launched produce a significant change in the way people think about business? Yes. Did it make people more or less willing to consider additional reforms? Obviously, much more willing.

We would argue that Clean Money Campaign Reform is also a "nonreformist reform." It proposes a reform that can be won, and one that if won will substantially weaken business power. By itself, will it transform American society? No. Will it have an impact? Yes. Will the end of corporate campaign contributions and the emergence of public financing make it easier or more difficult to make future political changes? Clearly, easier. Will continued struggle be necessary to elect good people and to fight business power? Certainly. Will electoral politics be enough? No. Business exercises power on many different fronts and that power must be opposed on every front.

■ DISCUSSION QUESTIONS

1. Smith claims that campaign contributors don't buy favors or votes from candidates but that contributions simply register support for candidates' political positions. How would Smith deal with the contention that contributions buy privileged access to candidates and that to get access requires contributions?

2. In *Buckley* v. *Valeo* (1976), the U.S. Supreme Court seemed to agree with Smith's idea that campaign contributions are protected by the First Amendment as free speech. Are proposals for public financing of campaigns such as those submitted by the authors of "Dollars and Votes" a violation of free speech?

3. In 1999, the congressional GOP leadership blocked campaign reform initiatives from coming to a vote. If money is such a corrupting influence in campaigns, why aren't voters more supportive of the kinds of initiatives proposed to limit its effects? What are the obstacles to forming a grassroots movement that supports finance reform?

4. Assuming that money has become crucial in modern campaigns, devise a plausible campaign strategy for a cash-poor but volunteer-rich candidate for a House seat. Could volunteers be used to balance the high-tech campaign? Under what circumstances?

SUGGESTED READINGS AND INTERNET RESOURCES

A comprehensive set of articles about campaign finance before 1997 is provided by Anthony Corrado, ed., *Campaign Finance Reform: A Sourcebook* (Washington, D.C.: Brookings Institution, 1997). For complete accounts of the 1996 money-raising excesses of both parties, see Gerald Pomper, ed., *The Election of 1996* (Chatham, N.J.: Chatham House, 1997). For a skeptical and thorough look at the effects of campaign finance reform, see Michael Malbin and Thomas Gais, *The Day After Reform: Sobering Campaign Finance Lessons from the States* (Albany, N.Y.: Rockefeller Institute Press, 1998). A devastating look at the corrosive effects of campaign finance and corporate lobbying is Elizabeth Drew, *The Corruption of American Politics* (Secaucus, N.J.: Carol Publishing, 1999). A short and effective set of proposals for campaign reforms are proposed in David Donnelly, Janice Fine, and Ellen Miller, *Money and Politics* (Boston: Beacon Press, 1999).

The Federal Election Commission (FEC)
www.fec.gov
The FEC's site provides access to the financial reports of all candidates for federal offices and press releases summarizing monthly trends in campaign fundraising.

The Center for Responsive Politics
www.opensecrets.org
The most comprehensive site for data and analysis of FEC data, with a concentration on the role of monied interests and their effects on the political process.

Public Campaign
www.publiccampaign.org
News and views from the major advocacy organization favoring public financing of political campaigns.

Democracy Network
www.dnet.org
League of Women Voters–sponsored site providing state-by-state access to candidate information and ways to contact and interact with campaign organizations.

Alliance for Better Campaigns
www.bettercampaigns.org
Funded by Pew Charitable Trusts and George Soros's Open Society Foundation, this site provides information and advocacy for more public airtime for quality debates, advertisements, and free media airtime.

CHAPTER 12

Political Participation: Are Generation Xers Political Slackers or Innovators?

The Baby Boomers, those born between 1947 and 1961, have dominated American culture for many years, and increasingly they are dominating politics as well. (Bill Clinton is the first Baby Boomer president.) The influence of the Boomers is partly based on their sheer numbers. After postponing children during the Depression and World War II, families began having more and more children in the late 1940s and into the 1950s. Births reached an all-time peak in 1957. Marketers and trend setters have kept their eyes on the Boomers, who, because of their demographic size, are sometimes referred to as the "pig in a python." Shaped by the monumental movements for civil rights and against the Vietnam War, Boomers are viewed as a politically engaged generation, with high ideals and participation, if not high accomplishments.

With no great defining event or experience, the generation born between 1961 and 1981 has always lived in the shadow of the Boomers. The upheavals of the 1960s, together with the worsening of the economy following the Arab oil boycott in 1973, led to a declining birth rate. The year 1975 marked the United States' lowest birth year since the end of World War II. The birth rate has picked up since then, and, with 80 million people representing about 30 percent of the U.S. population, this is hardly a generation to be ignored.

The generation following the Boomers has been given many names: Baby Busters, Slackers, New Lost Generation, the Free, the 13th Generation (the term used by the authors of our first selection). The name that has stuck the most is

Generation X, a term popularized by Douglas Coupland in his 1991 novel, *Generation X: Tales of an Accelerated Culture* (St. Martin's). Almost universally disliked by people in that generation, the term nevertheless accurately connotes a generation that is difficult to pin down, one often defined more by what it is not than what it is.

Clearly, Gen Xers grew up in more difficult economic times than the Boomers. In fact, Xers are probably the first generation of Americans to inherit a lower standard of living than their parents. Global competition has made job markets more turbulent and competitive. Since the 1970s, wages have generally declined for those with less than a college education. With corporate downsizing, even those who have graduated from college are less assured of stable jobs with job ladders and steady promotions. In addition, Gen Xers come out of college with, on average, about twice the debt of Boomers. The cynicism generated by restricted job opportunities is explored in the film *Reality Bites*. Winona Ryder plays a college valedictorian who is forced to take what Coupland refers to as a McJob, an assistant to an arrogant local TV personality who explodes when she fails to bring him his coffee. Gen Xers are often criticized for being whiners, but there is no doubt that until the boom of the mid-'90s, they had restricted economic opportunities compared to the Boomers.

Gen X has often been defined in opposition to the Baby Boomers. Gen Xers view the Boomer-dominated media as hostile, promoting a stereotype of Xers as apathetic, cynical, and alienated. Similarly, many Xers view Boomers as reckless, arrogant, and self-indulgent. They criticize Boomers for leaving them with a $5 trillion national debt. The issue that has irritated the most raw nerves, however, is Social Security. When Boomers start retiring *en masse* in 2010, the Social Security Trust Fund will be rapidly depleted. Unless something is done, there will be no money left when the Gen Xers retire. By the year 2030, there will be 63 Social Security recipients for every 100 workers; in order to maintain current benefits under the present system, workers in 2030 will have to pay as much as 40 percent of their income directly to the elderly. The main source of the problem is that Boomers never put aside enough money to fund their retirement, confirming the image many Xers have of them as self-indulgent. As Coupland sarcastically put it in an article in *Fortune:* "The last penny [in the Social Security Trust Fund] will be spent on a jewel-encrusted stereo system for Robin Williams's walker."

The selections in this chapter deal with the political orientations and involvements of Gen Xers. Using conventional measurements, Xers are clearly less involved in politics than previous generations. All young people vote at relatively low rates, but Xers have even lower turnouts than previous generations. For example, 48 percent of Boomers ages 18 to 20 reported voting in the 1972 presidential election compared to only 31 percent of 18- to 20-year-olds in the 1996 election. Harvard political scientist Robert Putnam has documented the steady decline in political involvement, group membership, and social trust for every generation born from the 1930s onward, with each generation, including the Boomers, being less civically involved than the previous generation. Putnam attributes declining civic involvements primarily to television.

The authors of our first selection, Neil Howe and Bill Strauss, acknowledge the declining civic involvements of Xers, whom they call the 13th Generation, but argue that Xer apathy is simply a response to the conditions they inherited from the Baby Boomers. Boomers pursued idealistic causes, Howe and Strauss argue, but ended up bequeathing to succeeding generations worse economic, social, and political conditions. Beginning in the 1970s, the job market deteriorated, rising rates of divorce and drug use created an environment that was not supportive of children, and new federal policies, including environment and anti-poverty policies, failed. (Howe and Strauss's argument is undermined by the unprecedented economic expansion that began in 1991.) The great protest movements of the 1960s and 1970s—the civil rights, environmental, and feminist movements—not only failed to solve society's problems but often made things worse. Gen Xers are viewed by Howe and Strauss as conservative, even reactionary, but for good reason: liberal programs, which rely on government, have failed over and over again. In short, the conservatism and reluctance of Xers to participate in social movements or even vote are not viewed by Howe and Strauss as expressions of apathy. Rather, a withdrawn and skeptical stance toward politics is interpreted as the height of realism.

Howe and Strauss acknowledge, as do most surveys, that Gen Xers are highly involved in small-scale voluntary efforts, but they don't give this trend much political significance. In contrast, Matthew Moseley attributes great political significance to the voluntary service movement among young people. Young people do care about where society is heading; they just don't buy into the present political system as a way of bringing about change. Moseley says that the political commitments of Gen Xers have been underappreciated because we have looked at the facts through the conventional lens of the public and private sectors. Society, says Moseley, is a three-legged stool: the public and private sectors are strong, but the third leg, civil society, is weak. Rooted in local voluntary commitments that are independent of big government and big corporations, a strong civil society, Moseley maintains, is necessary for a strong democracy. In short, Gen Xers are not apathetic, Moseley suggests; we have just been looking in the wrong place to find their political commitments and ideals.

The debate about the political involvements and orientations of Gen Xers is interesting because for the most part the two sides agree on the facts. Moseley would agree, for example, that Gen Xers are cynical about conventional politics. He stresses, however, that politics must be understood more broadly to include voluntary commitments and grassroots organizations. Why do Howe and Strauss give volunteerism little political significance? If civil society is built up, will it have implications for politics, as conventionally understood? In their selection Howe and Strauss stress that the Baby Boom Generation left Gen Xers a raw deal and that therefore young people's cynicism is understandable. Why does Moseley play down conflicts between the generations and suggest that the problem is not so much flawed private and public institutions as a weak civil society?

The 13th Generation:
Caring Less
for Good Reason[1]

NEIL HOWE
AND BILL STRAUSS

"**W**hen you get beneath the surface of their cheerfulness," observes Christopher Lasch, author of *The Culture of Narcissism*, "young people in the suburbs are just as hopeless as those in the ghetto ... living in a state of almost unbearable, though mostly inarticulate, agony. They experience the world only as a source of pleasure and pain." So what's left over, in between the extremes of pleasure or pain? For many, the only alternative is: boredom.

One of the most damning elder indictments of this generation is that they feel no connection to the broader social world beyond their own private interests. It's not so much whether they're smart or dumb, conservative or liberal, miserly or thriftless—but rather that none of the above really matters to them. Thirteeners get scolded for having no civic spirit; for feeling no stake in the nation's past crusades or future ideals; for seldom bothering to read newspapers, learn about public affairs, discuss big issues, or vote for candidates; for just *not caring*.

What about this 13er apathy? Has their civic virtue vanished along with the trucks and cowboys in those desert-mirage beer commercials? To find out, put yourself in the position of a 13er teenager.

You sit in civics and history classes day after day, and then you look around and see what today's adults have been up to lately. You can't help but notice that the last time Americans willingly sacrificed themselves to the public good was way back in the 1930s and '40s. That's decades before you were born, impossibly remote from your own time.

You gaze at the great hero-built edifices that have lasted from that era—NATO, the Pentagon, Social Security, network TV, Aid to Dependent Children, TVA pork barrel, ICBMs, marble post offices—[2]and what you

---

1. Howe and Strauss use the term *13th Generation* or 13ers, to refer to the generation born between 1961 and 1981. This generation, they maintain, is the 13th since the founding of the United States.
2. NATO stands for North Atlantic Treaty Organization; Aid to Dependent Children was the main federal welfare program that was ended as an entitlement in 1996; TVA stands for Tennessee Valley Authority, a New Deal innovation that aided economic development by building dams and generating electricity; and ICBM stands for Intercontinental Ballistic Missile.

mostly see are dysfunctional irrelevancies sagging with age. Through your eyes, they all seem like some old municipal aqueduct—massive beyond your comprehension, hoisted during some ancient era you can hardly imagine, intended for some grand purpose that no longer matters. Cracks in its concrete reveal a complex network of rusting wires and pipework designed long ago by some whistling young engineer. Maybe he cared about it back then, but he's long since retired on a generous federal pension paid for with the money deducted from your Pizza Hut paycheck.

You know that nobody is about to ask you to build anything to match that old edifice, or even to keep it in good repair. Instead, your task is simply to keep it barely functional, to run to and fro through the cracks—doing errands, delivering messages, fulfilling instant needs of every kind—while your elders are allowed to believe the old edifice still works fine and to reap whatever meager rewards it still has left to offer. Propping it up pays you little today and promises you nothing tomorrow. So you stop caring about the crumbling old thing—and then hear your very indifference used against you. *You're* the ignoramus who can't decipher its ancient inscriptions. *You're* the incompetent who wouldn't know how to rebuild it even if somebody gave you the money. *You're* the barbarian cavorting among its ruins. *YOU* must be the reason it's falling apart.

Then you listen to middle-aged people brag about their grand crusades—civil rights, the Peace Corps, Vietnam, women's lib, Earth Day, the toppling of Nixon—those shining moments when they, as youths, righteously challenged and conquered the great injustices of the world. Here, too, you find yourself at a disadvantage. You're well aware that you had no hand in any of that. You suspect that they're exaggerating, but you can't prove it. Watching those crusaders gray in place just ahead of you—ensconced in such culture bastions as college faculties, public radio stations, policy foundations, and trendy rural retreats—you notice how they've redefined every test of idealism in ways guaranteed to make you fail. You're expected to muster passions against political authority you've never felt, to search for truth in places you've never found useful, to solve world problems through gestures you find absurd.

As you assess the bewildering rhetorical legacy of those older crusaders (*make love not war, feed the poor, off the pigs, up against the wall*), here again you're left gazing at the seamy underside of social accomplishments gone awry. Here again you stop caring. And here again any disinterest on your part is interpreted as proof of your moral blight. No matter that it was the crusaders' own self-indulgence that let the system fall apart. The Decade of Greed is your fault. "Compassion Fatigue" is *your* fault. The hunger for sound bites (this from the crowd who once telegenically chanted "Ho, Ho, Ho Chi Minh!") is your fault. "The age of apathy"? Well, that motto, of course, has *YOUR* mindless graffiti splattered all over it.

If you take little interest in the institutional edifices and grand crusades that have always absorbed the energy of your elders, it's because you feel no

Percent Voting in Presidential Elections of 1972 and 1988

	1972	1988	Change
Age 18–20	48%	33%	–15%
Age 20–24	51%	38%	–12%
Age 25 and over	66%	61%	– 5%

Source: U.S. Bureau of the Census

stake or connection. You sense that much of the debate over the so-called "big issues" is irrelevant to your future—and that you're powerless to affect the outcome anyway. As such, you feel more alienated from the social legacy being handed to you than your elders were at like age. If you score higher on most measures of cynicism, it's because in your short life cycle you've already witnessed too many grand causes go bust. And because elders seem to think that everything you offer is negative.

Yes, maybe you don't much care about voting—not because you're uncivic in principle, but just because right now, as you see politics, it doesn't make one iota of difference who wins. Policy platforms mean nothing, politicians say anything to win, legislative bodies are gridlocked, and what few measures politicians do enact seldom amount to much (and certainly haven't done squat to fix your own problems). Having grown up in the age of Watergate and Abscam, you look at it this way: When you vote, maybe you'll waste your time, or worse, later feel doublecrossed.[3] If you pin too much hope on a candidate, you could end up feeling like a total sucker. On the other hand, when you give tangible help to your friends and neighbors, you're doing something that matters, if only on a small scale. So you like volunteering for little "c" causes—like bringing food to the homeless, recycling trash, cleaning up beaches, or tutoring the disadvantaged. You express your civic virtue one on one, meal by meal, regardless whether anybody is paying attention. The president of MIT has likened your civic attitude to that of the Lone Ranger: Do a good deed, leave a silver bullet, and move on.

Yes, maybe you don't much care about "current events"—those *boring* newsprinted artifacts that threaten to turn your brain into some overstuffed piece of Victorian luggage. This is an instinct you acquired young, a reaction against what teacher and author Patrick Welsh calls "a world of information overload." Hearing elders declare everything too complex for yes-or-no answers, you've struggled to filter out the noise, cut through the

---

3. Watergate was the scandal that caused Richard Nixon to resign the presidency in 1974; Abscam refers to a 1980 FBI sting operation in which seven members of Congress were filmed accepting cash in return for political favors.

rhetoric, and isolate the handful of practical truths that really matter. Maybe your "aliteracy" prevents you from competing for credentialed sinecures, or from discussing such MacNeil/Lehrer topics as new NTBs at the global phase-two GATT meetings. But it does enable you to forge boldly into the future—by traveling light, thinking fresh, and striking quickly. It's a style you figure elders could learn from. . . .

That's how many 13ers see, and justify, their attitude about public life. In 1989, as East German students poured over the Berlin Wall, newspaper accounts described high school kids as "left flat" and "utterly unmoved" by events that brought their teachers tears of joy. Yet again, older Americans took the opportunity to shake their heads at blasé youth. But what many called "apathy" might also have been described as the weary realism of a generation whose own first-hand experiences have taught them what can happen when barriers are blithely broken down; chaos, confusion, a new mess for somebody to clean up. Today, 13ers are less surprised than other Americans to hear that most of the news from Eastern Europe consists not of constitutions being written or factories being built, but of ethnic warfare, civilian bombardments, mass migrations, and economic panic.

Whatever their race, most 13ers are tired of being lectured on the subject of race relations—and believe they handle racial problems a whole lot better than their elders. Older generations take pride in having introduced an effusive rhetoric of group justice into such decorous forums as legislatures and universities, while fretting about 13er-style institutions—like small business, pro sports, and the military—where conversations are more to-the-point. Asked to speak their own mind, a lot of 13ers wouldn't mind pointing out the obvious: Where are you most likely to find different races actually eating together and working together, the typical army mess hall or the typical college cafeteria? But 13ers are rarely asked to speak their mind and are usually smart enough not to bother. They already know that the over-30 crowd cares more about what gets said than about what gets done. . . .

. . . For most of this generation, the accumulated failures of elder-built racial policies have led to a very different outcome: a profound skepticism about any social unit larger than the individual or family. Regardless of race, most 13ers rank their own success and mobility above the need to display racial solidarity.

As if to punctuate their skepticism, 13ers are transforming racial images in ways that strip pluralism of much of its earlier poetry and promise. To the youth of the mid-1960s, blacks and whites were symbolically complementary. Blacks (to whites) were rural and spiritual, authors of an expressive blues and folk culture; whites (to blacks) were powerful and disciplined, builders of big things. Trusted leaders spoke of deliverance, giving whites back their virtue and blacks their Promised Land. To 13er youths, all that symbolism has collapsed. Blacks (to whites) have become urban and kinetic, notable for gang violence and a culture of poverty; whites (to blacks) are incompetent and self-absorbed, unable to fix even the simplest public prob-

---

Percent agreeing that Ronald Reagan's
presidency will go down in history as
above-average:

age 18–29	70%
age 30–49	62%
age 50+	48%

Source: Gallup Poll (1989)

---

lem. Nowadays, no one trusts group leaders, and no one expects group deliverance. Individual whites affirm their virtue by tuning in to talk-radio,
and individual blacks reach their Promised Land by moving to the suburbs.
White or black, 13ers are coming of age in a world where, as many see it,
real racial progress coexists with a new racial cynicism. . . .

Press the generational rewind button. Back in the mid-1960s, *Mad* magazine ran a cartoon spoof about a "new generation gap" twenty years in
the future. Seen through the prism of that era, it couldn't have been more
bizarre. The middle-aged parents were portrayed as aging hipsters, funky
grand-daddios, and graying, free-love radicals; the teenagers as clean-cut
reactionaries who despised everything their parents stood for. Readers
laughed and shook their heads. Now press fast-forward to the mid-1980s,
and press pause at a new sitcom called *Family Ties*. The middle-aged parents? Talkative, sensitive, broadminded Democrats. The teenager? A cut-
the-bull young Republican who argues with dad about Reagan and packs
a *Wall Street Journal* under his arm. Viewers laughed, and this time they
nodded.

The conservative child of liberal parents. From fantasy to stereotype,
this has become the most striking popular image of the 13th Generation's
political identity.

Does the image hold? It certainly does if we compare today's 13ers with
their older siblings or parents at like age. Twenty years ago, back when
mop-haired Meathead was ripping into Archie Bunker, the young were far
more liberal than their parents; polls showed self-identified young "liberals"
outnumbering self-identified young "conservatives" by nearly three to one.
Now that millions of middle-aged Meatheads have their own college-age
children, polls show young people no more liberal than their parents—and
quite a bit more conservative on such bellwether issues as crime, defense
spending, drugs, and welfare. This is true for the poor as much as the rich,
for blacks as much as whites.

To understand what makes 13ers tick politically, go back and look carefully at the 1970s—that decade of cultural upheaval and institutional decline when grade-school Atari-wavers got their first glimpse of national life.
To older generations, this seemed a fine time to turn inward, cast off the

How would you describe your political views?

	College Freshmen in 1970	College Freshmen in 1991	Change
"Liberal" or "Far Left"	37%	26%	−11%
"Middle of the Road"	45%	54%	+ 9%
"Conservative" or "Far Right"	18%	20%	+ 2%

Source: "The American Freshman: Twenty-five Year Trends" (UCLA, 1991–1992)

burdens of social discipline, and put personal agendas ahead of the larger national interest. But to the opening wedge of the 13th Generation, there was nothing therapeutic in the spectacle of an entire nation letting go. To them, the 1970s unfolded like a grim and horrifying newsreel. Watergate. Oil embargo. The "Christmas without lights." Impeachment. Collapse of Vietnam. Stagflation. CIA and Lockheed scandals. Three Mile Island. A second oil embargo. More stag- and more -flation. Tehran hostages. Afghanistan. Yellow ribbons. Looking up from the turmoil in their families and schools, 13ers saw a mirror-image welter of political failure and sensed that adults were simply not in control of themselves or the country.

Along the way, with millions of new members reaching voting age each year, the 13th Generation has forged an attitude of political reaction. The 1992 election showed that this reaction can even be against the president and party they once helped elect—if they feel the incumbents just aren't delivering what was promised. Most of today's twentysomethings listen to the partisans of social justice, global compassion, and big government with sharp-eyed skepticism. ("Word, word, word," as a rapper would say.) They prefer the flesh-and-blood loyalties they can count on—family, platoon, gang—over abstract theories, bloated institutions, and political parties that, in their experience, sooner or later let you down. Come election day, most choose not to choose and simply don't vote.

America's Youth: New Forms of Political Engagement

MATTHEW MOSELEY

Remarkable change is occurring among American youth. An enormous resurgence of volunteerism and monumental efforts in rebuilding the civic structure of America are guiding the nation on a path toward revitalization and renewal. Political pundits and the media mistakenly paint a picture of lazy and apathetic youth. They could not be more wrong. It is time to wake up and shed old stereotypes. America must move beyond the misleading label of "Generation X" and all the negative stigmas attached to it. . . .

While there is no shortage of statistics indicating widespread political apathy on college campuses, the terminology used and types of questions asked often skew the result and lead to a negative conclusion. As Terrell Bell, former Secretary of Education in the Reagan Cabinet, and Hillary Rodham Clinton, listed then as a Little Rock attorney, wrote six years ago, "Young people have learned only half of America's story. Although they clearly appreciate the democratic freedoms, they fail to perceive a need to reciprocate by exercising the duties and responsibilities of good citizenship."

Misconceptions abound regarding young men and women. For example, a *Newsweek* article published on June 6, 1994, "Global Whining We're No. 1: U.S. Youth Still Outmoans All," described American youth as "passive" in their whining, as well as lazy and apathetic.

The current literature fails to acknowledge that social activism has replaced political activism as the principal form of youth involvement. Such books as Paul Loeb's *Generation at a Crossroads* and Neil Howe and Bill Strauss's *13th Gen* paint a dismal, if not inaccurate, portrait of American youth while failing to recognize the many positive contributions of youth service. Regretfully, they ignore the facts. An Independent Sector survey conducted in 1992 concluded that over *half* of all people between the ages of 18 and 24 volunteered during the preceding year. It is not hard to understand that youth of the 1990s have found it much easier to make a difference in the world if they start at the most basic level—their communities and neighborhoods.

The popular misconception . . . is that declining interest in partisan politics and a lack of interest in inside-the-beltway issues translates into political apathy. Politicians and the media would have us think that youth today are lazy and unconcerned with civic responsibility because they don't buy into the political system. They are sadly mistaken.

In a speech delivered at the National Press Club on February 9, 1995, Senator Bill Bradley described society as a three-legged stool. One leg represents government, which is firm and strong—perhaps too strong. Another leg is the equally strong private or corporate sector. The third leg is the civic sector, which is disproportionately weak. The fact that civil society is weak in relation to the government and corporate sectors has caused a great imbalance. But youth are stabilizing the system through significant and effective work in the civic sector of society.

And what is civil society? It is the place where we live and make our homes; it is our families, where we play sports, where we worship our God and teach our children. It is that place in society where we listen to music, view art, experience culture, appreciate theater, and hang out in coffee shops. Civil society consists of beauty parlors, front porches, Elks Clubs, Junior Leagues, and all of our various forms of groups and associations. Most significantly, it is the realm of our society that so desperately needs support and strength to stay alive and healthy—not hindrance and neglect.

There is a "movement" quietly occurring in America in which young people are taking an active role in repairing and building up this third and weakest leg. Consequently, the misunderstanding of how youth perceive their political role is drawn from the absence of youth involvement from the private and public legs of our societal stool. This movement is a broad, sweeping wave of youth action that builds upon that third leg, and not only brings America back into balance, but leaves a lasting mark on civic renewal in its wake.

Many young people have big hopes and exciting dreams for their lives. Many members of the younger generation may have given up on the super-success of high-paying jobs. Indeed, "twenty-somethings" have changed the way they measure their personal success. But they aren't as down and out as public opinion analysts and the media so often suggest. It isn't because jobs aren't as available as they were, because they are. On Sunday, June 4, 1995, Lisa Ganasci of the Associated Press published an article entitled "Grads Find Improved Market," in which she cited a 38-percent increase in recruiting for students with doctorates and master's degrees in science.

But enhanced campus-recruitment efforts—and higher bonuses for those students who *do* choose to sign-on with corporate America—indicate that young men and women are rejecting the idea that they must literally sell their souls for the almighty dollar. Nancy Nagy, career services director at Duke University's Fuqua School of Business, states, "With the market more competitive for graduates, many companies are offering 'signing bonuses' of anywhere from $2,000 to $50,000, bringing some salary packages to six figures. The average salary for a graduate this year [1995] is $63,500."

Clearly, the cost-benefit analysis has changed: Many feel it is no longer worth it to sit in the dismal, lifeless corporate cubicle that Douglas Coupland describes in *Generation X* as the "veal-fattening pen."

Rejection of the cradle-to-grave employment model shouldn't be interpreted as indifference. The hopes and dreams of youth today are different from those of previous generations, but they are just as important and far-reaching.

So what are young men and women doing? Southern Community Partners funds youth-driven initiatives in the South that are helping to revitalize urban and rural areas through key strategic efforts. *Who Cares* magazine, chronicler of the youth service movement, acts as a necessary clearinghouse for information and resources on youth-led and youth-serving nonprofit organizations. Partners in Education is forging partnerships between communities and schools, bringing community service into the classroom and tapping a valuable, previously under-utilized resource. COOL (Campus Outreach Opportunity League) provides a much-needed forum for community service at colleges and universities across the country. The list goes on: Public Allies, City Year, National Urban Coalition, Youth Service America, Teach for America, Americorps, Do Something, Black Student Leadership Network, Urban Service, Student Pugwash, Selma Do Something Fund, Bread for the World, and Campus Ecology, to name a few, all are agents of effective social change at the grass roots.

United through the Alliance for National Renewal, many of these organizations are joining forces and collaborating under the newly formed National Renewal Youth Alliance.

These organizations, along with countless others, represent fresh and innovative responses to the key emerging issues of our time that won't be heard on CNN or debated on C-SPAN. Oprah doesn't talk about them, and Letterman only has the occasional guest. These issues often lack the glamour worthy of big-time television. However, this negligence can be remedied. If people do have a genuine concern for the direction of society, it is crucial to understand the beliefs and motivations of young people, for they soon will become those of the entire nation.

There are three fundamental ways in which youth are changing the world today. First, the way they participate socially and politically has vastly changed over the last five to ten years. The way young men and women think of themselves as members of society and how they express their participation through various networks and associations is profoundly different from those of previous generations. For instance, youth have rejected political parties as an avenue of participation in the electoral process. Apathy toward Washington doesn't mean that youth just crumble up and die. All across the country, youth are banding together in diverse ways to change their communities and their lives. They are shifting their attention to other activities whereby they can really make a difference. It is likely to be close to home, in their own backyards: building housing for the homeless, working in soup kitchens, helping the elderly, advocating for youth, educating underprivileged kids, etc.

Second, the trend toward multiculturalism is having an enormous effect on youth and the institutions of the nation. Youth have waved goodbye to the All-American kid as a stereotype of what is "normal, mainstream Americana." This image has been pushed aside for a broader interpretation of American youth. With the proliferation of international students, at home and abroad, youth have struggled with diversity in the university classroom to witness a rapidly changing curriculum. Even Howe and Strauss agree in *13th Gen* that American youth today are de facto more tolerant, accepting and open to differences in race, ethnicity and gender than any other generation in the history of the world.

Third, the way people work to pay the bills has been modified for several reasons. The work ethic has changed dramatically over the last five to ten years. How, why and when people choose to work has shifted. Why are people moving out of the bigger cities and going to places like Telluride, Stowe or Lake Tahoe? It is because living in the apartment complex, shopping mall, corporate, or consumer mind-set isn't enough to keep their dreams alive. There must be more to life. This is not solely a factor of youth, but a phenomenon that is occurring throughout all age groups. It just so happens that youth are much more mobile and apt to pick up and move if they decide they don't like a particular place for social or economic reasons. This mobility is responsible for an emerging new class of technical migrants or—as they are called in the Rocky Mountain West—Modem Cowboys. It is possible today for people to live and work almost anywhere in the world if they structure their working environments the right way.

The young generation is rejecting the dichotomy between themselves and their elders—the classic breakdown between busters and boomers, the polarizing difference between "twenty-somethings" and "forty-somethings." Today's youth have never endorsed the catchy labels of Madison Avenue: 13ners, Gen X, slackers, the "me" generation. Part of the trend of fresh thinking among young and old alike is to break out of these damaging stereotypes.

It is time to cast issues in a new light. Youth are exiting an age of intense polarization; the debate between conservatives and liberals and Republicans and Democrats is withering. Many young Americans seek equitable and feasible public policies without the entrenched political baggage of previous generations. Young people today believe it is possible to find common ground on most issues, and are nearly unanimous of such issues as abortion, gun control and deficit reduction.

The political parties don't effectively represent and engage the American public and have nearly alienated youth. Ricki Seidman, executive director of Rock the Vote, a national voter registration campaign targeted at youth, believes that approximately 70 percent of voters between the ages of 18 and 24 are registered as Independents. Young men and women tend to view issues more in the context of what is right and good, rather than which political organization proposes the solutions.

A new type of leadership is quietly emerging from the ground up amid seemingly insurmountable problems in our communities. Young people are carefully redefining the American Dream and what it means to be a good citizen. They are rekindling the revolutionary spirit of our founding fathers.

It is through small, intensely localized efforts that young men and women are playing their cards now. They are throwing down their most valuable cards with courage and vision—not holding back in apathy. Today's youth are ready and willing to play the game. . . . [I]f utilized properly, the youth service movement will prove to be the trump card in our nation's effort to revitalize and renew American democracy. . . .

DISCUSSION QUESTIONS

1. Do you think young people today are cynical in general, or are they simply cynical about big government and corporations? Do you volunteer in your local community, and if so, why?

2. If someone volunteers at a homeless shelter or participates in a tutoring project, does this act have political significance, or is it simply a private matter of individuals helping individuals? If individuals volunteered much more than they presently do, would this change the way governments or private corporations behave?

3. Do you think that the protest movements of the 1960s and 1970s, led by Boomers, ultimately improved or weakened U.S. democracy? What sort of issues are best dealt with by protest movements, and what sorts are more appropriately handled by electoral politics or volunteerism?

4. What should the government do, if anything, to encourage civic volunteers? President Clinton began Americorps, which helps young people to pay for college if they volunteer to serve in needy communities. Do you think this is a good idea, or does government involvement and paying people ultimately corrupt voluntary activities?

5. Does it make sense to analyze politics in terms of generations, or does it make more sense to talk about the differences *within* generations among different classes, races, and ethnicities?

SUGGESTED READINGS AND INTERNET RESOURCES

The Howe and Strauss selection is from *13th Generation: Abort, Retry, Ignore, Fail?* (New York: Random House, 1993), which is full of cartoons, vignettes, and provocative quotes. In *Welcome to the Jungle: The Why Behind "Generation X"*

(New York: St. Martin's Press, 1995), Geoffrey T. Holtz takes a similar approach to Howe and Strauss, arguing that Gen X cynicism is largely justified, given the conditions handed down to them by the Baby Boomers. Allan Bloom's *The Closing of the American Mind: How Higher Education Has Failed Democracy and Impoverished the Souls of Today's Students* (New York: Simon and Schuster, 1987) touched off a heated controversy by blaming the faults of the younger generation on liberal professors who ignored the classics and taught mindless relativism in values. For a more uplifting picture of the political commitments of Gen Xers, see Paul Rogat Loeb's *Generation at the Crossroads: Apathy and Action on the American Campus* (New Brunswick, N.J.: Rutgers University Press, 1994) and Michele Mitchell's, *A New Kind of Party Animal: How the Young Are Redefining "Politics as Usual"* (New York: Simon and Schuster, 1998). The best collection of scholarly articles on the politics of Gen Xers is Stephen C. Craig and Stephen Earl Bennett, eds., *After the Boom: The Politics of Generation X* (Lanham, Md.: Rowman and Littlefield, 1997).

Generation X Coalition
http://members.aol.com/genxcoal/genxcoal.html
A useful web site that serves as a clearinghouse for articles and information on Generation X, including downloadable documents and articles.

X-PAC
http://www.clark.net/pub/x-pac/home.html
A nonpartisan political action committee dedicated to representing the political needs of Gen Xers, focusing particularly on Social Security reform.

Generation X
http://www.xgeneration.org/
Another site that encourages participation and change; it includes links to other sites giving the opportunity to contact parties, candidates, and interest groups.

Third Millennium
http://www.thirdmil.org/
Third Millennium is a national, nonpartisan, nonprofit organization launched by young adults to offer solutions to long-term problems facing the United States. Their mission is to promote sustainable reform of Social Security and Medicare by informing and mobilizing the nation's opinion leaders.

CHAPTER

Congress:
Can It Serve
the Public Good?

O
f the three branches of the national government, Congress provides the
most direct representation, and it is sometimes called "the people's
branch." But public disenchantment with Congress was on the rise in the
late 1980s and early 1990s. When members of Congress voted themselves
a pay raise in 1989, talk radio shows erupted with vehement denunciations
of the nation's legislators as a privileged elite out of touch with the citizens who
had sent them to Washington. The House banking scandal of 1992 added to
the image of privilege the taint of corruption. Meanwhile, congressional
inability to get mounting deficits under control or to pass major legislation
created a picture of a profligate and inefficient legislature. Then came the
electoral "earthquake" of 1994, when the voters took out their unhappiness on
the Democrats who had long controlled Congress and established a new
Republican majority pledged to transform the institution.

Under the leadership of the new Speaker of the House, Newt Gingrich, the
Republicans moved swiftly to enact a "revolution" in Congress. Playing to
popular democratic grievances, House Republicans took the lead in cutting
down some of the symbols of congressional privilege. More important,
congressional Republicans pushed a far-reaching conservative agenda that
would shift power away from Washington to the states and private industry, cut
taxes, and balance the budget through major spending cuts.

269

Perhaps the most remarkable aspect of the Republican "revolution" of 1995 was the attempt to transform fundamentally how Congress works. During the years of Democratic control, the most influential force in shaping congressional behavior had been the individual members, whose concern for reelection fostered close attention to district or state interests. Congress as an institution was relatively decentralized, with committees and subcommittees shaping legislation more than the parties or their leadership. It was the goal of Speaker Gingrich and his followers to change the congressional culture by placing the unifying forces of leadership and party above the fragmenting forces of committee power and individualism. Through new rules and bold assertions of authority, Gingrich and his team consolidated power and kept the focus on their party's agenda.

If the House was ready for revolution in 1995, however, the Senate, still characterized by individualism and decentralization, was slower to change. And Gingrich had not counted on forceful opposition to his conservative agenda from President Clinton. When Clinton won a showdown with the Republicans over the budget at the end of 1995, the steam went out of the Republican revolution. Nothing symbolized its failure so well as the declining fortunes of its leader, Newt Gingrich. In January 1997 he was reprimanded by the House for an ethics violation and ordered to pay a $300,000 fine. In November 1998, blamed by his fellow Republicans when their party suffered unexpected losses in the midterm elections, he resigned from Congress.

Congress after the revolution is more partisan and centralized than it had been prior to 1995. To that extent, Gingrich could claim some success in his effort to change the congressional culture. But the forces of individualism and committee influence have reasserted themselves in the postrevolutionary Congress, while the power of congressional leaders to gain agreement for a party agenda has waned. After the 1998 elections, Republicans in the Senate had a small but solid majority, but in the House, the Republican margin of control was razor thin. With a weak Speaker, Dennis Hastert, replacing Gingrich and with Republican moderates and pragmatic conservatives frequently squabbling with hard-line conservatives, the most that congressional Republicans could achieve was a deadlock with President Clinton.

Although political scientists who study Congress did not anticipate the electoral explosion of 1994 or the revolution of 1995, they have long been concerned with the problems of the institution. Many have agreed with the electorate that the contemporary Congress has not been working well. Others, however, believe that Congress has strengths that disenchanted citizens (and disenchanted political scientists) fail to recognize.

Morris P. Fiorina, the author of our first selection, believes that both legislators and the people who elect them are motivated by calculations of self-interest. For members of Congress, the goal of self-interested behavior is reelection. For their constituents, the goal of self-interested behavior is pork barrel projects, which bring federal dollars into their district, and assistance from the legislator in handling problems with federal bureaucrats ("casework"). Fiorina stresses how the bureaucratic state is a godsend to congressional incumbents, who get credit for establishing new programs that expand the bureaucracy and then win still further credit by denouncing the inevitable bureaucratic blunders that ensue. Note that in Fiorina's picture of congressional politics, neither representatives nor voters are paying much attention to legislation that seeks to address the nation's problems.

In the second selection, Joseph M. Bessette takes issue with Fiorina's sardonic account of Congress. Bessette argues that Congress still contains members who uphold James Madison's hopes for a deliberative and public-spirited legislature—elite democracy at its best. While not denying that the reelection motive affects members of Congress, he disputes the claim that it is the best explanation for congressional behavior. Bessette finds evidence that Congress is influenced by "serious lawmakers," who want to improve national well-being, seek the respect of their colleagues as much as the votes of their constituents, do the hard work of developing expertise in particular policy areas, sway fellow legislators through reasoned persuasion, and even are willing to take personal risks for the sake of the public good.

The debate between Fiorina and Bessette raises important questions about the character of representation in the contemporary Congress. It also may prove enlightening to set their accounts of Congress against the conception put forward during the Republican revolution of 1995. Are representatives and voters locked into a system of self-interested and short-term exchanges while no one devotes sufficient care to the long-term welfare of the nation? Can lawmakers engage in a deliberative search for the public good, and are there congressional reforms that will enhance such deliberation? Have the Republicans remedied the worst congressional ills, or have they substituted a narrowly partisan agenda for true deliberation about the public good?

The Rise of the Washington Establishment

MORRIS P. FIORINA

Dramatis Personae

I assume that most people most of the time act in their own self-interest. This is not to say that human beings seek only to amass tangible wealth but rather to say that human beings seek to achieve their own ends—tangible and intangible—rather than the ends of their fellow men. I do not condemn such behavior nor do I condone it (although I rather sympathize with Thoreau's comment that "if I knew for a certainty that a man was coming to my house with the conscious design of doing me good, I should run for my life"). I only claim that political and economic theories which presume self-interested behavior will prove to be more widely applicable than those which build on more altruistic assumptions.

What does the axiom imply when used in the specific context of this book, a context peopled by congressmen, bureaucrats, and voters? I assume that the primary goal of the typical congressman is reelection. Over and above the $57,000 salary plus "perks" and outside money, the office of congressman carries with it prestige, excitement, and power.[1] It is a seat in the cockpit of government. But in order to retain the status, excitement, and power (not to mention more tangible things) of office, the congressman must win reelection every two years. Even those congressmen genuinely concerned with good public policy must achieve reelection in order to continue their work. Whether narrowly self-serving or more publicly oriented, the individual congressman finds reelection to be at least a necessary condition for the achievement of his goals.

Moreover, there is a kind of natural selection process at work in the electoral arena. On average, those congressmen who are not primarily interested in reelection will not achieve reelection as often as those who are interested. We, the people, help to weed out congressmen whose primary motivation is not reelection. We admire politicians who courageously adopt the aloof role of the disinterested statesman, but we vote for those politicians who follow our wishes and do us favors.

---

1. The $57,000 salary was the salary for a member of Congress in 1977, when the first edition of Fiorina's book was published.

What about the bureaucrats? A specification of their goals is somewhat more controversial—those who speak of appointed officials as public servants obviously take a more benign view than those who speak of them as bureaucrats. The literature provides ample justification for asserting that most bureaucrats wish to protect and nurture their agencies. The typical bureaucrat can be expected to seek to expand his agency in terms of personnel, budget, and mission. One's status in Washington (again, not to mention more tangible things) is roughly proportional to the importance of the operation one oversees. And the sheer size of the operation is taken to be a measure of importance. As with congressmen, the specified goals apply even to those bureaucrats who genuinely believe in their agency's mission. If they believe in the efficacy of their programs, they naturally wish to expand them and add new ones. All of this requires more money and more people. The genuinely committed bureaucrat is just as likely to seek to expand his agency as the proverbial empire-builder.

And what of the third element in this equation, us? What do we, the voters who support the Washington system, strive for? Each of us wishes to receive a maximum of benefits from government for the minimum cost. This goal suggests maximum government efficiency, on the one hand, but it also suggests mutual exploitation on the other. Each of us favors an arrangement in which our fellow citizens pay for our benefits.

With these brief descriptions of the cast of characters in hand, let us proceed.

Tammany Hall Goes to Washington

What should we expect from a legislative body composed of individuals whose first priority is their continued tenure in office? We should expect, first, that the normal activities of its members are those calculated to enhance their chances of reelection. And we should expect, second, that the members would devise and maintain institutional arrangements which facilitate their electoral activities. . . .

For most of the twentieth century, congressmen have engaged in a mix of three kinds of activities: lawmaking, pork barreling, and casework. Congress is first and foremost a lawmaking body, at least according to constitutional theory. In every postwar session Congress "considers" thousands of bills and resolutions, many hundreds of which are brought to a record vote (over 500 in each chamber of the 93rd Congress). Naturally the critical consideration in taking a position for the record is the maximization of approval in the home district. If the district is unaffected by and unconcerned with the matter at hand, the congressman may then take into account the general welfare of the country. (This sounds cynical, but remember that "profiles in courage" are sufficiently rare that their occurrence inspires books and articles.) Abetted by political scientists of the pluralist school, politicians have propounded an ideology which maintains that the good of the country on any given issue is simply what is best for a majority of congressional districts.[2] This ideology provides a philosophical justification for what congressmen do while acting in their own self-interest.

A second activity favored by congressmen consists of efforts to bring home the bacon to their districts. Many popular articles have been written about the pork barrel, a term originally applied to rivers and harbors legislation but now generalized to cover all manner of federal largesse. Congressmen consider new dams, federal buildings, sewage treatment plants, urban renewal projects, etc. as sweet plums to be plucked. Federal projects are highly visible, their economic impact is easily detected by constituents, and sometimes they even produce something of value to the district. The average constituent may have some trouble translating his congressman's vote on some civil rights issue into a change in his personal welfare. But the workers hired and supplies purchased in connection with a big federal project provide benefits that are widely appreciated. The historical importance congressmen attach to the pork barrel is reflected in the rules of the House. That body accords certain classes of legislation "privileged" status: they may come directly to the floor without passing through the Rules Committee, a traditional graveyard for legislation. What kinds of legislation are privileged? Taxing and spending bills, for one: the government's power to raise and spend money must be kept relatively unfettered. But in addition, the omnibus rivers and harbors bills of the Public Works Committee and public lands bills from the Interior Committee share privileged status. The House will allow a civil rights or defense procurement or environmental bill to languish in the Rules Committee, but it takes special precautions to insure that nothing slows down the approval of dams and irrigation projects.

A third major activity takes up perhaps as much time as the other two combined. Traditionally, constituents appeal to their congressman for myriad favors and services. Sometimes only information is needed, but often constituents request that their congressman intervene in the internal workings of federal agencies to affect a decision in a favorable way, to reverse an adverse decision, or simply to speed up the glacial bureaucratic process. On the basis of extensive personal interviews with congressmen, Charles Clapp writes:

> Denied a favorable ruling by the bureaucracy on a matter of direct concern to him, puzzled or irked by delays in obtaining a decision, confused by the administrative maze through which he is directed to proceed, or ignorant of whom to write, a constituent may turn to his congressman for help. These letters offer great potential for political

---

2. Pluralist theory in political science argues that power in the United States is dispersed among many different groups, which compete for influence in a process marked by bargaining and compromise.

benefit to the congressman since they affect the constituent personally. If the legislator can be of assistance, he may gain a firm ally; if he is indifferent, he may even lose votes.

Actually congressmen are in an almost unique position in our system, a position shared only with high-level members of the executive branch. Congressmen possess the power to expedite and influence bureaucratic decisions. This capability flows directly from congressional control over what bureaucrats value most: higher budgets and new program authorizations. In a very real sense each congressman is a monopoly supplier of bureaucratic unsticking services for his district.

Every year the federal budget passes through the appropriations committees of Congress. Generally these committees make perfunctory cuts. But on occasion they vent displeasure on an agency and leave it bleeding all over the Capitol. The most extreme case of which I am aware came when the House committee took away the entire budget of the Division of Labor Standards in 1947 (some of the budget was restored elsewhere in the appropriations process). Deep and serious cuts are made occasionally, and the threat of such cuts keeps most agencies attentive to congressional wishes. Professors Richard Fenno and Aaron Wildavsky have provided extensive documentary and interview evidence of the great respect (and even terror) federal bureaucrats show for the House Appropriations Committee. Moreover, the bureaucracy must keep coming back to Congress to have its old programs reauthorized and new ones added. Again, most such decisions are perfunctory, but exceptions are sufficiently frequent that bureaucrats do not forget the basis of their agencies' existence. For example, the Law Enforcement Assistance Administration (LEAA) and the Food Stamps Program had no easy time of it this last Congress (94th). The bureaucracy needs congressional approval in order to survive, let alone expand. Thus, when a congressman calls about some minor bureaucratic decision or regulation, the bureaucracy considers his accommodation a small price to pay for the goodwill its cooperation will produce, particularly if he has any connection to the substantive committee or the appropriations subcommittee to which it reports.

From the standpoint of capturing voters, the congressman's lawmaking activities differ in two important respects from his pork-barrel and casework activities. First, programmatic actions are inherently controversial. Unless his district is homogeneous, a congressman will find his district divided on many major issues. Thus when he casts a vote, introduces a piece of nontrivial legislation, or makes a speech with policy content he will displease some elements of his district. Some constituents may applaud the congressman's civil rights record, but others believe integration is going too fast. Some support foreign aid, while others believe it's money poured down a rathole. Some advocate economic equality, others stew over welfare cheaters. On such policy matters the congressman can expect to make friends as well as enemies. Presumably he will behave so as to maximize the excess of the former over the latter, but nevertheless a policy stand will generally make some enemies.

In contrast, the pork barrel and casework are relatively less controversial. New federal projects bring jobs, shiny new facilities, and general economic prosperity, or so people believe. Snipping ribbons at the dedication of a new post office or dam is a much more pleasant pursuit than disposing of a constitutional amendment on abortion. Republicans and Democrats, conservatives and liberals, all generally prefer a richer district to a poorer one. Of course, in recent years the river damming and stream-bed straightening activities of the Army Corps of Engineers have aroused some opposition among environmentalists. Congressmen happily react by absorbing the opposition and adding environmentalism to the pork barrel: water treatment plants are currently a hot congressional item.

Casework is even less controversial. Some poor, aggrieved constituent becomes enmeshed in the tentacles of an evil bureaucracy and calls upon Congressman St. George to do battle with the dragon. Again Clapp writes:

> A person who has a reasonable complaint or query is regarded as providing an opportunity rather than as adding an extra burden to an already busy office. The party affiliation of the individual even when known to be different from that of the congressman does not normally act as a deterrent to action. Some legislators have built their reputations and their majorities on a program of service to all constituents irrespective of party. Regularly, voters affiliated with the opposition in other contests lend strong support to the lawmaker whose intervention has helped them in their struggle with the bureaucracy.

Even following the revelation of sexual improprieties, Wayne Hays won his Ohio Democratic primary by a two-to-one margin. According to a *Los Angeles Times* feature story, Hays's constituency base was built on a foundation of personal service to constituents:

> They receive help in speeding up bureaucratic action on various kinds of federal assistance—black lung benefits to disabled miners and their families, Social Security payments, veterans' benefits and passports.
>
> Some constituents still tell with pleasure of how Hays stormed clear to the seventh floor of the State Department and into Secretary of State Dean Rusk's office to demand, successfully, the quick issuance of a passport to an Ohioan.

Practicing politicians will tell you that word of mouth is still the most effective mode of communication. News of favors to constituents gets around and no doubt is embellished in the process.

In sum, when considering the benefits of his programmatic activities, the congressman must tote up gains and losses to arrive at a net profit. Pork barreling and casework, however, are basically pure profit.

A second way in which programmatic activities differ from casework and the pork barrel is the difficulty of assigning responsibility to the former as compared with the latter. No congressman can seriously claim that he is responsible for the 1964 Civil Rights Act, the ABM, or the 1972 Revenue Sharing Act.[3] Most constituents do have some vague notion that their congressman is only one of hundreds and their senator one of an even hundred. Even committee chairmen have a difficult time claiming credit for a piece of major legislation, let alone a rank-and-file congressman. Ah, but casework, and the pork barrel. In dealing with the bureaucracy, the congressman is not merely one vote of 435. Rather, he is a nonpartisan power, someone whose phone calls snap an office to attention. He is not kept on hold. The constituent who receives aid believes that his congressman and his congressman alone got results. Similarly, congressmen find it easy to claim credit for federal projects awarded their districts. The congressman may have instigated the proposal for the project in the first place, issued regular progress reports, and ultimately announced the award through his office. Maybe he can't claim credit for the 1965 Voting Rights Act, but he can take credit for Littletown's spanking new sewage treatment plant.

Overall then, programmatic activities are dangerous (controversial), on the one hand, and programmatic accomplishments are difficult to claim credit for, on the other. While less exciting, casework and pork barreling are both safe and profitable. For a reelection-oriented congressman the choice is obvious.

The key to the rise of the Washington establishment (and the vanishing marginals)[4] is the following observation: *the growth of an activist federal government has stimulated a change in the mix of congressional activities*. Specifically, a lesser proportion of congressional effort is now going into programmatic activities and a greater proportion into pork-barrel and casework activities. As a result, today's congressmen make relatively fewer enemies and relatively more friends among the people of their districts.

To elaborate, a basic fact of life in twentieth-century America is the growth of the federal role and its attendant bureaucracy. Bureaucracy is the characteristic mode of delivering public goods and services. Ceteris paribus, the more the government attempts to do for people, the more extensive a bureaucracy it creates. As the scope of government expands, more and more citizens find themselves in direct contact with the federal government. Consider the rise in such contacts upon passage of the Social Security Act, work relief projects, and other New Deal programs. Consider the millions of additional citizens touched by the veterans' programs of the postwar period. Consider the untold numbers whom the Great Society and its aftermath brought face to face with the federal government. In 1930 the federal bureaucracy was small and rather distant from the everyday concerns of Americans. By 1975 it was neither small nor distant.

---

3. The acronym ABM stands for antiballistic missile.
4. *Marginals* refers to congressional incumbents who barely hold on to their seats in close races; instead, most incumbents at the time Fiorina was writing were winning their races by large margins.

As the years have passed, more and more citizens and groups have found themselves dealing with the federal bureaucracy. They may be seeking positive actions—eligibility for various benefits and awards of government grants. Or they may be seeking relief from the costs imposed by bureaucratic regulations—on working conditions, racial and sexual quotas, market restrictions, and numerous other subjects. While not malevolent, bureaucracies make mistakes, both of commission and omission, and normal attempts at redress often meet with unresponsiveness and inflexibility and sometimes seeming incorrigibility. Whatever the problem, the citizen's congressman is a source of succor. The greater the scope of government activity, the greater the demand for his services.

Private monopolists can regulate the demand for their product by raising or lowering the price. Congressmen have no such (legal) option. When the demand for their services rises, they have no real choice except to meet that demand—to supply more bureaucratic unsticking services—so long as they would rather be elected than unelected. This vulnerability to escalating constituency demands is largely academic, though. I seriously doubt that congressmen resist their gradual transformation from national legislators to errand boy–ombudsmen. As we have noted, casework is all profit. Congressmen have buried proposals to relieve the casework burden by establishing a national ombudsman or Congressman Reuss's proposed Administrative Counsel of the Congress. One of the congressmen interviewed by Clapp stated:

> Before I came to Washington I used to think that it might be nice if the individual states had administrative arms here that would take care of necessary liaison between citizens and the national government. But a congressman running for reelection is interested in building fences by providing personal services. The system is set to reelect incumbents regardless of party, and incumbents wouldn't dream of giving any of this service function away to any subagency. As an elected member I feel the same way.

In fact, it is probable that at least some congressmen deliberately stimulate the demand for their bureaucratic fixit services. Recall that the new Republican in district A travels about his district saying:

> I'm your man in Washington. What are your problems? How can I help you?

And in district B, did the demand for the congressman's services rise so much between 1962 and 1964 that a "regiment" of constituency staff became necessary?[5] Or, having access to the regiment, did the new Democrat stimulate the demand to which he would apply his regiment?

---

5. Earlier in his book, Fiorina presented case studies of districts A and B.

In addition to greatly increased casework, let us not forget that the growth of the federal role has also greatly expanded the federal pork barrel. The creative pork barreler need not limit himself to dams and post offices—rather old-fashioned interests. Today, creative congressmen can cadge LEAA money for the local police, urban renewal and housing money for local politicians, educational program grants for the local education bureaucracy. And there are sewage treatment plants, worker training and retraining programs, health services, and programs for the elderly. The pork barrel is full to overflowing. The conscientious congressman can stimulate applications for federal assistance (the sheer number of programs makes it difficult for local officials to stay current with the possibilities), put in a good word during consideration, and announce favorable decisions amid great fanfare.

In sum, everyday decisions by a large and growing federal bureaucracy bestow significant tangible benefits and impose significant tangible costs. Congressmen can affect these decisions. Ergo, the more decisions the bureaucracy has the opportunity to make, the more opportunities there are for the congressman to build up credits.

The nature of the Washington system is now quite clear. Congressmen (typically the majority Democrats) earn electoral credits by establishing various federal programs (the minority Republicans typically earn credits by fighting the good fight). The legislation is drafted in very general terms, so some agency, existing or newly established, must translate a vague policy mandate into a functioning program, a process that necessitates the promulgation of numerous rules and regulations and, incidentally, the trampling of numerous toes. At the next stage, aggrieved and/or hopeful constituents petition their congressman to intervene in the complex (or at least obscure) decision processes of the bureaucracy. The cycle closes when the congressman lends a sympathetic ear, piously denounces the evils of bureaucracy, intervenes in the latter's decisions, and rides a grateful electorate to ever more impressive electoral showings. Congressmen take credit coming and going. They are the alpha and the omega.

The popular frustration with the permanent government in Washington is partly justified, but to a considerable degree it is misplaced resentment. *Congress is the linchpin of the Washington establishment.* The bureaucracy serves as a convenient lightning rod for public frustration and a convenient whipping boy for congressmen. But so long as the bureaucracy accommodates congressmen, the latter will oblige with ever larger budgets and grants of authority. Congress does not just react to big government—it creates it. All of Washington prospers. More and more bureaucrats promulgate more and more regulations and dispense more and more money. Fewer and fewer congressmen suffer electoral defeat. Elements of the electorate benefit from government programs, and all of the electorate is eligible for ombudsman services. But the general, long-term welfare of the United States is no more than an incidental by-product of the system.

Congress and Deliberative Democracy

JOSEPH M. BESSETTE

Deliberation Defined

The deliberation that lies at the core of the kind of democracy established by the American constitutional system can be defined most simply as *reasoning on the merits of public policy*. As commonly and traditionally understood, deliberation is a reasoning process in which the participants seriously consider substantive information and arguments and seek to decide individually and to persuade each other as to what constitutes good public policy. Thus, deliberation includes a variety of activities often called "problem solving" or "analytic": the investigation and identification of social, economic, or governmental problems; the evaluation of current policies or programs; the consideration of various and competing proposals; and the formulation of legislative or administrative remedies. In any genuine deliberative process the participants must be open to the facts, arguments, and proposals that come to their attention and must share a general willingness to learn from their colleagues and others.

So defined, the proximate aim of a deliberative process is the conferral of some public good or benefit. Such a benefit need not necessarily be national in scope (such as a healthy economy or a sound national defense); it may instead be a locally oriented good (such as a flood control project or a new highway), a good directed toward a broad class of citizens (as with civil rights laws or labor legislation), or even transnational in its reach (such as foreign aid). Thus, the existence of deliberation does not turn on the distinction between local and national interests. An overriding desire to serve one's local constituents does not in itself close a legislator to the persuasive effects of information and arguments, although such a legislator will respond to different kinds of appeals than one who seeks to promote national interests. This is true even if the desire to confer local benefits results directly from self-interested calculations, such as the representative's desire to be reelected; for the legislator who seeks singlemindedly to be reelected may well find that in some situations this goal requires him to give real consideration to the merits of legislative proposals designed to benefit his constituents.

Although legislators may deliberate about local, or partial, interests as well as those of a national dimension, there remains a relationship between the likelihood and nature of deliberation in Congress and the scope of the public benefits that legislators seek to confer. Consider, for example, legislators who deliberate about how to promote the well-being of specific interests. If such legislators see their job essentially in terms of doing good for external groups, they will be inclined to accept the groups' determination as to how this should be done; for who knows the groups' interests better than they do. The narrower and more specific the group (wheat farmers, auto workers, coal miners, etc.) the less difference of opinion or conflict there will be and therefore the less need for such a legislator to consider different arguments or to reason about alternative proposals. However, as the scope of the legislator's concerns widens, to encompass more or broader interests, the more difficult it will become to defer to the interests themselves for guidance. A variety of differing and often conflicting opinions will highlight the complexity of the issues at stake and place a greater obligation on the lawmaker to exercise some independent judgment. For the legislator who seeks to promote the national interest, personal deliberation will be essential; insofar as other legislators share the same goal, collective deliberation will be pervasive.

Personal deliberation by individual legislators does not require that others in the lawmaking body share the same goals. A member of the House, for example, could deliberate in a serious way about how the federal government could solve a transportation problem within his or her district even if no House members shared the same concern. Collective deliberation, however, necessarily requires some sharing of goals, purposes, or values. If legislators are to reason together about the merits of public policy, there must be some common ground for the arguments and appeals essential to deliberation. Whether the shared goal is quite specific and well defined (e.g., a national health insurance plan along the British model) or much broader and even somewhat vague (e.g., a healthy economy or a sound national defense), it will provide the basis for legislators, who may have little else in common, to share information and to reason and argue together about public policy.

Although the geographically based representation of the American system of government has a tendency to elevate localized interests and needs over broad programmatic concerns, district and state representation also provides a solid basis for the sharing of goals within Congress. Similar kinds of constituencies are likely to have common interests and needs and therefore similar desires or expectations for national policy. Inner-city residents throughout the nation are likely to have similar desires regarding social welfare policy. Farmers from the Midwest, South, and West are likely to agree on the need for price supports. Blue-collar workers in threatened industries across the country are likely to desire high tariffs or other protectionist measures. Those elected to Congress to represent these kinds of constituents will soon discover that many of their colleagues represent similar electorates and thus share many of the same policy goals. In some cases such like-minded legislators institutionalize and promote their shared policy interests through an informal caucus which helps them to share information and ideas and to coordinate policy efforts.

In describing what deliberation is, it is important to clarify what it is not; for policy deliberation is not just any kind of reasoning involved in the policy process. As understood throughout this book, policy deliberation necessarily involves reasoning about the substantive benefits of public policy, reasoning about some *public* good—some good external to the decision-makers themselves. "Reasoning on the merits" of public policy means reasoning about how public policy can benefit the broader society or some significant portion thereof. Thus, there is a sharp analytical distinction between deliberation and merely self-interested calculations (however complex the relationship between these two in practice). Similarly, deliberation does not include reasoning about legislative tactics, such as drafting a bill to facilitate its referral to a sympathetic committee or determining how to use the rules of the House or Senate to greatest advantage during the legislative process.

Although a deliberative process is per se rational or analytical, the values or dispositions that the participants bring to bear on the determination of good public policy may reflect a host of diverse influences: general upbringing, parental values, personal experiences, the views of friends and acquaintances, influential teachers, partisan attachments, social class, economic status, etc. Thus, it is not surprising that different individuals often reach quite opposed conclusions about the merits of policy proposals even when exposed to the same information and arguments. Such disagreement is not in itself evidence of the absence of deliberation.

Deliberation, as defined here, may take a variety of forms. It may be a largely consensual process in which like-minded individuals work together to fashion the details of a policy they all desire; or it may involve deep-seated conflicts over fundamental issues or principles. It may result in unanimity of view, where no votes are necessary; or it may reveal sharp disagreements that require formal voting to determine the majority view. It may range from private reflection in the quiet of an office or study to an emotionally charged exchange on the floor of the House or Senate. It may take the form of open and public discussions preserved in official records or of private exchanges hidden from public view. It may involve direct discussions among elected officials themselves or, perhaps more frequently, conversations among their staff. It may be limited to those who hold formal positions in the government, either elective or appointive; or it may include the ideas and opinions of interest groups, trade associations, national organizations, or the scholarly community.

Nonetheless, however diverse the various manifestations of deliberation, every deliberative process involves three essential elements: information, arguments, and persuasion. . . .

Bargaining and reelection theories are the two great pillars that support the widespread contemporary view that Congress is not a deliberative institution (at least in any fundamental sense) and, by implication, that American democracy is not a deliberative democracy. We have seen in the previous chapter how little support the case studies of policymaking within Congress provide for the belief that bargaining is the predominant device for reaching collective decisions in the House and Senate. What, then, of the reelection incentive as the principal explanation for individual desires and actions? No one can dispute the analytical attractiveness of *assuming* its dominance, but what does the empirical evidence tell us, fairly reviewed?

We must be careful how we frame the issue. The question here is not whether the reelection incentive matters in Congress. The vast majority of those who serve in the House and Senate give every indication that they desire to remain in office (although some voluntarily resign at each election). Thus, it is reasonable to call the reelection incentive an established fact. This incentive, then, inclines the members of Congress to engage in behaviors helpful to future electoral success. As we have seen, such behaviors are not limited to formal campaigning. They may occur throughout a legislative term (it is not unusual to hear House members complain about campaigning for reelection all the time) and may include activities that are clearly nonlegislative in character, such as tracking down missing Social Security checks, posing for photographs with delegations from home, and the like. That those who serve in the House and Senate devote a certain amount of their time and resources, especially staff time, to nonlegislative activities that will promote reelection is beyond dispute.

Thus the issue here is not whether the members of Congress pursue reelection but rather whether the reelection incentive squeezes out deliberative activities in a way that undermines, or even destroys, Congress's character as a deliberative institution. This could occur in two ways. First, reelection-oriented activities could so consume the time and resources of the member that nothing is left for serious reasoning about public policy. Second, the reelection incentive could intrude upon formal legislative activities in such a way as to distort otherwise deliberative behavior. For example, the committee member who single-mindedly plays to the cameras during some hearing on a controversial matter because it is good politics has allowed his private interests to overcome his deliberative responsibilities.

While it is certainly possible for the reelection incentive to undermine deliberation in these two ways, it is not necessary. The fact that the members of Congress do certain things to promote their reelection is hardly proof that they do not do other things to reach reasoned judgments about the merits of public policy. Indeed, as noted earlier, those who designed the American Congress saw no necessary incompatibility between the reelection incentive and deliberation. The framers believed not only that the legislator's desire to return to Congress would not disable him from engaging in genuine deliberation about national laws, but also that the reelection incentive was the vital link between deliberations in Congress and popular interests and attitudes. Indeed, to argue that the system of public accountability in the modern Congress makes genuine deliberation impossible is virtually the equivalent of saying that deliberation and democracy, as presently constituted in the United States, are incompatible.

It follows, then, that in assessing Congress as a deliberative institution the issue is not so much whether the reelection incentive is a powerful motive in influencing congressional behavior, but rather whether and to what degree legislators in the U.S. Congress embrace and act upon the independent desire to promote good public policy, the end for which deliberation is the means. How much evidence do we have that the ambitious and reelection-seeking members of Congress actually care about and work to promote good public policy? . . .

The High Art of Responsible Lawmaking

. . . A theory of legislative behavior that posits only the low motive of reelection cannot even provide the vocabulary to describe and explain the serious lawmaking evident in the accounts summarized here. To repeat a question asked above, how can the reelection incentive explain why any legislator would choose substance over symbols, hard work over posturing, or responsibility over popularity? And, most incongruous of all, why would any legislator moved primarily by the reelection incentive ever take any political risks for the sake of substantive policy goals?

Conversely, a full understanding and appreciation of the high art of lawmaking allows the low arts of mere self-seeking to reveal themselves fully for what they are. Could it even be said that it is only some sense of what constitutes serious lawmaking that makes it possible to understand fully the nature of the lower self-seeking arts (what Hamilton called "the little arts of popularity")? Consider "posturing," for example, a term that came up in several of the portraits. Lawmakers and those who observe and study lawmakers have little difficulty identifying posturing when they see it; but surely this is because in the back of their minds they possess a rather clear picture or model of what posturing is not: reasoned argument and effort at genuine persuasion. Posturing can be understood fully only in contrast to this thing which it is not, in contrast to something higher than itself.

What, then, are the principal characteristics of those who engage in serious lawmaking in the United States Congress? Insofar as the accounts reviewed here are an accurate guide, the following stand out:

- Serious lawmakers are not satisfied simply to serve in Congress and enjoy its many perks. They want to make a difference, to accomplish something of importance, to make the nation (and perhaps the world) a better place through their governing activities. They believe that there is a public interest, that it is knowable, and that their efforts in Congress can help to achieve it.

- By virtue of their office (membership in the House or Senate, committee and subcommittee chairmanships, leadership positions, etc.) they feel a sense of responsibility to something beyond their personal advantage, a duty to larger ends. It is the accomplishment of these larger ends that is the source of their deepest political satisfaction.

- They seek to earn the respect of their colleagues and of those outside Congress through their deliberative efforts and their substantive achievements. They want to be known as effective legislators. The respect they so earn from their colleagues is a principal source of their power in Congress.

- They develop substantive expertise in the areas under their jurisdiction through careful and thorough analysis, engaging in the hard work necessary to master a subject. Open to facts and arguments, they are willing to learn from others.

- They seek to influence others on legislative matters principally through reasoned persuasion. Although they recognize that raw political bargaining may be necessary to build majorities, their decided preference is to influence through facts and arguments, not through bargains.

- They try to protect the opportunities for responsible lawmaking from the consequences of unrestrained publicity seeking. They have little respect for "legislators" who seek only popularity and reelection.

- Although they wish and seek reelection to Congress, they are, nonetheless, willing to take some political risks for the sake of good public policy.

It would be an understatement to say that these kinds of characteristics are not well accounted for by the reigning self-interest theories of Congress or of American government more generally. Moreover, the point here is not that the 535 members of the House and Senate fall neatly into two categories: the merely ambitious who pursue only narrow self-interest and the high-minded who strive for the public good. Rather these represent something like the extremes of the continuum, from the low to the high, between which the various members of Congress can be found. As this exercise has tried to demonstrate, some members of the U.S. Congress, perhaps especially the leaders within the institution, look more like the serious lawmaker described by these characteristics than like the mere self-seeker we have come to view as the norm. If, as those who created the U.S. Congress believed, the serious lawmaker is nothing less than essential to the success of American democracy, then we ought to have a very great interest indeed in assessing the status and activities of such legislators in the contemporary

Congress: How many members of the institution behave like serious law-makers and has this changed over time? What electoral conditions promote the election of the serious-minded, public-spirited legislator as opposed to the mere self-seeking politician? How much influence do serious lawmakers have in the two branches? What are the forces that affect their lawmaking behavior? And what procedural or structural reforms, if any, would enhance the prospects of serious lawmaking in Congress? Although it is beyond the scope of this work to address systematically these various questions, a few additional points can be made.

A central issue is how many of our representatives and senators display the characteristics of the serious lawmaker described here—if not all of the time, then at least much of the time. That the serious lawmaker is not so rare as to be analytically uninteresting or irrelevant to the workings of Congress on major policy issues is amply demonstrated by the kinds of detailed portraits of legislators reviewed here, by the large body of evidence demonstrating the importance of the goal of promoting good public policy in attracting members of the House and Senate to many of the leading committees, and by such occasional episodes as the nearly united, and quite unpopular, stand by Senate Republicans in 1985 in favor of a COLA freeze on Social Security payments. . . .

In addition to the evidence that serious lawmakers are more prevalent within Congress than modern theories acknowledge, there is also reason for believing that they have a greater impact on policymaking than their mere numbers (and relative proportion of the membership) might suggest. One reason is that because the serious lawmaker undertakes the kind of substantive legislative work that does not interest the mere self-seeker, he will *ipso facto* influence the details of policy in a way that the self-seeker rarely will. After all, the legislator dominated by the reelection incentive has "only a modest interest in what goes into bills or what their passage accomplishes." He knows that "in a large class of undertakings the electoral payment is for positions rather than for effects." The second reason is that the serious lawmaker may be more prevalent among institutional leaders than among the membership generally. In part this is because the members of Congress may select as their leaders those with a reputation for legislative skill and seriousness of purpose. In addition, for formal leadership positions within committees and subcommittees, where selection is virtually automatic, the office itself may foster a sense of responsibility to ends larger than mere private advantage.

This latter point is one of the conclusions of Martha Derthick and Paul Quirk in their study of the deregulation movement of the Carter and Reagan years:

> There is an unmistakable pattern in our leading cases: presidents, commission chairmen, and congressional committee and sub-committee leaders generally advocated reform. We infer that such leaders are especially induced or constrained to serve broad,

encompassing, diffuse interests. Any officeholder faces conflicting pressures of personal conviction, desire for reputation, and political interest; some of these pressures will encourage service to broader, diffuse interests while others certainly will not. For leaders, the pressures that encourage such service are markedly enhanced by the very fact of leadership, which makes their actions visible to a wider public, exposes them to observation and comment among the political and governmental elite, and tends to elicit a more compelling sense of responsibility.

And as they say about congressional leaders in particular:

To the extent that a congressman finds or places himself in [a position of leadership on an issue] . . . , two related conditions follow, both of them likely to affect his response: his actions will be more consequential to the outcome; and because they will be more consequential, they will also be more widely observed. Leaders on an issue will be more prone to act on their conception of the public interest, because it is more irresponsible for those in a position of power to do otherwise.

It follows that even a handful of serious, responsible lawmakers in key positions within Congress may have a more consequential effect on the substance of public policy than a much larger number of mere self-seeking politicians who can pursue and achieve private advantage through nonlegislative means.

DISCUSSION QUESTIONS

1. What motivates members of Congress in their legislative behavior? What motivates constituents when they decide whom to vote for in a congressional contest? How do Fiorina and Bessette approach questions of motivation, and how do their respective approaches reflect different conceptions of human nature?

2. Can Congress initiate changes that will remove the causes of public disenchantment? Why is Fiorina skeptical about this possibility? How might Bessette explain public disenchantment with Congress? What reforms might he support that would enhance deliberation in Congress *and* the public's respect for the institution?

3. How do we explain lawmaking that serves narrow interests? Have members of Congress become too tied up with the self-seeking objectives of federal bureaucrats and their programs, as Fiorina argues? Or are there other reasons that better explain the inability of Congress to serve the national

interest, for example, the power of monied private interests to influence legislation?

4. To what extent have Newt Gingrich and the Republicans carried out a transformation of Congress? Would Fiorina and Bessette approve or disapprove of the Republican "revolution" in Congress?

SUGGESTED READINGS AND INTERNET RESOURCES

The central place of the electoral motive in congressional behavior is highlighted in David Mayhew, *Congress: The Electoral Connection* (New Haven, Conn.: Yale University Press, 1974). For a rich descriptive account of the interactions of representatives and their constituents, the classic work is Richard Fenno, *Home Style: House Members in Their Districts* (Boston: Little, Brown, 1978). A sophisticated analysis of why members of Congress sometimes support narrow interests and sometimes vote for a broader public interest is R. Douglas Arnold, *The Logic of Congressional Action* (New Haven, Conn.: Yale University Press, 1990). An important study of members' activities during the legislative process is Richard L. Hall, *Participation in Congress* (New Haven, Conn.: Yale University Press, 1996). And see Lawrence C. Dodd and Bruce I. Oppenheimer, eds., *Congress Reconsidered,* (6th ed.; Washington, D.C.: CQ Press, 1997), for thought-provoking essays on Congress, including insightful analyses of the new Republican era in Congress.

Free Congress Foundation
http://www.freecongress.org
A conservative perspective on Congress, offering numerous publications and Internet links.

National Committee for an Effective Congress
http://www.ncec.org/
A liberal perspective on Congress, with extensive coverage of liberal challengers to conservative incumbents.

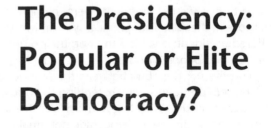

The Presidency: Popular or Elite Democracy?

he president of the United States is coming to your city. You may not like this president's personality, programs, or ideas, but you are likely to make an effort to see him (someday, her) in the flesh. Why? Because most Americans regard the president—any president—as the embodiment of our nation's history and greatness. The presidency is commonly seen as the personification of American democracy.

This equation of the presidency with democracy would have come as a surprise to the generation that established the American Republic. The men who drafted the U.S. Constitution believed that democracy had been carried too far in the revolutionary era. They conceived of the new president not as a democratic champion of the people but rather as a constitutional officer who would, by the length of his term and the loftiness of his stature, be insulated from the passions and pressures of ordinary citizens. Anti-federalist critics of the Constitution, on the other hand, feared that the president would be too remote from the people and too reminiscent of the arbitrary executive that the Revolution had banished.

Neither Federalists nor Anti-federalists viewed the executive as a democratic figure. In sharp contrast, modern presidents present themselves as the only elected representative of the whole people and the very embodiment of democracy itself. Other political actors—members of Congress, bureaucrats, political parties, interest groups—are taken to represent only partial and selfish interests. The president alone can claim to stand for the national interest and the public good.

The modern equation of the presidency with democracy began with Theodore Roosevelt and Woodrow Wilson and reached its zenith with Franklin Roosevelt. After Roosevelt, most journalists, political scientists, and historians came to believe that presidents were the principal agents of democratic purpose in the American political system. Modern media, especially television, offered presidents a vehicle to bring their dramas of democratic leadership directly into people's homes.

Yet even as the bond between the presidency and democracy was celebrated, presidents were extending their powers in ways that threatened democratic values. With the Vietnam War, the Watergate scandal, and later the Iran-contra affair, the undemocratic potential of executive power was revealed. A new and more skeptical perspective toward the presidency began to emerge. On the other hand, the perceived failures of most recent presidents also left many Americans eager to see a reassertion of an effective presidency as a champion of democracy.

The White House career of Bill Clinton exemplifies the ambiguous democratic character of the modern presidency. Focusing on Clinton's sensitivity to the problems of ordinary people, his town meetings, his concern for dialogue on race relations, or his policies to improve education and health care for the working and middle classes, one can readily make the case that this president is a popular democrat. Focusing on Clinton's cozy relations with the rich and powerful in search of campaign contributions, his courting of Wall Street elites on behalf of his economic program, his assertions of the "war power" in the cases of Haiti, Bosnia, and Kosovo, or his claims of executive privilege to hide his affair with Monica Lewinsky from the independent counsel investigating him, one can just as readily make the case that this president is an elite democrat. Champions and critics of presidential power can each find abundant material for their perspectives in Clinton's story.

Richard E. Neustadt's *Presidential Power* (retitled *Presidential Power and the Modern Presidents* in its most recent edition, published in 1990) is the classic argument for a strong president as the key to the health of the American political system. In the first part of our selection from his book, Neustadt suggests that presidents are not authoritative commanders but democratic persuaders. Functioning in a system where separated institutions share power, presidents can advance their own goals only by persuading other power holders to cooperate with them. Presidential persuasion has less to do with reasoned argument than with bargaining, as presidents use "the coin of self-interest" to win essential allies over to their cause. But why should "we the people" want, as Neustadt does, to see presidents maximize their power to bargain? In the second part of the selection, Neustadt answers this question by arguing that a power-maximizing president energizes the political process, promotes "viable" public policies, and ultimately serves democracy.

   Bruce Miroff takes issue with Neustadt's portrayal of the president as democratic champion. He does not dispute Neustadt's claim that presidents generally
have to rely on persuasion rather than command and to remain responsive to
public opinion. But he finds elements of elite democracy in the modern
presidency that are neglected or obscured in Neustadt's account. Drawing
examples mostly from the Clinton presidency, Miroff emphasizes five areas
where presidents tend to be elite democrats: lifestyle, campaign funding,
relations with the economic elite, war making and secrecy, and image making.
   Neustadt and Miroff differ in fundamental ways about the relationship of
the presidency and democracy. Is the president, as Neustadt suggests, so
dependent on winning the cooperation of others that he must stick to
democratic methods of persuasion and pursue policies agreeable to a broad
spectrum of interests and constituents? Or is the president, as Miroff suggests,
subject to elitist impulses of his own and to powerful pressures to satisfy
economic and national security elites? Is the presidency more often found
serving popular democracy or elite democracy?

The Power to Persuade

RICHARD E. NEUSTADT

T he limits on command suggest the structure of our government. The
Constitutional Convention of 1787 is supposed to have created a
government of "separated powers." It did nothing of the sort.
Rather, it created a government of separated institutions *sharing* powers. "I
am part of the legislative process," Eisenhower often said in 1959 as a re-
minder of his veto. Congress, the dispenser of authority and funds, is no
less part of the administrative process. Federalism adds another set of separated institutions. The Bill of Rights adds others. Many public purposes can
only be achieved by voluntary acts of private institutions; the press, for one,
in Douglass Cater's phrase, is a "fourth branch of government." And with
the coming of alliances abroad, the separate institutions of a London, or a
Bonn, share in the making of American public policy.
   What the Constitution separates our political parties do not combine.
The parties are themselves composed of separated organizations sharing
public authority. The authority consists of nominating powers. Our national parties are confederations of state and local party institutions, with a
headquarters that represents the White House, more or less, if the party has

a President in office. These confederacies manage presidential nominations. All other public offices depend upon electorates confined within the states. All other nominations are controlled within the states. The President and congressmen who bear one party's label are divided by dependence upon different sets of voters. The differences are sharpest at the stage of nomination. The White House has too small a share in nominating congressmen, and Congress has too little weight in nominating presidents for party to erase their constitutional separation. Party links are stronger than is frequently supposed, but nominating processes assure the separation.

The separateness of institutions and the sharing of authority prescribe the terms on which a President persuades. When one man shares authority with another, but does not gain or lose his job upon the other's whim, his willingness to act upon the urging of the other turns on whether he conceives the action right for him. The essence of a President's persuasive task is to convince such men that what the White House wants of them is what they ought to do for their sake and on their authority. (Sex matters not at all; for *man* read *woman*.)

Persuasive power, thus defined, amounts to more than charm or reasoned argument. These have their uses for a President, but these are not the whole of his resources. For the individuals he would induce to do what he wants done on their own responsibility will need or fear some acts by him on his responsibility. If they share his authority, he has some share in theirs. Presidential "powers" may be inconclusive when a President commands, but always remain relevant as he persuades. The status and authority inherent in his office reinforce his logic and his charm.

Status adds something to persuasiveness; authority adds still more. When Truman urged wage changes on his secretary of commerce while the latter was administering the steel mills, he and Secretary Sawyer were not just two men reasoning with one another.[1] Had they been so, Sawyer probably would never have agreed to act. Truman's status gave him special claims to Sawyer's loyalty or at least attention. In Walter Bagehot's charming phrase "no man can *argue* on his knees." Although there is no kneeling in this country, few men—and exceedingly few cabinet officers—are immune to the impulse to say "yes" to the President of the United States. It grows harder to say "no" when they are seated in his Oval Office at the White House, or in his study on the second floor, where almost tangibly he partakes of the aura of his physical surroundings. In Sawyer's case, moreover, the President possessed formal authority to intervene in many matters

---

1. To avert a threatened strike in the steel industry during the Korean War, President Harry Truman ordered the steel mills seized by the government. The owners sued, and the Supreme Court ruled that Truman's action was unconstitutional. Important actors in this drama included Charles S. Sawyer, secretary of commerce; Charles E. Wilson, head of the Office of Defense Mobilization; and Ellis Arnall, head of the Office of Price Stabilization.

of concern to the secretary of commerce. These matters ranged from juris-dictional disputes among the defense agencies to legislation pending before Congress and, ultimately, to the tenure of the secretary, himself. There is nothing in the record to suggest that Truman voiced specific threats when they negotiated over wage increases. But given his formal powers and their relevance to Sawyer's other interests, it is safe to assume that Truman's very advocacy of wage action conveyed an implicit threat.

A President's authority and status give him great advantages in dealing with the men he would persuade. Each "power" is a vantage point for him in the degree that other men have use for his authority. From the veto to appointments, from publicity to budgeting, and so down a long list, the White House now controls the most encompassing array of vantage points in the American political system. With hardly an exception, those who share in governing this country are aware that at some time, in some de-gree, the doing of *their* jobs, the furthering of *their* ambitions, may depend upon the President of the United States. Their need for presidential action, or their fear of it, is bound to be recurrent if not actually continuous. Their need or fear is his advantage.

A President's advantages are greater than a mere listing of his "powers" might suggest. Those with whom he deals must deal with him until the last day of his term. Because they have continuing relationships with him, his future, while it lasts, supports his present influence. Even though there is no need or fear of him today, what he could do tomorrow may supply today's advantage. Continuing relationships may convert any "power," any aspect of his status, into vantage points in almost any case. When he in-duces other people to do what he wants done, a President can trade on their dependence now and later.

The President's advantages are checked by the advantages of others. Continuing relationships will pull in both directions. These are relation-ships of mutual dependence. A President depends upon the persons whom he would persuade; he has to reckon with his need or fear of them. They too will possess status, or authority, or both, else they would be of little use to him. Their vantage points confront his own; their power tempers his.

Persuasion is a two-way street. Sawyer, it will be recalled, did not re-spond at once to Truman's plan for wage increases at the steel mills. On the contrary, the secretary hesitated and delayed and only acquiesced when he was satisfied that publicly he would not bear the onus of decision. Sawyer had some points of vantage all his own from which to resist presidential pressure. If he had to reckon with coercive implications in the President's "situations of strength," so had Truman to be mindful of the implications underlying Sawyer's place as a department head, as steel administrator, and as a cabinet spokesman for business. Loyalty is reciprocal. Having taken on a dirty job in the steel crisis, Sawyer had strong claims to loyal support. Be-sides, he had authority to do some things that the White House could ill afford. Emulating Wilson, he might have resigned in a huff (the removal power also works two ways). Or, emulating Ellis Arnall, he might have declined to sign necessary orders. Or he might have let it be known publicly that he deplored what he was told to do and protested its doing. By following any of these courses Sawyer almost surely would have strengthened the position of management, weakened the position of the White House, and embittered the union. But the whole purpose of a wage increase was to enhance White House persuasiveness in urging settlement upon union and companies alike. Although Sawyer's status and authority did not give him the power to prevent an increase outright, they gave him capability to undermine its purpose. If his authority over wage rates had been vested by a statute, not by revocable presidential order, his power of prevention might have been complete. So Harold Ickes demonstrated in the famous case of helium sales to Germany before the Second World War.[2]

The power to persuade is the power to bargain. Status and authority yield bargaining advantages. But in a government of "separated institutions sharing powers," they yield them to all sides. With the array of vantage points at his disposal, a President may be far more persuasive than his logic or his charm could make him. But outcomes are not guaranteed by his advantages. There remain the counterpressures those whom he would influence can bring to bear on him from vantage points at their disposal. Command has limited utility; persuasion becomes give-and-take. It is well that the White House holds the vantage points it does. In such a business any President may need them all—and more. . . .

To make the most of power for himself a President must know what it is made of. This book has treated power in the sense of personal influence and influence in the sense of effectiveness prospectively, looking toward tomorrow from today. That look conveys the essence of the task before a man who seeks to maximize his power. If he wants it for the future, he must guard it in the present. He mounts guard, as best he can, when he appraises the effects of present action on the sources of his influence. In making that appraisal he has no one to depend on but himself; his power and its sources are a sphere of expertise reserved to him. But the issues that present themselves for action day by day rarely show his personal risks upon their surface. His expertise must first help him to see beneath the surface if it is to help him weigh what may be there. The President as expert does himself a double service. Without the expertise he cannot do it.

The Presidency, to repeat, is not a place for amateurs. That sort of expertise can hardly be acquired without deep experience in political office. The Presidency is a place for men of politics. But by no means is it a place for every politician.

There is no reason to suppose that politicians, on the average, have the wherewithal to help themselves build presidential power. The men of poli-

---

2. Harold Ickes was secretary of the interior under President Franklin Roosevelt.

tics who specialize in organization work and party office scarcely qualify at all; governmental office is the relevant experience. For present purposes we can regard as politicians only those who build careers in public office. Yet skillful use of presidential power does not follow automatically from such experience. No post in government at any level necessarily equips a man to recognize the Presidency's peculiar sources of influence. Those sources have as many parts as a President has constituencies, foreign and domestic; the posts that furnish insights into one part often obscure others. Besides, past officeholding is no guarantee that any man brings with him to the White House the degree and kind of feeling for direction that can help him once he gets there. Former Commerce Secretary Hoover had a sense of purpose so precise as to be stultifying. Former Senator Harding seems to have had none at all. And mere experience, however relevant, is no assurance that a President will find the confidence he needs just when he needs it most. Such confidence requires that his image of himself in office justify an unremitting search for personal power. But it requires, also, that his image of himself allow for failures and frustration in the search.

FDR is said to have remarked that Lincoln "was a sad man because he couldn't get it all at once. And nobody can." If a President is to assist himself through the vicissitudes of four long years or eight, his source of confidence must make him capable of bearing Lincoln's sadness with good grace. The power seeker whose self-confidence requires quick returns and sure success might make a mess of everything including his own power. Grace calls for humor and perspective. Political experience does not assure those qualities. Indeed, it may diminish them in the degree it brings a taste for power. The officeholder who combines them with an insight into presidential influence and hunger for it is no average politician.

Expertise in presidential power seems to be the province not of politicians as a class but of extraordinary politicians. What sets such men apart? Mr. Justice Holmes once characterized Franklin Roosevelt as a "second-class intellect but a first-class temperament." Perhaps this is a necessary combination. The politics of well-established government has rarely been attractive to and rarely has dealt kindly with the men whom intellectuals regard as first-rate intellects. Temperament, at any rate, is the great separator. Experience will leave its mark on expertise; so will a man's ambitions for himself and his constituents. But something like that "first-class" temperament is what turns know-how and desire to his personal account. The necessary confidence is nourished by that temperament. It is a human resource not discovered every day among American politicians.

II

If skill in maximizing power for himself served purposes no larger than the man's own pride or pleasure, there would be no reason for the rest of us to care whether he were skillful or not. More precisely, there would be no reason except sentiment and partisanship. But a President's success in that endeavor serves objectives far beyond his own and far beyond his party's. For reasons I will come to in a moment, an expert search for presidential influence contributes to the energy of government and to the viability of public policy. Government is energized by a productive tension among its working parts. Policy is kept alive by a sustained transformation of intent into result. Energetic government and viable public policy are at a premium as we begin the seventh decade of the twentieth century. Expertise in presidential power adds to both. A President's constituents, regardless of their party (or their country, for that matter), have a great stake in his search for personal influence.

In the American political system the President sits in a unique seat and works within a unique frame of reference. The things he personally has to do are no respecters of the lines between "civil" and "military," or "foreign" and "domestic," or "legislative" and "executive," or "administrative" and "political." At his desk—and there alone—distinctions of these sorts lose their last shred of meaning. The expectations centered in his person converge upon no other individual; nobody else feels pressure from all five of his constituencies; no one else takes pressure in the consciousness that he has been elected "by the nation." Besides, nobody but the President lives day by day with his responsibility in an atomic age amid Cold War. And he alone can claim unquestionable right to everybody's information on the mysteries of that age and that war. His place and frame of reference are unique. By the same token, though, his power is mercurial. Since no one shares his place, nobody is committed to uphold what he may do there. The consequences are described by every illustration in this book.

The things a President must think about if he would build his influence are not unlike those bearing on the viability of public policy. The correspondence may be inexact, but it is close. The man who thinks about the one can hardly help contributing to the other. A President who senses what his influence is made of and who means to guard his future will approach his present actions with an eye to the reactions of constituents in Washington and out. The very breadth and sweep of his constituencies and of their calls upon him, along with the uncertainty of their response, will make him keen to see and weigh what Arthur Schlesinger has called "the balance of administrative power." This is a balance of political, managerial, psychological, and personal feasibilities. And because the President's own frame of reference is at once so all-encompassing and so political, what he sees as a balance for himself is likely to be close to what is viable in terms of public policy.

What he sees in terms of power gives him clues in terms of policy to help him search beneath the surfaces of issues.

Viability in policy has three ingredients. First is a purpose that moves with the grain of history, a direction consonant with coming needs. Second is an operation that proves manageable to the men who must administer it, acceptable to those who must support it, tolerable to those who must put up with it, in Washington and out. Timing can be crucial for support and acquiescence; proper timing is the third ingredient. The President who sees his power stakes sees something very much like the ingredients that make for viability in policy.

Our system affords nobody a better source of clues. Presidential expertise thus serves effective policy. Deciding what is viable has grown more critical and more complex with almost every turn of world events (and of home politics) since the Second World War. Substantive considerations have become so specialized that experts in one sphere lose touch with expertise in any other. Substantive appraisals have become so tricky that the specialists in every sphere dispute among themselves. In consequence the viability of policy may be the only ground on which a substantive decision can be reached. When that ground is itself inordinately complicated by the tendency of policies to interlock, and overlap, and to leap national boundaries, it becomes a sphere of expertness as specialized as others. In the sphere of viability our system can supply no better expert than a President intent on husbanding his influence—provided that he understands what influence is made of.

The more determinedly a President seeks power, the more he will be likely to bring vigor to his clerkship. As he does so he contributes to the energy of government. In Congress and the agencies and in the national parties, energy is generated by support or opposition. But first there must be something to support or to oppose. Most Washingtonians look to the White House for it. There often is no other place to look. The need of others for a President's initiatives creates dependence on him. Their dependence becomes his advantage. Yet he can only capture the advantage as he meets the need. An energetic clerk will energize all government; the man intent on influence will be that sort of clerk. (So may a man intent on history, provided that he has the heroes of a Harry Truman. But one cannot expect that many men will know their history as well as he, and even those who know it may choose other heroes.)

The contributions that a President can make to government are indispensable. Assuming that he knows what power is and wants it, those contributions cannot help but be forthcoming in some measure as by-products of his search for personal influence. In a relative but real sense one can say of a President what Eisenhower's first secretary of defense once said of General Motors: What is good for the country is good for the President, and vice versa. There is no guarantee, of course, that every President will keep an eye on what is "good" for him; his sense of power and of purpose and the source of his self-confidence may turn his head away. If so, his "contributions" could be lethargy not energy, or policy that moves against, not with, the grain of history. The way he sees his influence and seeks it will affect the rest of us, no matter what becomes of him.

The Presidency and Elite Democracy

BRUCE MIROFF

For almost forty years, students of the presidency have taken guidance from Richard E. Neustadt's classic, *Presidential Power*. Neustadt's approach to understanding the presidency, focusing on the skills and persuasive powers of individual incumbents, no longer dominates research on the presidency as it once did; many alternative approaches, emphasizing institutional, structural, and historical factors rather than differences between individual presidents, are now in wide use. Yet *Presidential Power* remains the most well-known work of political science on the presidency and the inevitable starting point for studying it. Its ideas and insights continue to be provocative and fruitful even as a succession of new chief executives have come along to test the validity of Neustadt's fundamental claims.

It is not my purpose in this essay to disparage *Presidential Power* or to discourage students from grappling with its powerful arguments. What I do wish to accomplish is to raise questions about Neustadt's assumption that presidential power is almost always going to be exercised in the service of American democracy. In *Presidential Power*, Neustadt urges executives to maximize their power but assures citizens that this power will not pose any threat to democracy. The compatibility of power maximization in the presidency and democracy is based on two key assumptions: (1) presidents must operate in a democratic fashion, persuading rather than giving orders to other political actors; (2) presidential objectives and the public interest are closely meshed (or as Neustadt puts it, "What is good for the country is good for the President, and vice versa"). The ideal chief executive, in Neustadt's analysis, is clearly an uncommon, elite figure (an "extraordinary politician"), but he uses the methods and serves the ends of popular democracy.

The thrust of this essay is that Neustadt is altogether too sanguine about the presidency as a servant of popular democracy. Far more than he acknowledges, the presidency is prone to elitist practices and is tied to elite interests in American society. In this essay, I will suggest five important respects in which the presidency should be considered closer to elite democracy than to popular democracy.

I

I do not want to overstate my case. In many arenas of presidential action, Neustadt's argument that presidents must use persuasion rather than command because other actors possess independent power remains undeniable. Indeed, if anything the constraints upon presidential action and the need to persuade an array of independent power holders have grown greater since he first wrote. As political parties have weakened, as special interests have proliferated, as media outlets have multiplied, presidents find themselves constantly struggling to overcome fragmentation and promote coherent policy direction. As divided government has become more the norm than the exception, Congress has complicated the president's persuasive tasks with partisan as well as institutional objections. Ask Bill Clinton, buried by interest group and congressional foes in his failed campaign for health-care reform in 1994, or bloodied but victorious in the budget showdown with Newt Gingrich and his followers in 1995, and he would no doubt confirm Neustadt's view that presidents can rarely command and often don't even have the resources they need to persuade.

There remains much truth, too, in Neustadt's assertion that presidents have to pursue ends that the public generally favors and that can be expected to advance the welfare of the majority. Indeed, presidents have become even more sensitive to measures of public opinion than Neustadt would probably desire. Concerned about their standing in the polls, their prospects for reelection, and their place in history, they keep a close watch over public sentiments. Many observers now lament that presidents have become too obsessed with public opinion, too inclined to define leadership as following the opinion polls. In its first year in office, the Clinton administration spent nearly $2 million on polling. Its frantic drive for cash before the 1996 election was rooted in the need for expensive polls that would indicate what themes to highlight in even more expensive television ads. According to Clinton's image guru in 1996, Dick Morris, the president even consulted the polls to decide where to take his summer vacation.

II

But exercises in persuasion and calculations of how to gratify the public are not the entirety of the modern presidency. Consider five aspects of the presidency that clash with Neustadt's portrayal of presidents as champions of democracy:

1. The presidential life-style;
2. The financing of presidential campaigns;
3. The president's need to placate holders of economic power;
4. The president's powers of secrecy and war making in international affairs;
5. The president's image-making capacities.

The Presidential Life-Style. Fearful that the American Revolution was about to be overturned by the framers of the new Constitution, Anti-federalist Patrick Henry warned that the office of the presidency "squints toward monarchy" and predicted that presidents would live in "extravagant magnificence." To counter charges of pseudo-monarchism, most presidents since the time of Andrew Jackson have trumpeted their modest democratic presumptions and practices. To cite only the most recent examples, the patrician George Bush made famous his liking for pork rinds, while his more genuinely down-home successor has wanted to be called just plain "Bill."

But presidents do not, in fact, live like the rest of us. George Reedy, once President Johnson's press secretary, portrayed the White House in monarchical terms. "There is built into the presidency," wrote Reedy, "a series of devices that tend to remove the occupant of the Oval Room from all of the forces which require most men to rub up against the hard facts of life on a daily basis. The life of the White House is the life of a court. It is a structure designed for one purpose and one purpose only—to serve the material needs and the desires of a single man."

Several stories from recent administrations suggest that Reedy was not exaggerating much. Touring a grocery store, President Bush professed amazement at the electronic scanners that read prices; here was a president who appeared totally unfamiliar with how families struggled with their food bills each week. Bill Clinton criticized Bush's elitism during the 1992 campaign, but his own image as a populist unraveled once he took office, tarnished by revelations that he was hanging out with Hollywood movie stars and moguls, and getting a $200 haircut from a Beverly Hills stylist. Perhaps these incidents might appear trivial from Neustadt's perspective. But we should consider the possibility that if a president's "extravagant" lifestyle cuts him off from the experiences of ordinary citizens, while throwing him mostly into the company of the powerful, the rich, and the famous, his perspective will likely be the view from above and not the view from among the American people.

The financing of presidential campaigns. When Neustadt first published *Presidential Power* in 1960, the selection of the president was largely a party affair. State-based party leaders, controlling blocs of delegates at the quadrennial national conventions, held in their hands the key to the nomination. Yet even in 1960, big money was starting to play a powerful role in presidential campaigns, as multimillionaire Joseph Kennedy bankrolled his son John's rapid ascent to the White House. By 1972, huge contributions from business "fat cats," most of them illegal, financed Richard Nixon's reelection steamroller.

Campaign finance reforms, a response to the Watergate scandal, were designed to take big money out of presidential elections. But they have been a woeful failure in this respect, and the pursuit of wealthy donors by presidential candidates and incumbent presidents has only escalated in recent years. President Bush and the Republican National Committee formed

"Team 100," an honorary organization whose membership requirement was a $100,000 contribution. Topping Bush, President Clinton invited rich contributors to become "Managing Trustees" for a mere $200,000. In his frenetic quest after campaign cash for the 1996 election, Clinton came up with even more attractive inducements: big contributors got to schmooze with the president at White House coffee klatches and even bigger contributors were treated to overnight stays in the Lincoln Bedroom. The president raised a reported $27 million in this fashion.

What do wealthy elites get for their lavish contributions to presidents? They don't usually get direct payoffs in favorable public policies; these would be too easy for the media to uncover, at considerable political embarrassment to the White House. They don't stop presidents from paying attention to issues of concern to the electorate at large. But money does bring access, the capacity to express one's concerns and advocate one's interests directly to the president. Even more important, it works as a constraint. Presidents who have come to depend on the campaign giving of corporate executives and other rich folk do not lead class-conscious crusades to help the many at the expense of the few. They do not bite the hand that feeds them.

The president's need to placate holders of economic power. Campaign contributions from the wealthy are neither the only nor even the most important factor that constrains presidents to pursue policies acceptable to holders of economic power. Since the New Deal of Franklin D. Roosevelt, it has become a legally mandated responsibility of the president to manage the American economy. His prescribed mission is to avoid economic downturns and to promote sustained growth accompanied by stable prices. Both the prosperity of the nation and the political health of the president and his party are contingent upon the success of this mission. But key ingredients of success lie outside the president's control, in the higher reaches of the corporate and financial sectors. It is there that the decisions on investments and interest rates that drive the economy are concentrated.

Some presidents have cordial relations with corporate America and are naturally in sync with corporate priorities. But for those whose electoral base and policy instincts point them in a more populist direction, the threat of a negative reaction from holders of economic power operates as a powerful constraint. No president wants to be vulnerable to charges of wrecking "business confidence," with the attendant drop in investment and rise in interest rates that supposedly will ensue. To be successful as an economic manager, the prescribed course is to avoid attacks on business, to limit reforms that business elites consider too costly or redistributive, and to promote policies that will encourage corporate investment and low interest rates from Wall Street.

The power of the "business confidence" factor to affect presidents has, not surprisingly, been most evident in Democratic administrations. In 1962, John F. Kennedy had to move against the leading corporations in the steel industry to force them to withdraw a surprise price increase that would have shattered the president's anti-inflation policy. Unhappy business leaders blamed Kennedy when, a month later, the stock market suffered a huge drop, and they began to predict a recession as the fruit of Kennedy's destruction of business confidence. Kennedy and his advisers felt that they had little choice but to retreat. Through a series of symbolic gestures and policy concessions, they bent over backwards to assure business leaders that they had meant no harm in the steel affair and that they knew where power truly lay in the political economy.

The most recent Democrat in the White House, Bill Clinton, has also felt the sting of the "business confidence" factor. Clinton's 1992 campaign featured a populist economic agenda, "Putting People First," with proposals for greater public spending on education, worker retraining, and infrastructure. But upon assuming office he felt compelled to change economic course: populist proposals were dropped in favor of a deficit-reduction strategy designed to placate Wall Street and the Federal Reserve so that they would lower interest rates and stimulate the economy. Hardly thrilled about the pressures that pushed a Democratic president into the arms of largely Republican business elites, Clinton exclaimed in frustration: "'We're Eisenhower [moderate] Republicans here, and we are fighting the Reagan [conservative] Republicans. We stand for lower deficits and free trade and the bond market. Isn't that great?'"

The president's powers of secrecy and war making in international affairs. Neustadt's image of the president as persuader may be valid for many arenas of presidential action, but it is not valid for all. Especially in the arena of American foreign relations, presidents have powers of secrecy and war making that look more like elitist command than democratic persuasion.

Writing during the height of the Cold War between the U.S.-led "Free World" and the communist "bloc," Neustadt was perhaps unaware of how extensive was the secret global apparatus that presidents had come to control. Commanding the Central Intelligence Agency (CIA), National Security Agency, and the military intelligence services, chief executives after World War II were freed from congressional oversight and public accountability as they pursued clandestine foreign policy strategies. Through the CIA in particular, they could intervene covertly in the politics of other nations, financing pro-American parties and subverting unfriendly ones, encouraging military coups against governments regarded as unfavorable to U.S. interests, even mounting assassination attempts against foreign leaders.

Secret action has been seductive to presidents. Bypassing the necessity of persuasion, it allows them to implement their foreign policy goals with methods that would raise ethical as well as constitutional problems if openly pursued. Ironically, however, secrecy has often led presidents into foolish moves—for example, assassination attempts against Cuba's Fidel Castro and the Iran-contra affair. These cases illustrate one of the prime pitfalls in secretive, elitist decision making: when a small group of individuals (the president and his aides) make decisions without consulting diverse sources or worrying about how larger audiences will react, their grip on political reality is likely to be weakened.

The Cold War gave presidents war making as well as secretive powers. Ignoring the constitutional mandate that Congress must decide if the U.S. is to engage in war, Cold War executives asserted their primacy over the "war power." In the cases of Korea (Truman) and Vietnam (Kennedy, Johnson, and Nixon), dispatching American troops into overseas combat and keeping them there became a presidential prerogative. And when congressional and public opposition emerged, presidents relied not on persuasion but on manipulation and deceit to keep the lid on dissent. Congress tried to recapture some of its lost authority by passing the War Powers Resolution in 1973 over President Nixon's veto, but this resolution has not changed executive practices since it was adopted.

The end of the Cold War has made hardly any difference in the control over war making. President Clinton has claimed the same prerogative as his Cold War predecessors: to send American troops into theaters of military conflict without first persuading Congress to authorize the venture. In 1994, he defied Congress—and public opinion—by dispatching American forces to Haiti. As constitutional law expert Louis Fisher observes, "Clinton's interpretation of presidential war power would have astonished the framers of the Constitution." Decisions about war and peace are the most consequential ones that any nation makes—yet in this critical area the maximization of presidential power certainly has not increased democracy.

The president's image-making capacities. In Neustadt's account, presidents direct most of their persuasive efforts toward other power holders in the "Washington community." He regards the larger public as inattentive to presidential actions except insofar as they impinge on people's daily lives; presidents must therefore guard their public prestige mainly by holding the public's expectations to a realistic level. But since Neustadt first wrote *Presidential Power*, presidents have paid greater attention to mobilizing public support in order to increase their leverage in the increasingly fragmented world of the "Washington community." In the well-known phrase of presidency scholar Samuel Kernell, they are "going public" with growing frequency. This new approach might be considered a gain for democracy—if presidents were "going public" to educate their audiences and to stimulate greater civic participation. Instead, the White House has improved its image-making capabilities so that presidents can cloak themselves in appealing symbols that obscure the substance of their actions and programs.

President Kennedy was the first to demonstrate how presidents could exploit the new medium of television. President Nixon was awkward on TV, but he was more innovative than Kennedy in the institutional management of the media, creating the White House Office of Communications to manipulate or circumvent the press. Some of their successors have been clumsy in "going public" (Ford, Carter, and Bush), while others have been very skillful (Reagan and Clinton). Yet all of these presidents have placed image making at the heart of the modern presidential enterprise.

The public presidency today is about spectacle and not about persuasion. Aided by an extensive public-relations machine in the White House, the president presents himself as a larger-than-life character, with impressive qualities magnified far beyond what viewers or readers can imagine themselves as possessing. Many actions are designed less to accomplish policy ends than to send signals to the public audience that the president is intelligent, determined, courageous, and dedicated to the common welfare. Ronald Reagan "standing tall" in the invasion of Grenada, George Bush bringing the Panamanian dictator and drug lord Manuel Noriega to justice, Bill Clinton "feeling the pain" of unemployed, uninsured, or unhealthy Americans—these are among the memorable images that constitute the contemporary spectacle of presidential leadership.

III

Presidents should not be viewed as tools of elites. They respond to many political forces besides the wealthy and the powerful. Their own political preferences, their desire for public support and votes, and their concern with the verdict of history all point them toward objectives that transcend the interests of a narrow elite. Yet their sensitivities to the currents of democratic politics are not the whole of the story. It has been the argument of this essay that they live and act in an elite realm, are constrained by elite pressures, are dependent for their success on elite approval. Richard E. Neustadt's picture of the president as democratic persuader and servant of the public welfare is thus incomplete. We need to add to his picture the contrasting shades of elite democracy in the White House.

Just how much presidents are bound to elite democracy will depend, above all, on their political situation. If they are to serve popular democracy rather than elite democracy, it will not be because they are skilled at maximizing their power. Rather, presidents can be pushed toward popular democracy by the forces of public sentiment, grassroots activism, and social movements. It was a mobilized and militant civil rights movement that overcame President Kennedy's caution and propelled him to sponsor a landmark civil rights bill. It was a blossoming environmental movement that broke through President Nixon's indifference and led him to sign the Environmental Protection Act. Contrary to Neustadt's conception, presidents will rarely lead the American people toward greater popular democracy on their own. To overcome the elitist elements of the presidency, the people have to lead the president.

■ DISCUSSION QUESTIONS

1. What is the relationship between presidential power and democracy? Does a strong presidency enhance democracy by energizing the political process and promoting the public welfare? Or does presidential power tempt executives into undemocratic acts and serve the wealthy and powerful who make the key investment decisions and campaign donations?
2. Where are presidents most constrained by other political forces, most dependent on their limited powers of persuasion? Where are they most free to act as they choose?
3. How does the president's relationship to democracy affect other parts of the American political system? How does Neustadt's power-maximizing president affect the role that Congress plays in democracy? What do Miroff's criticisms suggest about the ways that the media should examine the presidency?
4. Do the end of the Cold War and the limited domestic successes of Presidents Bush and Clinton suggest that both Neustadt and Miroff exaggerate the role of the president? Are presidents becoming less important in American politics? Or are we still dependent on presidential leadership?

■ SUGGESTED READINGS AND INTERNET RESOURCES

For a view of presidential effectiveness that is more skeptical than Neustadt's, see Theodore Lowi, *The Personal President* (Ithaca, N.Y.: Cornell University Press, 1985). The growing tendency of presidents to cultivate mass support is analyzed in Samuel Kernell, *Going Public: New Strategies of Presidential Leadership,* 3rd ed. (Washington, D.C.: CQ Press, 1997). For a powerful historical analysis of presidential power as shaped by "political time," see Stephen Skowronek, *The Politics Presidents Make: Leadership from John Adams to Bill Clinton* (Cambridge, Mass.: Harvard University Press, 1997). Portraits of both elite democratic and popular democratic leadership can be found in Bruce Miroff, *Icons of Democracy: American Leaders as Heroes, Aristocrats, Dissenters, and Democrats* (Lawrence: University Press of Kansas, 2000). The strengths and dangers of presidential leadership both receive detailed attention in Thomas E. Cronin and Michael A. Genovese, *The Paradoxes of the American Presidency* (New York: Oxford University Press, 1998).

The White House
http://www.whitehouse.gov/
The president's web site, containing speeches, documents, press briefings, and assorted information on the administration and offering e-mail communication with the White House.

Center for the Study of the Presidency
http://www.cspresidency.org/
A nonpartisan organization that holds student conferences and publishes a scholarly journal, *Presidential Studies Quarterly;* its web site offers publications and provides numerous links to research sites on the presidency.

15

Bureaucracy: Should It Be "Banished" from Democracy?

ew political terms carry so much negative baggage as *bureaucracy*. What comes to mind when you hear this word? A government form written in organizational gobbledygook that you must laboriously fill out? A dreary motor vehicle or unemployment office where you must endure a long wait before encountering a surly clerk? If images like these occur to you, you are one of many Americans who believe that bureaucracy is an affront to freedom and democracy.

Political scientists usually put forward a more neutral account of bureaucracy. Drawing from the pioneering discussion of bureaucracy by the great German sociologist Max Weber, they define it as a corps of administrators, organized in a hierarchy, governed by impersonal rules, and divided up by specialized functions, who conduct the work of government. (Since similar features characterize most large organizations, we can speak of private bureaucracies as well as government ones.) Despite the prevalent negative feelings toward bureaucracy, it has been one of the most prominent features of American life in the twentieth century. And most political scientists agree that, whatever its flaws, bureaucracy in some form is an inevitable component of a complex, modern society.

If bureaucracy is hard to escape, it is easy to attack. Political activists and analysts on both the right and the left dislike bureaucracy. To conservatives, bureaucracy represents the heavy, clumsy hand of government interfering with individual choice and free enterprise. Wherever possible, they argue, private markets should be preferred to government programs implemented by government agencies. To liberals and radicals, bureaucracy is the rule of an unaccountable elite that protects special interests and perpetuates the status quo. Wherever possible, they argue, ordinary citizens should reclaim the power that has been removed from their control by secretive bureaucratic experts.

In recent years, it has largely been the conservatives who have spearheaded an assault on bureaucracy. If such presidents as Theodore Roosevelt, Woodrow Wilson, Franklin D. Roosevelt, and Lyndon Johnson were builders of the American administrative state, Ronald Reagan, the conservative hero, was the prime antibureaucracy president in modern U.S. history. Reagan told the American people that government in the United States (by which he meant bureaucratic government) was not the solution to our problems but the problem itself. Both in his disparaging rhetoric and in his attempts to weaken government agencies that he perceived as wedded to liberal missions, he launched an unprecedented presidential attack on the federal bureaucracy. Congress and the courts blunted much of Reagan's attack. But it has been renewed with vigor by Reagan's heirs, the conservative Republicans who took over Congress in 1995.

Inspired by a best-seller, *Reinventing Government: How the Entrepreneurial Spirit is Transforming the Public Sector,* written by David Osborne and Ted Gaebler, President Clinton took a different tack. Critical of the bureaucracy, but not favoring its wholesale dismantling in the spirit of Reagan, Clinton appointed Vice President Al Gore to head a National Performance Review to come up with a blueprint for bureaucratic transformation. Gore touted his achievement in "reinventing government" when he ran for president in 2000.

The first of the selections that follow is from the book that inspired Clinton's proposed reform of the bureaucracy. To David Osborne and Ted Gaebler, bureaucracy may have been an efficient mechanism in the old industrial era, but in the postindustrial, high-tech world of today it is a dinosaur. If public agencies are to overcome the inefficiency, waste, and downright torpor that have turned so many citizens against government, they must shed the bankrupt bureaucratic model and replace it with an entrepreneurial approach. The two authors claim political neutrality: they argue that they do not seek bigger (liberal) government or smaller (conservative) government, but only want to foster better government.

The second selection, from Charles Goodsell's *The Case for Bureaucracy,* provides a spirited argument on behalf of an unpopular cause. According to Goodsell, the bureaucracy that everyone loves to criticize is a mythical creature. Unlike the abstract bureaucracy of myth, real American bureaucracies, he claims, have many positive features. Citing numerous studies in his book, Goodsell sets out to knock down the criticisms of bureaucracy point by point. In his view, Americans should be proud of their bureaucracies, which are the best in the world. In the last part of the selection, Goodsell takes on the challenge to bureaucracy posed by Osborne and Gaebler. The real thrust of their ideas, he suggests, is to revive Reagan's bureaucracy bashing in a more so-phisticated form.

The debate that pits Osborne and Gaebler against Goodsell raises fundamental issues about the place of bureaucracy in American democracy. Are the common criticisms of bureaucracy based on a real appreciation of inherent bureaucratic flaws, or do stereotypes and myths prevent us from seeing that most American administrative agencies do a good job? Will a more entrepreneurial approach improve the quality of government services and the morale of government employees, or will it lead to cuts in personnel, decreases in public services, and perhaps profits for private businesses at the public's expense? Is bureaucracy *the* big problem in modern American government, or is it a convenient scapegoat for others (politicians? special interests? the wealthy?) who attack it to divert attention from their own purposes and power?

Reinventing Government

DAVID OSBORNE
AND TED GAEBLER

s the 1980s drew to a close, *Time* magazine asked on its cover: "Is Government Dead?"

As the 1990s unfold, the answer—to many Americans—appears to be yes.

Our public schools are the worst in the developed world. Our health care system is out of control. Our courts and prisons are so overcrowded that convicted felons walk free. And many of our proudest cities and states are virtually bankrupt.

Confidence in government has fallen to record lows. By the late 1980s, only 5 percent of Americans surveyed said they would choose government service as their preferred career. Only 13 percent of top federal employees said they would recommend a career in public service. Nearly three out of four Americans said they believed Washington delivered less value for the dollar than it had 10 years earlier. . . .

Yet there is hope. Slowly, quietly, far from the public spotlight, new kinds of public institutions are emerging. They are lean, decentralized, and innovative. They are flexible, adaptable, quick to learn new ways when conditions change. They use competition, customer choice, and other non-bureaucratic mechanisms to get things done as creatively and effectively as possible. And they are our future. . . .

. . . Our thesis is simple: The kind of governments that developed during the industrial era, with their sluggish, centralized bureaucracies, their preoccupation with rules and regulations, and their hierarchical chains of command, no longer work very well. They accomplished great things in their time, but somewhere along the line they got away from us. They became bloated, wasteful, ineffective. And when the world began to change, they failed to change with it. Hierarchical, centralized bureaucracies designed in the 1930s or 1940s simply do not function well in the rapidly changing, information-rich, knowledge-intensive society and economy of the 1990s. They are like luxury ocean liners in an age of supersonic jets: big, cumbersome, expensive, and extremely difficult to turn around. Gradually, new kinds of public institutions are taking their place.

Government is hardly leading the parade; similar transformations are taking place throughout American society. American corporations have spent the last decade making revolutionary changes: decentralizing authority, flattening hierarchies, focusing on quality, getting close to their customers—all in an effort to remain competitive in the new global marketplace. Our voluntary, nonprofit organizations are alive with new initiatives. New "partnerships" blossom overnight—between business and education, between for-profits and nonprofits, between public sector and private. It is as if virtually all institutions in American life were struggling at once to adapt to some massive sea change—striving to become more flexible, more innovative, and more entrepreneurial.

The Bankruptcy of Bureaucracy

It is hard to imagine today, but 100 years ago the word *bureaucracy* meant something positive. It connoted a rational, efficient method of organization—something to take the place of the arbitrary exercise of power by authoritarian regimes. Bureaucracies brought the same logic to government work that the assembly line brought to the factory. With their hierarchical authority and functional specialization, they made possible the efficient undertaking of large, complex tasks. Max Weber, the great German sociologist, described them using words no modern American would dream of applying:

> The decisive reason for the advance of bureaucratic organization has always been its purely technical superiority over any other form of organization. . . .
>
> Precision, speed, unambiguity, . . . reduction of friction and of material and personal costs—these are raised to the optimum point in the strictly bureaucratic administration.

In the United States, the emergence of bureaucratic government was given a particular twist by its turn-of-the-century setting. A century ago, our cities were growing at breakneck speed, bulging with immigrants come to labor in the factories thrown up by our industrial revolution. Boss Tweed and his contemporaries ran these cities like personal fiefdoms: In exchange for immigrant votes, they dispensed jobs, favors, and informal services. With one hand they robbed the public blind; with the other they made sure those who delivered blocs of loyal votes were amply rewarded. Meanwhile, they ignored many of the new problems of industrial America—its slums, its sweatshops, its desperate need for a new infrastructure of sewers and water and public transit.

Young Progressives like Theodore Roosevelt, Woodrow Wilson, and Louis Brandeis watched the machines until they could stomach it no more. In the 1890s, they went to war. Over the next 30 years, the Progressive movement transformed government in America. To end the use of government jobs as patronage, the Progressives created civil service systems, with written exams, lockstep pay scales, and protection from arbitrary hiring or dismissal. To keep major construction projects like bridges and tunnels out of the reach of politicians, they created independent public authorities. To limit the power of political bosses, they split up management functions, took appointments to important offices away from mayors and governors, created separately elected clerks, judges, even sheriffs. To keep the administration of public services untainted by the influence of politicians, they created a profession of city managers—professionals, insulated from politics, who would run the bureaucracy in an efficient, businesslike manner.

Thanks to Boss Tweed and his contemporaries, in other words, American society embarked on a gigantic effort to *control* what went on inside government to keep the politicians and bureaucrats from doing anything that might endanger the public interest or purse. This cleaned up many of our governments, but in solving one set of problems it created another. In making it difficult to steal the public's money, we made it virtually impossible to *manage* the public's money. In adopting written tests scored to the third decimal point to hire our clerks and police officers and fire fighters, we built mediocrity into our work force. In making it impossible to fire people who did not perform, we turned mediocrity into deadwood. In attempting to control virtually everything, we became so obsessed with dictating *how* things should be done—regulating the process, controlling the inputs—that we ignored the outcomes, the *results*.

The product was government with a distinct ethos: slow, inefficient, impersonal. This is the mental image the word *government* invokes today; it is what most Americans assume to be the very essence of government. Even government buildings constructed during the industrial era reflect this ethos: they are immense structures, with high ceilings, large hallways, and ornate architecture, all designed to impress upon the visitor the impersonal authority and immovable weight of the institution.

For a long time, the bureaucratic model worked—not because it was efficient, but because it solved the basic problems people wanted solved. It provided security—from unemployment, during old age. It provided stability, a particularly important quality after the Depression. It provided a basic sense of fairness and equity. (Bureaucracies, as Weber pointed out, are designed to treat everyone alike.) It provided jobs. And it delivered the basic, no-frills, one-size-fits-all services people needed and expected during the industrial era: roads, highways, sewers, schools.

During times of intense crisis—the Depression and two world wars— the bureaucratic model worked superbly. In crisis, when goals were clear and widely shared, when tasks were relatively straightforward, and when virtually everyone was willing to pitch in for the cause, the top-down, command-and-control mentality got things done. The results spoke for themselves, and most Americans fell in step. By the 1950s, as William H. Whyte wrote, we had become a nation of "organization men."

But the bureaucratic model developed in conditions very different from those we experience today. It developed in a slower-paced society, when change proceeded at a leisurely gait. It developed in an age of hierarchy, when only those at the top of the pyramid had enough information to make informed decisions. It developed in a society of people who worked with their hands, not their minds. It developed in a time of mass markets, when most Americans had similar wants and needs. And it developed when we had strong geographic communities—tightly knit neighborhoods and towns.

Today all that has been swept away. We live in an era of breathtaking change. We live in a global marketplace, which puts enormous competitive pressure on our economic institutions. We live in an information society, in which people get access to information almost as fast as their leaders do. We live in a knowledge-based economy, in which educated workers bridle at commands and demand autonomy. We live in an age of niche markets, in which customers have become accustomed to high quality and extensive choice.

In this environment, bureaucratic institutions developed during the industrial era—public *and* private—increasingly fail us.

Today's environment demands institutions that are extremely flexible and adaptable. It demands institutions that deliver high-quality goods and services, squeezing ever more bang out of every buck. It demands institutions that are responsive to their customers, offering choices of non-standardized services; that lead by persuasion and incentives rather than commands; that give their employees a sense of meaning and control, even ownership. It demands institutions that *empower* citizens rather than simply *serving* them.

Bureaucratic institutions will work in some circumstances. If the environment is stable, the task is relatively simple, every customer wants the same service, and the quality of performance is not critical, a traditional public bureaucracy can do the job. Social security still works. Local government agencies that provide libraries and parks and recreational facilities still work, to a degree.

But most government institutions perform increasingly complex tasks, in competitive, rapidly changing environments, with customers who want quality and choice. These new realities have made life very difficult for our public institutions—for our public education system, for our public health care programs, for our public housing authorities, for virtually every large, bureaucratic program created by American governments before 1970. It was no accident that during the 1970s we lost a war, lost faith in our national leaders, endured repeated economic problems, and experienced a tax revolt. In the years since, the clash between old and new has only intensified. The result has been a period of enormous stress in American government.

In some ways, this is a symptom of progress—of the disruptive clash that occurs when new realities run headlong into old institutions. Our information technologies and our knowledge economy give us opportunities to do things we never dreamed possible 50 years ago. But to seize these opportunities, we must pick up the wreckage of our industrial-era institutions and rebuild. "It is the first step of wisdom," Alfred North Whitehead once wrote, "to recognize that the major advances in civilization are processes which all but wreck the society in which they occur."

The Emergence of Entrepreneurial Government

The first governments to respond to these new realities were local governments—in large part because they hit the wall first. On June 6, 1978, the voters of California passed Proposition 13, which cut local property taxes in half. Fed by the dual fires of inflation and dissatisfaction with public services, the tax revolt spread quickly. In 1980, Ronald Reagan took it national—and by 1982, state and local governments had lost nearly one of every four federal dollars they received in 1978. During the 1982 recession, the deepest since the Depression, state governments began to hit the wall.

Under intense fiscal pressure, state and local leaders had no choice but to change the way they did business. Mayors and governors embraced "public-private partnerships" and developed "alternative" ways to deliver services. Cities fostered competition between service providers and invented new budget systems. Public managers began to speak of "enterprise management," "learning organizations," and "self-reliant cities." States began to restructure their most expensive public systems: education, health care, and welfare. . . .

Over the past five years, as we have journeyed through the landscape of governmental change, we have sought constantly to understand the underlying trends. We have asked ourselves: What do these innovative, entrepreneurial organizations have in common? What incentives have they changed, to create such different behavior? What have they done which, if other governments did the same, would make entrepreneurship the norm and bureaucracy the exception?

The common threads were not hard to find. Most entrepreneurial governments promote *competition* between service providers. They *empower* citizens by pushing control out of the bureaucracy, into the community. They measure the performance of their agencies, focusing not on inputs but on *outcomes*. They are driven by their goals—their *missions*—not by their rules and regulations. They redefine their clients as *customers* and offer them choices—between schools, between training programs, between housing options. They *prevent* problems before they emerge, rather than simply offering services afterward. They put their energies into *earning* money, not simply spending it. They *decentralize* authority, embracing participatory management. They prefer *market* mechanisms to bureaucratic mechanisms. And they focus not simply on providing public services, but on *catalyzing* all sectors—public, private, and voluntary—into action to solve their community's problems.

We believe that these ten principles . . . are the fundamental principles behind this new form of government we see emerging: the spokes that hold together this new wheel. Together they form a coherent whole, a new model of government. They will not solve all of our problems. But if the experience of organizations that have embraced them is any guide, they will solve the major problems we experience with bureaucratic government.

Why Government Can't Be "Run Like A Business"

Many people, who believe government should simply be "run like a business," may assume this is what we mean. It is not.

Government and business are fundamentally different institutions. Business leaders are driven by the profit motive; government leaders are driven by the desire to get reelected. Businesses get most of their money from their customers; governments get most of their money from taxpayers. Businesses are usually driven by competition; governments usually use monopolies.

Differences such as these create fundamentally different incentives in the public sector. For example, in government the ultimate test for managers is not whether they produce a product or profit—it is whether they please the elected politicians. Because politicians tend to be driven by interest groups, public managers—unlike their private counterparts—must factor interest groups into every equation.

Governments also extract their income primarily through taxation, whereas businesses earn their income when customers buy products or services of their own free will. This is one reason why the public focuses so intensely on the cost of government services, exercising a constant impulse to *control*—to dictate how much the bureaucrats spend on every item, so they cannot possibly waste, misuse, or steal the taxpayers' money.

All these factors combine to produce an environment in which public employees view risks and rewards very differently than do private employees. "In government all of the incentive is in the direction of not making mistakes," explains Lou Winnick of the Ford Foundation. "You can have 99 successes and nobody notices, and one mistake and you're dead." Standard business methods to motivate employees don't work very well in this kind of environment.

There are many other differences. Government is democratic and open; hence it moves more slowly than business, whose managers can make quick decisions behind closed doors. Government's fundamental mission is to "do good," not to make money; hence cost-benefit calculations in business turn into moral absolutes in the public sector. Government must often serve everyone equally, regardless of their ability to pay or their demand for a service; hence it cannot achieve the same market efficiencies as business. . . .

The fact that government cannot be run just like a business does not mean it cannot become more *entrepreneurial,* of course. Any institution, public or private, can be entrepreneurial, just as any institution, public or private, can be bureaucratic. Few Americans would really want government to act just like a business—making quick decisions behind closed doors for private profit. If it did, democracy would be the first casualty. But most Americans would like government to be less bureaucratic. There is a vast continuum between bureaucratic behavior and entrepreneurial behavior, and government can surely shift its position on that spectrum.

A Third Choice

Most of our leaders still tell us that there are only two ways out of our repeated public crises: we can raise taxes, or we can cut spending. For almost two decades, we have asked for a third choice. We do not want less education, fewer roads, less health care. Nor do we want higher taxes. We want better education, better roads, and better health care, for the same tax dollar.

Unfortunately, we do not know how to get what we want. Most of our leaders assume that the only way to cut spending is to eliminate programs, agencies, and employees. Ronald Reagan talked as if we could simply go into the bureaucracy with a scalpel and cut out pockets of waste, fraud, and abuse.

But waste in government does not come tied up in neat packages. It is marbled throughout our bureaucracies. It is embedded in the very way we do business. It is employees on idle, working at half speed—or barely working at all. It is people working hard at tasks that aren't worth doing, following regulations that should never have been written, filling out forms that should never have been printed. . . .

Waste in government is staggering, but we cannot get at it by wading through budgets and cutting line items. As one observer put it, our governments are like fat people who must lose weight. They need to eat less and exercise more; instead, when money is tight they cut off a few fingers and toes.

To melt the fat, we must change the basic incentives that drive our governments. We must turn bureaucratic institutions into entrepreneurial institutions, ready to kill off obsolete initiatives, willing to do more with less, eager to absorb new ideas.

The lessons are there: our more entrepreneurial governments have shown us the way. Yet few of our leaders are listening. Too busy climbing the rungs to their next office, they don't have time to stop and look anew. So they remain trapped in old ways of looking at our problems, blind to solutions that lie right in front of them. This is perhaps our greatest stumbling block: the power of outdated ideas. As the great economist John Maynard Keynes once noted, the difficulty lies not so much in developing new ideas as in escaping from old ones.

The old ideas still embraced by most public leaders and political reporters assume that the important question is *how much* government we have—not *what kind* of government. Most of our leaders take the old model as a given, and either advocate more of it (liberal Democrats), or less of it (Reagan Republicans), or less of one program but more of another (moderates of both parties).

But our fundamental problem today is not too much government or too little government. We have debated that issue endlessly since the tax revolt of 1978, and it has not solved our problems. Our fundamental problem is that we have *the wrong kind of government*. We do not need more government or less government, we need *better* government. To be more precise, we need better *governance*.

The Case for Bureaucracy

CHARLES T. GOODSELL

To make the case for bureaucracy. What a ridiculous idea! . . . Only the devil himself would make a case for evil. Only a lunatic would come to the defense of the indefensible.

I hope, dear reader, that you will eventually lay aside any such initial suspicions about your author's character or sanity. Several pages may have to be turned before you do so.

Admittedly, to convince you to accept my case for bureaucracy, I have a large task ahead. We have all heard about police raids that are brutal, welfare departments that are heartless, defense contracts that waste billions, and public schools that graduate illiterates. Also, we have all personally encountered individual bureaucrats who are arrogant, rude, lazy, condescending, apathetic, and incapable of writing in clear English. How, then, can any self-respecting professor write a book in *defense* of bureaucracy? . . .

Bureaucracy As Bungler

. . . Conservative theorists produce well-developed arguments for why bureaucracy cannot perform well. These center on what might be called its lack of "market exposure." Few, if any, incentives are said to exist to reduce costs, increase productivity, and produce a product or service that people actually want. Public bureaucracy not only escapes the need to sell its outputs, according to this position, it operates as a monopoly devoid of competition. As a consequence, bureaucracy is supposedly wasteful, not attuned to the desires of its "customers," unmotivated to innovate, and inimical to an efficient allocation of society's resources. Without a need to beat out competitors and satisfy customers and investors, this line of thinking goes, those in charge of bureaucracies need only survive, promote expansion for its own sake, and appease important political constituencies.

This "business is superior" school of thought is based largely on a pro-market premise. The notion of bureaucracy as bungler is also, however, related to patterns of control and authority. Government imposes more legal restrictions and accountability channels on its managers and workers, it is said. As a result, bureaucrats are said to have less autonomy, flexibility, and motivation than business entrepreneurs. The lack of clear, consistent, and quantifiable goals in government means its leaders have less reason or opportunity to assure high levels of performance within the organization. The merit system constitutes a specific obstacle to performance by blocking discretion in hiring, firing, and promoting. This both undercuts executive control and reduces the incentives of subordinates, it is said. Further, the rigidity of bureaucratic rules and the political safety found in "not rocking the boat" supposedly make bureaucracy inherently uncreative, rigid, and non-dynamic in comparison with the private business world.

Let us respond to this viewpoint by offering some observations that are relatively axiomatic yet necessary to clear the air before looking at the empirical evidence. First, distinctions between government and business are not always that obvious. The dichotomy of private versus public enterprise is vivid enough in classroom debates on capitalism and socialism. But in the modern industrial world the interaction between sectors is so complex, and mixed entities so numerous, that the borderline between public and private becomes fuzzy, and the notion of a dichotomy itself almost approaches irrelevancy. This point alone would seem to downgrade the importance of which sector performs better, but is not a good reason to duck the issue.

Second, business corporations are themselves organized bureaucratically. Hence comparative public-private statistics are not truly between bureaucracy and nonbureaucracy but between different kinds of bureaucracy.

Critics of the contemporary American corporation frequently allege that the supposed diseases once regarded as endemic only in government (e.g., wholesale waste, lack of innovation, and conserving strategies) badly infect American big business as well. . . . "Bureaucracy" in the sense of systematic and professional management may not be all that bad in business either.

Third, the presupposition that the private sector is disciplined by the market while the public sector escapes such discipline hides important truths. For one thing, perfect competition among firms is explained elegantly in economics texts but is not found in most of the real business world. To suggest, furthermore, that bureaucracies are unexposed to a harsh external environment is to confess ignorance about the nature of the public sector. Government agencies are faced with long-standing rivalries, periodic turf battles, continuous budget competition over scarce resources, frequent audits and investigations by skeptical outsiders, and pugnacious press scrutiny at any hint of embarrassment or scandal. Indeed, the bureaucratic environment contains plenty of performance-demanding compulsion too, although—like marketplace competition—its results are not always predictable.

A final preliminary point is that comparisons between the two sectors run into inevitable "apples versus oranges" problems. Public bureaucracy is not created to perform according to economic or managerial criteria alone. Government is given tasks that the private sector would not touch or has abandoned. Government must not only be economical and efficient but also carry out statutory intent; observe due process; follow election returns; seek the participation of citizens; pursue justice; and symbolize an open, caring, and honest government. Thus, to compare public bureaucracies with private businesses merely on the basis of productive output or tight management is to stack the argument, in advance, in favor of business. . . .

Anatomy of a Falsehood

Our starting point for making the case for bureaucracy, and thereby exposing the great falsehood about American government, is the proposition that bureaucracy's true nature is discovered not in campaign rhetoric or newspaper horror stories, or even much of the academic writing on the subject, but in the *understandings of citizens*. It is here that we can best learn the quality of what government does, for these "students" of public administration do not approach the subject as a political or theoretical plaything, but as a set of real-life institutions on which they depend for obtaining crucial services. As we found, client surveys, exit interviews, and mailed questionnaires all repeat the same basic finding: The large majority of encounters are perceived as satisfactory, with many highly rated. Bureaucracy is reported as *very often* providing the services sought and expected. *Most of the time* it lives up to acceptable standards of efficiency, courtesy, and fairness. Sometimes government agencies perform poorly, of course; innumerable acts of sloth, injustice, incompetence, and common rudeness are committed daily in government offices around the country. No one is claiming perfection for bureaucracy. At the same time, the basic conclusion of satisfactory citizen treatment as the *norm* rather than the *exception* flies radically in the face of most literature on the subject. That success is normal in American public administration is substantiated, moreover, by quantifiable evidence obtained from measures of bureaucratic performance having nothing to do with citizen perceptions, such as on-time measures, error rates, external observation of transactions, and productivity data.

The relatively good performance of American bureaucracy is made even clearer when we study it comparatively. The intellectual poverty of viewing the Weberian form of organization as deterministic of only "bureaucratic" behavior in the negative sense of that word is revealed when formally identical organizations behave very differently.[1] Even the most convincing negative stereotypes (e.g., condescending application forms and dreary welfare waiting rooms) are seen on close examination to vary enormously. Then too, the long-standing expectation by political liberals that urban bureaucracies systematically discriminate against the poor and racial minorities is discovered to be not merely an oversimplification but plain wrong. The commonly accepted view of political conservatives that government never performs as well as business is also shown to be a patent falsehood. Moreover, a comparison of American bureaucracy to that of other countries reveals that we experience one of the best levels of service in the world, light years ahead of that endured by most national populations.

A major cause for chronic underestimation of American bureaucratic performance is our tendency to hold unrealistic expectations for it. Belonging to a culture accustomed to optimism and habituated to progress, we Americans tend to assume that if bureaucracies do not succeed in changing the world in the ways we wish, they have somehow failed. But in reality we often "set up" bureaucracy in such a way as to make complete success impossible. We give administrative organizations inconsistent or contradictory goals, creating disappointments no matter what happens. We make effective implementation of laws unduly difficult in many policy areas by holding several different organizations responsible for the job, through grants, loans, and contracts. The resulting "proxy" administration adds to the complexity of administration and can lead to decreased accountability, hollowed out agencies, and added layers of control. Bureaucracy is further handicapped by the tendency of Americans to expect it to solve any and all problems, no matter how solvable or unsolvable they may be, even when the bureaucrats have no control whatever over the causes of the problems. We also expect bureaucracy to carry out all the social changes we happen to endorse, denouncing any and all departures from this behavior as unforgivable support for the status quo.

---

1. The reference here is to sociologist Max Weber's ideal type of bureaucracy.

Our misleading stereotypes of bureaucracy extend to the human beings who staff them. Roughly 20 million Americans work for government. We all recognize that this huge slice of the population does not consist solely of lazy bums, incompetents, or the psychologically malformed. These Americans are very similar to the population as a whole in many respects, although racial minorities are found among them in greater numbers and in higher positions than in private employment. With respect to political opinions, the bureaucrats seem to tip slightly to the liberal side but they are hardly radicals. Nor are they inherently arrogant, rulebound, or conservative in their conduct toward clients, or for that matter alienated, fearful, or psychologically warped from working in a hierarchy.

Several misconceptions also prevail about bureaucracy's tendencies with respect to organizational size, growth, aging, and power. Loose talk of giantism—based on the huge overall size of employment rolls or budgets—misrepresents the range of bigness versus smallness found in American public administration. Most of the individual government offices and facilities at which citizens work and do business are, in fact, surprisingly small. Moreover, bureaucratic organizations do not inevitably grow in size or "build empires"; some get bigger, some remain stable, others actually get smaller, especially in an era of tight budgets. Regardless of changes in size, no evidence supports the contention that growth or bigness automatically leads to inefficiency or rigidity. Also unsupported is the notion that, over time, bureaucracies necessarily become ossified or captured by political clients.

While bureaucracies obviously possess political power—they could not do their jobs without it—this power is by no means unrestrained. Indeed, one could argue that, because of the peculiarities of our constitutional separation of powers and hyperpluralistic political system, American bureaucracies tend to be excessively restricted in what they can do. Study after study shows that the bureaucrats are constrained from every direction and subject to innumerable counterchecks. Despite this, they attempt to respond to new directions received from elected officials and stand ready to advocate whatever new cause is elevated by the political process to the governmental agenda. In short, American bureaucracy is of American politics and not above it, exactly as a democracy requires.

If American bureaucracy turns out not to be a societal curse after all, but actually a valuable asset of our nation, why then do we tend to regard it so falsely? Why does such a chasm separate the reality of bureaucratic performance and our abstract images of it? How can such a great falsehood live on, year after year and decade after decade, especially when the gap between belief and reality is not just a few degrees of disagreement but a nearly inverse contradiction? And this in a culture where critical questioning of every orthodoxy—and the endless cycle of intellectual revisionism—never stops?

The only possible explanation is that the falsehood fulfills important functions for the society. Let us explore possibilities here.

One possible function of the great falsehood of American government could be termed *validation*. By this I mean granting reassurance to individuals whose constructions of reality are not compatible with the objective world. To illustrate the concept of validation from another context, the falsehood of white supremacy reassures racists, just as does the falsehood of male superiority for male chauvinists. Applying the idea to bureaucracy, when for whatever reason a person fails to achieve a personal goal vis-à-vis a government office, such as being turned down for help, information, faster service, or a job, one can avoid self-blame by pinning the trouble on "the bureaucracy." This is reassuring even if the true cause of the turndown is legal prohibitions, inadequate funding, low test scores, or a bypassed deadline. By the same token, if we work for the bureaucracy, it is easier to accept a rejected promotion or ignored advice or rewritten memo if the cause is not our own inadequacies but a "closed" or "hide-bound" bureaucracy.

The great bureaucratic falsehood also validates questionable actions in which we partake from time to time. If administrative agencies are seen as nests of vipers, the most aggressive investigative tactics an enterprising journalist can invent are deemed honorable. Deliberate internal sabotage of a government program—that is, organizational disloyalty—can also be rationalized. If bureaucracy is viewed as captured by selfish private interests, self-appointed spokespersons for the public good can justify the most outrageous militancy, even to the extent of breaking the law. Similarly, the image of a compulsively wasteful bureaucracy can insert an unattractive, self-righteous moralism into the hearts of auditors, budget examiners, inspectors general, and management consultants.

A second function of the great bureaucratic falsehood is *justification*. In this instance the belief not merely reassures the believer, but reassures others. A false belief that the bureaucracy oppresses the poor and is captured by business reassures liberals. A false belief that the bureaucracy harasses business and wastes money reassures conservatives. The extreme ends of the political spectrum can be truly creative in their imaginings about bureaucracy, with the left seeing it as associated with fascist authoritarianism and the right regarding it as part and parcel of socialism.

Other uses of the falsehood for justification are completely nonideological, available to any candidate for public office to use for self-promotion. Bloated bureaucracy becomes a source of naive proposals for painless budget cutting. Gross inefficiency allows us to urge more spending without raising taxes or the deficit, by "cutting out the fat." Obstructionist bureaucracy furnishes a ready explanation for why our favored programs, which we have claimed would work miracles, have not achieved all that was promised.

In both validation and justification, bureaucracy serves as a most effective enemy. Enemies are useful tools to advocates of almost any idea or interest. They justify righteousness and a sense of urgency. They intensify feelings, focus effort, divert attention, and silence critics. And bureaucracy is the perfect enemy. It is abstract enough to fit anyone's value system, from the taxpayer's anger over the complexity of the revenue code to the environmentalist's disgust over compromised air-quality standards. Moreover, bureaucracy as an enemy is very dependable because it is never defeated and never disappears—and thus its availability as an enemy is never terminated. In addition, bureaucracy's imputed association with huge size, impersonality, and mysterious technology, plus its backing by the sovereign power of the state, make it a particularly ominous and hence potent object of hatred. Note the threatening tone in the following statement against gun control:

> *The time to use your guns is when the government comes to get them.* When they come for the guns it is time to act. More than anything else, this is what Washington fears. And along these lines, friends, if you think the bureaucratic goons are arrogant now, imagine how they would behave if they knew you were helpless.

Bureaucracy probably performs validation and justification functions in every nation and culture in the world. No doubt some interesting variations occur in this regard. In totalitarian countries, never-ending denunciations of bureaucracy are sometimes welcomed by the authorities because they deflect antiregime sentiment in a relatively harmless way. In many low-income countries, bureaucracy conveniently "explains" why development plans never work out. These peculiarities are also country specific. In France, denigrating humor about bureaucracy allows Frenchmen to mock themselves while secretly admiring the state. In Germany, making fun of bureaucratic orderliness ironically fosters pride in a strong and dependable fatherland. In Britain, bureaucracy's middle-class reliability offers the perfect counterfoil to haughty but nimble amateurism, admired by the upper crust.

As for the United States, the presence of bureaucracy provides ongoing fuel for Americans' habitual suspicion of government and corresponding commitment to market capitalism. In our business-oriented culture, bureaucracy stands as the antithesis of a self-reliant, free, and entrepreneurial America. Here it is the target of jokes, yes—but also plain disdain. One might argue that, generically, public bureaucracy does not "fit" American culture well; the obverse of this point is that the great falsehood about American government fits it perfectly.

Reactions to the Falsehood

The "reinventing" argument of Osborne and Gaebler is based on the assumption that, because of modern technology, the information age, contemporary customer wants, and global economics, government must radically change the way it does things. The current way government works is a discredited kind of "industrial era" bureaucracy, that is, in-house program implementation of programs delivered to clients by hierarchically organized departments directed by managers according to operational rules and fiscal checks. All this must now be changed, they say. Government bureaucracies must "steer" and not "row," that is, work through other organizations via contracts and other devices. They must be converted into flat, participative organizations with incentives that encourage risk, imaginative innovation, customer service, and competitive entrepreneurialism. . . .

Following the 1992 election, Osborne proposed that when Clinton took office a high-level "reinventing-government group" should be established in the White House. He even urged that the president's first executive order be a one-page vision statement on reinventing government and that this document be framed and hung above the desk of every new agency head. This did not happen, but nonetheless the administration took his ideas seriously. Impressed with a five-month performance review that the Texas comptroller performed in the Lone Star State, Clinton gave Vice-President Al Gore the assignment of heading a six-month National Performance Review. . . . [C]urrent federal employees were mobilized to investigate ideas for change, kicked off by a series of "town meetings" held in Washington and around the country. The vice-president, who conducted these meetings, termed the performance review "historic." He asserted, "I want to ask all of you to mark this date: President Clinton is starting a revolution in government right here and now."

The Gore report that emerged contained several good ideas, such as instituting a two-year budget, decentralizing personnel administration, simplifying government procurement, and ending the monopoly of the Government Printing Office. Other proposals, framed in general terms, call for more decentralized management, better "customer service," and additional user fees. These ideas are stated in general terms and cannot be assessed until they are specified. The proposed closing of numerous government field offices, laboratories, and overseas missions will certainly save money, but at the cost of reducing what services government renders where. Indeed, any big savings are likely to come only by cutting programs, not by reinventing government.

This is because most of the reinventions have already been invented. For years, American bureaucracy has been, in various degrees and places, contracting out (as we know); improving management; bidding for services; engaging in partnerships; employing performance review; forming quality circles; enhancing service to clients; charging fees; transcending line-item budgets; and awarding incentive bonuses. As far as being innovative, competitive, and entrepreneurial is concerned, these qualities have always been exhibited by the best of our public executives, at all levels of government. The remaining specifics offered by Osborne and Gaebler, for example, test marketing, loan pools, profit centers, and allowing appropriations to hold over to the next fiscal year, will hardly "revolutionize" American public administration. But they won't ruin it either.

The reinvention movement has, however, accomplished one thing. It has turned the Washington establishment and much of the public management fraternity back in the direction of the mind-set of the Reagan era. Once again we are assuming that public servants do not serve and that bureaucracy does not work. Even though Clinton's head of OPM is publicly casting himself as an ally of the federal worker, the overall emphasis of the administration has been to revert to the posture of correcting problems, not building on strengths.[2] The vice-president's claim on the day before his report was presented that American government is "failing the American people" captures this sentiment succinctly.

The great falsehood of American government has thus returned to its high status of popular and academic orthodoxy. Although the language and tactics of disparagement of American bureaucracy have evolved, the failure to acknowledge its proportionate degrees of success and comparative levels of achievement has not. To assume that American government does not work is again *au courant*.

DISCUSSION QUESTIONS

1. What are the general views of bureaucracy prevalent in American politics and media? What have been your actual experiences in dealing with bureaucratic agencies of federal, state, or local government? Have your experiences been consistent with the commonly held and largely negative perception of bureaucracy?

2. Should American government be "reinvented" along the lines proposed by Osborne and Gaebler? Will their proposals make the public sector leaner, more flexible, and more capable of giving citizens what they want? Or will they foster even greater public skepticism about government, justify further reductions in public services, and diminish attention to the economically disadvantaged?

3. If Goodsell is right that Americans should take pride in a bureaucracy that is the best in the world, why don't they exhibit that pride? Is the prevailing negative view of bureaucracy a "great falsehood," or has Goodsell exaggerated bureaucracy's virtues and underestimated its vices?

4. Can a modern democracy do without bureaucracy? Can it do without the large organizations, impersonal rules designed to check corruption and ensure equitable treatment, and professional expertise that characterize bureaucracy? Will a shift toward private markets and "entrepreneurial" public agencies improve or diminish the workings of democratic government?

---

2. The acronym OPM stands for Office of Personnel Management.

SUGGESTED READINGS
AND INTERNET RESOURCES

A further elaboration of the "reinventing government" approach, with many American and international examples, can be found in David Osborne and Peter Plastrik, *Banishing Bureaucracy: The Five Strategies for Reinventing Government* (Reading, Mass: Addison Wesley Longman, 1997). For the Clinton administration version of "reinventing government," see Al Gore, *Report of the National Performance Review* (New York: Times Books, 1994). The successes and failures of the alternatives to bureaucracy are discussed in Joel F. Handler, *Down from Bureaucracy: The Ambiguity of Privatization and Empowerment* (Princeton, NJ: Princeton University Press, 1996). A systematic treatise on bureaucracy, more sympathetic than critical, is James Q. Wilson, *Bureaucracy: What Government Agencies Do and Why They Do It* (New York: Basic Books, 1989). A scorching treatment of bureaucrats is Ralph P. Hummel, *The Bureaucratic Experience* (3rd ed.; New York: St. Martin's Press, 1987).

National Performance Review
http://www.npr.gov/
The homepage for Al Gore's "reinventing government" program; provides commentary, goal statements, case studies, and research tools.

Regulation
http://www.regulation.org/
A conservative site that comments on problems with regulation; provides links to conservative think tanks that criticize big government.

American Society for Public Administration
http://www.aspanet.org/
This site provides current news and research tools for those in the profession of public administration.

16

The Judiciary: What Should Its Role Be in a Democracy?

A mericans like to think of the justices of the Supreme Court as grave and learned elders of the law, engaged in a search for justice that has little to do with the selfish interests and ambitions that we so often associate with politics. The justices themselves encourage this view, holding court in a marble temple (the Supreme Court Building), wearing black robes, shrouding their decision-making processes in secrecy. Yet an institution that makes authoritative decisions about many of the most troublesome issues of our times—abortion, affirmative action, the rights of the accused, the relationship between church and state—cannot be kept aloof from politics. Thus, the Supreme Court's role in the political system has become one of the central issues in current debates about American democracy.

From one perspective, the Supreme Court is not really a democratic institution at all. The nine justices of the Supreme Court are not elected; they are nominated by the president and confirmed by the Senate. They serve during good behavior—that is, until they retire, die, or are impeached by the House and convicted by the Senate. Composed exclusively of one profession, lawyers, the Court can use its power of judicial review to strike down laws passed by legislatures that have been elected by the majority.

From another perspective, however, the Supreme Court is an essential component of American democracy. Its most important role is as a guardian of the Constitution, which is the fundamental expression of the people's will.

According to this view, the Court sometimes must oppose the wishes of a temporary majority in the name of the abiding principles and values contained in the Constitution.

During the last several decades, landmark decisions by the Supreme Court have often evoked democratic debates. Some decisions by the Court have been approved by a majority of Americans but have been fiercely resisted by intense minorities. Among these have been *Brown* v. *Board of Education* (1954), ordering school desegregation, and *Roe* v. *Wade* (1973), guaranteeing the right of a woman to choose to have an abortion. Other decisions have been opposed by a large majority. Among these have been *Engel* v. *Vitale* (1962), which forbade prayer in public schools, and *Miranda* v. *Arizona* (1966), which required police to inform criminal suspects of their rights before they could be interrogated.

Decisions such as these have led critics to charge the Court with overstepping its proper role in the political system. The most prominent critic has been Edwin Meese III, the attorney general of the United States during Ronald Reagan's presidency. In a series of speeches in 1985 (one of which is excerpted here), Meese accused the Court of substituting its own preferences and prejudices for the principles of the Constitution. Springing to the defense of the Court against Meese was Justice William Brennan, Jr., who played an influential role in crafting many of the decisions that Meese was condemning. The debate between Meese and Brennan has been a profoundly important one because it cuts to the most basic issues concerning the judiciary's role in American democracy.

Meese insists that the justices of the Supreme Court should be strictly guided by the words of the Constitution and the laws and by the intentions of those who drafted them (he calls this a "jurisprudence of original intention"). This emphasis on the original intention of the Framers calls into question the Court's recent decisions on the rights of racial minorities, women, and persons accused of crimes. Meese wants the Supreme Court to play a more restrained role and to defer whenever possible to the elected branches of government.

Brennan rejects each of Meese's arguments. He suggests that the original intention of the Framers cannot be known and that while justices must respect the past, they must ultimately be guided in their interpretations by what the words of the Constitution mean today. He believes that Meese's position is a cloak for a conservative political agenda, the aim of which is to reverse recent advances in our understanding of the constitutional rights of previously disadvantaged groups. Brennan denies that democracy requires a deferential judiciary: the Court, he argues, has a democratic responsibility to uphold the nation's founding "aspiration to social justice, brotherhood, and human dignity."

Among the three branches of the national government, the judiciary is clearly the most elite in its selection process, composition, and form of deliberation. Yet in the debate between Meese and Brennan, each tries to associate his view of the judiciary with a popular democratic position. You can decide for yourself whose position in this debate deserves to be identified with popular democracy by considering the following questions. Can we be guided in interpreting the Constitution by the original intention of its Framers, or must we read the Constitution in a more adaptive and modern fashion? Should our understanding of constitutional rights be squarely rooted in the text of the Constitution, or should we apply constitutional values to the protection of rights for individuals and groups that the Framers never thought to protect? Must the Court, as an unelected branch of government, avoid undemocratic action by acting with deference toward the elected branches, or must it actively pursue the democratic aspirations of the Constitution even when this brings the judiciary into conflict with the elected branches?

A Jurisprudence of Original Intention

EDWIN MEESE III

A large part of American history has been the history of Constitutional debate. From the Federalists and the Anti-Federalists, to Webster and Calhoun, to Lincoln and Douglas, we find many examples. Now, as we approach the bicentennial of the framing of the Constitution, we are witnessing another debate concerning our fundamental law. It is not simply a ceremonial debate, but one that promises to have a profound impact on the future of our Republic. . . .

Today I would like to discuss further the meaning of constitutional fidelity. In particular, I would like to describe in more detail this administration's approach.

Before doing so, I would like to make a few commonplace observations about the original document itself. It is easy to forget what a young country America really is. The bicentennial of our independence was just a few years ago, that of the Constitution still two years off. The period surrounding the creation of the Constitution is not a dark and mythical realm. The young America of the 1780's and 90's was a vibrant place, alive with pamphlets, newspapers and books chronicling and commenting upon the great issues of the day. We know how the Founding Fathers lived, and much of what they read, thought, and believed. The disputes and compromises of the Constitutional Convention were carefully recorded. The minutes of the Convention are a matter of public record. Several of the most important participants—including James Madison, the "father" of the Constitution—

wrote comprehensive accounts of the convention. Others, Federalists and Anti-Federalists alike, committed their arguments for and against ratification, as well as their understandings of the Constitution, to paper, so that their ideas and conclusions could be widely circulated, read, and understood.

In short, the Constitution is not buried in the mists of time. We know a tremendous amount of the history of its genesis. The Bicentennial is encouraging even more scholarship about its origins. We know who did what, when, and many times why. One can talk intelligently about a "founding generation." . . .

Our approach to constitutional interpretation begins with the document itself. The plain fact is, it exists. It is something that has been written down. Walter Berns of the American Enterprise Institute has noted that the central object of American constitutionalism was "the effort" of the Founders "to express fundamental governmental arrangements in a legal document—to 'get it in writing.'" Indeed, judicial review has been grounded in the fact that the Constitution is a written, as opposed to an unwritten, document. In *Marbury* v. *Madison*, [5 U.S. 137 (1803),] John Marshall rested his rationale for judicial review on the fact that we have a written constitution with meaning that is binding upon judges. "[I]t is apparent," he wrote, "that the framers of the Constitution contemplated that instrument as a rule for the government of *courts*, as well as of the legislature. Why otherwise does it direct the judges to take an oath to support it?"

The presumption of a written document is that it conveys meaning. As Thomas Grey of the Stanford Law School has said, it makes "relatively definite and explicit what otherwise would be relatively indefinite and tacit."

We know that those who framed the Constitution chose their words carefully. They debated at great length the most minute points. The language they chose meant something. They proposed, they substituted, they edited, and they carefully revised. Their words were studied with equal care by state ratifying conventions. This is not to suggest that there was unanimity among the framers and ratifiers on all points. The Constitution and the Bill of Rights, and some of the subsequent amendments, emerged after protracted debate. Nobody got everything they wanted. What's more, the Framers were not clairvoyants—they could not foresee every issue that would be submitted for judicial review. Nor could they predict how all foreseeable disputes would be resolved under the Constitution. But the point is, the meaning of the Constitution can be known.

What does this written Constitution mean? In places it is exactingly specific. Where it says that Presidents of the United States must be at least 35 years of age it means exactly that. (I have not heard of any claim that 35 means 30 or 25 or 20). Where it specifies how the House and Senate are to be organized, it means what it says.

The Constitution also expresses particular principles. One is the right to be free of an unreasonable search or seizure. Another concerns religious liberty. Another is the right to equal protection of the laws.

Those who framed these principles meant something by them. And the meanings can be found. The Constitution itself is also an expression of certain general principles. These principles reflect the deepest purpose of the Constitution—that of establishing a political system through which Americans can best govern themselves consistent with the goal of securing liberty.

The text and structure of the Constitution is instructive. It contains very little in the way of specific political solutions. It speaks volumes on how problems should be approached, and by *whom*. For example, the first three articles set out clearly the scope and limits of three distinct branches of national government, the powers of each being carefully and specifically enumerated. In this scheme it is no accident to find the legislative branch described first, as the Framers had fought and sacrificed to secure the right of democratic self-governance. Naturally, this faith in republicanism was not unbounded, as the next two articles make clear.

Yet the Constitution remains a document of powers and principles. And its undergirding premise remains that democratic self-government is subject only to the limits of certain constitutional principles. This respect for the political process was made explicit early on. When John Marshall upheld the Act of Congress chartering a national bank in *McCulloch* v. *Maryland* [17 U.S. 316 (1819)], he wrote: "The Constitution [was] intended to endure for ages to come, and, consequently, to be adapted to the various crises of human affairs." But to use *McCulloch*, as some have tried, as support for the idea that the Constitution is a protean, changeable thing is to stand history on its head. Marshall was keeping faith with the original intention that Congress be free to elaborate and apply constitutional powers and principles. He was not saying that the Court must invent some new constitutional value in order to keep pace with the times. In Walter Berns' words: "Marshall's meaning is not that the Constitution may be adapted to the 'various crises of human affairs,' but that the legislative powers granted by the Constitution are adaptable to meet these crises."

The approach this administration advocates is rooted in the text of the Constitution as illuminated by those who drafted, proposed, and ratified it. In his famous Commentary on the Constitution of the United States, Justice Joseph Story explained that: "The first and fundamental rule in the interpretation of all instruments is, to construe them according to the sense of the terms, and the intention of the parties."

Our approach understands the significance of a written document and seeks to discern the particular and general principles it expresses. It recognizes that there may be debate at times over the application of these principles. But it does not mean these principles cannot be identified.

Constitutional adjudication is obviously not a mechanical process. It requires an appeal to reason and discretion. The text and intention of the Constitution must be understood to constitute the banks within which constitutional interpretation must flow. As James Madison said, if "the sense in which the Constitution was accepted and ratified by the nation . . .

be not the guide in expounding it, there can be no security for a consistent and stable government, more than for a faithful exercise of its powers."

Thomas Jefferson, so often cited incorrectly as a framer of the Constitution, in fact shared Madison's view: "Our peculiar security is in the possession of a written Constitution. Let us not make it a blank paper by construction." Jefferson was even more explicit in his personal correspondence:

> On every question of construction [we should] carry ourselves back to the time, when the constitution was adopted; recollect the spirit manifested in the debates; and instead of trying [to find], what meaning may be squeezed out of the text, or invented against it, conform to the probable one, in which it was passed.

In the main, jurisprudence that seeks to be faithful to our Constitution—a Jurisprudence of Original Intention, as I have called it—is not difficult to describe. Where the language of the Constitution is specific, it must be obeyed. Where there is a demonstrable consensus among the framers and ratifiers as to a principle stated or implied by the Constitution, it should be followed. Where there is ambiguity as to the precise meaning or reach of a constitutional provision, it should be interpreted and applied in a manner so as to at least not contradict the text of the Constitution itself.

Sadly, while almost every one participating in the current constitutional debate would give assent to these propositions, the techniques and conclusions of some of the debaters do violence to them. What is the source of this violence? In large part I believe that it is the misuse of history stemming from the neglect of the idea of a written constitution.

There is a frank proclamation by some judges and commentators that what matters most about the Constitution is not its words but its so-called "spirit." These individuals focus less on the language of specific provisions than on what they describe as the "vision" or "concepts of human dignity" they find embodied in the Constitution. This approach to jurisprudence has led to some remarkable and tragic conclusions.

In the 1850's, the Supreme Court under Chief Justice Roger B. Taney read blacks out of the Constitution in order to invalidate Congress' attempt to limit the spread of slavery. The *Dred Scott* decision, famously described as a judicial "self-inflicted wound," helped bring on the Civil War. There is a lesson in this history. There is danger in seeing the Constitution as an empty vessel into which each generation may pour its passion and prejudice.

Our own time has its own fashions and passions. In recent decades many have come to view the Constitution—more accurately, part of the Constitution, provisions of the Bill of Rights and the Fourteenth Amendment—as a charter for judicial activism on behalf of various constituencies. Those who hold this view often have lacked demonstrable textual or historical support for their conclusions. Instead they have "grounded" their rulings in appeals to social theories, to moral philosophies or personal notions of human dignity, or to "penumbras," somehow emanating ghostlike from various provisions—identified and not identified—in the Bill of Rights.[1] The problem with this approach, as John Hart Ely, Dean of the Stanford Law School has observed with respect to one such decision, is not that it is bad constitutional law, but that it is not constitutional law in any meaningful sense, at all.

Despite this fact, the perceived popularity of some results in particular cases has encouraged some observers to believe that any critique of the methodology of those decisions is an attack on the results. This perception is sufficiently widespread that it deserves an answer. My answer is to look at history.

When the Supreme Court, in *Brown* v. *Board of Education* [347 U.S. 483 (1954)], sounded the death knell for official segregation in the country, it earned all the plaudits it received. But the Supreme Court in that case was not giving new life to old words, or adapting a "living," "flexible" Constitution to new reality. It was restoring the original principle of the Constitution to constitutional law. The *Brown* Court was correcting the damage done 50 years earlier, when in *Plessy* v. *Ferguson* [163 U.S. 537 (1896)], an earlier Supreme Court had disregarded the clear intent of the Framers of the Civil War amendments to eliminate the legal degradation of blacks, and had contrived a theory of the Constitution to support the charade of "separate but equal" discrimination.

Similarly, the decisions of the New Deal and beyond that freed Congress to regulate commerce and enact a plethora of social legislation were not judicial adaptations of the Constitution to new realities. They were in fact removals of encrustations of earlier courts that had strayed from the original intent of the Framers regarding the power of the legislature to make policy.

It is amazing how so much of what passes for social and political progress is really the undoing of old judicial mistakes. Mistakes occur when the principles of specific constitutional provisions—such as those contained in the Bill of Rights—are taken by some as invitations to read into the Constitution values that contradict the clear language of other provisions.

Acceptances to this illusory invitation have proliferated in recent decades. One Supreme Court justice identified the proper judicial standard as asking "what's best for this country." Another said it is important to "keep the Court out in front" of the general society. Various academic commentators have poured rhetorical grease on this judicial fire, suggesting that constitutional interpretation appropriately be guided by such standards as whether a public policy "personifies justice" or "comports with the notion of moral evolution" or confers "an identity" upon our society or was consistent with "natural ethical law" or was consistent with some "right of equal citizenship."

---

1. Meese's use of *penumbras* refers to Justice William O. Douglas's opinion in *Griswold* v. *Connecticut* (1965), which established a constitutional right to privacy. Douglas argued that although this right was not explicitly stated in the Bill of Rights, it could be found in the penumbras of several of the first ten amendments.

Unfortunately, as I've noted, navigation by such lodestars has in the past given us questionable economics, governmental disorder, and racism— all in the guise of constitutional law. Recently one of the distinguished judges of one of our federal appeals courts got it about right when he wrote: "The truth is that the judge who looks outside the Constitution always looks inside himself and nowhere else" [Robert H. Bork, *Traditions and Morality in Constitutional Law* (1984)]. Or, as we recently put it before the Supreme Court in an important brief: "The further afield interpretation travels from its point of departure in the text, the greater the danger that constitutional adjudication will be like a picnic to which the framers bring the words and the judges the meaning" [Brief for the United States as *amicus curiae* at 24, *Thornburgh* v. *American College of Obstetricians and Gynecologists*, No. 844-95, June 11, 1986].[2]

In the *Osborne* v. *Bank of United States* [22 U.S. 738 (1824)], decision 21 years after *Marbury*, Chief Justice Marshall further elaborated his view of the relationship between the judge and the law, be it statutory or constitutional:

> Judicial power, as contradistinguished from the power of the laws, has no existence. Courts are the mere instruments of the law, and can will nothing. When they are said to exercise a discretion, it is a mere legal discretion, a discretion to be exercised in discerning the course prescribed by law; and, when that is discerned, it is the duty of the Court to follow it.

Any true approach to constitutional interpretation must respect the document in all its parts and be faithful to the Constitution in its entirety. What must be remembered in the current debate is that interpretation does not imply results. The Framers were not trying to anticipate every answer. They were trying to create a tripartite national government, within a federal system, that would have the flexibility to adapt to face new exigencies—as it did, for example, in chartering a national bank. Their great interest was in the distribution of power and responsibility in order to secure the great goal of liberty for all.

A jurisprudence that seeks fidelity to the Constitution—a Jurisprudence of Original Intention—is not a jurisprudence of political results. It is very much concerned with process, and it is a jurisprudence that in our day seeks to de-politicize the law. The great genius of the constitutional blueprint is found in its creation and respect for spheres of authority and the limits it places on governmental power. In this scheme the Framers did not see the courts as the exclusive custodians of the Constitution. Indeed, because the document posits so few conclusions it leaves to the more political branches the matter of adapting and vivifying its principles in each generation. It also leaves to the people of the states, in the 10th amendment,

---

2. *Amicus curiae* means friend of the court. Legal briefs of this kind are filed by those who are not the actual parties in a lawsuit.

those responsibilities and rights not committed to federal care. The power to declare acts of Congress and laws of the states null and void is truly awesome. This power must be used when the Constitution clearly speaks. It should not be used when the Constitution does not.

In *Marbury* v. *Madison*, at the same time he vindicated the concept of judicial review, Marshall wrote that the "principles" of the Constitution "are deemed fundamental and permanent," and, except for formal amendment, "unchangeable." If we want a change in our Constitution or in our laws we must seek it through the formal mechanisms presented in that organizing document of our government.

In summary, I would emphasize that what is at issue here is not an agenda of issues or a menu of results. At issue is a way of government. A jurisprudence based on first principles is neither conservative nor liberal, neither right nor left. It is a jurisprudence that cares about committing and limiting to each organ of government the proper ambit of its responsibilities. It is a jurisprudence faithful to our Constitution.

By the same token, an activist jurisprudence, one which anchors the Constitution only in the consciences of jurists, is a chameleon jurisprudence, changing color and form in each era. The same activism hailed today may threaten the capacity for decision through democratic consensus tomorrow, as it has in many yesterdays. Ultimately, as the early democrats wrote into the Massachusetts state constitution, the best defense of our liberties is a government of laws and not men.

Reading the Constitution as Twentieth-Century Americans

WILLIAM J. BRENNAN, JR.

It will perhaps not surprise you that the text I have chosen for exploration is the amended Constitution of the United States, which, of course, entrenches the Bill of Rights and the Civil War amendments, and draws sustenance from the bedrock principles of another great text, the Magna Carta. So fashioned, the Constitution embodies the aspiration to social justice, brotherhood, and human dignity that brought this nation into being. The Declaration of Independence, the Constitution and the Bill of Rights solemnly committed the United States to be a country where the dignity and rights of all persons were equal before all authority. In all candor we must concede that part of this egalitarianism in America has been more pretension than realized fact. But we are an aspiring people, a people with faith in progress. Our amended Constitution is the lodestar for our aspirations. Like every text worth reading, it is not crystalline. The phrasing is broad and the limitations of its provisions are not clearly marked. Its majestic generalities and ennobling pronouncements are both luminous and obscure. This ambiguity of course calls forth interpretation, the interaction of reader and text. The encounter with the constitutional text has been, in many senses, my life's work. . . .

When Justices interpret the Constitution they speak for their community, not for themselves alone. The act of interpretation must be undertaken with full consciousness that it is, in a very real sense, the community's interpretation that is sought. Justices are not platonic guardians appointed to wield authority according to their personal moral predelictions. Precisely because coercive force must attend any judicial decision to countermand the will of a contemporary majority, the Justices must render constitutional interpretations that are received as legitimate. The source of legitimacy is, of course, a wellspring of controversy in legal and political circles. At the core of the debate is what the late Yale Law School professor Alexander Bickel labeled "the counter-majoritarian difficulty." Our commitment to self-governance in a representative democracy must be reconciled with vesting in electorally unaccountable Justices the power to invalidate the expressed desires of representative bodies on the ground of inconsistency with higher law. Because judicial power resides in the authority to give meaning to the Constitution, the debate is really a debate about how to read the text, about constraints on what is legitimate interpretation.

There are those who find legitimacy in fidelity to what they call "the intentions of the Framers." In its most doctrinaire incarnation, this view demands that Justices discern exactly what the Framers thought about the question under consideration and simply follow that intention in resolving the case before them. It is a view that feigns self-effacing deference to the specific judgments of those who forged our original social compact. But in truth it is little more than arrogance cloaked as humility. It is arrogant to pretend that from our vantage we can gauge accurately the intent of the Framers on application of principle to specific, contemporary questions. All too often, sources of potential enlightenment such as records of the ratification debates provide sparse or ambiguous evidence of the original intention. Typically, all that can be gleaned is that the Framers themselves did not agree about the application or meaning of particular constitutional provisions, and hid their differences in cloaks of generality. Indeed, it is far from clear whose intention is relevant—that of the drafters, the congressional disputants, or the ratifiers in the states?—or even whether the idea of an original intention is a coherent way of thinking about a jointly drafted document drawing its authority from a general assent of the states. And apart from the problematic nature of the sources, our distance of two centuries cannot but work as a prism refracting all we perceive. One cannot help but speculate that the chorus of lamentations calling for interpretation faithful to "original intention"—and proposing nullification of interpretations that fail this quick litmus test—must inevitably come from persons who have no familiarity with the historical record.

Perhaps most importantly, while proponents of this facile historicism justify it as a depoliticization of the judiciary, the political underpinnings of such a choice should not escape notice. A position that upholds constitutional claims only if they were within the specific contemplation of the Framers in effect establishes a presumption of resolving textual ambiguities against the claim of constitutional right. It is far from clear what justifies such a presumption against claims of right. Nothing intrinsic in the nature of interpretation—if there is such a thing as the "nature" of interpretation—commands such a passive approach to ambiguity. This is a choice no less political than any other; it expresses antipathy to claims of the minority rights against the majority. Those who would restrict claims of right to the values of 1789 specifically articulated in the Constitution turn a blind eye to social progress and eschew adaptation of overarching principles to changes of social circumstance.

Another, perhaps more sophisticated, response to the potential power of judicial interpretation stresses democratic theory: because ours is a government of the people's elected representatives, substantive value choices should by and large be left to them. This view emphasizes not the transcendent historical authority of the framers but the predominant contemporary authority of the elected branches of government. Yet it has similar consequences for the nature of proper judicial interpretation. Faith in the majoritarian process counsels restraint. Even under more expansive formulations of this approach, judicial review is appropriate only to the extent of ensuring that our democratic process functions smoothly. Thus, for example, we would protect freedom of speech merely to ensure that the people are heard by their representatives, rather than as a separate, substantive value. When, by contrast, society tosses up to the Supreme Court a dispute that would require invalidation of a legislature's substantive policy choice, the Court generally would stay its hand because the Constitution was meant as a plan of government and not as an embodiment of fundamental substantive values.

The view that all matters of substantive policy should be resolved through the majoritarian process has appeal under some circumstances, but I think it ultimately will not do. Unabashed enshrinement of majority will would permit the imposition of a social caste system or wholesale confiscation of property so long as a majority of the authorized legislative body, fairly elected, approved. Our Constitution could not abide such a situation. It is the very purpose of a Constitution—and particularly of the Bill of Rights—to declare certain values transcendent, beyond the reach of temporary political majorities. The majoritarian process cannot be expected to rectify claims of minority right that arise as a response to the outcomes of that very majoritarian process. As James Madison put it:

The prescriptions in favor of liberty ought to be levelled against that quarter where the greatest danger lies, namely, that which possesses the highest prerogative of power. But this is not found in either the Executive or Legislative departments of Government, but in the body of the people, operating by the majority against the minority (I Annals 437).

Faith in democracy is one thing, blind faith quite another. Those who drafted our Constitution understood the difference. One cannot read the text without admitting that it embodies substantive value choices; it places certain values beyond the power of any legislature. Obvious are the separation of powers; the privilege of the Writ of Habeas Corpus; prohibition of Bills of Attainder and *ex post facto* laws; prohibition of cruel and unusual punishments; the requirement of just compensation for official taking of property; the prohibition of laws tending to establish religion or enjoining the free exercise of religion; and, since the Civil War, the banishment of slavery and official race discrimination. With respect to at least such principles, we simply have not constituted ourselves as strict utilitarians. While the Constitution may be amended, such amendments require an immense effort by the People as a whole.

To remain faithful to the content of the Constitution, therefore, an approach to interpreting the text must account for the existence of these substantive value choices, and must accept the ambiguity inherent in the effort to apply them to modern circumstances. The Framers discerned fundamental principles through struggles against particular malefactions of the Crown; the struggle shapes the particular contours of the articulated principles. But our acceptance of the fundamental principles has not and should not bind us to those precise, at times anachronistic, contours. Successive generations of Americans have continued to respect these fundamental choices and adopt them as their own guide to evaluating quite different historical practices. Each generation has the choice to overrule or add to the fundamental principles enunciated by the Framers; the Constitution can be amended or it can be ignored. Yet with respect to its fundamental principles, the text has suffered neither fate. Thus, if I may borrow the words of an esteemed predecessor, Justice Robert Jackson, the burden of judicial interpretation is to translate "the majestic generalities of the Bill of Rights, conceived as part of the pattern of liberal government in the eighteenth century, into concrete restraints on officials dealing with the problems of the twentieth century" *Board of Education* v. *Barnette* [319 U.S. 624, 639 (1943)].

We current Justices read the Constitution in the only way that we can: as Twentieth Century Americans. We look to the history of the time of framing and to the intervening history of interpretation. But the ultimate question must be, what do the words of the text mean in our time. For the genius of the Constitution rests not in any static meaning it might have had in a world that is dead and gone, but in the adaptability of its great principles to cope with current problems and current needs. What the constitutional fundamentals meant to the wisdom of other times cannot be their measure to the vision of our time. Similarly, what those fundamentals mean for us, our descendants will learn, cannot be the measure to the vision of their time. This realization is not, I assure you, a novel one of my own creation. Permit me to quote from one of the opinions of our Court, *Weems* v. *United States* [217 U.S. 349], written nearly a century ago:

> Time works changes, brings into existence new conditions and purposes. Therefore, a principle to be vital must be capable of wider application than the mischief which gave it birth. This is peculiarly true of constitutions. They are not ephemeral enactments, designed to meet passing occasions. They are, to use the words of Chief Justice John Marshall, "designed to approach immortality as nearly as human institutions can approach it." The future is their care and provision for events of good and bad tendencies of which no prophecy can be made. In the application of a constitution, therefore, our contemplation cannot be only of what has been, but of what may be.

Interpretation must account for the transformative purpose of the text. Our Constitution was not intended to preserve a preexisting society but to make a new one, to put in place new principles that the prior political community had not sufficiently recognized. Thus, for example, when we interpret the Civil War Amendments to the charter—abolishing slavery, guaranteeing blacks equality under law, and guaranteeing blacks the right to vote—we must remember that those who put them in place had no desire to enshrine the status quo. Their goal was to make over their world, to eliminate all vestige of slave caste.

Having discussed at some length how I, as a Supreme Court Justice, interact with this text, I think it time to turn to the fruits of this discourse. For the Constitution is a sublime oration on the dignity of man, a bold commitment by a people to the ideal of libertarian dignity protected through law. Some reflection is perhaps required before this can be seen.

The Constitution on its face is, in large measure, a structuring text, a blueprint for government. And when the text is not prescribing the form of government it is limiting the powers of that government. The original document, before addition of any of the amendments, does not speak primarily of the rights of man, but of the abilities and disabilities of government. When one reflects upon the text's preoccupation with the scope of government as well as its shape, however, one comes to understand that what this text is about is the relationship of the individual and the state. The text marks the metes and bounds of official authority and individual autonomy. When one studies the boundary that the text marks out, one gets a sense of the vision of the individual embodied in the Constitution.

As augmented by the Bill of Rights and the Civil War Amendments, this text is a sparkling vision of the supremacy of the human dignity of every individual. This vision is reflected in the very choice of democratic self-governance: the supreme value of a democracy is the presumed worth of each individual. And this vision manifests itself most dramatically in the specific prohibitions of the Bill of Rights, a term which I henceforth will apply to describe not only the original first eight amendments, but the Civil War amendments as well. It is a vision that has guided us as a people throughout our history, although the precise rules by which we have protected fundamental human dignity have been transformed over time in response to both transformations of social condition and evolution of our concepts of human dignity. . . .

In general, problems of the relationship of the citizen with government have multiplied and thus have engendered some of the most important constitutional issues of the day. As government acts ever more deeply upon those areas of our lives once marked "private," there is an even greater need to see that individual rights are not curtailed or cheapened in the interest of what may temporarily appear to be the "public good." And as government continues in its role of provider for so many of our disadvantaged citizens, there is an even greater need to ensure that government act with integrity and consistency in its dealings with these citizens. To put this another way, the possibilities for collision between government activity and individual rights will increase as the power and authority of government itself expands, and this growth, in turn, heightens the need for constant vigilance at the collision points. If our free society is to endure, those who govern must recognize human dignity and accept the enforcement of constitutional limitations on their power conceived by the Framers to be necessary to preserve that dignity and the air of freedom which is our proudest heritage. Such recognition will not come from a technical understanding of the organs of government, or the new forms of wealth they administer. It requires something different, something deeper—a personal confrontation with the well-springs of our society. Solutions of constitutional questions from that perspective have become the great challenge of the modern era. All the talk in the last half-decade about shrinking the government does not alter this reality or the challenge it imposes. The modern activist state is a concomitant of the complexity of modern society; it is inevitably with us. We must meet the challenge rather than wish it were not before us.

The challenge is essentially, of course, one to the capacity of our constitutional structure to foster and protect the freedom, the dignity, and the rights of all persons within our borders, which it is the great design of the Constitution to secure. During the time of my public service this challenge has largely taken shape within the confines of the interpretive question whether the specific guarantees of the Bill of Rights operate as restraints on the power of State government. We recognize the Bill of Rights as the primary source of express information as to what is meant by constitutional liberty. The safeguards enshrined in it are deeply etched in the foundation of America's freedoms. Each is a protection with centuries of history behind it, often dearly bought with the blood and lives of people determined to prevent oppression by their rulers. The first eight Amendments, however, were added to the Constitution to operate solely against federal power. It was not until the Thirteenth and Fourteenth Amendments were added, in 1865 and 1868, in response to a demand for national protection against abuses of state power, that the Constitution could be interpreted to require application of the first eight amendments to the states.

It was in particular the Fourteenth Amendment's guarantee that no person be deprived of life, liberty or property without process of law that led us to apply many of the specific guarantees of the Bill of Rights to the States. In my judgment, Justice Cardozo best captured the reasoning that brought us to such decisions when he described what the Court has done as a process by which the guarantees "have been taken over from the earlier articles of the federal bill of rights and brought within the Fourteenth Amendment by a process of absorption . . . [that] has had its source in the belief that neither liberty nor justice would exist if [those guarantees] . . . were sacrificed" {*Palko* v. *Connecticut* [302 U.S. 319, 326 (1937)]}. But this process of absorption was neither swift nor steady. As late as 1922 only the Fifth Amendment guarantee of just compensation for official taking of property had been given force against the states. Between then and 1956 only the First Amendment guarantees of speech and conscience and the Fourth Amendment ban of unreasonable searches and seizures had been incorporated—the latter, however, without the exclusionary rule to give it force. As late as 1961, I could stand before a distinguished assemblage of the bar at New York University's James Madison Lecture and list the following as guarantees that had not been thought to be sufficiently fundamental to the protection of human dignity so as to be enforced against the states: the prohibition of cruel and unusual punishments, the right against self-incrimination, the right to assistance of counsel in a criminal trial, the right to confront witnesses, the right to compulsory process, the right not to be placed in jeopardy of life or limb more than once upon accusation of a crime, the right not to have illegally obtained evidence introduced at a criminal trial, and the right to a jury of one's peers.

The history of the quarter century following that Madison Lecture need not be told in great detail. Suffice it to say that each of the guarantees listed above has been recognized as a fundamental aspect of ordered liberty. Of course, the above catalogue encompasses only the rights of the criminally accused, those caught, rightly or wrongly, in the maw of the criminal justice system. But it has been well said that there is no better test of a society than how it treats those accused of transgressing against it. Indeed, it is because we recognize that incarceration strips a man of his dignity that we demand strict adherence to fair procedure and proof of guilt beyond a reasonable doubt before taking such a drastic step. These requirements are, as Justice Harlan once said, "bottomed on a fundamental value determination of our society that it is far worse to convict an innocent man than to let a guilty man go free" {*In re Winship* [397 U.S. 358, 372 (1970)] (concurring opinion)}. There is no worse injustice than wrongly to strip a man of his dignity. And our adherence to the constitutional vision of human dignity is so strict that even after convicting a person according to these stringent standards, we demand that his dignity be infringed only to the extent appropriate to the crime and never by means of wanton infliction of pain or deprivation. I interpret the Constitution plainly to embody these fundamental values.

Of course the constitutional vision of human dignity has, in this past quarter century, infused far more than our decisions about the criminal process. Recognition of the principle of "one person, one vote" as a constitutional one redeems the promise of self-governance by affirming the essential dignity of every citizen in the right to equal participation in the democratic process. Recognition of so-called "new property" rights in those receiving government entitlements affirms the essential dignity of the least fortunate among us by demanding that government treat with decency, integrity and consistency those dependent on its benefits for their very survival. After all, a legislative majority initially decides to create governmental entitlements; the Constitution's Due Process Clause merely provides protection for entitlements thought necessary by society as a whole. Such due process rights prohibit government from imposing the devil's bargain of bartering away human dignity in exchange for human sustenance. Likewise, recognition of full equality for women—equal protection of the laws—ensures that gender has no bearing on claims to human dignity.

Recognition of broad and deep rights of expression and of conscience reaffirm the vision of human dignity in many ways. They too redeem the promise of self-governance by facilitating—indeed demanding—robust, uninhibited and wide-open debate on issues of public importance. Such public debate is of course vital to the development and dissemination of political ideas. As importantly, robust public discussion is the crucible in which personal political convictions are forged. In our democracy, such discussion is a political duty, it is the essence of self-government. The constitutional vision of human dignity rejects the possibility of political orthodoxy imposed from above; it respects the right of each individual to form and to express political judgments, however far they may deviate from the mainstream and however unsettling they might be to the powerful or the elite. Recognition of these rights of expression and conscience also frees up the private space for both intellectual and spiritual development free of government dominance, either blatant or subtle. Justice Brandeis put it so well sixty years ago when he wrote: "Those who won our independence believed that the final end of the State was to make men free to develop their faculties; and that in its government the deliberative forces should prevail over the arbitrary. They valued liberty both as an end and as a means" {*Whitney* v. *California* [274 U.S. 357, 375 (1927)] (concurring opinion)}.

I do not mean to suggest that we have in the last quarter century achieved a comprehensive definition of the constitutional ideal of human dignity. We are still striving toward that goal, and doubtless it will be an eternal quest. For if the interaction of this Justice and the constitutional text over the years confirms any single proposition, it is that the demands of human dignity will never cease to evolve.

■ DISCUSSION QUESTIONS

1. Should justices of the Supreme Court be guided by the original intention of those who wrote the Constitution and the laws? What are the advantages of this approach to constitutional interpretation? What problems might justices face in trying to ascertain original intention?

2. If original intention is not to be the standard for constitutional interpretation, what can the standard be? How might Brennan respond to Meese's argument that if original intention is rejected, the door is opened to justices arbitrarily pouring their own values and goals into their decisions while claiming to base them on the Constitution?

3. Does the Constitution guarantee only those rights that are specified in its text? Can we derive such things as a right to privacy (the basis for Supreme Court decisions on contraception and abortion) from constitutional values even when the Constitution says nothing about such a right?

4. What is the place of the judiciary in American democracy? Does the Supreme Court's status as an unelected branch require that it play a limited and restrained role? Or does its claim to be the guardian of the Constitution warrant a more active role for the Court on behalf of democratic principles and values?

5. Is it possible to depoliticize the Supreme Court? Can the Supreme Court be removed from the central political controversies of American life?

■ SUGGESTED READINGS AND INTERNET RESOURCES

In *The Tempting of America: The Political Seduction of the Law* (New York: Free Press, 1990), Robert Bork develops a view of constitutional interpretation similar to Meese's and presents a scathing conservative critique of an activist judiciary. Leonard Levy elaborates on Brennan's skeptical view of original intention in his *Original Intent and the Framers' Constitution* (New York: Macmillan Co., 1988). A skeptical argument that the judiciary cannot be the agent of social justice that Brennan envisions can be found in Gerald Rosenberg, *The Hollow Hope: Can Courts Bring About Social Change?* (Chicago: The University of Chicago Press, 1991). The judiciary has been criticized from the left as well as from the right; for radical perspectives, see David Kairys, ed., *The Politics of Law: A Progressive Critique,* 3rd ed. (New York: Basic Books, 1998). An argument for a populist constitutional law that would deny the judicial branch the exclusive authority to interpret the Constitution is Mark Tushnet, *Taking the Constitution Away from the Courts* (Princeton, N.J.: Princeton University Press, 1999).

The Federalist Society
http://www.fed-soc.org/
The web site of a prominent organization of conservative lawyers, offering perspectives on recent Supreme Court cases and other legal issues.

The American Civil Liberties Union
http://www.aclu.org/
Legal issues and court cases viewed from the perspective of the group that has argued many of the most prominent civil liberties issues before the U.S. Supreme Court.

University of Pittsburgh School of Law
http://www.jurist.law.pitt.edu
This site provides Supreme Court opinions and stories on constitutional law.

17

Economic Inequality: A Threat to Democracy?

The United States has always prided itself on being a land of opportunity. Unlike the class-divided societies of Europe, American society is viewed as being more fluid and open to individual ambition. In the United States you can rise from "rags to riches," as the saying goes. The "American Dream," which is defined in many different ways but almost always involves economic success, is supposedly within everyone's grasp. Millions of immigrants have been drawn to our shores by the lure of the "American Dream." Not only is the United States a land of opportunity and upward mobility, but it is generally believed that we lack the extremes of wealth and poverty that characterize other societies. The United States is viewed as basically a middle-class society.

Almost everyone agrees that equal opportunity and a strong middle class are essential to the healthy functioning of American society and its political system. Throughout U.S. history, however, debates have periodically erupted about how to guarantee equal opportunity and how much economic inequality should be tolerated in a democracy before government needs to take action. One of the first such debates was between two giants of American political history, Thomas Jefferson and Alexander Hamilton. Jefferson argued that the stability of American democracy rested on the backs of small farmers who, because they made a living through their own efforts on their own land, were free to speak out and participate fully in politics without any fears. Jefferson felt

that manufacturing and large cities created wide inequalities and dangerous de-
pendencies that corrupted democracy. His opponent, Alexander Hamilton, was
much less fearful of economic inequalities. In his *Report on Manufactures,*
Hamilton argued that the government should encourage manufacturing as a
way to tie the wealthy classes to government, thus providing a check against
the turbulence of the masses.

In the long run, Hamilton's vision of industrial expansion prevailed over Jefferson's agricultural ideal. After the Civil War (1861–1865), industry really
began to take off. Entrepreneurs, like Andrew Carnegie and John D. Rockefeller,
amassed huge fortunes the likes of which had never been seen before in the
New World. At the same time, millions of immigrants poured into U.S. cities to
work in industry at low wages and long hours. Many observers believed that
events were proving Jefferson's fears correct. Mark Twain called the "Gilded
Age" a time of money lust. Muckraking journalists exposed the ways that
Robber Barons corrupted the political process, sometimes buying off whole
state legislatures. The Populist movement of the late nineteenth century fought
to protect the small farmer and limit the power of corporations. It proposed
antitrust legislation to break up the large corporations, expanding the money
supply to ease the debt burden on the small farmers, and a federal income tax
to redistribute wealth.

The opponents of the Populists vigorously denied that industrialism was
creating unfair inequalities that threatened American democracy. They did not
deny that some people were very rich and others quite poor, but they argued
that these inequalities were a natural result of economic competition that
brought great benefits to all of society. Social Darwinists applied Charles
Darwin's theory of human evolution to society, arguing that inequalities were a
result of economic competition which resulted in the "survival of the fittest."
Great wealth was the result of hard work and entrepreneurial genius. As the
prominent Social Darwinist William Graham Sumner put it: "No man can
acquire a million without helping a million men to increase their little fortunes
all the way down all through the social grades." The United States was a land of
opportunity where self-made men could rise up out of the working class to
great riches. Indeed, there were many examples, besides Carnegie and
Rockefeller, to point to. The principles of Social Darwinism were spread to the
broad public by a "success" literature that told vivid stories of poor boys rising
up out of poverty through hard work and moral uprightness. A Unitarian minister by the name of Horatio Alger published 106 such rags-to-riches books from
1868 to 1904, many of which became best-sellers.

A century later the democratic debate about economic inequality is once
again heating up, albeit in very different economic circumstances. From World
War II until the 1970s, most observers agree that economic inequalities
remained the same or even shrank somewhat. Sometime in the 1970s,
however, wages began to stagnate and even fall for most workers. Many
reasons have been offered for this. Global competition has put downward pressure on U.S. industrial wages, which now must often compete with wages in
Third World countries. It is not so much the decline in manufacturing wages as

the shift from manufacturing to services that is hurting wages for many workers. Manufacturing employment has declined as jobs have migrated abroad and workers are replaced by machines, including industrial robots. Wages in the expanding service sector are generally lower than in manufacturing. Partly driven by the spread of computers into practically every workplace, education and skills have become even more important to earning a good wage. The wages of those with a high school education and less have fallen, while those with postgraduate degrees have seen their salaries soar. You can no longer earn a decent wage simply by having a strong back and being willing to work hard.

Like the Gilded Age, in the present period at the same time that many workers are struggling to get by, huge fortunes are being amassed at the top. The incredible bull market on Wall Street that began in the late 1980s has brought fantastic returns for those who hold stocks. Technological breakthroughs in computer technology have generated tremendous opportunities for daring entrepreneurs to accumulate vast wealth. Personal computers, software, and the development of the internet have created wealth more rapidly than at any time in American history. Some internet companies, such as Amazon.com, saw their stock values soar into the billions even though they had never earned a profit. Bill Gates, the founder of Microsoft, which supplies the operating system for most personal computers, is now the richest man in the world, worth well over $100 billion (that's billion, not million!). His fortune, even after correcting for inflation, is many times that of John D. Rockefeller. Reminiscent of the government's effort to break up Rockefeller's Standard Oil Trust, the federal government is prosecuting Microsoft for antitrust violations.

As with the inequalities generated by nineteenth-century industrialism, the inequalities of the so-called postindustrial economy have prompted a spirited political and policy debate. When deindustrialization hit with a vengeance in the 1980s, many people called for the United States to engage in industrial planning, similar to that done by Japan. National industrial planning never took off, however. Instead, led by President Ronald Reagan (1981–1989), the United States pursued a very different approach. Reagan argued that government regulation and high taxes were choking off economic growth. Reagan's supply-side economics recommended cutting taxes in order to increase incentives to work hard and invest. Inequalities were necessary as a goad to work hard and in the long run everyone would benefit from a growing economy. "A rising tide would lift all boats."

Bill Clinton campaigned for the presidency in 1992 on a call for the government to address inequalities. Among other things, Clinton called for a national health insurance program and greater investments in education and job training for American workers. Although Clinton lost on health insurance and largely jettisoned his proposals to invest in American workers in order to reduce the deficit, throughout his presidency he advocated government programs, such as increasing the minimum wage, to help those who were being left behind by the booming economy. Clinton strongly supported free trade, but many, most notably Pat Buchanan and Ross Perot, attacked free trade for exporting U.S. jobs (Perot's "giant sucking sound").

The two selections that follow address the contemporary inequality debate in our rapidly changing economy. The first excerpt is from a 1999 book entitled *Myths of Rich and Poor* by W. Michael Cox, chief economist at the Federal Reserve Bank of Dallas, and Richard Alm. Acknowledging that some statistics show wide and widening income inequalities (Figures 1 and 2), they maintain that these inequalities are not threatening. According to Cox and Alm, we should not concentrate on the gap between the top and the bottom, but instead we should focus on whether those at the bottom are better or worse off. In the book from which this excerpt is taken, the authors make a convincing case that those at the bottom generally are better off in terms of *consumption*. Breakthroughs in technology mean that we have more conveniences than ever, like VCRs, color TVs, and telephone answering machines. In addition, these devices which enhance the quality of our lives are more efficient and powerful than ever (consider the improvement in home computers in recent years). In the section we have chosen, Cox and Alm make the point that snapshots of inequality at one point in time do not capture the movement of people out of poverty over their lifetimes. It is still a land of opportunity, they argue.

Paul Krugman, an iconoclastic MIT economist, argues in our other selection that it is precisely the gap between the rich and the poor that we should be focusing on. A middle-class nation, Krugman says, is a nation where "most people live more or less the same kind of life." Increasingly, however, those at the top are living very different lives from the rest of us; they are withdrawing into residential enclaves that make them feel little connection to the lives of ordinary people. For Krugman, rising inequalities are partly caused by economic factors, such as global competition and new technologies. For the rest of the story, he says, we must look to changing values by corporations and the power they wield compared to the declining power of labor unions. The danger, Krugman suggests, is that growing inequalities reinforce themselves in a vicious cycle of spiraling inequality that could tear American society apart. What we need are new public policies, like those of Franklin Roosevelt's New Deal, that can reverse the process of widening inequalities.

Before reading the two selections, you may want to look back at the discussion of inequality in the Introduction to this book. Do the authors take a process orientation toward equality or a results orientation? Why do Cox and Alm think we should focus on what those at the bottom are able to consume, whereas Krugman says little about this and instead concentrates on the gap between the top and the bottom? Krugman clearly thinks that it is the political power of those at the top that is partly responsible for rising inequalities. What do Cox and Alm say is the cause of income differences?

Myths of Rich and Poor

W. MICHAEL COX
AND RICHARD ALM

"Land of Opportunity." Anywhere in the world, those three words bring to mind just one place: the United States of America.

Opportunity defines our heritage. The American saga entails waves of immigrant farmers, shopkeepers, laborers, and entrepreneurs, all coming to the United States for the promise of a better life. Some amassed enormous fortunes—the Rockefellers, the Carnegies, the DuPonts, the Fords, the Vanderbilts, to name just a few. Even today, America's opportunity is always on display. Bill Gates in computer software, Ross Perot in data processing, Bill Cosby and Oprah Winfrey in entertainment, Warren Buffett in investing, Sam Walton in retailing, Michael Jordan in sports, and Mary Kay Ash in cosmetics could head a list of the many thousands who catapulted from society's lower or middle ranks to the top. Many millions more, descendants of those who arrived with little more than the clothes on their backs and a few bucks in their pockets, took advantage of an open economic system to improve their lot in life through talent and hard work.

Even pessimists acknowledge that the Gateses, Perots, Cosbys, Winfreys, Buffetts, Waltons, Jordans, and Ashes are getting filthy rich, along with Wall Street's wheeler-dealers, Hollywood moguls, and big-league ballplayers. At the nation's 350 largest companies, top executives' median total compensation in 1996 was $3.1 million, or 90 times what a typical factory hand earns. We often hear that ordinary Americans aren't keeping up, that success isn't as easy, or at least not as democratic, as it once was. At the close of the twentieth century, one disturbing vision portrays the United States as a society pulling apart at the seams, divided into separate and unequal camps, an enclave of fat cats gorging themselves on the fruits of others' labor surrounded by a working class left with ever more meager opportunities.

The most-cited evidence of ebbing opportunity is the *distribution of income*—the slicing up of the American pie. Examining the data, analysts seize on two points. First, there's a marked inequality in earnings between society's haves and have-nots. Second, and perhaps more ominous, the gap between the richest and poorest households has widened over the past two decades. The Census Bureau provides the statistical ballast for these claims. In 1997, the top 20 percent of American households received almost half of the nation's income. Average earnings among this group are $122,764 a year. The distribution of income to the four other groups of 20 percent was as follows: The second fifth had 23.2 percent, with average earnings of $57,582; the third fifth had 15.0 percent, with average earnings of $37,177; the fourth fifth had 8.9 percent, with average earnings of $22,098. The bottom 20 percent earned 3.6 percent of the economic pie, or an average of $8,872 a year (Figure 1).

The case for the existence of a growing rift between rich and poor rests on longer-term trends in the same Census Bureau data. Since 1975, only the top 20 percent of Americans managed to expand their allotment of the nation's income—from 43.2 percent to 49.4 percent. Over the same period, the distribution to the middle three groups slipped slightly. The share going to the lowest 20 percent of income earners fell from 4.4 percent to 3.6 percent. The shift of income toward the upper end of the distribution becomes even more striking when it's put in dollars. After adjusting for inflation, the income of households in the bottom 20 percent increased by only $207 from 1975 to 1997. The top tier, meanwhile, jumped by $37,633 (Figure 2).

Once again, the pessimists have it wrong. The income distribution only reveals how one group is doing relative to others at a particular moment. That kind of you-vs.-me score keeping has little to do with whether any American can get ahead. By its very nature, opportunity is individual rather than collective. Even for an individual, the concept can't be divorced from

FIGURE 1—Slicing Up the American Pie

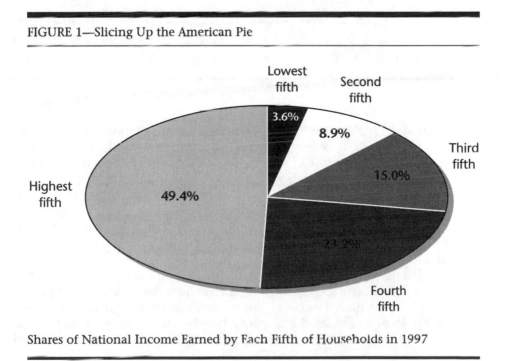

Shares of National Income Earned by Each Fifth of Households in 1997

FIGURE 2—A Caste Society?

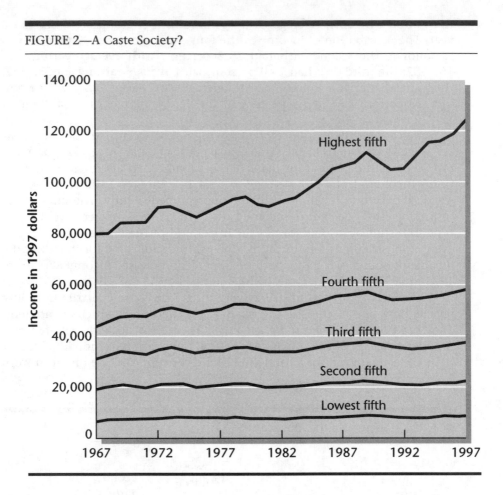

its time element, an assessment of how well someone is doing today relative to yesterday, or how he can expect to do tomorrow compared to today. How many of us worked our way up? How quickly did we move from one rung to the next? How many of us fell? Studies of income inequality cannot say whether individuals are doing better or worse. They lump together Americans who differ in age, educational level, work effort, family and marital status, gender and race. The sample never stays the same from one year to another, and researchers haven't a clue about what happened to any individual in the income distribution.

Annual snapshots of the income distribution might deserve attention if we lived in a caste society, with rigid class lines determining who gets what share of the national income—but we don't live in a caste society. It takes a heroic leap to look at the disparity between rich and poor and conclude that any one individual's chances of getting ahead aren't what they used to be. Even the most sophisticated income-distribution statistics fail to tell us what we really want to know: Are the majority of Americans losing their birthright—a chance at upward mobility? Static portraits, moreover, don't tell us whether low-income households tend to remain at the bottom year after year. By definition, a fifth of society will always inhabit the lowest 20 percent of the income distribution. We don't know, however, whether individuals and families stay there over long periods. It's no great tragedy if the bottom rung is where many Americans start to climb the ladder of success. To argue that upward mobility is being lost, we would have to show that the poorest remain stuck where they are, with little hope of making themselves better off. Nothing could be further from the truth. . . .

Making It from Bottom to Top

The Treasury Department affirms that most Americans still have a good shot at upward mobility. In a 1992 analysis covering nine years, researchers found that 86 percent of those in the lowest 20 percent of income earners in 1979 had moved to a higher grouping by 1988. Moreover, 66 percent reached the middle tier or above, with almost 15 percent making it all the way to the top fifth of income earners. Among Americans who started out above the bottom fifth in 1979, the Treasury found the same movement up the income ladder. Nearly 50 percent of those in the middle tier, for example, rose into the top two groupings, overwhelming whatever downward mobility that took place. . . .

In addition to confirming that most Americans are still getting ahead in life, the Treasury study verifies that the quickest rise occurs among the young, an antidote to the prevailing ennui among the so-called Generation X. It also found that wage and salary income was primarily responsible for pushing people upward in the distribution, indicating that work, not luck, is the widest path to opportunity. Ours is not a *Wheel of Fortune* economy, where a few lucky individuals win big, leaving paltry gains to the great mass of people. Most of us get ahead because we strive to make ourselves and our families better off.

By carefully tracking individuals' incomes over many years, . . . the Treasury study show[s] that our economic system is biased toward success. These results should go a long way toward quelling fears of an America polarized between privileged rich and permanently poor. The rich may indeed be getting richer. We ought to have little problem with that. The poor are also getting richer. We ought to celebrate that. Indeed, what's so encouraging is the ability of those who start out in the lowest income brackets to jump into the middle and upper echelons. There's evidence that most Americans are making their way up the income distribution through education, experience, and hard work.

That's what the American Dream, a dream of opportunity, is all about. . . .

The Common Thread: Lifetime Earnings

If so many Americans are rising through the income ranks, and if only a few of us stay stuck at the bottom, who makes up the lowest fifth of today's income earners? One group is the downwardly mobile, those who once took in enough money to be in a higher echelon. Descent can be voluntary, usually a result of retirement, or it can be involuntary, resulting from layoffs or other hard luck. Just changing jobs sometimes results in a dip in earnings. We've already seen, though, that downward mobility happens to only a small segment of the population. By far the largest number of low-income earners are new entrants into the world of work, mostly young people. Many of us begin our working lives as part of the bottom 20 percent, either as students with part-time jobs or as relatively unskilled entrants to the labor force. Many immigrants, whatever their age, start off with low incomes.

Although they usually start at the bottom, the young tend to rise through the income distribution as they become better educated, develop skills, and gain experience. In fact, income tends to follow a familiar pattern over a person's lifetime: It rises rapidly in the early years of working, peaks during middle age, then falls toward retirement. When the average earnings at each age are placed side by side, it creates a lifetime earnings profile, shaped like a pyramid.

The changes in lifetime earnings over the past four decades tell us quite a bit about the evolution of our economy. In 1951, workers reached their peak earning years in ages 35 to 44, when their average annual earnings were 1.6 times the income of those in the 20-to-24 age group. By 1973, the ratio had risen to 2.4 to 1. By 1993, the peak earning years had shifted to ages 45 to 54, and workers in this highly paid group earned almost 3.2 times more than the 20-to-24-year-olds. . . .

A steeper lifetime earnings profile reflects greater opportunity. One way to see that is to imagine a perfectly flat pattern of lifetime income, with workers earning the same income every year. Paychecks for the middle years of life would match those for the early twenties. This would be a world devoid of upward mobility, offering workers no prospect of getting ahead during their lifetimes, no matter what their effort, no matter how much they improve their worth on the job.

What is behind the faster rise in Americans' lifetime earnings? Most likely, it's the by-product of broad changes in the way we work. When the economy was largely industrial, Americans worked with their hands and their backs. Today, more Americans than ever owe their paychecks to brainpower. The skills of the mind, unlike those of the body, are cumulative. Mental talents continue to sharpen long after muscles and dexterity begin to falter. These facts of physiology and economic development probably explain why the peak earning years have shifted to older age groups in the past two decades. As the United States retools itself for a more knowledge-intensive era, as the country moves from a blue-collar economy to a white-collar one, the rewards for education and experience are increasing.

The lifetime earnings profile is the thread that sews together recent trends in upward mobility and income inequality. As today's workers reap greater rewards for what they've learned on the job, earnings become sharply higher with experience. It's not that today's young workers are falling behind their counterparts of earlier generations. On the contrary, older workers are doing so much better than they used to. The result is an increase in the gap between youth and middle age. In the end, the steepening of lifetime earnings leads us to a surprising conclusion: Upward mobility may well be an important factor in the widening gap in income distribution.

All told, this isn't the harsh world seen by those who say the rich are getting richer and the poor are getting poorer. Both rich and poor are becoming better off. Are most of us going nowhere? Quite the contrary; the majority of Americans are busy climbing the income ladder. Greater returns to education and experience can skew income toward the upper end, but we would be foolhardy indeed to become so obsessed with the pecking order that we lose sight of what's really important—opportunity.

A steeper lifetime earnings profile also puts a different slant on the notion of a vanishing middle class. The center of the income distribution isn't a destination. It's just one step on the ladder of upward mobility. Forty years ago, with a flatter earnings profile, families spent most of their working lives in the middle income brackets. Today's more rapid rise in incomes means they move to the top faster, spending less time defined as "middle class." Worries about Generation X's future can be put to rest, too. Those entering the labor force in the 1900s may look at their parents' income and wonder how they will ever attain such heights. They should, however, find a steeper earnings profile encouraging. During their first two or three decades in the labor market, young workers are likely to see their incomes rise more quickly than their parents' did.

In the United States, getting ahead isn't a great mystery. The economy provides opportunity—more, in fact, than ever before—but it's up to each of us to grab it. Success isn't random. Luck and Daddy's money aren't the way most Americans get to the top. More often than not, the rewards go to education, experience, talent, ambition, vision, risk taking, readiness to change, and just plain hard work. Young people aren't guaranteed success any more than their parents were. Their chances will improve, though, if they make the right choices in life. Opportunity lies in the advice given by generations of parents and teachers: Study, work hard, and save. In short, the best advice for economic success is this: Listen to your elders. . . .

Inequality Is Not Inequity

Judging from the public debate, at least some Americans would prefer a more equal distribution of income to a less equal one, perhaps on moral grounds, perhaps as a part of an ideal of civic virtue. There's no *economic* reason, however, to prefer one pattern of income distribution over another.

In fact, the income statistics do little but confirm what's obvious: America isn't an egalitarian society. It wasn't designed to be. Socialism, a failed and receding system, sought to impose an artificial equality. Capitalism, a successful and expanding system, doesn't fight a fundamental fact of human nature—we vary greatly in capabilities, motivation, interests, and preferences. Some of us are driven to get ahead. Some of us are just plain lazy. Some of us are willing to work hard so we can afford a lifestyle rich in material goods. Some of us work just hard enough to provide a roof overhead, food, clothes, and a few amenities. It shouldn't come as a surprise that our incomes vary greatly.

Income inequality isn't an aberration. Quite the opposite, it's perfectly consistent with the laws that govern a free-enterprise system. In the early 1970s, three groups of unemployed Canadians, all in their twenties, all with at least 12 years of schooling, volunteered to participate in a stylized economy where the only employment was making woolen belts on small hand looms. They could work as much or as little as they liked, earning $2.50 for each belt. After 98 days, the results were anything but equal: 37.2 percent of the economy's income went to the 20 percent with the highest earnings. The bottom 20 percent received only 6.6 percent. This economic microcosm tells us one thing: Even among similar people with identical work options, some workers will earn more than others.

In a modern economy, incomes vary for plenty of reasons having little to do with fairness or equity. Education and experience, for example, usually yield higher pay. As industry becomes more sophisticated, the rewards to skilled labor tend to rise, adding to the number of high-income earners. Location matters. New Yorkers earn more than Mississippians. Lifestyle choices play a part, too. Simply by having an additional paycheck, two-income families make more money than those with a single breadwinner. Longer retirements, however, will add to the number of households with low income, even if many senior citizens live well from their savings. Demographic changes can twist the distribution of income. As the Baby Boom enters its peak earning years, the number of high-income households ought to rise. Economic forces create ripples in what we earn. The ebb and flow of industries can shift workers to both ends of the income distribution. Layoffs put some Americans into low-income groups, at least temporarily. Companies with new products and new technologies create jobs and, in most cases, share the bounty by offering workers higher pay. In technology industries, bonuses and stock options are becoming more common. Higher rates of return on investments—with, for example, a stock-market boom— will create a windfall for households with money riding on financial markets.

In and of itself, moreover, income distribution doesn't say much about the performance of an economy or the opportunities it offers. A widening gap isn't necessarily a sign of failure, nor does a narrowing one guarantee that an economy is functioning well. As a matter of fact, it's quite common to find a widening of income distribution in boom times, when almost everyone's earnings are rising rapidly. All it takes is for one segment of the workforce to become better off faster than others. However, the distribution can narrow in hard times, as companies facing declining demand cut back on jobs, hours, raises, and bonuses. In fact, we often see a compression of incomes in areas where people are sinking into poverty.

There's no denying that our system allows some Americans to become much richer than others. We must accept that, even celebrate it. Opportunity, not equality of income, is what made the U.S. economy grow and prosper. It's most important to provide equality of opportunity, not equality of results. There's ample evidence to refute any suggestion that the economy is no longer capable of providing opportunity for the vast majority of Americans. At the end of the twentieth century, upward mobility is alive and well. Even the lower-income households are sharing in the country's progress. What's more, data suggest that the populist view of America as a society torn between haves and have-nots, with rigid class lines, is just plain wrong. We are by no means a caste society.

The Spiral
of Inequality

PAUL KRUGMAN

Ever since the election of Ronald Reagan, right-wing radicals have insisted that they started a revolution in America. They are half right. If by a revolution we mean a change in politics, economics, and society that is so large as to transform the character of the nation, then there is indeed a revolution in progress. The radical right did not make this revolution, although it has done its best to help it along. If anything, we might say that the revolution created the new right. But whatever the cause, it has become urgent that we appreciate the depth and significance of this new American revolution—and try to stop it before it becomes irreversible.

The consequences of the revolution are obvious in cities across the nation. Since I know the area well, let me take you on a walk down University Avenue in Palo Alto, California.

Palo Alto is the de facto village green of Silicon Valley, a tree-lined refuge from the valley's freeways and shopping malls. People want to live here despite the cost—rumor has it that a modest three-bedroom house sold recently for $1.6 million—and walking along University you can see why. Attractive, casually dressed people stroll past trendy boutiques and restaurants; you can see a cooking class in progress at the fancy new kitchenware store. It's a cheerful scene, even if you have to detour around the people sleeping in doorways and have to avoid eye contact with the beggars. (The town council plans to crack down on street people, so they probably won't be here next year, anyway.)

If you tire of the shopping district and want to wander further afield, you might continue down University Avenue, past the houses with their well-tended lawns and flower beds—usually there are a couple of pickup trucks full of Hispanic gardeners in sight. But don't wander too far. When University crosses Highway 101, it enters the grim environs of East Palo Alto. Though it has progressed in the past few years, as recently as 1992 East Palo Alto was the murder capital of the nation and had an unemployment rate hovering around 40 percent. Luckily, near the boundary, where there is a cluster of liquor stores and check-cashing outlets, you can find two or three police cruisers keeping an eye on the scene—and, not incidentally, serving as a thin blue line protecting the nice neighborhood behind them.

Nor do you want to head down 101 to the south, to "Dilbert Country" with its ranks of low-rise apartments, the tenements of the modern proletariat—the places from which hordes of lower-level white-collar workers drive to sit in their cubicles by day and to which they return to watch their VCRs by night.

No. Better to head up into the hills. The "estates" brochure at Coldwell Banker real estate describes the mid-Peninsula as "an area of intense equestrian character," and when you ascend to Woodside-Atherton, which the *New York Times* has recently called one of "America's born-again Newports," there are indeed plenty of horses, as well as some pretty imposing houses. If you look hard enough, you might catch a glimpse of one of the new $10 million-plus mansions that are going up in growing numbers.

What few people realize is that this vast gap between the affluent few and the bulk of ordinary Americans is a relatively new fixture on our social landscape. People believe these scenes are nothing new, even that it is utopian to imagine it could be otherwise.

But it has not always been thus—at least not to the same extent. I didn't see Palo Alto in 1970, but longtime residents report that it was a mixed town in which not only executives and speculators but schoolteachers, mailmen, and sheet-metal workers could afford to live. At the time, I lived on Long Island, not far from the old *Great Gatsby* area on the North Shore. Few of the great mansions were still private homes then (who could afford the servants?); they had been converted into junior colleges and nursing homes, or deeded to the state as historic monuments. Like Palo Alto, the towns contained a mix of occupations and education levels—no surprise, given that skilled blue-collar workers often made as much as, or more than, white-collar middle managers.

Now, of course, Gatsby is back. New mansions, grander than the old, are rising by the score; keeping servants, it seems, is no longer a problem. A couple of years ago I had dinner with a group of New York investment bankers. After the business was concluded, the talk turned to their weekend homes in the Hamptons. Naively, I asked whether that wasn't a long drive: after a moment of confused silence, the answer came back: "But the helicopter only takes half an hour."

You can confirm what your eyes see, in Palo Alto or in any American community, with dozens of statistics. The most straightforward are those on income shares supplied by the Bureau of the Census, whose statistics are among the most rigorously apolitical. In 1970, according to the bureau, the bottom 20 percent of U.S. families received only 5.4 percent of the income, while the top 5 percent received 15.6 percent. By 1994, the bottom fifth had only 4.2 percent, while the top 5 percent had increased its share to 20.1 percent. That means that in 1994, the average income among the top 5 percent of families was more than 19 times that of the bottom 20 percent of families. In 1970, it had been only about 11.5 times as much. (Incidentally, while the change in distribution is most visible at the top and bottom, families in the middle have also lost: The income share of the middle 20 percent of families has fallen from 17.6 to 15.7 percent.) These are not abstract numbers. They are the statistical signature of a seismic shift in the character of our society.

The American notion of what constitutes the middle class has always been a bit strange, because both people who are quite poor and those who are objectively way up the scale tend to think of themselves as being in the middle. But if calling America a middle-class nation means anything, it means that we are a society in which most people live more or less the same kind of life.

In 1970 we were that kind of society. Today we are not, and we become less like one with each passing year. As politicians compete over who really stands for middle-class values, what the public should be asking them is, *What* middle class? How can we have common "middle-class" values if whole segments of society live in vastly different economic universes?

If this election was really about what the candidates claim, it would be devoted to two questions: Why has America ceased to be a middle-class nation? And, more important, what can be done to make it a middle-class nation again?[1]

The Sources of Inequality

Most economists who study wages and income in the United States agree about the radical increase in inequality—only the hired guns of the right still try to claim it is a statistical illusion. But not all agree about why it has happened.

Imports from low-wage countries—a popular villain—are part of the story; but only a fraction of it. The numbers just aren't big enough. We invest

---

1. This was written just before the 1996 presidential election between Bill Clinton and Bob Dole.

billions in low-wage countries—but we invest trillions at home. What we spend on manufactured goods from the Third World represents just 2 percent of our income. Even if we shut out imports from low-wage countries (cutting off the only source of hope for the people who work in those factories), most estimates suggest it would raise the wages of low-skill workers here by only 1 or 2 percent.

Information technology is a more plausible villain. Technological advance doesn't always favor elite workers, but since 1970 there has been clear evidence of a general "skill bias" toward technological change. Companies began to replace low-skill workers with smaller numbers of high-skill ones, and they continue to do so even though low-skill workers have gotten cheaper and high-skill workers more expensive.

These forces, while easily measurable, don't fully explain the disparity between the haves and the have-nots. Globalization and technology may explain why a college degree makes more difference now than it did 20 years ago. But schoolteachers and corporate CEOs typically have about the same amount of formal education. Why, then, have teachers' salaries remained flat while those of CEOs have increased fivefold? The impact of technology and of foreign trade do not answer why it is harder today for most people to make a living but easier for a few to make a killing. Something else is going on.

Values, Power, and Wages

In 1970 the CEO of a typical Fortune 500 corporation earned about 35 times as much as the average manufacturing employee. It would have been unthinkable to pay him 150 times the average, as is now common, and downright outrageous to do so while announcing mass layoffs and cutting the real earnings of many of the company's workers, especially those who were paid the least to start with. So how did the unthinkable become first thinkable, then doable, and finally—if we believe the CEOs—unavoidable?

The answer is that values changed—not the middle-class values politicians keep talking about, but the kind of values that helped to sustain the middle-class society we have lost.

Twenty-five years ago, prosperous companies could have paid their janitors minimum wage and still could have found people to do the work. They didn't, because it would have been bad for company morale. Then, as now, CEOs were in a position to arrange for very high salaries for themselves, whatever their performance, but corporate boards restrained such excesses, knowing that too great a disparity between the top man and the ordinary worker would cause problems. In short, though America was a society with large disparities between economic classes, it had an egalitarian ethic that limited those disparities. That ethic is gone.

One reason for the change is a sort of herd behavior: When most companies hesitated to pay huge salaries at the top and minimum wage at the bottom, any company that did so would have stood out as an example of greed; when everyone does it, the stigma disappears.

There is also the matter of power. In 1970 a company that appeared too greedy risked real trouble with other powerful forces in society. It would have had problems with its union if it had one, or faced the threat of union organizers if it didn't. And its actions would have created difficulties with the government in a way that is now unthinkable. (Can anyone imagine a current president confronting a major industry over price increases, the way John F. Kennedy did the steel industry?)

Those restraining forces have largely disappeared. The union movement is a shadow of its former self, lucky to hold its ground in a defensive battle now and then. The idea that a company would be punished by the government for paying its CEO too much and its workers too little is laughable today: since the election of Ronald Reagan the CEO would more likely be invited to a White House dinner.

In brief, much of the polarization of American society can be explained in terms of power and politics. But why has the tide run so strongly in favor of the rich that it continues regardless of who is in the White House and who controls the Congress?

The Decline of Labor

The decline of the labor movement in the United States is both a major cause of growing inequality and an illustration of the larger process under way in our society. Unions now represent less than 12 percent of the private workforce, and their power has declined dramatically. In 1970 some 2.5 million workers participated in some form of labor stoppage; in 1993, fewer than 200,000 did. Because unions are rarely able or willing to strike, being a union member no longer carries much of a payoff in higher wages.

There are a number of reasons for the decline of organized labor: the shift from manufacturing to services and from blue-collar to white-collar work, growing international competition, and deregulation. But these factors can't explain the extent or the suddenness of labor's decline.

The best explanation seems to be that the union movement fell below critical mass. Unions are good for unions: In a nation with a powerful labor movement, workers have a sense of solidarity, one union can support another during a strike, and politicians take union interests seriously. America's union movement just got too small, and it imploded.

We should not idealize the unions. When they played a powerful role in America, they often did so to bad effect. Occasionally they were corrupt, often they extracted higher wages at the consumer's expense, sometimes they opposed new technologies and enforced inefficient practices. But unions helped keep us a middle-class society—not only because they forced greater equality within companies, but because they provided a counterweight to the power of wealthy individuals and corporations. The loss of that counter-weight is clearly bad for society.

The point is that a major force that kept America a more or less unified society went into a tailspin. Our whole society is now well into a similar downward spiral, in which growing inequality creates the political and economic conditions that lead to even more inequality.

The Polarizing Spiral

Textbook political science predicts that in a two-party democracy like the United States, the parties will compete to serve the interests of the median voter—the voter in the middle, richer than half the voters but poorer than the other half. And since ordinary workers are more likely to lose their jobs than strike it rich, the interests of the median voter should include protecting the poor. You might expect, then, the public to demand that government work against the growing divide by taxing the rich more heavily and by increasing benefits for lower-paid workers and the unemployed.

In fact, we have done just the opposite. Tax rates on the wealthy—even with Clinton's modest increase of 1993—are far lower now than in the 1960s. We have allowed public schools and other services that are crucial for middle-income families to deteriorate. Despite the recent increase, the minimum wage has fallen steadily compared with both average wages and the cost of living. And programs for the poor have been savaged: Even before the recent bipartisan gutting of welfare, AFDC payments for a typical family had fallen by a third in real terms since the 1960s.[2]

The reason why government policy has reinforced rather than opposed this growing inequality is obvious: Well-off people have disproportionate political weight. They are more likely to vote—the median voter has a much higher income than the median family—and far more likely to provide the campaign contributions that are so essential in a TV age.

The political center of gravity in this country is therefore not at the median family, with its annual income of $40,000, but way up the scale. With decreasing voter participation and with the decline both of unions and of traditional political machines, the focus of political attention is further up the income ladder than it has been for generations. So never mind what politicians say; political parties are competing to serve the interests of families near the 90th percentile or higher, families that mostly earn $100,000 or more per year.

Because the poles of our society have become so much more unequal, the interests of this political elite diverge increasingly from those of the typical family. A family at the 95th percentile pays a lot more in taxes than a family at the 50th, but it does not receive a correspondingly higher benefit

---

2. The acronym AFDC stands for Aid to Families with Dependent Children, the main federal welfare program from 1935 to 1996.

from public services, such as education. The greater the income gap, the greater the disparity in interests. This translates, because of the clout of the elite, into a constant pressure for lower taxes and reduced public services.

Consider the issue of school vouchers. Many conservatives and even a few liberals are in favor of issuing educational vouchers and allowing parents to choose among competing schools. Let's leave aside the question of what this might do to education and ask what its political implications might be.

Initially, we might imagine, the government would prohibit parents from "topping up" vouchers to buy higher-priced education. But once the program was established, conservatives would insist such a restriction is unfair, maybe even unconstitutional, arguing that parents should have the freedom to spend their money as they wish. Thus, a voucher would become a ticket you could supplement freely. Upper-income families would realize that a reduction in the voucher is to their benefit: They will save more in lowered taxes than they will lose in a decreased education subsidy. So they will press to reduce public spending on education, leading to ever-deteriorating quality for those who cannot afford to spend extra. In the end, the quintessential American tradition of public education for all could collapse.

School vouchers hold another potential that, doubtless, makes them attractive to the conservative elite: They offer a way to break the power of the American union movement in its last remaining stronghold, the public sector. . . . The leaders of the radical right want privatization of schools, of public sanitation—of anything else they can think of—because they know such privatization undermines what remaining opposition exists to their program.

If public schools and other services are left to deteriorate, so will the skills and prospects of those who depend on them, reinforcing the growing inequality of incomes and creating an even greater disparity between the interests of the elite and those of the majority.

Does this sound like America in the '90s? Of course it does. And it doesn't take much imagination to envision what our society will be like if this process continues for another 15 or 20 years. We know all about it from TV, movies, and best-selling novels. While politicians speak of recapturing the virtues of small-town America (which never really existed), the public—extrapolating from the trends it already sees—imagines a *Blade Runner*-style dystopia, in which a few people live in luxury while the majority grovel in Third World standards.

Strategies for the Future

There is no purely economic reason why we cannot reduce inequality in America. If we were willing to spend even a few percent of national income on an enlarged version of the Earned Income Tax Credit, which supplements the earnings of low-wage workers, we could make a dramatic impact on both incomes and job opportunities for the poor and near-poor—bringing a greater number of Americans into the middle class. Nor is the money for such policies lacking: America is by far the least heavily taxed of Western nations and could easily find the resources to pay for a major expansion of programs aimed at limiting inequality.

But of course neither party advanced such proposals during the electoral campaign. The Democrats sounded like Republicans, knowing that in a society with few counterweights to the power of money, any program that even hits at redistribution is political poison. It's no surprise that Bill Clinton's repudiation of his own tax increase took place in front of an audience of wealthy campaign contributors. In this political environment, what politicians would talk of taxing the well-off to help the low-wage worker?

And so, while the agenda of the GOP would surely accelerate the polarizing trend, even Democratic programs now amount only to a delaying action. To get back to the kind of society we had, we need to rebuild the institutions and values that made a middle-class nation possible.

The relatively decent society we had a generation ago was largely the creation of a brief, crucial period in American history: the presidency of Franklin Roosevelt (1933–1945), during the New Deal and especially during the war. That created what economic historian Claudia Goldin called the Great Compression—an era in which a powerful government, reinforced by and in turn reinforcing a newly powerful labor movement, drastically narrowed the gap in income levels through taxes, benefits, minimum wages, and collective bargaining. In effect, Roosevelt created a new, middle-class America, which lasted for more than a generation. We have lost that America, and it will take another Roosevelt, and perhaps the moral equivalent of another war, to get it back.

Until then, however, we can try to reverse some of the damage. To do so requires more than just supporting certain causes. It means thinking strategically—asking whether a policy is not only good in itself but how it will affect the political balance in the future. If a policy change promises to raise average income by a tenth of a percentage point, but will widen the wedge between the interests of the elite and those of the rest, it should be opposed. If a law reduces average income a bit but enhances the power of ordinary workers, it should be supported.

In particular, we also need to apply strategic thinking to the union movement. Union leaders and liberal intellectuals often don't like each other very much, and union victories are often of dubious value to the economy. Nonetheless, if you are worried about the cycle of polarization in this country, you should support policies that make unions stronger, and vociferously oppose those that weaken them. There are some stirrings of life in the union movement—a new, younger leadership with its roots in the service sector has replaced the manufacturing-based old guard, and has won a few political victories. They must be supported, almost regardless of the merits of their particular case. Unions are one of the few *political* counterweights to the power of wealth.

Of course, even to talk about such things causes the right to accuse us of fomenting "class warfare." They want us to believe we are all members of a broad, more or less homogeneous, middle class. But the notion of a middle-class nation was always a stretch. Unless we are prepared to fight the trend toward inequality, it will become a grim joke.

DISCUSSION QUESTIONS

1. Poll your class. Do most members of your class think they will be economically better off or worse off than their parents? Define *better off* and *worse off.*

2. Women (especially single mothers) and minorities are disproportionately poor. Part of the debate on inequality concerns whether existing inequalities reflect people's talents and work efforts or whether there is still significant racial and gender discrimination in job markets. What do you think, and how does your conclusion affect your attitude toward present inequalities?

3. No one favors a complete leveling of income and wealth, nor does anybody want all wealth to be concentrated in a few hands. But where do we draw the line? What level of inequality should be tolerated in our democracy before government is required to take action?

4. Do you think the present level of economic inequality is corrupting our political processes? Would campaign finance laws protect the system from the unaccountable power of money, or do we need to reduce economic inequality itself?

5. In their book, Cox and Alm suggest that, because of technological advances, the average American is better off today than a millionaire was in the 1890s. Agree or disagree.

SUGGESTED READINGS AND INTERNET RESOURCES

For further elaboration of Cox and Alm's argument that nearly everyone is benefiting from our dynamic economy, see their *Myths of Rich and Poor: Why We're Better Off Than We Think* (New York: Basic Books, 1999) from which our excerpt was taken. The best compilation of data on the changing distribution of income and wealth (which can be viewed as a rejoinder to Cox and Alm) is *The State of Working America 1998–99* (Ithaca, N.Y.: Cornell University Press, 1999) by Lawrence Mishel, Jared Bernstein, and John Schmitt. In one of the most controversial books in recent years, *The Bell Curve: Intelligence and Class Structure in American Life* (New York: Free Press, 1994), Richard J. Herrnstein and Charles

Murray argue that economic inequalities in our technological society fairly reflect differences in people's intelligence, or IQ. In *Illusions of Opportunity: The American Dream in Question* (New York: Norton, 1997), John E. Schwarz argues that the "American Dream" is out of reach for many people because there is a shortage of 16 million jobs with decent enough wages to support a family ($7.60 an hour in 1994 dollars, plus health coverage).

United for a Fair Economy
http://www.stw.org/
United for a Fair Economy is a national, nonpartisan organization that spotlights the dangers of growing income and wealth inequality in the United States and coordinates action to reduce the gap.

Economic Policy Institute
http://www.epinet.org/
The Economic Policy Institute is a nonprofit, nonpartisan think tank that seeks to broaden the public debate about strategies to achieve a strong economy. The Institute stresses real world analysis and a concern for the living standards of working people, and it makes its findings accessible to the general public, the media, and policy makers.

The Heritage Foundation
http://www.heritage.org/library/welfare.html
The Heritage Foundation is a conservative think tank whose mission is to formulate and promote public policies based on the principles of free enterprise, limited government, individual freedom, traditional American values, and a strong national defense.

The Cato Institute
http://www.cato.org/
The Cato Institute seeks to broaden the parameters of public policy debate to allow consideration of more options that are consistent with the traditional American principles of limited government.

CHAPTER 18

The United States and the Global Economy: Serving Citizens or Corporate Elites?

F or nearly forty years after World War II, U.S. foreign policymakers fought a Cold War to contain Communism. The costs were often great: massive casualties in Vietnam and Korea, a militarization of U.S. society, and the continuous threat and fear of nuclear holocaust. Fighting the Cold War abroad often endangered democracy at home, as the values of open debate were often victims of governmental secrecy and McCarthyism. Yet by 1991, the Cold War was over. With the collapse of the Soviet Union and nearly all Communist regimes, U.S. foreign policy had apparently won a smashing victory.

Yet the end of simple anti-Communism as a foundation of U.S. foreign policy has posed perplexing new questions. What roles, if any, should the United States play in stemming the seemingly intractable religious and ethnic conflicts and atrocities in places like Bosnia, Kosovo, Chechnya, and Rwanda? Should the United States act alone, with other states, or not at all when rogue states like Yugoslavia and Iraq threaten regional security? And when, if at all, should the United States balance human rights concerns against its economic and security interests?

If often during the Cold War "politics stopped at the water's edge," in the 1990s answers to such questions have sparked spirited debate, fierce partisanship, and frequent policy shifts and uncertainty. "New isolationists," with perennial presidential candidate Pat Buchanan in the lead, are suspicious of government cooperation with international organizations like the United

Nations. Others, like Clinton's Secretary of State Madeleine Albright, call for a new projection of U.S. power in the world and a coordinated political, economic, and military strategy to do so. A third and much less influential group remains skeptical about U.S. global activism, arguing that the military and intelligence agencies formed to fight the Cold War remain both too powerful and expensive now.

These traditional divisions and concerns are important. Yet they all share the increasingly dubious assumption that national governments are the sovereign or at least major actors in the international arena. As the new century dawns, these national governments are seen by many as no longer the primary or even chief actors on the international stage. Perhaps more than ever, what nation-states do, how citizens work, and what they consume are not guided by governments but by the powerful actors that shape the global economy. From the media empires of Rupert Murdoch, Disney, and Time Warner to the operating systems of the world's Microsoft computers, transnational corporations and their investors and managers determine what we know, how we work, and what's fun. Financial institutions—from banks, mutual funds, and currency dealers—have the power to invest, disinvest, employ people, or "downsize" them out of their jobs altogether.

In 1997 and 1998, the burgeoning economic "tigers" of East Asia learned this lesson all too well, as their collapsing currencies and growing debt burdens signaled a sudden "lack of confidence" by global capitalists and investors. Governments and international institutions like the International Monetary Fund (IMF) stepped in to prop up the economies of these countries, but more as firefighters than as doctors. The United States and other wealthy countries lent the East Asian economies new money, in the hopes that international investors would return. However, all this came at a high price to the East Asian workers and creditors, often pushed into unemployment or poverty, and financial loss or ruin by the terms posed by international organizations and investors.

The effects of a new globalized economy dominated by transnational corporations and investors are hardly limited to developing countries like Mexico, South Korea, or Thailand. Reminiscent of the Cold War era, the United States remains the biggest and most powerful economy in the New World. It is the biggest producer and consumer of goods, the headquarters of the bulk of the most important banks and financial and equity markets, and a worldwide innovator in many of the high-technology industries of the future. From Wall Street, and from Capitol Hill and the White House as well, economic globalization looks not only inevitable but a benign force that bolsters U.S. power, prestige, and wealth.

Yet these industries may have little loyalty to the United States and its communities; to keep investors happy, the United States has to continually produce the incentives for people to invest. From a different perspective, the power held by corporations, banks, and investors poses a threat, not only to people's livelihoods and security but also to democracy, the environment, and the dignity and status of labor and citizenship. When investors, banks, and corporations can prowl the world in search of cheap labor, when businesses can come and go from any country with few restraints, and when the price of attracting business may be environmental degradation, economic globalization appears in a very different light.

While Wall Street and Silicon Valley boom, most U.S. wage earners work more hours and for wages that are often less than those in the 1970s. Universal health care, a secure retirement, quality public education, and a healthy environment are for many low- and middle-income workers illusive dreams. In late 1999, the member countries of the World Trade Organization (WTO) met to decide on the next round of rules aiding free trade and the uninterrupted flow of capital and goods in and out of countries. They were met by 50,000 protestors, from European farmers to world environmentalists, from U.S. labor unions to activist students. The protestors demanded more access and more power in the decisions made by states and corporations that affect the lives of the world's population. From their perspective, economic globalization and its effects were the primary and vexing issues facing the U.S. and the world.

Does economic globalization threaten democracy and prosperity or enhance both? In its present form, is it the people's choice or the tyranny of the rich? Can democratic politics control the forces that make for economic globalization? Should it?

The two selections reprinted here present contrasting answers to these questions. The first is written by Thomas Friedman, a *New York Times* columnist and author of the best-selling *The Lexus and the Olive Tree*. Friedman argues that economic globalization is inevitable and that its basic outlines can't be altered by the older structures of the nation-state. A benign but revolutionary process increasing at warp speed, globalization is said to benefit the United States, the country with the political and social institutions and entrepreneurial culture most appropriate to success. Globalization produces some dangers of strife, but its disadvantages are far outweighed by its production of vast new wealth and individual freedom.

David Korten, author of *When Corporations Rule the World* and a political activist, would certainly agree with Friedman about globalization's importance. Yet his perspective on its implications and roots couldn't be more different. Korten sees globalization as the extension of the elite-centered, pro-corporate policies established by the United States and its Allies after World War II. Rather than a world of economic opportunity, Korten sees a planet lurching toward ecological suicide and authoritarian corporate rule over workers and people. Like many who protested at the 1999 WTO meetings in Seattle, Korten envisions a people-centered reinvention of local and regional economies and governments, where workers and consumers can curtail the power of corporate giants and the new international rules that sustain them. Korten's essay is drawn from a speech he gave in Bretton Woods, New Hampshire, site of the famous 1944 conference that established the international economic institutions of the post–World War II capitalist world.

As you read the two essays, consider the following questions: Do the authors have contrasting definitions of economic globalization? How might Korten and Friedman define democracy? Why, for Friedman, is globalism inevitable while for Korten it isn't? When each author speaks of U.S. power, which people and institutions are included and excluded?

Revolution Is U.S.

THOMAS FRIEDMAN

T oday's era of globalization, which replaced the Cold War, is [an] international system with its own unique attributes.

To begin with, the globalization system, unlike the Cold War system, is not static, but a dynamic ongoing process. Globalization involves the inexorable integration of markets, nation-states and technologies to a degree never witnessed before—in a way that is enabling individuals, corporations and nation-states to reach around the world farther, faster, deeper and cheaper than ever before, and in a way that is also producing a powerful backlash from those brutalized or left behind by this new system.

The driving idea behind globalization is free-market capitalism—the more you let market forces rule and the more you open your economy to free trade and competition, the more efficient and flourishing your economy will be. Globalization means the spread of free-market capitalism to virtually every country in the world. Globalization also has its own set of economic rules—rules that revolve around opening, deregulating and privatizing your economy.

Unlike the Cold War system, globalization has its own dominant culture, which is why it tends to be homogenizing. In previous eras this sort of cultural homogenization happened on a regional scale. . . . Culturally speaking, globalization is largely, though not entirely, the spread of Americanization—from Big Macs to iMacs to Mickey Mouse—on a global scale.

Globalization has its own defining technologies: computerization, miniaturization, digitization, satellite communications, fiber optics and the Internet. And these technologies helped to create the defining perspective of globalization. If the defining perspective of the Cold War world was "division," the defining perspective of globalization is "integration." The symbol of the Cold War system was a wall, which divided everyone. The symbol of the globalization system is a World Wide Web, which unites everyone. The defining document of the Cold War system was "The Treaty." The defining document of the globalization system is "The Deal." . . .

While the defining measurement of the Cold War was weight—particularly the throw weight of missiles—the defining measurement of the globalization system is speed—speed of commerce, travel, communication and innovation. The Cold War was about Einstein's mass-energy equation, $e = mc^2$. Globalization is about Moore's law, which states that the computing power of silicon chips will double every eighteen to twenty-four months. In the Cold War, the most frequently asked question was: "How big is your missile?" In globalization, the most frequently asked question is: "How fast is your modem?" . . .

. . . If the Cold War were a sport, it would be sumo wrestling, says Johns Hopkins University foreign affairs professor Michael Mandelbaum. "It would be two big fat guys in a ring, with all sorts of posturing and rituals and stomping of feet, but actually very little contact, until the end of the match, when there is a brief moment of shoving and the loser gets pushed out of the ring, but nobody gets killed."

By contrast, if globalization were a sport, it would be the 100-meter dash, over and over and over. And no matter how many times you win, you have to race again the next day. And if you lose by just one-hundredth of a second it can be as if you lost by an hour. . . .

To paraphrase German political theorist Carl Schmitt, the Cold War was a world of "friends" and "enemies." The globalization world, by contrast, tends to turn all friends and enemies into "competitors." . . .

In the Cold War we reached for the hot line between the White House and the Kremlin—a symbol that we were all divided but at least someone, the two superpowers, was in charge. In the era of globalization we reach for the Internet—a symbol that we are all connected but nobody is in charge. The defining defense system of the Cold War was radar—to expose the threats coming from the other side of the wall. The defining defense system of the globalization era is the X-ray machine—to expose the threats coming from within.

Globalization also has its own demographic pattern—a rapid acceleration of the movement of people from rural areas and agricultural lifestyles to urban lifestyles more intimately linked with global fashion, food, markets and entertainment trends.

Last, and most important, globalization has its own defining structure of power, which is much more complex than the Cold War structure. The Cold War system was built exclusively around nation-states, and it was balanced at the center by two superpowers: the United States and the Soviet Union.

The globalization system, by contrast, is built around three balances. The first is the traditional balance between nation-states. In the globalization system, the United States is now the sole and dominant superpower and all other nations are subordinate to it to one degree or another. . . .

The second balance in the globalization system is between nation-states and global markets. These global markets are made up of millions of investors moving money around the world with the click of a mouse. I call them "the Electronic Herd," and this herd gathers in key global financial centers, such as Wall Street, Hong Kong, London and Frankfurt, which I call "the Supermarkets." The attitudes and actions of the Electronic Herd and the Supermarkets can have a huge impact on nation-states today, even to the point of triggering the downfall of governments. . . .

The third balance that you have to pay attention to in the globalization system—the one that is really the newest of all—is the balance between individuals and nation-states. Because globalization has brought down many of the walls that limited the movement and reach of people, and because it has simultaneously wired the world into networks, it gives more power to individuals to influence both markets and nation-states than at any time in history. . . .

Five Gas Stations

I believe in the five gas stations theory of the world.

That's right: I believe you can reduce the world's economies today to basically five different gas stations. First there is the Japanese gas station. Gas is $5 a gallon. Four men in uniforms and white gloves, with lifetime employment contracts, wait on you. They pump your gas. They change your oil. They wash your windows, and they wave at you with a friendly smile as you drive away in peace. Second is the American gas station. Gas costs only $1 a gallon, but you pump it yourself. You wash your own windows. You fill your own tires. And when you drive around the corner four homeless people try to steal your hubcaps. Third is the Western European gas station. Gas there also costs $5 a gallon. There is only one man on duty. He grudgingly pumps your gas and unsmilingly changes your oil, reminding you all the time that his union contract says he only has to pump gas and change oil. He doesn't do windows. He works only thirty-two hours a week, with ninety minutes off each day for lunch, during which time the gas station is closed. He also has six weeks' vacation every summer in the South of France. Across the street, his two brothers and uncle, who have not worked in ten years because their state unemployment insurance pays more than their last job, are playing boccie ball. Fourth is the developing-country gas station. Fifteen people work there and they are all cousins. When you drive in, no one pays any attention to you because they are all too busy talking to each other. Gas is only 35 cents a gallon because it is subsidized by the government, but only one of the six gas pumps actually works. The others are broken and they are waiting for the replacement parts to be flown in from Europe. The gas station is rather run-down because the owner lives in Zurich and takes all the profits out of the country. The owner doesn't know that half his employees actually sleep in the repair shop at night and use the car wash equipment to shower. Most of the customers at the developing-country gas station either drive the latest-model Mercedes or a motor scooter. The place is always busy, though, because so many people stop in to use the air pump to fill their bicycle tires. Lastly there is the communist gas station. Gas there is only 50 cents a gallon—but there is none, because the four guys working there have sold it all on the black market for $5 a gallon. Just one of the four guys who is employed at the communist gas station is actually there. The other three are working at second jobs in the underground economy and only come around once a week to collect their paychecks.

What is going on in the world today, in the very broadest sense, is that through the process of globalization everyone is being forced toward America's gas station. If you are not an American and don't know how to pump your own gas, I suggest you learn. With the end of the Cold War, globalization is globalizing Anglo-American-style capitalism. It is globalizing American culture and cultural icons. It is globalizing the best of America and the worst of America. It is globalizing the American Revolution and it is globalizing the American gas station. . . .

Rational Exuberance

. . . Since I spend a great deal of time overseas and away from Wall Street—looking at my country from the outside in—I am constantly exposed to the rational exuberance about America in the rest of the world. This rational exuberance is built on the following logic: If you look at globalization as the dominant international system today, and you look at the attributes that both companies and countries need to thrive in this system, you have to conclude that America has more assets, and fewer liabilities, in relation to this system than any other major country. This is what I call rational exuberance. It is the intuition among global investors that while many in Europe and Asia were still trying to adjust their societies to globalization, and some were barely up to the starting line, Uncle Sam was already around the first turn and in full sprint.

A useful way to analyze this rational exuberance is to ask the following question: If 100 years ago you had come to a visionary geo-architect and told him that in the year 2000 the world would be defined by a system called "globalization," what sort of country would he have designed to compete and win in that world? The answer is that he would have designed something that looks an awful lot like the United States of America. Here's what I mean:

First of all, he would have designed a country that was in an ideally competitive geographic position. That is, he would have designed a country that was both an Atlantic and a Pacific power, looking comfortably in both directions; and at the same time connected by landmass to both Canada and Latin America, so that it could easily interact with all three key markets of the world—Asia, Europe, and the Americas. That would come in handy.

He would have designed a country with a diverse, multicultural, multi-ethnic, multilingual population that had natural connections to all continents of the globe, but was, at the same time, bound together by a single language—English—which would also be the dominant language of the Internet. He would also have bestowed upon this country at least five different regional economies joined by a single currency, the dollar, which would also be the reserve currency for the rest of the world. Having a single country with different regional economies is a great asset because when one region might be slumping the other could be surging, helping to smooth out some of the peaks and valleys of the business cycle. All of that would be helpful.

He would have designed a country with extremely diverse, innovative and efficient capital markets, where venture capitalism was considered a noble and daring art, so that anyone with a reasonable (or even ridiculous) invention in his basement or garage could find a venture capitalist somewhere to back it. That would be nice. . . . If you compare a list of the twenty-five biggest companies in Europe twenty-five years ago with a list of the twenty-five biggest European companies today, the two lists are almost the same. But if you take a list of the twenty-five biggest companies in America twenty-five years ago and compare it with a list of the twenty-five biggest American companies today, most of the companies are different. Yes, America's financial markets, with their constant demands for short-term profits and quarterly earnings, often won't let corporations "waste money" by focusing on long-term growth. That's true. But these same markets will give someone with a half-baked idea $50,000 overnight to try to turn it into the next Apple computer. Massachusetts has a bigger venture capital industry than all of Europe combined. Venture capitalists are very important people in this day and age, and not just as a source of money. The best of them provide real expertise for start-up companies. They see a lot of them and they understand the stages through which companies have to go in order to develop, and they can help carry them through, which is often as important as seed money.

Our geo-architect would certainly have designed a country with the most honest legal and regulatory environment in the world. In this country, both domestic and foreign investors could always count on a reasonably level playing field, with relatively little corruption, plenty of legal safeguards for any foreigner who wants to make an investment and take out his profits at any time, and a rule of law that enables markets and contracts to work and protects and encourages innovation through patent protection. The U.S. capital markets today are not only more efficient than those of any other country, they are also the most transparent. The U.S. stock markets simply will not tolerate secrecy, so every listed company must file timely earnings reports, along with regularly audited financial statements, so that mismanagement and misallocation of resources is easily detected and punished.

He would have designed a country with a system of bankruptcy laws and courts that actually encourages people who fail in a business venture to declare bankruptcy and then try again, perhaps fail again, declare bankruptcy again, and then try again, before succeeding and starting the next Amazon.com—without having to carry the stigma of their initial bankruptcies for the rest of their lives. . . .

In Europe, bankruptcy carries a lifelong stigma. Whatever you do, do not declare bankruptcy in Germany: you, your children and your children's children will all carry a lasting mark of Cain in the eyes of German society.

If you must declare bankruptcy in Germany, you are better off leaving the country. (And you'll be welcomed with open arms in Palo Alto.)

On that subject, our geo-architect would certainly have designed a country that was hard-wired for accepting new immigrants, so that anyone could come to its shores and be treated as constitutionally equal to anyone else, thus enabling that country to be constantly siphoning off the best brains in the world and bringing them together in its companies, medical centers and universities. Roughly one-third of Silicon Valley's scientists and engineers today are foreign-born immigrants, who then turn around and project Silicon Valley values and products all over the world. According to University of California at Berkeley urban affairs expert AnnaLee Saxenian, research by the Public Policy Institute of California found that in 1996, 1,786 Silicon Valley technology companies, with $12.6 billion in sales and 46,000 employees, were run by Indian or Chinese immigrant executives alone. . . . To be a Japanese you pretty much have to be born a Japanese. To be a Swiss you pretty much have to be born a Swiss. To be an American you just have to want to be an American. That doesn't mean that we let everyone in who wants to be an American, but when citizenship is a legal question not an ethnic, racial or national one, it makes it much easier for a country to absorb new talent. . . .

The more knowledge workers you can attract to your shores, the more successful you will be. As far as America is concerned, I say bring 'em in, and not only the rich, educated entrepreneurs. I would never turn back a single Haitian boat person. Anyone who has the smarts and energy to build a raft out of milk cartons and then sail across the Atlantic to America's shores is someone I want as a new immigrant. . . .

Our geo-architect certainly would have designed a country with a democratic, flexible federal political system that allows for a high degree of decentralized political decisionmaking that enables different regions and localities to adjust themselves to world trends without waiting for the center to move. Indeed, a federal system—with fifty states all having an incentive to compete and experiment in finding solutions to the intertwined problems of education, welfare and health care—is an enormous asset in the era of globalization, when such problems can be highly complex and you rarely get the right answer without experimenting a few times.

Our geo-architect certainly would have designed a country with the most flexible labor market in the world—one that enables workers to move easily from one economic zone to another, and one that enables employers to hire and fire workers with relative ease. The easier it is to fire workers, the more incentive employers have to hire them. Compare the millions of jobs eliminated in America in the 1990s and the many millions more created in America in the 1990s with the virtually stagnant job turnover rate in Western Europe. In America, lose your job in Maine one day and, if one is available, you can get a new one in San Diego the next day. Lose your job in Tokyo one day and I wouldn't recommend looking for one in Seoul the next. Lose your job in Munich one day and, even with a common European currency market, it is not so easy to get one the next day in Milan.

Our geo-architect would have designed a country where government-protected cartels are abhorred, so every company and bank has to fight and stand on its own, and monopolies will not be tolerated. That would be important. Even when a U.S. firm becomes a much-envied, world-class gem, like Microsoft, it still has to answer to a Justice Department antitrust lawyer making $75,000 a year.

Our geo-architect would have designed a country that is tolerant of the oddball, the guy with the ponytail or the gal with the ring in her nose who is also a mathematical genius or software whiz. America is a country where the minute one person stands up and says, "That's impossible," someone else walks in the door and announces, "We just did it." Says Intel vice president Avram Miller: "The Japanese don't get it, because they are focused on homogeneity. When it was building a gazillion of all the same thing, they were the world experts and we mistook it for some special genius. But the world does not want a lot of the same thing today, and in a world where everyone wants something different—and the technology that will give them something perfectly tailored [to their own needs and specifications]—America has a real advantage."

Our geo-architect would have designed a country whose corporate sector, unlike Europe's or Japan's, had, by the mid-1990s, already gone through most of the downsizing, privatizing, networking, deregulation, reengineering, streamlining and restructuring required to fully adjust to, and exploit, the democratizations of finance, technology and information and to avoid Microchip Immune Deficiency. Just as America won the space race, it is now winning the cyberspace race. American companies spend more on information technology per capita than any others in the world.

He also would have designed a country with a deeply rooted entrepreneurial culture and a tax system that allows the successful investor or innovator to hold on to a large share of his or her capital gains, so there is a constant incentive to get enormously rich. In our ideal country, Horatio Alger is not a mythical character but sometimes your next-door neighbor, who just happened to get hired as an engineer at Intel or America Online when they were getting started and ended up being paid in stock options that are now worth $10 million.

Our geo-architect certainly would have designed a country that still had a lot of environmentally attractive, wide-open spaces and small towns, to attract knowledge workers. Because today, thanks to the Internet, fax machines and overnight package delivery, high-tech firms and knowledge workers can escape from urban centers and settle virtually anywhere they want. So having lots of lush green valleys not far from oceans or mountains can be a real asset. That's why states like Idaho, Washington, Oregon, Minnesota and North Carolina have booming high-tech sectors today.

He would have designed a country that values the free flow of information so much that it defends the rights of the worst pornographers and the most incendiary racists to do their things. That would be an asset. Because in a world in which information, knowledge, goods and services will flow with increasing speed across the Fast World or through cyberspace, those countries comfortable with such openness, and the cacophony and chaos that sometimes attend it, those countries comfortable competing on the basis of imagination, not behind walls of protection, will have a real advantage. America, with its Freedom of Information Act, which barely allows the government to keep secrets for long, has nurtured this culture of openness from its foundation.

And, most important, our geo-architect would have designed a country whose multinational companies and little entrepreneurs are increasingly comfortable thinking big and thinking globally, and excel now in virtually every fast, light, networked, knowledge-intensive field of endeavor. America today excels at software design, computing, Internet design, Internet marketing, commercial banking, E-mail, insurance, derivatives, genetic engineering, artificial intelligence, investment banking, high-end health care, higher education, overnight package delivery, consulting, fast food, advertising, biotechnology, media, entertainment, hotels, waste management, financial services, environmental industries and telecommunications. It's a postindustrial world, and America today is good at everything that is postindustrial.

. . . The publisher and editor of this book, Jonathan Galassi, called me one day and said, "I was telling some friends of mine that you're writing a book about globalization and they said, 'Oh, Friedman, he loves globalization.' What would you say to that?" I answered Jonathan that I feel about globalization a lot like I feel about the dawn. Generally speaking, I think it's a good thing that the sun comes up every morning. It does more good than harm. But even if I didn't much care for the dawn there isn't much I could do about it. I didn't start globalization, I can't stop it—except at a huge cost to human development—and I'm not going to waste time trying. All I want to think about is how I can get the best out of this new system, and cushion the worst, for the most people.

When Corporations
Rule the World

DAVID C. KORTEN

T
he fame of Bretton Woods and of this hotel dates from July 1944, when the United Nations Monetary and Financial Conference was held here. . . . The economic leaders who quietly gathered at this hotel were looking beyond the end of the war with hopes for a world united in peace through prosperity. Their specific goal was to create the institutions that would promote that vision.

By the end of this historic meeting, the World Bank and the International Monetary Fund (IMF) had been founded, and the groundwork had been laid for what later became GATT [General Agreement on Tariffs and Trade]. In the intervening years, these institutions have held faithfully to their mandate to promote economic growth and globalization. Through structural adjustment programs (SAPs),[1] the World Bank and the IMF have pressured countries of the South to open their borders and change their economies from self-sufficiency to *export* production. Trade agreements negotiated through GATT have reinforced these actions and opened economies . . . to the increasingly free importation of goods and money.

As we look back fifty years later, we can see that the Bretton Woods institutions have indeed met their goals. Economic growth has expanded fivefold. International trade has expanded by roughly twelve times, and foreign direct investment has been expanding at two to three times the rate of trade expansion. Yet, tragically, while these institutions have met their goals, they have failed in their purpose. The world has more poor people today than ever before. We have an accelerating gap between the rich and the poor. Widespread violence is tearing families and communities apart nearly everywhere. And the planet's ecosystems are deteriorating at an alarming rate.

Yet the prevailing wisdom continues to maintain that economic growth offers the answer to poverty, environmental security, and a strong social fabric, and that *economic globalization*—erasing economic borders to allow free flow of goods and money—is the key to such growth. Indeed, the more

---

1. SAPs, or structural adjustment programs, are the requirements the IMF imposes on nations in return for the Fund's assistance. Usually, SAPs have required governments to cut social spending and consumption, open markets to foreign investors, and reduce wages in order to stimulate investor and banker confidence.

severe the economic, environmental, and social crises, the stronger the policy commitment to these same prescriptions, even as evidence mounts that they are not working. In fact, there is a growing consensus outside of official circles that they cannot work, for reasons I will explain.

Ecological Limit to Growth

. . . The human economy is embedded in and dependent on the natural ecosystems of our planet. Until the present moment in human history, however, the scale of our economic activity relative to the scale of the ecosystems has been small enough so that, in both economic theory and practice, we could, up to a point, afford to ignore this fundamental fact.

Now, however, we have crossed a monumental historical threshold. Because of the fivefold economic expansion since 1950 the environmental demands of our economic system have filled up the available environmental space of the planet. In other words, we live in a "full world.". . .

The first environmental limits that we have confronted and possibly exceeded are . . . the limits to renewable resources and to the environment's *sink functions*—its ability to absorb our wastes. These are limits related to the loss of soils, fisheries, forests, and water; to the absorption of CO_2 emissions; and to destruction of the ozone layer. We could argue whether a particular limit was hit at noon yesterday or will be passed at midnight tomorrow, but the details are far less important than the basic truth that we have no real option other than to adapt our economic institutions to the reality of a "full world."

The structure and ideology of the existing Bretton Woods system is geared to an ever-continuing expansion of economic output—*economic growth*—and to the integration of national economies into a seamless global economy. The consequence is to intensify competition for already overstressed environmental space. In a "full world," this intensified competition accelerates destruction of the regenerative capacities of the ecosystem on which we and future generations depend; it crowds out all forms of life not needed for immediate human consumption purposes; and it increases competition between rich and poor for control of ecological resources. In a free market—which responds only to money, not needs—the rich win this competition every time. We see it happening all over the world: Hundreds of millions of the financially disenfranchised are displaced as their lands, waters, and fisheries are converted to uses serving the wants of the more affluent.

As long as their resources remain, the demands of the rich can be met—which may explain why so many of the rich see no problem. The poor experience a very different reality, but in a market economy their experience doesn't count.

The market cannot deal with questions relating to the appropriate scale of economic activity. There are no price signals indicating that the poor are going hungry because they have been forced off their lands; nor is there any price signal to tell polluters that too much CO_2 is being released into the air, or that toxins should not be dumped into soils or waters. Steeped in market ideology and highly responsive to corporate interests, the Bretton Woods institutions have demonstrated little capacity to give more than lip service either to environmental concerns or to the needs of the poor. Rather, their efforts have . . . centered on ensuring that people with money have full access to whatever resources remain—with little regard for the broader consequences.

A new Bretton Woods meeting to update the international system would serve a significant and visionary need—if its participants were to accept that economic growth is no longer a valid public policy priority. Indeed, whether the global economy grows or shrinks is largely irrelevant. Having crossed the threshold to a full world, the appropriate concern is whether the available planetary resources are being used in ways that: (1) meet the basic needs of all people; (2) maintain biodiversity; and (3) ensure the sustained availability of comparable resource flows to future generations. Our present economic system fails on all three counts.

Economic Injustice

In *How Much Is Enough?* Alan Durning divided the world into three consumption classes: overconsumers, sustainers, and marginals. The overconsumers are the 20 percent of the world's people who consume roughly 80 percent of the world's resources—that is, those of us whose lives are organized around automobiles, airplanes, meat-based diets, and wastefully packaged disposable products. The marginals, also 20 percent of the world's people, live in absolute deprivation.

If we turn to measurements of *income* rather than *consumption,* the figures are even more stark. The United Nations Development Program (UNDP) *Human Development Report* for 1992 introduces the champagne glass as a graphic metaphor for a world of extreme economic injustice. The bowl of the champagne glass represents the abundance enjoyed by the 20 percent of people who live in the world's richest countries and receive 82.7 percent of the world's income. At the bottom of the stem, where the sediment settles, we find the poorest 20 percent of the world's people, who barely survive on 1.4 percent of the total income. The combined incomes of the top 20 percent are nearly sixty times larger than those of the bottom 20 percent. Furthermore, this gap has doubled since 1950, when the top 20 percent enjoyed only thirty times the income of the bottom 20 percent. And the gap continues to grow.

These figures actually understate the true inequality in the world, because they are based on national averages rather than actual individual incomes. If we take into account the very rich people who live in poor countries and the very poor people who live in rich countries, the incomes of the richest 20 percent of the world's people are approximately 150 times those of the poorest 20 percent. That gap is growing as well.

Robert Reich, the [former] U.S. Secretary of Labor in the Clinton administration, explained in his book *The Work of Nations* (1991), that the economic globalization the Bretton Woods institutions have advanced so successfully has served to separate the interests of the wealthy classes from a sense of national interest and thereby from a sense of concern for and obligation to their less fortunate neighbors. A thin segment of the super rich at the very lip of the champagne glass has formed a stateless alliance that defines *global interest* as synonymous with the personal and corporate financial interests of its members.

This separation has been occurring in nearly every country in the world to such an extent that it is no longer meaningful to speak of a world divided into northern and southern nations. The meaningful divide is not geography—it is class.

Whether intended or not, the policies so successfully advanced by the Bretton Woods institutions have inexorably empowered the super rich to lay claim to the world's wealth at the expense of other people, other species, and the viability of the planet's ecosystem.

Freeing Corporations from Control

The issue is not the market per se. Trying to run an economy without markets is disastrous, as the experience of the Soviet Union demonstrated. However, there is a fundamentally important distinction between markets and free markets.

The struggle between two extremist ideologies has been a central feature of the twentieth century. Communism called for all power to the state. Market capitalism calls for all power to the market—a euphemism for giant corporations. Both ideologies lead to their own distinctive form of tyranny. The secret of Western success in World War II and the early postwar period was not a free market economy; it was the practice of democratic pluralism built on institutional arrangements that sought to maintain balance between the state and the market and to protect the right of an active citizenry to hold both accountable to the public interest.

Contrary to the claims of ideologues who preach a form of corporate libertarianism,[2] markets need governments to function efficiently. It is well established in economic theory and practice that markets allocate resources efficiently only when markets are competitive and when firms pay for the social and environmental impact of their activity—that is, when they *internalize* the costs of their production. This requires that governments set and

---

2. Libertarianism is a doctrine that perceives government as the major threat to individual freedom.

enforce the rules that make cost internalization happen, and, since successful firms invariably grow larger and more monopolistic, governments regularly step in to break them up and restore competition.

For governments to play the necessary role of balancing market and community interests, governmental power must be equal to market power. If markets are national, then there must be a strong national government. By expanding the boundaries of the market beyond the boundaries of the nation-state through economic globalization, the concentration of market power moves inevitably beyond the reach of government. This has been a most important consequence of both the structural adjustment programs of the World Bank and IMF and the trade agreements negotiated under GATT. As a result, governance decisions are transferred from governments, which at least in theory represent the interests of all citizens, to transnational corporations, which by their nature serve the interests only of their dominant shareholders. Consequently, societies everywhere on the planet are no longer able to address environmental and other needs.

Enormous economic power is being concentrated in the hands of a very few global corporations relieved of constraints to their own growth. Antitrust action to restore market competition by breaking up the concentrations is one of the many casualties of globalization. Indeed, current policy encourages firms to merge into ever more powerful concentrations to strengthen their position in global markets.

The rapid rate at which large corporations are shedding employees has created an impression in some quarters that the firms are losing their power. It is a misleading impression. The Fortune 500 firms shed 4.4 million jobs between 1980 and 1993. During this same period, their sales increased 1.4 times, assets increased 2.3 times, and CEO compensation increased 6.1 times. Of the world's one hundred largest economies, fifty are now corporations, not including banking and financial institutions.

Any industry in which five firms control 50 percent or more of the market is considered by economists to be highly monopolistic. The *Economist* recently reported that five firms control more than 50 percent of the global market in the following industries: consumer durables, automotive, airlines, aerospace, electronic components, electricity and electronics, and steel. Five firms control over 40 percent of the global market in oil, personal computers, and—especially alarming in its consequences for public debate on these very issues—media.

Forums for Elite Domination

. . . The forums within which corporate and government elites shape the global policies of the Western world were not limited to Bretton Woods. . . .

. . . The Trilateral Commission was formed in 1973 by David Rockefeller, chair of Chase Manhattan Bank, and Zbigniew Brzezinski, who served as the commission's director/coordinator until 1977 when he became national security advisor to President Jimmy Carter.

The members of the Trilateral Commission include the heads of four of the world's five largest nonbanking transnational corporations; top officials of five of the world's six largest international banks; and heads of major media organizations. U.S. presidents Jimmy Carter, George Bush, and Bill Clinton were all members of the Trilateral commission, as was Thomas Foley, former speaker of the House of Representatives. Many key members of the Carter administration were . . . Trilateral Commission members. Many of President Clinton's cabinet and other appointments are former members of the Trilateral Commission.

. . . The Trilateral Commission has provided forums in which top executives from the world's leading corporations meet regularly, informally, and privately with top national political figures and opinion leaders to seek consensus on immediate and longer-range problems facing the most powerful members of the Western Alliance.

To some extent, the meetings help maintain "stability" in global policies, but they also deprive the public of meaningful participation and choice—as some participants explicitly intend. Particularly significant about these groups is their bipartisan political membership. Certainly, the participation of both George Bush and Bill Clinton in the Trilateral Commission makes it easier to understand the seamless transition from the Republican Bush administration to the Democratic Clinton administration with regard to U.S. commitment to pass GATT and NAFTA. Clinton's leadership in advancing what many progressives saw as a Bush agenda won him high marks from his colleagues on the Trilateral Commission.

Instruments of Control

Corporations have enormous political power, and they are actively using it to reshape the rules of the market in their own favor. The GATT has now become one of the corporations' most powerful tools for reshaping the market. Under the new GATT agreement, a World Trade Organization, the WTO, has been created with far-reaching powers to provide corporations the legal protection they feel they need to continue expanding their far-flung operations without the responsibility to serve any interest other than their own bottom line. . . .

The WTO hears disputes brought against the national or local laws of any country that another member country considers to be a trade barrier. Secret panels made up of three unelected trade experts will hear the disputes, and their rulings can be overturned only by a unanimous vote of the member countries. In general, any health, safety, or environmental standard that exceeds international standards set by industry representatives is likely to be considered a trade barrier, unless the offending government can prove that the standard has a valid scientific basis.

As powerful as the large corporations are, they themselves function increasingly as agents of a global financial system that has become the world's most powerful governance institution. The power in this system lies within a small group of private financial institutions that have only one objective: to make money in massive quantities. A seamless electronic web allows anyone with proper access codes and a personal computer to conduct instantaneous trade involving billions of dollars on any of the world's financial markets. The world of finance itself has become a gigantic computer game. In this game the smart money does not waste itself on long-term, high-quality commitments to productive enterprises engaged in producing real wealth to meet real needs of real people. Rather, it seeks short-term returns from speculation in erratic markets and from simultaneous trades in multiple markets to profit from minute price variations. In this game the short-term is measured in microseconds, the long-term in days. The environmental, social, and even economic consequences of financial decisions involving more than a trillion dollars a day are invisible to those who make them.

Joel Kurtzman, former business editor of the *New York Times* and currently editor of the *Harvard Business Review*, estimates that for every $1 circulating in the productive economy today, $20 to $50 circulates in the world of pure finance. Since these transactions take place through unmonitored international computer networks, no one knows how much is really involved. The $1 trillion that changes hands each day in the world's international currency markets is itself twenty to thirty times the amount required to cover daily trade in actual goods and services. If the world's most powerful governments act in concert to stabilize exchange rates in these same markets, the best they can manage is a measly $14 billion a day—little more than pocket change compared to the amounts mobilized by speculators and arbitrageurs. . . .

The corporations that invest in *real* assets (as opposed to ephemeral financial assets) are forced by the resulting pressures to restructure their operations in order to maximize immediate short-term returns to shareholders. One way to do this is by downsizing, streamlining, and automating their operations, using the most advanced technologies to eliminate hundreds of thousands of jobs. The result is jobless economic growth. Contemporary economies simply cannot create jobs faster than technology and dysfunctional economic systems can shed them. In nearly every country in the world there is now a labor surplus, and those lucky enough to have jobs are increasingly members of a contingent work force without either security or benefits. The resulting fear and insecurity make the jobs-versus-environment issue a crippling barrier to essential environmental action.

Another way to increase corporate profits is to externalize the cost of the firm's operations on the community, pitting localities against one another in a standards-lowering competition to offer subsidies, tax holidays, and freedom from environmental and employment standards. Similarly, workers are pitted against one another in a struggle for survival that pushes wages down to the lowest common denominator. This is the true meaning of *global competitiveness*—competition among localities. Large corporations, by contrast, minimize their competition through mergers and strategic alliances.

Any corporation that does not play this game to its limit is likely to become a takeover target by a corporate raider who will buy out the company and profit by taking the actions that the previous management—perhaps in a fit of social conscience and loyalty to workers and community—failed to take. The reconstruction of the global economic system makes it almost impossible for even highly socially conscious and committed managers to operate a corporation responsibly in the public interest.

✳✳✳

We are caught in a terrible dilemma. We have reached a point in history where we must rethink the very nature and meaning of human progress; yet the vision and decisions that emerged some fifty years ago catalyzed events that have transformed the governance processes of societies everywhere such that the necessary changes in thought and structure seem very difficult to achieve. It has happened so quickly that few among us even realize what has happened. The real issues are seldom discussed in a media dependent on corporate advertising.

. . . What is the alternative? Among those of us who are devoting significant attention to this question, the answer is the opposite of economic globalization. It lies in promoting greater economic localization—breaking economic activities down into smaller, more manageable pieces that link the people who make decisions in ways both positive and negative. It means rooting capital to a place and distributing its control among as many people as possible.

Powerful interests stand resolutely in the way of achieving such a reversal of current trends. The biggest barrier, however, is the limited extent of public discussion on the subject. The starting point must be to get the issues on the table and bring them into the mainstream policy debates in a way that books like this may help to achieve.

■ DISCUSSION QUESTIONS

1. Despite their big differences, both authors argue that nation-states and their governments are less powerful in the new globalized economic order than they used to be. Yet Friedman appears to welcome this development, while Korten is less sure. Is the decline of government power beneficial or detrimental to democracy?
2. Friedman argues that economic globalization creates vast new wealth, while Korten says that it creates new inequalities. How would Friedman justify these new inequalities? How would Korten deal with the issue of producing new wealth?

3. Friedman seems to argue that the U.S. national interest consists of encouraging free trade, technological innovation, and greater individual entrepreneurship. Korten argues that a democratic foreign policy would return power to the voters and communities. How might citizens better control the movement of capital around the globe? If globalization is inevitable, is Korten's plea idealistic and impractical? Why or why not?

4. Recently, European and Japanese consumers have refused to buy genetically engineered food products, most of them concocted by U.S. companies like Monsanto. How would Friedman deal with such protests? How would Korten?

■ SUGGESTED READINGS AND INTERNET RESOURCES

Two prominent works that look favorably at the outlines of economic globalization are Jeffrey Garten, *The Big Ten: The Big Emerging Markets and How They Will Change Our Lives* (New York: Basic Books, 1998), and Daniel Yergin and Joseph Stanislaw, *The Commanding Heights* (New York: Simon and Schuster, 1998). Perhaps the best critical account of globalization's effects on the United States is Thomas Palley, *Plenty of Nothing* (Princeton, N.J.: Princeton University Press, 1999). See also William Greider, *One World, Ready or Not* (New York: Simon and Schuster, 1997). Should the United States erect trade barriers and encourage its citizens to buy U.S.-produced goods? Answers via an historical examination of this question are provided in Dana Frank, *Buy American: The Untold Story of Economic Nationalism* (Boston: Beacon Press, 1999). An excellent and wide-ranging critique of the undemocratic aspects of globalization and proposals for alternative forms of economic growth is Jerry Mander and Edward Goldsmith, eds., *The Case Against the Global Economy* (New York: Sierra Club Books, 1997).

International Affairs Resources Network Home Page
www.ucis. pitt.edu/dbinfo
Developed by the University of Pittsburgh and its strong international studies program, this site provides a comprehensive guide to public and private economic and political institutions worldwide.

Global Exchange
www.globalexchange.org
Best site for labor, environmental, and other activists who seek links to international groups opposing trade, labor, and economic practices.

World Trade Organization (WTO)
www.wto.org

Official site of the WTO, with links to government and business sites interested in the relaxation of trade barriers.

The International Bank for Reconstruction and Development (World Bank)
www.worldbank.org
Vast data base of the World Bank, established in 1944. Includes bank reports on world social and economic indicators, including the bank's often controversial loan priorities. Links with associated international organizations, including the International Monetary Fund (IMF).

CREDITS

BESSETTE, JOSEPH M.: From *The Mild Voice of Reason: Deliberative Democracy and American National Government,* by Joseph M. Bessette. Copyright © 1994 by the University of Chicago Press. Reprinted with permission.

BOWLES, SAMUEL, AND RICHARD EDWARDS: "The Market Erodes Democratic Government" from *Understanding Capitalism* (pages 411, 413, 418–423, 430–439). © 1993 Addison Wesley Longman, Inc. Reprinted by permission of the authors.

CLAWSON, DAN, ALAN NEUSTADTL, AND MARK WELLER: Excerpted and reprinted from the chapters entitled "Follow the Money" and "Scandal or System?" included in *Dollars and Votes: How Business Campaign Contributions Subvert Democracy* by Dan Clawson, Alan Neustadl, and Mark Weller, by permission of Temple University Press. © 1998 by Temple University. All rights reserved.

CORRADO, ANTHONY: Copyright © 1996 by the Aspen Institute. Originally published as "Elections in Cyberspace: Prospects and Problems" in *Elections in Cyberspace: Toward a New Era in American Politics.* Anthony Corrado and Charles Firestone, eds. Queenstown, Md: The Aspen Institute, 1996.

COX, MICHAEL W., AND RICHARD ALM: From *Myths of Rich & Poor* by W. Michael Cox and Richard Alm. Copyright © 1999 by W. Michael Cox and Richard Alm. Reprinted by permission of Basic Books, a member of Perseus Books, L.L.C.

DONAHUE, JOHN D.: From *Disunited States* by John D. Donahue. Copyright © 1997 by John D. Donahue. Reprinted by permission of Basic Books, a member of Perseus Books, L.L.C.

EGGERS, WILLIAM D., AND JOHN O'LEARY: Reprinted with the permission of The Free Press, a Division of Simon & Schuster, Inc., from *Revolution at the Roots: Making Our Government Smaller, Better, and Closer to Home* by William D. Eggers and John O'Leary. Copyright © 1995 by William D. Eggers and John O'Leary.

FIORINA, MORRIS P.: From *Congress: Keystone of the Washington Establishment* by Morris P. Fiorina. Copyright © 1989 by Yale University Press. Reprinted with permission.

FRANKEL, MARVIN E.: Excerpt from Chapter 4 "Piety Versus 'Secular Humanism': A Phony War" from *On Faith and Freedom* by Marvin E. Frankel. Copyright © 1995 by Marvin E. Frankel. Reprinted by permission of Hill and Wang, a division of Farrar, Straus and Giroux, L.L.C.

FRIEDMAN, MILTON: From *Capitalism and Freedom* by Milton Friedman. Copyright © 1982 by the University of Chicago Press. Reprinted by permission.